Reprints of Economic Classics

PUBLIC AND PRIVATE ECONOMY

PUBLIC AND PRIVATE ECONOMY

BY

THEODORE SEDGWICK

IN THREE PARTS

1836-1839

WITH AN INTRODUCTION
THEODORE SEDGWICK
FROM FEDERALISM TO JACKSONIANISM
By JOSEPH DORFMAN

LIBRARY
WEST LIBERTY STATE COLLEGE
WEST LIBERTY, WV 26074

AUGUSTUS M. KELLEY • PUBLISHERS
CLIFTON 1974

First Published in This Edition 1974
First Edition 1836-1839
(*New York*: Harper & Brothers, *No. 82,
Cliff-Street*, 1836-1839)

Reprinted 1974 by
Augustus M. Kelley Publishers
Clifton New Jersey 07012

Library of Congress Cataloguing in Publication Data

Sedgwick, Theodore, 1780-1839.
PUBLIC AND PRIVATE ECONOMY, Illustrated by Observations Made in England in the Year 1836.
With an Introduction: Theodore Sedgwick; from Federalism to Jacksonianism, *by* Joseph Dorfman.

(Reprints of Economic Classics).
Reprint of the 1836-1839 edition published by Harper, New York.
1. Economics. 2. Great Britain--Economic conditions--1760-1860. 3. United States--Economic conditions. I. Title.
HB161.S44   1974   330   68-27855
ISBN 0 678 01258 X

MAR 6 '75

PRINTED IN THE UNITED STATES OF AMERICA
by SENTRY PRESS, NEW YORK, N. Y. 10013
Bound by A. HOROWITZ & SON, CLIFTON, N. J.

THEODORE SEDGWICK:
From Federalism to Jacksonianism

In recent times no period of American history has been more widely discussed by historians than those years between Andrew Jackson's accession to the Presidency and the outbreak of the Civil War. Controversy has centered in good part on interpretation of the economic thinking of the Jacksonians, especially of those influential in policy making. To be sure, all good Jacksonians subscribed to the doctrine of Thomas Jefferson: the less government the better.

But, as the sage of Monticello himself had demonstrated, this proposition was not always to be interpreted literally or narrowly. Thus there were differences among the Jacksonian thinkers as well as among their present day interpreters. Among the more sophisticated and complex was Theodore Sedgwick (1780-1839), who was described in an obituary in a high level, powerful Jacksonian organ as "an enlightened political economist and zealous philanthropist" as well as "influential democrat."[1]

---

[1] Anonymous, "Political Portraits No. 17: Theodore Sedgwick," *The United States Magazine and Democratic Review*, February 1840, pp. 129, 136.

Two years later the journal printed a condensed version of the essay, "Political Portraits with Pen and Pencil, No. 31: The Late Theodore Sedgwick," *The United*

Sedgwick was well acquainted with the great works in economics, especially in British economic theory. He kept abreast of the latest publications both in England and in the United States, and also of continental European studies generally through English translations; he read the leading quarterlies, both British and American. He wrote much on economic theory and policy through the media of the newspaper article, the pamphlet, the legislative report, and most notably *Public and Private Economy* (3 vols., 1836-1839) which is reprinted below.

Sedgwick came of a distinguished old Massachusetts family and was related to such other leading colonial and Revolutionary War families as the Jays, the Livingstons, the Cabots and the Dwights. His father, Theodore Sedgwick [no. 1], after attending Yale had become a successful lawyer in Berkshire county in western Massachusetts. He served in the Continental Congress and in the first six congresses under the Constitution (1789-1801)—the last as speaker of the

---

States Magazine and Democratic Review, July 1842.

Anti-Jackson organs also noted in obituaries that Sedgwick was a ''political economist of some eminence.'' (*New Yorker*, reprinted in the *Massachusetts Eagle*, November 21, 1839). The *Eagle* had run its own enthusiastic account a week before.

We shall at times refer to him as ''Theodore Sedgwick no. 2,'' in order to distinguish him as does the Massachusetts Historical Society from two other prominent Theodore Sedgwicks: no. 1, his father, and no. 3, his son. The Massachusetts Historical Society is the main repository of the Sedgwick family papers.

FROM FEDERALISM TO JACKSONIANISM 7

House of Representatives—and then from 1802 to his death in 1813 he was an associate justice of the Supreme Judicial Court of Massachusetts. The senior Sedgwick is best known as a founder of the Federalist Party, a defender of Alexander Hamilton's economic program, including the establishment of the Bank of the United States as the fiscal agent of the federal government; he was a bitter critic of Jefferson and his Republican Party.[2] As a descendant put it in the 1890's,

---

[2] As we have noted elsewhere with respect to the Bank, its ''stockholders were to have a limited liability; it was to be backed by the government's participation in ownership and by the acceptance of its notes for public dues, but it was to be privately operated and its profits were to go elsewhere than to the Treasury.'' [Joseph Dorfman and Rexford G. Tugwell, *Early American Policy: Six Columbia Contributors* (New York: Columbia University Press, 1960) pp. 29-30].

In the words of a biographer, the senior Sedgwick contended that: ''Banks were especially important to a young nation like our own. The disparity between the commercial enterprise of our merchants and the size of their capitals required that all steps possible be taken to utilize what metallic currency we had to the fullest extent, and to limit any large-scale exportation of it. A bank was needed whose paper could circulate throughout the entire country, and that bank should be one in which the national government had an interest.'' [Richard E. Welch Jr., *Theodore Sedgwick, Federalist: A Political Portrait* (Middletown, Conn.: Wesleyan University Press, 1965) p. 99]. This, he maintained, could not be done by the few local—state-chartered—banks. He asked of those who urged the use of such banks: ''Do they believe that those banks possess any powers by which they can give a projectile force to their paper, so as to extend its circulation throughout the United States? Or do they really wish to

"it was impossible for him to recognize any value politically in the Democrats whom he invariably referred to in his letters and conversation as Jacobins." The writer declared that his conspicuous characteristic as a statesman was his ardent belief first in executive government "and second in a liberal political *economy*," which to him meant opposition to any "needless or extra-

have the [Federal] Government repose itself on institutions with which they have not intimate connection, and over which they have no control?" To the charge that some of the terms promised the stockholders unduly large gains, Sedgwick replied that "as Government must rely principally on merchants to obtain the proposed stock, it would be necessary to afford to them sufficient motives to withdraw from their commercial pursuits a part of their capitals." ["Bank Bill," February 4, 1791, in *Annals of Congress* (Washington: Gales and Seaton, 1834) p. 1964].

On the other hand, Jefferson argued that "the National Bank Act . . . placed the circulating medium of the country at the mercy of the speculative interests which controlled the Bank. The value of specie, [David] Hume had taught him, was fixed by the natural laws of commerce and the supply varied in each country according to its commercial needs. The bank notes would inevitably be overissued. The paper by raising labor costs and prices would destroy the foreign markets. Specie would be drained from agriculture for use in speculation, thus upsetting the former." [Dorfman, *The Economic Mind in American Civilization*, 5 volumes (1946-1959; New York: Augustus M. Kelley Publishers, 1967, 1969) I, 438-439].

Jefferson's argument later became the basis of the Jacksonian opposition to the Second Bank of the United States and all other banks of issue, except that Jackson held more definitely that the specie was drained not only from agriculture but from all sober enterprise, for highly speculative projects in the nature of gambling.

vagant appropriations... proposed in congress."[3] Such was the heritage of the son, Theodore Sedgwick no. 2, who remained a Federalist long after the party was shattered.

This Theodore Sedgwick was born in Sheffield, Berkshire county, in 1780, spent his youth at his father's mansion at nearby Stockbridge, and graduated from Yale in 1798. This was the Yale of the presidency of the Reverend Timothy Dwight, who was popularly known as "the Pope of Federalism." Young Sedgwick went on to study for the law first with his eminent father and then with a lawyer in New York. After being admitted to the bar in 1801, he began practising in Albany in partnership with Harmanus Bleecker, a lifelong friend who was also active in politics—at the time as a Federalist and a confidant of the elder Sedgwick.[4]

---

[3] H. D. Sedgwick, "The Sedgwicks of Berkshire," Berkshire Historical and Scientific Society, *Collections*, volume III, No. 2, 1899-1913 (Pittsfield, Mass.: Sun Printing Co., 1915) pp. 96, 97.

[4] Bleecker served in the twelfth congress March 4, 1811, to March 3, 1813, and in the New York State Assembly 1814, 1815. Like Sedgwick no. 2 he later switched to the Democratic Party. It was doubtless through Bleecker that Sedgwick became a close friend of Martin Van Buren. Van Buren referred to Bleecker as "his personal and afterwards political friend." [*The Autobiography of Martin Van Buren*, edited by John C. Fitzpatrick (1920; New York: Augustus M. Kelley Publishers, 1969) p. 429]. When Van Buren became president, he appointed Bleecker *Chargé d'Affaires* to the Netherlands where he served from May 12, 1837, to June 28, 1842. It was Bleecker who

Sedgwick no. 2 quickly emerged as an ardent, leading Federalist. During the War of 1812, he carried on his father's bitter opposition to the Jeffersonians. In a Federalist public meeting of "the friends of Liberty, Peace and Commerce," he declared: "We have no confidence in the talents and patriotism of the present [Madison] administration."[5] On specific economic policies the occasion was notable for Sedgwick's energetic support of free trade. Resolutions which he drew up for the Albany meeting declared: "That the system of commercial restrictions which have been adopted and pursued by the late and present administration [Jefferson's and Madison's] has obstructed the pursuit of commerce, dried up the most fruitful sources of the public revenue, and

---

[5] "Public Meeting," Albany *Gazette,* reprinted in New York *Evening Post,* September 14, 1812.

On the eve of the war the father wrote to Bleecker that in order to prevent the conflict with England, the Federalists in Congress must expose "'the meanness, the baseness and partiality of the administration [towards France].'" [Sedgwick to Bleecker, January 23, 1812, in Richard E. Welch Jr., *Theodore Sedgwick, Federalist,* p. 247].

Shortly afterwards the son and Bleecker were commiserating with each other that, as Bleecker put it, "'we have no hope of relief from the principle of democracy.'" (Bleecker to Sedgwick, June 12, 1812, Sedgwick no. 2 Papers, Massachusetts Historical Society).

---

in 1821 brought about the reconciliation between Van Buren and the famed dissident Republican leader, John Randolph of Roanoke. [Norman K. Risjord, *The Old Republicans: Southern Conservatism in the Age of Jefferson* (New York: Columbia University Press, 1965) p. 306].

weakened the confidence of the commercial states in the wisdom and impartiality of the councils of the Union. . . . That it has ruined the pecuniary interests of the nation, impoverished numerous and meritorious classes of citizens, and subserved the views of one of the belligerents who was, at the same time, waging a . . . destructive predatory war on our lawful commerce. . . . That commerce and agriculture are handmaid to each other; when the former is depressed the latter must languish; and therefore the restrictive system [protective tariffs, embargoes, etc.] operates as a consuming fire to the wealth and prosperity of this state.''

Ill health forced Sedgwick to leave Albany and the practice of law in 1823; he returned to the family home at Stockbridge, to live the life of an active ''country gentleman,'' and engaged in a variety of enterprises some of which were in what he called a ''sister state where my mature life was spent.''[6] By this time the opposition of the Federalist Party to the War of 1812, among other developments, had led to its practical disappearance as a political force; and most of its members drifted into the Jeffersonian Republican Party. Meanwhile, the Republican Party gradually split up into two main factions that very roughly corresponded to or were akin to the Federalists and the pre-war Republicans; by 1830 they were com-

---

[6] *An Address . . . Delivered before the Berkshire Association for the Promotion of Agriculture and Manufactures* (Pittsfield, Mass.: Allen, 1823) p. 9.

monly referred to as the National Republican (later to be the Whig Party) and the Democratic Party. The latter, which claimed with some credibility to be the true heir of the party of Jefferson, took its name and general form as the party which swept Jackson to victory in 1828. The National Republicans and Whigs also claimed to be Jeffersonian. Sedgwick no. 2, however, did not become identified with any political party until the middle 1830's. Indeed, in an anonymous pamphlet in 1823, he denounced parties as cabals and factions of bigots seeking "a party president and a party government." He exclaimed, while referring to the ill fate of the Federalists, that "personal merit, the most distinguished talents, the greatest capacity for business, the purest love of rational liberty, are no grounds with them [the party bigots] of restoration to favor provided a man's opinions have once been unfortunate."[7]

This did not prevent Sedgwick no. 2 from serving with distinction as a Stockbridge member of the Massachusetts House of Representatives in the General Court, first in 1823 and continuously

---

[7] *Hints for the People, with Some Thoughts on the Presidential Election.* Rusticus. (n.p.: 1823) pp. 10-11.

The party bigots, he complained, were admirers of Mandeville's *Fable of the Bees:* "'Private vices . . . are public blessings; and [for them] it is argument enough for war, that the art of surgery is improved, and that the people are kept in practice, provided always, however, that the rich epaulettes grace their shoulders and the fat contracts enlarge their domains.'" (p. 10).

from 1827 to 1830. Neither did this prevent him from supporting the National Republican John Quincy Adams in his successful campaign for the presidency in 1824 and in the unsuccessful one in 1828.[8] His opinion of the victor was hardly flattering at the time. Thus in May 1829, when Jackson had been in office barely two months, Sedgwick no. 2 wrote his ardent Jacksonian son (Sedgwick no. 3) then a Columbia College senior: "I fear that your President is to do himself no great honor—I always feared, that he wanted a sound mind, and this I considered the substantial objection to him—So it seems to turn out—But he may redeem himself—If so, no one will rejoice more than I shall. A Republican Government administered upon pure personal party politics is a misfame—a thing to abhor, and loathe."[9] By 1830, however, he was expressing in a public address what became in principle the dominant Jacksonian view. He declared that the "truths essential to good government" make up "the science of *self*-government." This is founded upon the simple idea "that a man knows what his own interests require, generally, better than it is possible for another man to know them." This di-

---

[8] A local Adams newspaper in May 1828 declared that Sedgwick "is a friend of the [Adams] administration . . . an administration which it is to be hoped will not be prematurely changed." (*Berkshire Star and County Republican*, May 15, 1828).

[9] To Theodore Sedgwick no. 3, May 9, 1829, Sedgwick no. 2 Papers.

rectly leads "among an *enlightened* people, [to] the notion of a Republican Government." Among the American people nothing remains to be done but to simplify further this idea. This would be accomplished "by having as few public establishments and officers as possible, and these, with small exceptions, are to be chosen by the people. This strikes at once at the root of party, and official corruption. . . . In getting rid of these, all improper restraints upon our actions, business, trade, intercourse, fall of course." In light of this view, he enthusiastically welcomed the French Revolution of 1830. He exclaimed that "the intelligence which we have so lately received from France of the downfall . . . of despotic rule in that beautiful country, has brightened every eye in this wide spread land."[10] He wrote his son in 1833: "By Reform I mean Economical Reform —The Democratic policy . . . has no other aim than Economical Reform—What is Free Trade—Opposition to the [Second] Bank [of the United States]—to [federal] Internal Improvements—to Corporations—What are State Right claims—but claims to be cheaply governed?—And, what is monopoly other than the one class getting all they can?"[11]

---

[10] *An Address, Delivered before the Berkshire Agricultural Society*, October 7, 1830 (Pittsfield, Mass.: Allen, 1830) p. 20.

[11] To Sedgwick no. 3, March 21, 1833, Sedgwick no. 2 Papers.

At this time Sedgwick no. 2 began to play an important role in national policy-making as an adviser and confidant of Van Buren, who as Bleecker put it, "well knew his worth."[12] Beginning with the election of 1836 Sedgwick was clearly and publicly attached to the Democratic Party.[13] He ran unsuccessfully for the federal house of representatives under the party's ticket headed by Van Buren. He suffered the same fate in his attempt to obtain the Massachusetts lieutenant governorship the next two years. He

---

[12] Bleecker to Van Buren, February 24, 1840, Van Buren Papers, Library of Congress.

His sister, Catherine Maria Sedgwick, who achieved fame as the first notable American woman novelist, met President Jackson in 1831 and was impressed. "'Mr. Van Buren [then Secretary of State] . . . had offered to call to take me and introduce me to the President. He came in his beautiful coach, servants in livery, elegant horses, and two most beautiful dogs. We drove to the palace, entered a large cold salon and then a drawing-room, in which is a fine full-length picture of General Washington. . . . The President was not in the drawing room when we entered. He came immediately, apologized for not having been there to receive us, as he had been that moment called out, and was very courteous and quite plain and pleasing. He has a wooden face, but honest and pretty good." [Catherine M. Sedgwick to R. M. Sedgwick, February 5, 1831, *Life and Letters of Catherine M. Sedgwick*, edited by Mary E. Dewey (New York: Harper, 1871) pp. 215-216].

[13] By this time Sedgwick was convinced that Jackson as in the case of Jefferson, had before becoming president believed that it was the greatest of errors to administer government "'too much upon party principles,'' but after entering office ''they were overruled.'' (To Van Buren, November 26, 1837, Van Buren Papers).

declined the nomination in 1839, but stumped vigorously for the state ticket and died in the midst of the campaign.

Much of Sedgwick's energies, including a good deal of his political activity, went into the promotion of economic development, especially of western Massachusetts. As his presidential addresses in 1823 and 1830 before the county agricultural societies amply attest, he took a decided interest in the improvement of agriculture.[14] As a substantial farmer he was closely associated with "other large farmers,"[15] and he proclaimed rural life the most conducive to the development of good character. He strongly believed that the prosperity of agriculture required the development of manufactures—the factory and the mill —and transportation, especially the new mode— railroads. Often in association with Theodore S. Pomeroy, Sedgwick was active in promoting various manufacturing and other industrial enterprises—fire insurance, gaslights, railroads, to name a few[16]

---

[14] *An Address . . . Delivered before the Berkshire Agricultural Association for the Promotion of Agriculture and Manufacturers.* (1823). *An Address, Delivered before the Berkshire Agricultural Society* (1830).

[15] Mrs. Theodore Sedgwick to Mrs. Maria Jay Banyer, December 11, 1828, John Jay Papers, Columbia University Libraries.

Mrs. Sedgwick also achieved some reputation as a writer, especially of novels and children's stories.

[16] Joseph E. A. Smith, *The History of Pittsfield, Massa-*

Underlying Sedgwick's general social philosophy was his belief that "the world would not be greatly improved, till all were obliged to respect the pure habits that belong to the middling classes," the classes that "have been the most virtuous in every age," as evidenced by their industriousness and saving, the accumulation and respect for property.[17] Believing that education and economic growth were closely intertwined, Sedgwick zealously promoted education of all the people in the arts and sciences and especially political economy. But the good books on the subject, he complained, were written for scholars, philosophers, statesmen, politicians and

---

[17] *Hints to My Countrymen.* An American. (New York: Seymour, 1823) pp. 146-147.

This anonymous work was written in the form of observations on "manners and ways" in New England and New York, made by a "farmer" and his friend, by an interesting choice a travelling "book-merchant." Like *Hints for the People* signed Rusticus, it is largely devoted to giving advice to the rural populace, and, according to the dedication, it was intended for "the *plainer* class of readers."

It was printed at his own expense, which came to $189.97 (Jonathan Seymour to Sedgwick, June 26, 1826, Sedgwick no. 2 Papers).

---

chusetts, from the Year 1800 to the Year 1876, 2 vols. (Springfield, Mass.: Bryan, 1876) II, 382. Sedgwick promoted at least one bank, and held stock in the Bank of the United States. (Theodore S. Pomeroy to Theodore Sedgwick no. 2, January 5, 1825; Robert Sedgwick to Theodore Sedgwick no. 2, October 5, 1824, Sedgwick no. 2 Papers). He had property in at least three states—Maryland, Massachusetts and New York.

gentlemen. The need, he declared in 1826, was "a popular work on American Political Economy, written expressly for the people,"[18] by which he meant "the people of middling property, including laborers for moderate wages."[19] That demand he sought to satisfy with his major treatise *Public and Private Economy*. After publishing the first part in 1836, he visited England for medical advice, and toured the country to get a clearer perspective of the American scene, as the expanded title of volumes II and III stated: *Public and Private Economy, Illustrated by Observations in England in the Year 1836*.[20]

[18] *Hints to My Countrymen*, p. 35.
[19] *Public and Private Economy*, 3 vols. (New York: Harper, 1836-1839) I, 243.
"These may be called *the people*, in the sense that they make up nine-tenths of *the people*." *Public and Private Economy*, I, 243.
[20] Sedgwick also made at the time a short excursion to France. Bleecker found his observations exceedingly useful for his diplomatic work in the Netherlands.
In a letter of 1838 to Horace Mann suggesting that the two volumes of *Public and Private Economy* already published be used in the schools of Massachusetts, he wrote: "I am aware that the subject of them is not popular, or generally captivating, but I think I cannot be mistaken in supposing that it ought to be so, and that the sooner judicious efforts are made to render it so, the better. . . . It seems to me to have one merit, that of being an *American* book upon *American* Economy and to be plain and intelligible to young minds. I know that many valuable works have been written in other countries, and in this, upon *Political Economy*—. But this is a book on *public and private Economy* and admits of the introduction of other subjects, and a different mode of treating them—. In such a book, I

For the prosecution of his economic studies, Sedgwick had an extensive library. This was supplemented by access to what would roughly correspond to the periodical reading room of the large modern private university club.[21]

---

[21] In 1828, his wife after noting in a letter to a Jay cousin that she had been occupied partly by "a little reading in the newspapers, Reviews, and Encyclopedias," went on to say: "I mention the Reviews, because they seem to take up the spare time of most of us. Here I will mention to you a circumstance which is a good deal characteristic of our Society. We have a Book association, and as we are fond of great names, it has been styled the *Philomathean Association.*—Set on foot, and continued *for about one year,* by five persons; to wit—one clerk in a country shop—one young tavern keeper—one shoe maker, and two young farmers—Since that period, the no. of subscribers is enlarged to about twenty, and now includes by *favor,* among others, two lawyers, one East India Gentleman Farmer, dropped down in these obscure regions by some unknown fate, and one lawyer retired from business—The circle of books in that time has also been enlarged, and we now take *The Edinburgh* [*Review*], *The North American* [*Review,* published in Boston], *The Southern Review* [printed at Charleston, S. C.]— The Library of Useful Knowledge—*The Museum of Foreign Literature—*...and one Christian Review. We are now about adding to our list, the Philadelphia [*American*

---

did not think it respectable to omit the subject of *slavery,* but I cannot believe, that my opinions upon a matter so unsettled, however erroneous, ought to be deemed a serious objection to its introduction into the schools. There is no subject upon which the community is more divided, and it can never be expected, that the [Massachusetts] Board [of Education] should give its sanction to every sentiment contained in a book, but rather to its general character.'' (Sedgwick to Horace Mann, December 1, 1838, Horace Mann Papers, Massachusetts Historical Society).

Of the quarterlies available to Sedgwick, *The Edinburgh Review* was the leading organ of the British Whig (later called the Liberal) Party and *The Quarterly Review* occupied a similar position for the Tory (later called the Conservative) Party. Both *The North American Review* and the *American Quarterly Review* were anti-Jackson, when Sedgwick began writing on economic theory in the 1820's. *The Southern Review* was more sympathetic to the general.

Sedgwick at the time appears to have favored the anti-Jackson *North American Review*. In writing of the Boston free English Grammar Schools in 1826, to which children were admitted at the age of seven, he declared that their object was among other things to teach the children to read the proverbs of Solomon, newspapers, "and to enable them, now and then, if they can afford five dollars a year, to take a peep into *The North American Review* and there get some lessons from Mr. [Edward] Everett and Mr. [Jared] Sparks upon political economy."[22]

---

[22] *Hints to My Countrymen*, p. 203. Both these Harvard professors were anti-Jackson.

Quarterly] Review and the London *Quarterly [Review]*— So you see, that though we have not all the advantages of a City Reading Room, we are now making approaches to them—under the interesting circumstance too, that our spirited young farmers and mechanics have set the plan on foot." (Mrs. Theodore Sedgwick to Mrs. Maria Jay Banyer, December 11, 1828, John Jay Papers).

The books Sedgwick read in economic theory ranged from the writings of Benjamin Franklin to the more formal treatises of the late eighteenth and early nineteenth centuries. Broadly speaking, he followed the British classical school— Adam Smith, Henry Thornton, David Ricardo, James Mill—and its French counterpart as represented by J. B. Say. These views centered around hard money and *laissez-faire,* or as Sedgwick preferred to call it, "free competition," and more specifically "freedom of exchange."[23] Sedgwick saluted the author of *The Wealth of Nations* as "the father of the science of political economy . . . [whose] discoveries on the earth were like those of Newton in the heavens."[24] This "apostle of free trade," he especially praised for having "discovered the great principle of the wealth of

---

[23] *Public and Private Economy,* I, 84. Parke Godwin, *A Biography of William Cullen Bryant with Extracts from his Private Correspondence,* 2 vols. (New York: Appleton, 1883) I, 184, 185.

William Cullen Bryant was a sort of protegé of Sedgwick, and his biographer noted: "Either following his [Sedgwick's] lead or impelled by his own researches, Mr. Bryant took the same view." The poet while still a Federalist had become in the early 1820's deeply interested in economics. As the zealous Jacksonian editor of the New York *Evening Post* beginning in 1829, he played a large role in influencing public opinion along Jacksonian lines.

[24] *Public and Private Economy,* II, 119.

nations in the division of labor."²⁵ He highly commended David Ricardo's *On the Principles of Political Economy and Taxation*,²⁶ and also praised his disciples James Mill and J. R. McCulloch, and the American Ricardian, the Reverend John McVickar of Columbia College. On policy matters Sedgwick was especially impressed with another Ricardian, who occupied high posts in the British Tory government in the 1820's. This was William Huskisson, who supported hard money and helped lead England towards freer trade.²⁷

---

²⁵ *Public and Private Economy*, I, 37.

The phrase "apostle of free trade" I take from an anonymous writer in the Jacksonian school who used it to characterize what he felt was Adam Smith's outstanding contribution to the furthering of economic science. ("The History and Moral Relations of Political Economy," *The United States Magazine and Democratic Review*, October 1840, p. 303).

²⁶ The anonymous writer to whom reference has just been made described Ricardo as the "most accomplished and influential modern teacher of the science." ("The History and Moral Relations of Political Economy," *The United States Magazine and Democratic Review*, October 1840, p. 304).

²⁷ Parke Godwin, *A Biography of William Cullen Bryant*, I, 184.

On Huskisson's death in 1830, the dominant Massachusetts Jacksonian organ, the Boston *Statesman*, reprinted an obituary from the Ricardian London *Morning Chronicle:* "During the agitation of the Bullion question, he [Huskisson] wrote a pamphlet [in support of a return to specie payments] which produced a great impression, at the time, and procured for him considerable reputation

Sedgwick believed that there were "many . . . general principles" in economics, applicable to all countries; but drawing upon the comparative historical approach of the Reverend Richard Jones, as expressed in *An Essay on the Distribution of Wealth, and on the Sources of Taxation* (1831), he also maintained that account should be taken of the fact that "every country has its own peculiar public economy, arising from its having habits, institutions, and modes of government peculiar to itself."[28] The peculiarities he conceived of primarily as qualifications and modifications of the fundamental principles that had to be taken into account in the economic development of a nation. Sedgwick subscribed to the Ricardian theory of value as presented by

---

[28] *Public and Private Economy*, I, 33.
Sedgwick had earlier used the terms "political economy" and "domestic economy."

---

as a political economist. . . . He was the most active ministerial member of the committee which reported at such length in 1820, and is understood to have made himself unpopular with the country gentlemen [the rural landlords seeking greater restrictions on the importation of grain] at that time on account of the steadfastness with which he advocated a more liberal system in opposition to them. He had a firm supporter in Mr. Ricardo, to whom he was, on several occasions, greatly indebted at that time." ("Mr. Huskisson," Boston *Statesman*, November 20, 1830). Sedgwick was a reader of the *Chronicle;* see *Public and Private Economy*, I, 34.

James Mill's *Elements of Political Economy* (3rd ed., 1826).[29]

Sedgwick contended that "the amount of labor put upon a thing determines its value, compared with other things . . . , [since] labor procures nearly all things. Labor, therefore, is . . . the regulator of value, 'and the first price of all things'. In other words, the cost of production regulates the exchangeable value of commodities."[30] After asserting that capital like nearly all other wealth proceeds from labor, that it is hoarded or "accumulated labor," he carefully detailed the manifold advantages of capital in the production of wealth. Among them was that "As capital is that which enables us to labor to advantage, it is that also which enables us to employ laborers. . . . Laborers, therefore, are always interested in saving and increasing capital, by which alone their wages are paid."[31]

[29] Sedgwick wrote his son in 1829: "When in New York call upon Mr. McVickar and ask him if I can find Mill's book on political economy in town. I want to see it very much. Tell him that I have sent to England for it, and in the meantime, if I can borrow it of him or any other person I should be very glad—This I must leave to your diplomacy." (To Sedgwick no. 3, September 16, 1829, Sedgwick no. 2. Papers),.

[30] *Public and Private Economy*, I, 148. Sedgwick quoted from Mill, chapter 2, section 3. He had apparently wanted Mill in order to dispose of that great heresy to classical economists; namely, the possibility of a general overproduction or a "general glut," as it was called then. See *An Address, Delivered before the Berkshire Agricultural Society*, pp. 12-14.

[31] *Public and Private Economy*, I, 140, 141.

Sedgwick was a pioneer in his emphasis on the importance of human capital: "'A poor man's capital may be said to consist of his education, his skill, his capacity to do business; this is his stock in trade.'"[32] He went so far as to argue that knowledge, especially of the advance of the arts, was as important if not more important than physical capital. He bluntly exclaimed in 1830: "There is no better investment of money than in the acquisition of knowledge of the best and cheapest way of achieving an object. Knowledge is a capital that does not waste, neither moth nor rust corrupts it; it brightens in using. . . . But knowledge has its price, and must be paid for.'"[33]

More conventional was his analysis of interest. Sedgwick had an embryonic, crude productivity theory of interest. Payment for the loan of money is just as valid as paying for the use of a horse. The borrower of the horse "can make money from the labor of the horse," and the borrower of money "'may exchange his money for a horse, and thus make more money"; similarly the borrower can use the money to buy wheat, "put it in the ground and produce more wheat." Laws fixing

---

[32] *Public and Private Economy*, I, 140.

From this he concluded that to direct the laborer "where, when, how, and for what wage he shall labour, is as cruel and unjust, as to seize by violence, the iron chest of the rich man."

[33] *An Address . . . Delivered before the Berkshire Association for the Promotion of Agriculture and Manufactures*, pp. 8, 10.

a maximum rate of interest were absurd because, to use an example, "a bushel of wheat and a dollar, and everything else may be made more valuable, by being made to earn more in the hands of the borrower at one time and place, than another."[34]

Accepting a sophisticated form of the wages fund doctrine Sedgwick laid down as a first principle of wages that *"the rate of wages depends upon the number of laborers, compared with the business to be done."*[35] In this sense, "Wages are generally in proportion to the prosperity and riches of a country.... Where there is a great deal of property there is a great deal of work to be done."[36] Another principle is that wages "are regulated, in a great measure, by the intelligence, education, good conduct, and independent condition of the laborers." By "independent condition," Sedgwick meant that if the laborers saved and placed the funds in savings banks or other forms of property, and thereby became capitalists, they would not be at the mercy of their employers in the competition in the labor market where "the employer desires to get wages as cheap as he can, and the employed to get as much as he can." This competition "has ever existed" and "is always going on." Since "the employer is a man of property . . . [,] a capitalist," he can suspend opera-

---

[34] *Public and Private Economy*, I, 138.
[35] *Public and Private Economy*, I, 38.
[36] *Public and Private Economy*, II, 133.

tions if necessary for a period, "'as we know now (1837) to be the case in consequence of the money distress in the country. Therefore, when things get to the worst, and the parties fall out, the owner lays up his ship, and the manufacturer stops his mill, till the laborer can be brought to terms, which, generally, is quickly done, for the laborer . . . has laid up nothing.'"[37]

Sedgwick had no difficulty in applying his theory or theories of wages to those in the public service. He boldly declared that "there is but one rule, and that is the same, which prudent people adopt on their farms, and in their workshops—to pay as much as will obtain the most competent, skillful, and faithful persons." He developed this application to meet the charge that the state's highest judicial officers were overpaid. He replied that "Considering . . . the immense difference in this station between one man and another, in learning, sense and capacity to dispatch business, which latter qualification alone, is a compensation to the people for almost any salary they may give, and applying the rule . . . to the whole State, to the towns as well as the country, thus giving the Commonwealth, the power of selection, the people have, as I think, with propriety, acquiesced in their salaries, as now established."[38]

---

[37] *Public and Private Economy*, II, 34-35.

[38] *An Address, Delivered before the Berkshire Agricultural Society*, pp. 19-20.

As Sedgwick surveyed the history of civilization, he exclaimed that "*the most remarkable feature of the present times is . . . the elevation of the laboring classes,*" especially in the United States.[39] But as he added in a letter to President Van Buren in 1837, he meant the elevation of "those who are, I think, properly called the 'laboring' classes, if that word is well understood, and not perverted." He maintained that "the laboring classes" included all those who were not members of the "aristocracy," and this class he defined somewhat vaguely as "those who either from principle, habit, or association do not sympathize strongly with the laboring classes."[40] In fact to him there were few in America who were not "laborers." "We are . . . yet in our infancy; ardent, enterprising, intelligent, and free from that curse of all curses, which seems to render the condition of many parts of the world hopeless, a dependent, ignorant, vulgar, overgrown population."[41] To the cry of some radicals of the day that the "only producers of wealth," were "the farmers, mechanics, manufacturers, and others whom they call laborers," Sedgwick retorted that since this was a "lamentable error, that creates heart burnings in different classes, it must be

---

[39] *Public and Private Economy*, II, 195.
[40] Sedgwick to Van Buren, November 26, 1837, Van Buren Papers.
[41] *An Address . . . Delivered before the Berkshire Association for the Promotion of Agriculture and Manufactures*, p. 7.

wholly rooted out of the country."⁴² Thus Sedgwick, like Jefferson and the Jacksonians in general, thought of the modern "class" struggle in terms of the middle ages, as between nobility and "laborers," and the latter included farmers, merchants, industrial employers as well as wage earners.

Sedgwick granted that much poverty and poor working conditions still existed even in the United States both in the urban and in the rural areas— among the settlers on new lands, farmers, immigrants and journeymen mechanics. In the factories, the "hirelings" hardly had an ideal life. There is the exploitation of the company stores, the miserable housing conditions, the long hours for women and children. Speaking of wage earners, both in England and in the United States, he exclaimed: "Many of them being ... doomed to work twelve, fourteen or more hours in a day have no leisure either for the proper improvement of the mind or for those recreations which are indispensable to recruit the wasted and exhausted strength of the body.... Their ignorance is deplorable; they can neither add a row of figures,

---

⁴² *Public and Private Economy*, I, 235.

See the discussion of the meaning of "workingman" in the Jacksonian era, in Joseph Dorfman, "The Jackson Wage-Earner Thesis," *The American Historical Review*, January 1949. A "workingman," according to Sedgwick, was a man who "must work to get his living ... [who] must live by effort and anxiety of mind, and toil of body." (*Public and Private Economy*, I, 221).

nor read the signs over the shop-doors, nor the names on the door plates."[43]

The wretched condition of the working people, however, is largely their own fault. Attempting to follow the fashions of those much richer than themselves, they spend much of their wages and property upon gewgaws, short-lived finery, and especially "low sensuality," such as beer, hard liquor and gambling "which either enfeebles or destroys their working faculties." He sadly commented that "the working people have a very feeble conception of the extent to which poverty and the unequal distribution of property proceeds from their vices."[44] The basic remedy

---

[43] *Public and Private Economy,* I, 79.

[44] *Public and Private Economy,* I, 131; II, 196.

It seems that his friend and relative, Mark Hopkins, the famed president of Williams College, was at least in part responsible for Sedgwick's emphasis in volume II on the ill effects of what Veblen would call "conspicuous waste." On receiving the first volume in 1836, Hopkins wrote Sedgwick that "If I were to mention another subject on which I think it important that your ideas should prevail, it would be the possibility of employing mankind upon something useful. It is a very common impression that people are well employed when they are producing any thing that will sell well, however trifling, and thus cause a circulation of property. Industry is necessary to virtue, and I should be very slow to think that it cannot be practised without ministering to those propensities and tastes to which virtue is opposed. In regard to this it is evident that true reform must commence among the employers. So long as the mass of the rich are selfish and vain, and prefer to spend their money for mere badges of distinction, that is, for fashion in any form, it must be

was temperance but this could be achieved only by voluntary action by the individual and persuasion, not by the compulsory power of law, because, as a party organ put it, Sedgwick believed that "the principle of *freedom*" was the greatest "practical agent for working out the highest possible degree of social amelioration."[45] Sedgwick himself declared: "The law never did nor ever will counteract the vicious habits of society, that consist in *indigence*. . . . No, it is the public sentiment the moral feeling, the religious conviction that is to afford us any hope."[46]

Sedgwick was exceptional in expressing sympathy for labor unions, especially in their efforts to lower the hours of toil; provided, that they built on temperance as the foundation. "Let the working people, then, whenever they combine, as they have a right and ought to do for all worthy

---

[45] "Political Portraits, No. 17: Theodore Sedgwick," *The United States Magazine and Democratic Review*, February 1840, pp. 137-138.
[46] *An Address . . . Delivered before the Berkshire Association for the Promotion of Agriculture and Manufactures*, p. 15.

---

expected that those who labor will produce such articles as they prefer, but when they, and indeed all classes, shall learn that there is a higher pleasure in being economical for the sake of being benevolent and public spirited, than for the sake of being *somebody*, then a reform will follow of course.

"Society has certainly a step to take on this point both in economy and morals, for I hold that good economy is a part of good morals." (Hopkins to Sedgwick, March 2, 1836, Sedgwick no. 2 Papers).

purposes, proclaim temperance as their watchword, and mutual respect for each other's virtues as the law of their order."⁴⁷

Sedgwick, however, became so distressed over the amount of labor wasted in catering to low sensuality that he exclaimed: "I have heard of many a strike on account of hours and wages, but not because of the contemptible, unworthy, wasteful employments in which laboring men are every day engaged, which would often be more to the purpose."⁴⁸

He contended that the foundation of higher and lower classes is ordained by nature and providence, but the lowly individual need not remain in his assigned place. The difference depended in large part on the amount of mental labor put forth: "If one man gets more knowledge than another, he will be greater, . . . more powerful; he will get more property, and property is power." The only sound way of rising is by "the acquisition of property, virtue, and education; but . . . property . . . gives the means of education, which, in its turn, creates more property . . . When industrious, virtuous, young men rise in this comtry, it is nine times in ten by husbanding

---

⁴⁷ "The working people form trades' unions and combinations to lessen their hours of toil. All this is well, if well done; but what signify, increased wages, if the money which a man earns is spent in those sinks of corruption, dramshops, in vice and debauchery." (*Public and Private Economy*, II, 196).

⁴⁸ *Public and Private Economy*, II, 132.

their wages and thus furnishing them with a capital for a higher and larger business." Thus if the depressed and over-worked eastern wage earners would stop wasting their earnings in gaudy displays, luxuries and drink, and instead observe Benjamin Franklin's *"Poor Richard's* economical code," with its emphasis on frugality and industry, they could in a few years either "settle as farmers in the new states, or . . . undertake an independent business in the old."[49]

This did not mean free grants of land to would-be settlers. On the contrary Sedgwick denounced the squatters on the western public and private "wild" lands. Originally, he said, when the Indians were troublesome in the frontier territory, it was expedient to allow squatters to occupy the public lands in order to settle the country, but most of the Indians have been removed, "or [are] in the course of removal." The lands, he insisted, were for the poorer and least fortunate people, who should be able by industrious labor

---

[49] *Public and Private Economy*, I, 224-226; *Hints for the People*, p. 31.

"[T]he more a man *labors* with his mind, which is mental labor, and the less with his hands, which is bodily labor, the higher he is in the scale of laborers . . . It is upon this ground, that there ever have been, and ever will be, high and low, rich and poor, masters and servants, officers and their men, masters of ships and their crews, farmers and their laborers, master mechanics and journeymen, manufacturers and their workmen. These are a part of the higher and lower classes in every country." (*Public and Private Economy*, I, 226-327).

to acquire in a few years sufficient funds—say $1000—to purchase "wild" land for cultivation. He contended that some of these squatters or "claimants" having settled on the best lands wait for government sales and then "by combination and threats of violence," against would-be higher bidders obtain their lands at the minimum price of one dollar and a quarter an acre. Worse still, according to Sedgwick, was the practice of poor squatters on public lands who could not furnish the minimum; these, after selling their claims often for trifling sums to speculators, would then serve as dummy purchasers at the government sales for the benefit of the speculators. Thus the law allowing a squatter a preemption right generally deprived individuals of their happiness from property honestly acquired. Certainly "no good and honest man will seize upon property which belongs to another."[50]

Sedgwick noted the existence of great private fortunes, but these, he maintained, were earned by their possessors or inherited from those who had earned them. He recounted in *Hints to My Countrymen* that he had heard in Boston that ten gentlemen, nearly all inheritors of great wealth, who had accidentally assembled at a dinner table were worth a total of $6,000,000. This amount was not dangerous; "for . . . the butchers, tailors, coach-makers, etc., will take care that it performs

---

[50] *Public and Private Economy*, I, 122-124.

FROM FEDERALISM TO JACKSONIANISM 35

the various useful offices which God designed for it in this country. Who can question an American's title to wealth? God gave the country, industry gives him the money." Put in another way, "The rich among us are generally made so by the laws of God, which give to knowledge, diligence and frugality, their sure rewards; not by that law of man, by which [as in England] millions are entailed upon an idiot, a madman or brute." Being very rich the people of Boston could afford great houses resembling castles. Some cost $40-$50,000 and one "not less than ninety thousand dollars! . . . But these very great houses are in bad taste for the people of Boston, and do not correspond with their general character—for they are great *political economists*"; that is, economical and saving.[51] In fact, the buyers and sellers of expensive, gaudy things were generally not the men who enjoy lordly inheritances; on the contrary, "their practice is to divide their property equally among their children, or nearly so."[52]

Sedgwick as an early proponent of industrialization strongly supported the development of the factory system. He applauded large, successful textile corporations, such as those at Waltham, Massachusetts. He explained that New England had taken the lead in "manufactories" largely

---

[51] *Hints to My Countrymen*, pp. 187, 188; *Hints for the People*, p. 5.

[52] *Public and Private Economy*, II, 126.

because of the ingenuity of its educated people, including their "spirit of enterprise." Here he made use of the historical method and emphasized education: "Every country has its peculiar character; nature perhaps creates it, institutions may greatly modify and add to its improvement. For the foundation of the sober, patient, discreet, sagacious character of our people, we may look to our early history, our rigid climate, stubborn hills, and iron bound coasts. The institutions for learning, have done the rest. What nature has denied, ingenuity supplies. How else can we account for the fact, that *we* should have taken the lead in manufactures, when other states are richer and in many parts possess the same natural advantages of water power?" Sedgwick prophesied that "the manufactures of New England, will constitute much of its riches and power. Yes, power, for a State *without riches, cannot have power*.... The manufacturing ability of Massachusetts just begins to show itself.... Already, those who are at the head of these establishments, enjoy salaries that far exceed the professional emoluments of gentlemen of the first reputation."[53] He noted some undesirable accompaniments of

---

[53] Massachusetts Commissioners on Establishment of Institutions of Instruction in Practical Arts and Sciences [Theodore Sedgwick, Chairman], *Report of the Commissioners Appointed by a Resolve of the 22 February, 1825.* (Boston: Commonwealth of Massachusetts. General Court, 1826) pp. 40-41. Hereafter referred to as Sedgwick *et al., Report of the Commissioners.*

the development of the factory system but he felt that they were the necessary price of progress and would eventually disappear. Thus he publicly stated in 1828, that "In the present condition of the world, the abstract question of the propriety, the necessity, the utility of manufactures is not one, that three words need be wasted upon. They are *indispensable* to a flourishing state. There are difficulties, objections to them, and so there is to every improvement, which brings wealth, and changes the state of society. Our moral people cannot bear to see their children at a tender age, turned off from father and mother, before they have learned to be useful in a domestic way, into these manufactories." This to Sedgwick was "a great evil," but he argued that "we must take the bad with the good. God has so ordered it. These are not the most favorable situations for health, but who has that choice always? New countries must be settled in the very face of pestilence; laborers in digging canals must toil through mire and swamps; cities must be cleansed of their impurities." To Sedgwick, "there is no option left for us in such cases. Those who object to manufactories, must first bring us back to log houses, and tow shirts. No; the arts which enable a common man to put a blue or a black coat upon his back, are changing the face of the world in government, morals, religion, every thing." At the same time, Sedgwick left open the use of various forms of social control to curb the evils of the factory system. He contended that "As to the *morals* of these manufactories, the eye of the public, of the state, of all good and religious men, should be upon them immediately, now in the onset, upon their regulations, police, schools."[54]

Strengthening Sedgwick's faith in industrialism was his finding on his tour of England that the intelligent laboring people were in the manufacturing districts, such as Manchester. "Such a fact," he wrote, "ought to go far to diminish the fears of the people of the United States as to the evils of their manufacturing population."[55] This meant all the more necessity of "*moral and intellectual cultivation,*" which he felt was the basis of the "certain prosperity of all institu-

---

[54] [Sedgwick], *Brief Remarks on the Rail Roads, Proposed in Massachusetts.* Berkshire. (Stockbridge, Mass.: Webster, 1828) p. 19. A decade later, he declared that the "growth of manufactures is inevitable here," and he contended that "all that is left to us is to educate the manufacturing people as highly as we can." (*Public and Private Economy*, II, 161).

The term police was defined by a contemporary Supreme Court Justice as follows: "A police measure, in common parlance, often relates to something connected with public morals. . . . But in law, the word *police* is much broader, and includes all legislation for the internal policy of a state." [Levi Woodbury, "On Taxes by States on Passengers in Vessels from Abroad, to Support Paupers," dissenting opinion in case of *Norris v. City of Boston* and *Smith v. Turner*, January term, Supreme Court of the United States, 1849; reprinted in Woodbury, *Writings of Levi Woodbury*, 3 volumes (Boston: Little Brown, 1852) II, 110.

[55] *Public and Private Economy*, II, 161.

tions." The salutary but "slow way of education and religious discipline" involved training in the arts and sciences, including political economy, broadly conceived to include government and ethics.[56] The working men, he declared, are greatly interested in physical science. "Simple as the labors of many of them are, their prosperity depends upon the progress of science. In those countries where science does not exist, they are the most miserable of all men."[57]

He believed that the state could do little directly to improve the condition of the factory operatives, but he commended as honorable men as well as good business men factory owners that did so. He declared that in this connection the factories of Lowell, "by far the most important manufacturing place in the United States appeared (1833) to great advantage. Very few children were then employed in the factories, in some scarcely any. The working hours were twelve or twelve and a quarter."[58] But even at Lowell in

---

[56] *Hints to My Countrymen*, p. 160.

[57] *Public and Private Economy*, I, 169.

[58] Sedgwick complained of the lack of adequate statistical information on manufactures, including the wages of operatives. He wrote his son in 1833: "I find a great defect of statistical information, which is essential to my design—And it is a kind of information, which I cannot get from books—It is only to be had from enquiry and actual observation,—particularly of the manufactures. I mean therefore in the course of the year, if possible to go in quest of it." (March 24, 1833, Sedgwick no. 2 Papers). The very same month he seems to have begun sending

the company houses "some rooms contained two or three beds, and sometimes three girls slept in a bed."[59]

In view of Sedgwick's emphasis on industrialization, his continued strong support of free trade was rather novel, even if it was in accord with classical political economy. He declared in 1826 "We are a commercial people, and as the interests of trade are better understood, the freedom of intercourse among nations will increase."[60] Sedgwick was a leader in the opposition to the establishment of a permanent protective policy. He was one of the promoters and participants of the great convention of September 1831 in Philadelphia "for the purpose of securing the efficient cooperation of the friends of Free Trade,

---

[59] *Public and Private Economy*, I, 111.

[60] Sedgwick *et al.*, *Report of the Commissioners*, p. 7.

---

questionnaires to informed people in various manufacturing communities. He asked of them the number and wages of operatives in each type of industry. Wages were classified according whether for "males over 16," "males under 16," and "women and girls." (Charles Older to Sedgwick, March 25, 1833, Sedgwick no. 2 Papers). This informant lived in the nearby village of South Lee. The fact that only one such questionnaire is in Sedgwick's papers seems to indicate that he must have had serious difficulties obtaining replies; in addition to the more general problems inherent in attempting to conduct a one-man statistical research bureau at the time.

throughout the United States, in procuring the repeal of the Restrictive System."[60a]

Brother Charles wrote to brother Robert in 1835: "I wish you would tell Theodore to establish a system of living while he is in New York, especially not to get up too early.... He overlooks the greatest blessing of the free trade principle, when he tries to regulate private affairs before 10 o'clock, A.M."[61]

Rather novel, at least in phrasing, was his contention "that to have a rich commerce, we must have rich customers; that nations are profited by the peaceful policy of each other; that all plans to monopolize the trade of a world, are but the poor devices of hucksters, pedlars and forestallers; that to enrich our own fields, it is not necessary to spread desolation over those of our neighbors."[61a]

Doubtless Sedgwick's faith in free trade was strengthened by his learning from people "who

---

[60a] "Minutes of the Free Trade Meeting," June 1831, in Condy Raguet, *The Principles of Free Trade* (2nd edition, 1849; New York: Augustus M. Kelley Publishers, 1969) p. 433.

[61] [*Letters of Charles Sedgwick to his Family and Friends,* edited by Catherine Maria Sedgwick (Boston: privately printed, 1871) p. 77]. The editor in a note commented that "The above is a playful allusion to the family infirmity of feeling miserable and reformatory before breakfast. My brother Theodore was grievously beset with this dyspeptic symptom." (p. 78).

[61a] Sedgwick et al., *Report of the Commissioners,* p. 39.

have the best means of forming an opinion'' that labor in the American textile mills was not dearer than in the English. This was so, because (1) of the greater proportion of females in the labor force, (2) the females could perform operations here which in England only men did, and (3) because of ''the regular, orderly, and virtuous character of the laborers,'' as against the ''notorious profligacy of the females in the manufacturing establishments in Manchester.''[61b]

Though Sedgwick opposed government intervention in international as well as domestic trade, he was a strong believer in state aid for improved means of domestic transportation, or what was called ''internal improvements.'' The local Adams organ in 1828, in congratulating Sedgwick on being reelected to the Massachusetts House of Representatives, stated that ''he is a friend to internal improvements, on which, wisely planned, and judiciously advanced, depend the prosperity of the individual, the State and the Country.''[61c]

Sedgwick following Adam Smith long maintained that a basic economic function of the state was to provide for ''internal improvements which are indispensable to the prosperity of all.''[62] But

---

[61b] *Hints to My Countrymen*, pp. 159-160.
[61c] *Berkshire Star and County Republican*, May 15, 1828.
[62] *Hints for the People*, p. 31.

what distinguished him was his pioneer role in the recognition of the importance of railroads for economic development, in particular for industrialization. Beginning in 1826, he was one of the most zealous advocates both in the press and in the Massachusetts State Legislature for the construction of a railroad across the state—the Western Railroad—from Boston to the western line and continuing to the Hudson River at or near Albany, a project that became the Boston and Albany Railroad.[63] He noted the advantage to the

[63] Nathan Hale, the leading Boston advocate of the project, declared that "in no part of the state has a warmer zeal been manifested for the establishment of the western railroad than in the county of Berkshire." [*Remarks on the Practicability and Expediency of Rail Roads from Boston to the Hudson River, and from Boston to Providence* (Boston: Lewis, 1829) p. 24]. This pamphlet was composed of articles originally published by Hale in his anti-Jackson Boston *Daily Advertiser,* in the summer of 1827.

A select committee of the House reported on January 13, 1827, that in connection with the determination of the most eligible route for a railway from Boston to the Hudson: "On ONE route at least a survey has been made from the Connecticut River to the Hudson by an intelligent and enterprising citizen of Berkshire, and by him a Railway had been pronounced not only practicable but highly expedient." [*Report of the Select Committee of the House of Representatives of Massachusetts on the Practicability and Expediency of constructing a Rail Way from Boston to the Hudson River, at or near Albany,* January 14, 1827, House Document no. 13 (1827) p. 24].

See also Charles L. Hodge, "Economic Beginnings of the Boston and Albany Railroad, 1831-1867," in *Facts and Factors in Economic History,* articles by former students of Edwin Francis Gay (1932; New York: Augustus M. Kelley Publishers, 1968) p. 449.

state of Massachusetts of such a railroad, and in particular to the county of Berkshire. The county has, he declared, an unlimited supply of water power, but it is worthless in the absence of such manufacturing and other enterprises that a railroad would encourage. So too it would make possible markets for Berkshire's timber, marble and iron as well as agricultural produce. In general by breaking "down the barriers between the Cities and the country," the railroads would induce the flow from the eastern centers of capital for investment on a large scale [into the region]. Thus it would develop the country area and build up interior cities.[64]

Sedgwick originally argued for state construction and management. He maintained that "Roads . . . belong to the community, and the railroad, so far as public use is designed by it, is the gift of the arts to states. It is among the few improvements, that a state can most successfully manage. What is intended for the beneficent use of the great public, should never be placed in private hands." He contended that a private company would place underdeveloped areas like Berkshire county at the mercy of the eastern capitalists. He said: "The mode of constructing the road; its direction; its connection with other communications; the regulation of the travel; of

---

[64] *Brief Remarks on the Rail Roads, Proposed in Massachusetts,* p. 16.

the tolls whether high or low; whether upon tonnage and passengers, or upon either alone, are all *public concerns*, and this . . . [should not] be left to the decision of *owners* living at Salem, Boston, Worcester, Springfield, etc." Finally Sedgwick declared that the "road will be worth all that it will cost, and a good deal more," in the sense, that it would be an *"advantageous, profitable,* undertaking."[65]

Facing too strong opposition to an exclusively public road, Sedgwick in September 1829 proposed a mixed enterprise, "a union between the State and individuals"; that is, a state chartered corporation, in which the state would be a stockholder and/or lend its credit and would exercise supervision, or what Sedgwick called the recognition of the supremacy of the state.[66] In the course of the debate on the measure in the House of Representatives, January 1830, Sedgwick introduced

---

[65] *Brief Remarks on the Rail Roads, Proposed in Massachusetts,* pp. 12, 14, 22.

[66] Sedgwick, "To the Public," no. 8, *Berkshire Journal,* September 17, 1829, reprinted in the Boston *Daily Advertiser,* September 24, 1829.

Internal improvements,—chiefly canals and railroads—are designed "to cheapen the transportation of persons and property. This is the great machinery, the greatest by far, in an age in which machinery has produced changes, with which, in the same time, nothing in former periods, bears comparison. It is the machinery of the public, for public uses, on the Public High Ways." Therefore the state would never surrender "her control of the subject." ("To the Public," no. 10, *Berkshire Journal,* December 3, 1829).

the heretical argument that such public works would serve to stimulate business recovery. In fact his position has almost a "Keynesian" flavor. He declared: "it is the duty of the state to do something for giving employment to the people, at a time when private investment of capital has been so disastrous, and the general stagnation of business was so severely felt."[67] There is still sufficient private capital "which if employed in this undertaking will give an impulse to business, and by its effects on the industry of the country will be worth all that the railroad will cost."[68]

The account in the Boston *Daily Advertiser* is a sort of summary of a great part of the Sedgwick address. There is fortunately an account of his views that he supplied the *Berkshire Journal* about three months earlier. This clarifies certain aspects of his intriguing discussion of "overproduction and employment." He began by saying that journals critical of the project argue that since the country was suffering from general overproduction there could be no economic justification for the railroad venture, at least at present. He replied: "Trade and manufactures have their fortunate and their unfortunate periods—we are

---

[67] He claimed also in the same debate that the tariff was similarly treated from the standpoint of employment. "The tariff policy is founded on the principle that it is for the interest of the country to furnish employment as far as it is practicable to all its citizens."

[68] Editorial, "Massachusetts Rail Road," Boston *Daily Advertiser*, January 22, 1830.

now experiencing the latter; people are alarmed, there is a panic, and men know not what to believe. It is said, that there is *overproduction,* and that this is likely in a state of peace to continue."

Then Sedgwick drew a distinction between "permanent overproduction" and "temporary overproduction" which he seemed to identify with partial overproduction. As he put it "there cannot be overproduction, permanently, so as to interfere *ruinously* with the industry of a country. . . . There may be overproduction at a given period, and doubtless now is in regard to certain products, for instance, woolen and cotton goods, and perhaps others." But overproduction permanently, or what would be the same thing, stagnation in the industry of the world for the want of demand for its products, is impossible, for no limit could be "assigned to men's wants. He wants all that his ingenuity can contrive"; that is, man's wants are insatiable. This somewhat familiar orthodox doctrine is also found earlier in *Brief Remarks on the Rail Roads* (1828). There he repeated that "The most senseless enterprises have been justified upon the ground, that they would *scatter money among the people,* and I recollect well, to have heard while the New York Canal was going forward, a language like this, that if it should fail altogether, still it would be no great loss, as the money would be spent among themselves. It would have been an immense loss; nearly a dead loss—just as though it is possible for a state to employ profitably a hundredth part of its population in picking up straws, and laying them down again. It is so much capital dead and gone. The community is so much the poorer for it. Though it has come directly from the pockets of the rich, the poor have so much less means to work with. In all great shocks of public credit and losses to the community, people of small means, are the first and greatest sufferers. Let it be distinctly understood therefore, that the Rail Road, is recommended upon its own merits, and not because it *scatters money*, as fools scatter it. It is the fool only, that comes to poverty by waste; the wise man wastes not a cent, nor does a wise state." (p. 22).

To return to the *Berkshire Journal*, Sedgwick argued that despite differences of opinion as to the cause of the present stagnation, there was general agreement that it existed; in short "that there is distress for the want of profitable employment; that some portion of the people are wholly out of employ, and others partly so. . . . In such a state of things, to employ men who are idle, in a work of decent, moderate utility to the public, is clear gain. . . . A thousand dollars expended now in useful, public works, will be of more value to the people than ten times the amount at a more prosperous period. A few hundred thousand dollars in a year like this, judiciously expended by the state, would put a new face on things." Instead therefore, of using the depression as an excuse for postponing the work "this is the moment in which public enterprise will have a tenfold value, and furnish a most seasonable relief to people, who are suffering severely." In any event this venture to construct "the best roads known to modern improvement" would prove "a money making and money saving business" to the people of New England.[69]

In an address at about the same time, he maintained that in "an older, but still progressive society," as was Massachusetts, "those improvements . . . which are for the good of a majority; which naturally belong to the public to take care of; which demand public encouragement in order to be successfully commenced, must be fostered by the state, in some way or other."[70] To this end, he supported state grants to agricultural societies. "The small fund granted by your [Massachusetts] legislature . . . really does not impoverish the State," for the funds are used to encourage

---

[69] "To the Public," no. 9, *Berkshire Journal*, October 29, 1829.

Sedgwick continued to charge that "some of the eminent political economists even at the present day, do justify the wasteful expenditures of governments in the support of otherwise useless armies and navies, prodigious church establishments, and hosts of useless officers," on the ground "that in no other way would there be a sufficient stimulus to industry, and demand for labor." (*An Address, Delivered before the Berkshire Agricultural Society*, p. 12).

[70] *An Address, Delivered before the Berkshire Agricultural Society*, p. 18.

the development and dissemination of advanced processes, that is, to advance knowledge which is often the scarce factor, rather than want of capital. "The improvements introduced by the dissemination of agricultural knowledge, are almost as free as the air."[71]

This applied to manufactures as well as agriculture. As he declared in his presidential address of 1830 before the Berkshire Agricultural Society, "Everything possible must be done to bring our resources to light. This Society should look through the remotest parts of the County, to see if there be not some new occupation, or trade, just springing up, which demands encouragement."[72]

The state financing of the construction of railroads and other large public improvements, Sedgwick granted, meant an increase in public debt at least temporarily, whether construction was on public account or by a "mixed" enterprise. But Sedgwick like the classical economists had denounced both private and public debt as wasteful burdens. Thus he wrote in *Hints to My Countrymen* that for the individual "debt and slavery are all one."[73] He informed his son in 1830: "[A]s a universal rule, as a matter of Economy,

---

[71] *An Address . . . Delivered before the Berkshire Association for the Promotion of Agriculture and Manufactures*, pp. 4, 10, 11.

[72] *An Address, Delivered before the Berkshire Agricultural Society*, p. 18.

[73] *Hints to My Countrymen*, p. 145.

FROM FEDERALISM TO JACKSONIANISM 51

I wish you 'to pay as you go'—Then there is nothing paid for *Credit*.—*Cash* and *Credit* are two things, even where the debtor is known to be quite good—That is, generally.''[74] As for the national debt, he had a farmer's son say in *Hints to My Countrymen* (1826). ''Our Agricultural Society, you know, has determined to send a deputation to Congress, as soon as the national debt is paid off, to thank those, under whose administration it takes place, in the name of the laborers of America, and I might say of the world, for the part they have taken in exhibiting to mankind the glorious sight of one nation not in chains.''[75] As a general principle expenditures by government, Sedgwick maintained, were a subtraction from the national income, or as he put it, they ''must be made out of the aggregate wealth of the community; it is only the diversion of so much money from one object to another.''[76] ''When rulers ... spend, it is generally what other people have

---

[74] To Sedgwick no. 3, April 18, 1830, Sedgwick no. 2 Papers.

[75] *Hints to My Countrymen*, pp. 145-146.

Earlier, in 1823, he exclaimed ''a great [federal] debt of ninety millions, a horrible charge upon the industry and enterprise of a young country just starting into life, demands our attention.'' (*Hints for the People*, p. 31). He added in 1830: ''The most prodigal of all people are generally those who are in debt, and so sensible is the country of this truth, that public sentiment has declared, that the national debt shall be paid and as speedily as possible.'' (*An Address, Delivered before the Berkshire Agricultural Society*, p. 19).

[76] Sedgwick *et al.*, *Report of the Commissioners*, p. 28.

earned."[76a] Sedgwick, however, did not condemn public debts for internal improvements that would yield at least sufficient net revenue to meet interest and amortization payments; that is, they would be a financial success and were therefore productive. Thus, in speaking of "savings ... that appertain to the public at large," he noted that New York's publicly constructed canals "will soon be paid for, and are a great property laid up; such evidence of the sagacity and forethought of a people, afford the best evidence that they are destined to be great." Sedgwick placed canals, railroads, common roads, ship building establishments, etc., among the items of "savings that appertain to the public at large." In the same category he also placed fortresses, war munitions, military roads, but with this comment: "it is a melancholy reflection, to consider how much of the property of the public commonly consists in superfluous masses of the implements of destruction, piled up year after year, without reference to the military wants of the country."[77]

Sedgwick was ahead of his day in his interest in what is now called urban economics. He was aware of the ills of cities, but these were overbalanced by the benefits. To use his words, "We, country folks, are not a little proud of our great cities for we, in fact, consider them as the best

---

[76a] *An Address, Delivered before the Berkshire Agricultural Society*, p. 19.
[77] *Public and Private Economy*, I, 170-171.

evidence of our own industry and enterprise."[78] These benefits were largely the advantages of "a dense, happy population of industrious beings. ... Wherever there are great numbers, there may be, and most often are, the advantages of a *nice division of labor,* which enables us to obtain manufactured articles at vastly less cost than we otherwise should." In short it makes goods cheap. This benefit "arises from the dexterity which a man acquires by doing one thing alone, which was pointed out by Xenophon more than 2000 years ago, as plainly it ever has been since."[79]

Another major advantage of large cities is that a "dense population is most favorable to arts, sciences, discoveries, inventions, and to many of the beautiful and useful refinements of life."[80] Then Sedgwick turned to the grave problems of cities, especially the lot of the urban poor.

Pointing to the European cities, he declared that much of their wretchedness and crime pro-

---

[78] *Hints for the People,* p. 19.

"Instead of envying the wealth and greatness of their capital [Boston], they are proud of that too, and with reason." (*An Address . . . Delivered before the Berkshire Association for the Promotion of Agriculture and Manufactures,* p. 9).

[79] *Public and Private Economy,* III, 138, 139, 140.

Sedgwick quoted Xenophon from the now famous heterodox economist, the Earl of Lauderdale's *An Inquiry into the Nature and Origins of Public Wealth* (1804; New York: Augustus M. Kelley Publishers, 1962) pp. 282-284.

[80] *Public and Private Economy,* III, 140.

ceeded from lack of education, "the people being huddled together, neglected by the rich, corrupted by their example, and left without such accomodations as pure water, baths, pavements, lights, public squares, and space enough in streets, alleys, lanes, to admit of cleanliness, ventilation, and health." He thought it would be fine charity "to light the lamps, clear out the rubbish, fill mud holes and pave the streets" in city slums. London was the worst. He complained that if "London had generally the spacious streets of Washington, the noble avenues of NewYork, and public squares in proportion, and if the population of it were spread over ten times the present surface, the improved comfort, morals and happiness of the people arising from such a circumstance, would more than compensate for the supposed advantage in riches of crowding them together for the purpose of continguity and a nice division of labor." Then he suddenly exclaimed that "all cities are too crowded. A miserable population is a burden, and not a profit; happiness is the true standard of wealth, not numbers."[81] He declared that "we are not far from . . . [Jefferson's] belief in supposing, that . . . [great cities] are often in a state very much liable to fester and inflame."[82]

---

[81] *Public and Private Economy*, III, 149-151.

[82] *Hints for the People*, p. 19.

He later pointed out that "Jefferson . . . does not say 'that great cities are great sores,' as has been imputed to him; though he does say 'that the *mobs* of great cities add

FROM FEDERALISM TO JACKSONIANISM 55

After pointing out that American cities were by no means free of the ills of European centers, Sedgwick said in 1837 that "New York . . . after being settled about two hundred years, is now making for the first time, an effectual effort to introduce pure and wholesome water for the people, and which, as yet, is not as well paved or lighted as London."[83] He expressed alarm too that like all cities New York had many indigents; in 1837 it had three thousand paupers in its poor houses. The basic remedy, he contended, for the elimination of "the wretched pauper system" would be the abolition of public poor relief, the accepted view of dominant Anglo-American classical economics.[84]

---

[83] *Public and Private Economy*, II, 126.

[84] "The number of our paupers both in the town and country, is a disgrace to so young a people." (*An Address . . . Delivered before the Berkshire Association for the Promotion of Agriculture and Manufactures*, p. 7).

---

just as much to the support of pure government, as sores do to the strength of the human body.' " In short, said Sedgwick, "'large cities are not evils or sores, of course, but the vicious and unnecessary parts of large cities are evils." [*Public and Private Economy*, III, 121, 138. Quotation from Jefferson from *Notes on the State of Virginia* (1787; New York: Harper and Row, 1964) p. 158].

He then laid down principles of state intervention that had far reaching implications. To be sure, "what they [the poor] can do for themselves, it is best, as a general rule, that they should do, and the less as a rule they are treated as paupers, the better for them; but, then, there are things which they cannot do for themselves: this should be done from taxation, if taxation be necessary, that is, property should do it. There is no economical truth more certain than that these appropriations of property, if prudently made, leave us richer and not poorer."[85]

Sedgwick hoped that the American people would very "early accustom themselves to the enjoyment of *good and respectable things of every kind*," and that they would not, as in the case of London's famed 400 acre Hyde Park, bar out of their parks and pleasure grounds those who could not afford to ride in coaches. He also hoped that the American people would furnish "parks and pleasure grounds for those poor people who cannot provide them for themselves, which is far from being the case at present. If so, we shall . . .

---

[85] *Public and Private Economy*, III, 149.

According to a summary of his address on pauperism before the New York Society for the Prevention of Pauperism that same year, Sedgwick proposed as "the most effectual remedies of pauperism—the destruction of the system of gratuitous support, and the instruction, especially the religious instruction of the poor." ("Pauperism," *Berkshire Star*, March 6, 1823).

be able to furnish *profitable and respectable work* for all the working people, and thus save both rich and poor from spending so much of their money in the silly, selfish way they do in England. . . . This is one of the remedies by which we propose to rescue the people from so much over breeding and pauperism as there is in England and Ireland"[86] He commended the wealthy of Boston for providing for the construction of hospitals where sick travellers with moderate funds could get rooms and treatment at reasonable charges, instead of being impoverished by the medical cost.[87]

To prevent "overgrown cities" more directly, he suggested that among other things states encourage the construction of roads, canals, railroads to build up interior cities. "It is, then, plainly the interest of the country to carry *inward* those public improvements which tend to equalize the population, the value of land, and its products. It is also a great public object to afford the means of a cheap removal of the foreign population from the seaboard to the interior."[88]

Sedgwick boldly contended that government as

---

[86] *Public and Private Economy*, III, 113-114.

[87] In one such hospital there were several persons "who paid, some two, some three dollars a week for their accommodations, including the best medical and surgical aid. These persons . . . by a three months' sickness in the city, with a few hundred dollars only in their pockets, would have been ruined." (*Hints to My Countrymen*, p. 188).

[88] *Public and Private Economy*, III, 141-142.

well as private individuals or associations should encourage the fine arts, for these make for the refinement of the people. The products of these arts—music, architecture, painting, statuary, etc.,—"'are among the most enduring possessions, and they are calculated to give pleasure to all mankind. Instead, however, of being possessions enjoyed by the people, rich and poor, for the improvement of their common nature, they have been monopolized by those who have engrossed every other kind of wealth.'"[89] He enthusiastically complimented an association of Boston gentlemen for their "noble and patriotic gift" to the people of Boston of a beautiful statue of Washington in the State House, Boston, and he applauded Congress's action in ordering another for the capitol "to be executed, by our countryman [Horatio] Greenough, in Italy, at an estimated expense of $25,000."[90]

---

[89] *Public and Private Economy*, I, 169.

President Mark Hopkins of Williams College was disturbed by the general charge of monopoly made by the "Jacksonians." In the letter praising Sedgwick for his comments on the "working man" and "rank" in volume I, he added: "I hope you will be equally discriminating and happy on the subject of monopolies in [the forthcoming] part 2, for there is also great need of definite ideas in regard to that. My present impression is that there is an undue prejudice against them, or rather that many things are called monopolies which are not, and which, as the olfactories of the public are now set, would smell much sweeter with another name. I am sure you will give them a candid examination." (Hopkins to Sedgwick, March 2, 1836, Sedgwick no. 2 Papers).

[90] *Public and Private Economy*, I, 169-170.

Then by an analysis closely akin to his justification of the salaries of judges, he proceeded to show how the American people might "safely and wisely, under their democratic government, become the patrons of the *fine arts.*" He warned first of all that they will, however, very "wisely determine that the useful arts shall come first." The "farmers, mechanics, merchants and manufacturers," are the practitioners of the useful arts, but these are not the only "workingmen," the only producers of wealth. For example, is not the doctor who heals the workingman and so enables him to work again, "the cause of wealth"? The question then arises "who furnish the funds, who earn the money, that supports these working people that are neither farmers, mechanics, merchants, or manufacturers? The answer is plain: they, the working people . . . Some of them are the public men, magistrates, lawyers, physicians, etc. . . . that no great and prosperous country can live without." Some are the producers of the many beautiful art objects that the workers in the useful arts "cannot produce but are willing to buy and to pay for *out of that surplus which they create* . . . This explains . . . the rise and progress of all the arts, which spring up as soon as the merchants, farmers, mechanics, and manufacturers, are supplied with the common conveniences and necessaries of life; that is, after obtaining these, they are willing to work for something more. . . . Thus, we see, too, how the working-men, in the United States, *combined,* pay Greenough twenty-five thousand dollars for a statue of Washington."[91]

The vague surplus defined some sort of limit for government expenditure for the fine arts, but more intriguing was the introduction of the idea that the demand for "public goods" rested on the same economic theory as the demand for private goods. They satisfied the wants of the public through the acts of its representatives. In other words, under our democratic government, Congress's gift to Greenough for the statue, was in effect a gift by "the working-men of the United States, *combined*" for a good purpose.

Sedgwick stated the basic underlying welfare principles, in his report to the legislature in 1826 which called for increased state aid for education and the improvement of especially the common school. He contended that *"the standard of knowledge and taste in the common schools does not comport with the spirit of the age."*[92]

To the great majority of children the advanced knowledge available in the modern manuals—especially mathematics, the physical sciences and political economy broadly conceived —is a sealed book. The rich, however, spared no

---

[91] *Public and Private Economy,* I, 170, 235-236.

[92] Sedgwick *et al, Report of the Commissioners,* p. 29. He said that the level of subjects and the curricula was that found in *The Wealth of Nations,* which was fifty years old.

expense in providing their children with this knowledge. "They are right, too, for it is in this way only, that they can maintain their rank in society. No man is at liberty to abandon the rational privileges, which God has given him in opportunities of superior knowledge. . . . It is plain that the mass of our people have not a just sensibility upon this subject. It is the duty of their legislators to inspire them with it. As the taste for a higher and better education advances, books will be written and provided to gratify that taste, the demand for them will create them."[93]

On the paramount issue of his last years, the monetary and banking system, Sedgwick was a "hard money" Jacksonian, but like most he was no extremist. He held that the purpose of money "was to serve as a medium by which all things might be valued that were to be bought and sold." On the basis of his labor theory of value he granted, that at present (1836) gold and silver provided the best money. "They are valuable because they are obtained with labor; because they answer a purpose which nothing else will; and . . . they are valuable in proportion to the labor expended in obtaining them." He hoped that changes might occur that would result in something better than gold and silver for the same purpose; and the saving of "the immense expenditure of labor," now required for their acquisition.[94] Irredeem-

---
[93] Sedgwick *et al.*, *Report of the Commissioners*, p. 31.
[94] *Public and Private Economy*, I, 136, 139.

able paper money, however, has so far proved disastrous, by leading to inflation and subsequent depression. Paper currency convertible into hard money on demand was desirable with proper safeguards. "The advantages of a paper circulation," he shrewdly wrote, "have been so great in the United States that it will never be dispensed with." It was unfortunate "that many honest people have been deluded by the idea of the possibility of an exclusive metallic currency. When, however, paper money is the *regulating medium*," wages lag behind the rise in prices as at present (1837). "Then . . . the poor, who have *nothing to sell*, and nearly all who live by wages," unjustly suffer. Referring to bank notes especially, he wrote that a great scourge to the poor was "that of irresponsible paper money, which, by some bad management or other, cannot be converted into gold and silver," that is, inconvertible paper money, "Those who are allowed to make any portion of the currency, which becomes a *debt* due from individuals or companies to the people at large, ought to be compelled to give the public the greatest security possible for its redemption; and this will be best done through a proper system of *free private banking*."[95]

This did not mean to Sedgwick that anyone could issue banknotes—but rather the abolition of the requirement that the promoters of a bank

---

[95] *Public and Private Economy*, II, 94-95.

obtain a charter by special act of the state legislature in each case, and the substitution of a *general* act; that is, all were *freely* allowed to engage in banking provided the uniform qualifications prescribed by the act were met. For Sedgwick it also included the repeal of the Restraining Acts in various states including New York. These acts strictly interpreted prohibited anyone from engaging in *any* branch of banking without a state charter. In a letter to Vice President Van Buren in 1834, which was notable for his use of the historical approach, Sedgwick wrote: These acts should be repealed ''upon that great principle of free trade and no monopoly, which is as applicable with few limitations to money, as to anything else, at a proper stage of the civilization, wealth and credit of a country.''[96]

The use of credit, especially bank credit, Sedg-

---

[96] Sedgwick no. 2 to Van Buren, March 11, 1834, Van Buren Papers.

Professor John McVickar was one of the pioneer advocates of a free banking act. See Joseph Dorfman and Rexford G. Tugwell, *Early American Policy; Six Columbia Contributors,* pp. 136-138. McVickar's proposal to the New York legislature, *Hints on Banking* (1827), is reprinted as an appendix in the reprint of McVickar's *Outlines of Political Economy* (1825; New York: Augustus M. Kelley Publishers, 1966). McVickar's scheme was substantially embodied in the New York State Banking Act of 1838, which Sedgwick approved. To Bleecker, Sedgwick wrote in February of the following year: ''I do not apprehend the same evil effects from the free bank privileges, that some do.'' (Sedgwick to Bleecker, February 14, 1839, Sedgwick no. 2 Papers).

wick maintained, was one of the secrets of the economic development of the nation. "In most countries individual enterprise is powerless, without capital," but in the United States, a well-educated person, that is, educated in the required skills, especially in mercantile and manufacturing pursuits, can with industry command it. "He finds those who are willing to furnish that, which is better employed by him than by them. The one has a fortune already accumulated, and only desires an investment of his money, in the hands of prudence, economy, and industry. It is by this process, that *here*, credit is a new power, the value of which cannot be fully understood in other countries."[97]

On the great national controversy over the Second Bank of the United States, he eventually followed Presidents Jackson and Van Buren. Thus Sedgwick supported President Jackson's veto in 1832 of the recharter of the Bank, which was the successor of the bank which his father had helped to establish. And he supported but reluctantly the transfer of government deposits in 1833 to selected state banks.

When a money panic swept the country in May 1837, accompanied by the suspension of specie payments and followed by a serious depression and intensification of the demand for restoration of the Second Bank of the United States or some-

---

[97] Sedgwick *et al., Report of the Commissioners,* pp. 41-42.

FROM FEDERALISM TO JACKSONIANISM 65

thing like it, Sedgwick supported President Van Buren's proposal to the special session of Congress in September 1837 for the Independent Treasury or Sub-Treasury System. Under this scheme the federal government would cease using state banks as fiscal agents and thereby cut off the means which presumably enabled the state banks to issue excessive amounts of banknotes followed by inflation and then a money panic and depression. Instead, government would hold, receive, and disburse its funds in hard money by means of its own Treasury and projected Sub-Treasuries. The measure was described by one of Sedgwick's admirers as "The separation of bank and state, and the independent safe-keeping of the public money for public uses."[98]

Sedgwick in replying to the President's request for his opinion of the plan,[99] expressed some dis-

[98] Quoted from obituary in Providence, Rhode Island, *Republican Herald* in "Political Portraits, No. 17, Theodore Sedgwick," *The United States Magazine and Democratic Review*, February 1840, pp. 142-143.

The key developer and promoter of the Sub-Treasury system was William M. Gouge, a clerk in the U.S. Treasury at the time and for most of his mature life. On Gouge, see Joseph Dorfman, "William M. Gouge and the Formation of Orthodox American Monetary Policy," introductory essay to Gouge, *A Short History of Paper Money and Banking in the United States* (1833; New York: Augustus M. Kelley Publishers, 1968) pp. 5-26.

[99] The President had written to Sedgwick on September 7: "Tell me frankly how near the [message to Congress] came to what you think it ought to be." (Sedgwick no. 2 Papers).

appointment that the President had not discussed the desirability of reform of the state banks in the message. "The reasons which you give, why the government ought to have nothing to do with the naturally free exchanges of commerce, are unanswerable—At the same time, as I believe, that the ideas of our people are in great confusion about the true notions of banking, I did suppose, as stated in my letter, that you would upon this occasion say, what would have greatly tended to help them out of the hobble. I am perfectly aware, however, that as the true measures must originate from the states, objections would arise in the minds of many, to your having anything to say about the matter." He agreed that the president's proposal was excellent and would do much to end permanently banks' suspension of specie payments, or, to use his language, "will forever render a recurrence of the present disgraceful state of bankruptcy impossible."[100]

Thenceforth, Sedgwick devoted most of his efforts to securing enactment of the Sub-Treasury bill. He wrote the President in November: "The warfare that we are carrying on is not against banks rightly constituted, nor against credit, but against paper money strictly, which has proved

---

[100] Sedgwick no. 2 to Van Buren, September 11, 1837, Van Buren Papers.

Sedgwick also stated in the letter that "'my son who is not a little hypercritical in such affairs writes with great enthusiasm about the message."

one of the greatest curses that have ever afflicted the industrious classes. It is against the whole system of monopoly banking. This being the case, all my convictions are confirmed against a Bank of the United States, and in favor of the plan proposed in your message, which is in harmony with all our ideas, and we cannot abandon it for anything yet proposed.'"[101]

In his last address, as he campaigned for the state Democratic ticket in November 1839, he was reported as giving his chief attention to the country's monetary affairs. ''The conduct of the banks was arraigned . . . the proper basis of the credit system presented, its importance admitted, and the folly of charging the Government with any attempt to destroy it. 'The credit system,' he said, 'we must have and shall have—the public ought not to suffer from bank suspension; they have yielded large profits, and if necessary they ought to make sacrifices, rather than that the public should suffer.' ''[102]

As for *Public and Private Economy* itself, it came closest to expressing the general principles of the classical economics of the dominant Jacksonian wing. This is evidenced by the anonymous

---

[101] Sedgwick to Van Buren, November 26, 1837, Van Buren Papers.

[102] ''Political Portraits, No. 17: Theodore Sedgwick,'' *The United States Magazine and Democratic Review*, February 1840, p. 139.

review which appeared in *The United States Magazine and Democratic Review* in 1839. It stated that "adapting, with great judgment and success, many of the recondite principles of economical science, 'to the business and bosoms' of individuals engaged in every pursuit of life, this work cannot fail to exert a salutary and permanent influence whenever it shall become known. . . . [P]erhaps his allusions to the evils inflicted upon society by the abuse of paper money, and the pointing out its deleterious influence upon the comfort of the productive classes, in consequence of enhancing the prices of the necessaries of life, always in a greater ratio than the rise of wages, may be regarded as an indication of his entertaining views similar with those of the present administration of the General Government."[103]

Even the book's specific objective ran in terms

---

[103] "Causes of Poverty," *The United States Magazine and Democratic Review*, May 1839, p. 448.

The author of the unsigned review article was most likely Richard Ela, a clerk in the United States Treasury and a braintruster to Levi Woodbury, Secretary of the Treasury. The review article on Sedgwick along with eleven other unsigned articles from the same journal comprise a bound volume which is in the Seligman collection, Special Collections, Columbia University Libraries. In the university's card catalogue it is listed under Ela's name, and is titled "Collection of Articles on Cotton, Credit, Currency and Philadelphia Banking, 1838-1840." Augustus M. Kelley plans in the near future to reproduce the volume. In the introduction I will supply a more complete identification and account of this contributor to American economic thought and policy, who has escaped the historian.

of the egalitarian individualism of the new economics of Adam Smith, Ricardo and James Mill. According to Bryant, Sedgwick sought "to promote an object which lay nearest the heart of its author—that of narrowing more and more the limits of poverty, ignorance, and vice among his countrymen—of inspiring them with the love of personal independence, giving them habits of reflection, teaching them reverence for each other's rights, and thus bringing about that equality of condition which is the most favorable to the morals and happiness of society, and to the working of our political institutions.''[104]

A most interesting "review" took the form of a private letter to Sedgwick. It was written by a recently arrived British Owenite, an itinerant printer at Harper's while volume I was in process of publication. William M. McDiarmid wrote: "Chance having thrown in my way a glance at your valuable work now going through the Press upon Political Economy, the first thing that struck me was an assertion of yours in the first Chapter, which determined me to write you upon the subject. The assertion was this—'There always have been rich and poor,' and not satisfied with this, you crown it with saying—'There must be rich and poor,' and, as a corollary,—'The people have

---

[104] William Cullen Bryant, ''Theodore Sedgwick,'' in *The Biographical Annual, Containing Memoirs of Eminent Persons, Recently Deceased*, edited by Rufus W. Griswold (New York: Linen and Fennell, 1841) pp. 18-19.

been most miserable in those countries where there are no rich.' This, Sir, in my opinion is one of the most mischievous dogmas that ever entered the heads of modern writers upon Political Economy; and, strange to say, they almost all indulge in the same doctrine.'' He had however great praise for Sedgwick for fearlessly pointing out that the United States was by no means free of poverty and related ills. He concluded with: ''[E]very reflecting mind, every eye in the civilized world is turned towards America, to see what she will do—what she can do encompassed about with her liberal institutions.''[105]

Broadly speaking, *Public and Private Economy* was an advanced attempt to adapt the British classical political economy to American conditions. It is by no means free of inconsistencies and even downright contradictions. These flowed in part from Sedgwick's failure at times to integrate policy conclusions based on his keen observations of current conditions into the classical doctrines which remained fundamental to his own thinking as well as that of the Jacksonians in general.[106]

---

[105] To Sedgwick, December 19, 1835, Sedgwick no. 2 Papers. McDiarmid described himself as a liberal.

[106] ''It is now [1826] fifty years since Adam Smith wrote his *Wealth of Nations*, (the *Wealth of Nations*, it is justly called) and to this day multitudes of the enlightened portion of his countrymen, understand little of his principles, much less have they been able to bring them to bear upon existing regulations.

''The first edition of Mr. *Say's* treatise upon this subject was published at Paris in the year 1803, since which

Yet not a little of the attraction of his publication for the economist of today lies in the novel analysis and positive proposals for achieving industrialization and coping with its problems, and raising the standards of taste and knowledge. Specifically, there is much to be learned from his insights on the role of collective action in the development and improvement of education, transportation, the factory system, the arts—both useful and fine—and urban life.

JOSEPH DORFMAN

Columbia University

February 1973

---

time, it has been introduced into many of the universities of Europe, and into some in this country, and still in public discussions in our National Hall, these rational, enlightened friends of mankind, have been, by way of derision, called *Philosophers,* as though true philosophy, and the principles of business, could by any possibility, be at war with each other. Of the truths of this science, no American citizen, of any public stature whatever, should be ignorant." (Sedgwick *et al., Report of the Commissioners,* pp. 38-39.)

"As to *agrarianism,* in a country where so many have property, and so many can easily acquire it, it is the 'shadow of a ghost.' People ought to be ashamed to be frightened at it, or even to talk of it." (*Public and Private Economy,* II, p. 88).

PUBLIC AND PRIVATE ECONOMY

BY

THEODORE SEDGWICK

PART FIRST

[1836]

AUGUSTUS M. KELLEY • PUBLISHERS
CLIFTON 1974

First Edition 1836

(*New York:* Harper & Brother, *No. 82, Cliff Street*, 1836)

PUBLIC

AND

PRIVATE ECONOMY.

BY THEODORE SEDGWICK.

PART FIRST.

NEW-YORK:
PUBLISHED BY HARPER & BROTHERS,
No. 82, Cliff-street.
....
1836.

Entered, according to Act of Congress, in the year 1836, by HARPER & BROTHERS, in the Clerk's Office for the Southern District of New-York.

TO

JAMES WADSWORTH,

OF

GENESEO, NEW-YORK,

WHOSE LABORIOUS ENTERPRISE, SUCCESSFUL LIFE, AND
LIBERAL DEVOTION TO THE EDUCATION AND
PROSPERITY OF THE PEOPLE, PRACTICALLY
ILLUSTRATE THE LEADING VIEWS
OF THE FOLLOWING PAGES,

THIS VOLUME

IS INSCRIBED, AS A SLIGHT TRIBUTE OF THE REGARD AND
RESPECT OF

THE AUTHOR.

Jan., 1836.

TABLE OF CONTENTS.

CHAPTER I.

Value and uses of Property—Property is power—Is cause of happiness—Abused Wealth—Disproportioned Wealth—Civilization is Property--Property principal means of doing good—Uses of Property; in building houses, manufactories, paying wages, providing for poor foreigners, providing tools, engines, and all means of improvement in the arts, &c.; provides for enjoyments of mind also—Loose instruction about Property—Love of Property natural appetite—Advantage of Property in securing independence—Christian Religion foundation of Wealth 14

CHAPTER II.

What Political Economy is—Another name for Public Economy—Political Economy is Science of Wealth, trade—What Political Economy is in United States—Education part of Political Economy—What Public Economy teaches—Difference between good laws and good Public Economy—No two nations have the same Economy—Public Economy of United States; Wages, division of Labonr, rule as to Wages 27

CHAPTER III.

History of Property—History best teacher of Economy—Land most important Property—Land is real Estate—Value of even small portions of the earth—Size of Farms in Tuscany and Naples—Different interests in Land, as the fee, tenancy for life, &c.—How Lands held in England—Power and liberty of the people have depended greatly upon the terms upon which they have held the Lands—Tenures of Land in Asia, under the Mahomedan Law; Laws of Menu—Of Sandwich Islands; condition of people there—Division of mankind into Landlords and Tenants—Rents, how divided—Labour, Metayer, Ryot, Money Rents—Serf Rents—How Labour Rent takes place—Labour Rents in Russia, &c.—Comparison of Labourers in Russia and England—Poles under Labour Rents—What Metayer Rent is —What Ryot Rents are—What Money Rents—Irish Absentees —Money Rents in England—Grandeur of Owners of Land in England—Mr. Coke's Farm—Tenures of Northern Nations that over-ran the Roman empire—Oath of Fealty—Feudal System —Primogeniture 40

CHAPTER IV.

History of Property continued—Condition of people on discovery of America—Slaves, Villeins, Freemen—First dawn of liberty among Slaves, arose from Slaves saving their Wages—Early concessions to Slaves—Tyranny exercised over labouring people in early times—Statutes regulating Labour—Diet and Apparel—Price of books in the dark ages—Condition of the world when America was discovered—Tenures of Land first granted here—How Tenancies began—Law of Primogeniture in New-York and Southern Colonies—American Revolution—How carried forward by the Property of the people—Mr. Burke, his eulogium on New England—Condition of people when Revolution began—Lessons to be derived from this history of Property 59

CHAPTER V.

History and marks of Poverty—History of Poverty is the history of mankind—So much Poverty not necessary—Dr. Johnson's opinion as to Poverty—Difference between man and brute— *First* Mark of the Poor—Excessive Labour—Manufacturing population of New England, how many hours they work— Working hours in Scotland—*Second* Mark of Poor—No time for improvement of their minds—*Third*, Bad Food—Adulterated food—What articles are adulterated—Dupin's statement of how the French live—Ireland, M'Cullock's statement of how the Irish live—England, condition of Poor there—Poor Law Commissioners' Report—M'Cullock's description of Irish cabins, &c. —*Fourth* Mark of Poor—Bad habitation—*Fifth* Mark—Deficient and bad fuel—*Sixth* Mark of the Poor—Buying on credit

CONTENTS.   ix

—*Seventh* Mark—Greater mortality of the Poor—*Eighth* Mark
—Vices of the Poor—Our ignorance of the Poor—Diminution
of disease 72

CHAPTER VI.

Poverty in the United States—Poverty of Day-labourers in the
United States—Day-labourers in the cities—What proportion
own lots or houses—Their condition in the cities—Clothes—
Fuel—Day-labourers in the country—What proportion own
Land—or a Cow—or Garden—Their houses—Clothes—Intel-
lectual pleasures—What Education they have in the common
Schools—Want of books, &c.—Poverty of Farmers in United
States—What their Education—Houses—Out-houses, Gardens,
Farms, Cattle—Cattle in Ohio—Poverty of Manufacturing
class—How Manufactories supplied with hands—Manufacturers
—How far destitute of Land, Gardens, Cows, &c.—Their con-
dition at Lowell—Store-pay—What Store-pay is—Poverty of
Journeymen Mechanics—Mechanics in Pittsburgh—Poverty to
be prevented by saving Wages—Fashionable expensive Poor—
Who they are in the United States—How they live 94

CHAPTER VII.

Poverty in the United States continued—Another class of Poor—
Poor Emigrants—Their passage across the Lakes—Hardships
of it—Hardships of a journey by land—Prairies of Illinois—
Their beauty—Log-houses of Emigrants—Their cost—Diseases
of Emigrants—Difficulties in obtaining medical aid—Poverty of
Emigrants who cannot buy Government Land—Government
Land composed of Timber Land and Prairie Land—Character
of Prairie Land—How to be cultivated—Wild Lands belonging
to individuals—Squatters—Claimants—Manner in which they
take possession of Government Land—Objects to which the
Lands of Government ought to be appropriated—Virtues of
people who settle new countries—Detroit, its situation—Michigan Territory—Enterprise of the people in making rail-roads,
&c.—Folly of people of United States in the excessive use of
expensive wines—Price of Champagne in United States—In
France—Practical lessons to be derived from this account of
Poverty 116

CONTENTS.

CHAPTER VIII.

What is Wealth?—Definitions of—Wealth obtained by Labour—Items of Wealth—Money—Precious Metals—Gold and Silver—Different articles used as money in different countries—Foundation of the value of the precious metals is labour of obtaining them—Precious metals are merchandize—Capital, what it is—Proceeds from Labour—Produces Wealth, and how—Fixed Capital—Circulating Capital 132

CHAPTER IX.

How is Wealth obtained?—By Labour and Economy—Poverty of our First Parents—Of Savages—Command of God to "replenish" the Earth 143

CHAPTER X.

Labour determines the value of things—Labour first price of all things—Barter—Exceptions to the principle that Labour determines the value of things—Scarcity—Supply and Demand—Principles of Political Economy intelligible to common people—Nature of Wealth to increase—New sources of Wealth discovered yearly 148

CHAPTER XI.

Consumption; or, what must be consumed, and what can or cannot be laid up or saved—Death and burial of African king, Tom Bassa: shows how Property is consumed; shows how Poverty is caused—Productive and Unproductive Consumption—Farmers, &c., not the only producers—Laws of Nature that show that Consumption is always going on: illustrated in the Pyramids—Succession of Improvements, one kind of Consumption—What can be laid up or saved—Particulars of Savings—Saving and Spending, illustrated by the case of a New Settler . . . 157

CHAPTER XII.

Causes of Poverty—Many Causes of Poverty—Malthus' Opinions as to Causes of Poverty—Intemperance—Temperance Re-

CONTENTS. xi

form—Laws of Nature, cause of Poverty—Principal Cause of Poverty, that people do not produce the means of living—Labourers, who are independent, can work at what occupations they choose—Vicious employments, cause of Poverty—Frivolous employments, also—Fashion, cause of Poverty—Fashion of Midshipman's Dress in American Navy—What Fashion is—Fashion Trade—Quantity of gold and silver used in trinkets, &c. 175

CHAPTER XIII.

Brief History of Labour—What is meant by History of Labour—History, best teacher of Economy—Gibbon's Opinions—In what Reform consists—A Reform of Labour—Quotation from Paley—Ancient Labour—Labour on the Pyramids—Use of the Pyramids—Romans, what they laboured at—Their Labour expended in sensuality, in fashion, in vicious sports, &c.—Fate of Rome as described by Gibbon—War, cause of Poverty—History of Louis XIV., of France, shows the Causes of Poverty—Fête in honour of Mademoiselle de la Vallière 195

CHAPTER XIV.

Labour in the United States—Labour spent for much we do not want—Power of people of middling property in the United States—Whence this power springs—Voters in England, in France, in United States—Labour a different thing in the United States from what it is in most other countries—Who are working people in United States—Definitions given of labouring people—Who live by wages—Farmers in United States, their character—Servants in United States—Higher and lower classes—What is meant by a Manual Labourer—What the farmer is—His condition in the United States—Artists, sculptors, musicians, &c., are Labourers—Producers of Wealth, also—Necessity of Labour, great distinction of people of United States—Idle classes in England—Table of Rank and Precedence there 214

CHAPTER XV.

Labour in the United States, continued—Man an active being—Causes that compel most people to labour in United States—Equal division of property—Equal education—Equal political privileges—Facility of obtaining wild land—Small number here that can live without work—Illustrated in the town of Stockbridge, county of Berkshire—Laws not principal cause of just distribution of Property—Power of people of middling Property in the United States—How this power to be exercised . . . 237

CHAPTER XVI.

Slavery—Subjects discussed in this work—Slaves in United States—Question how far Slavery is to be discussed—If Slavery a good thing ought to be pointed out—Ideas that Slavery has inculcated as to Labour—Ancient Slavery—State of it—How universal Slavery was in Europe—Experience against Slavery—Number of Slaves among the ancients—In Athens—Former condition of Slavery in Europe—How far extinguished—Slavery, natural enemy of the labouring man—How the poor white man considered in the Southern States—Exhausted state of some parts of the Slave States—Varieties into which human race is divided—White people at the head of the human families—Amalgamation—Miserable state of Coloured People in free States—Gradual emancipation and gradual removal, true remedy for the evil—Southern people will liberate the Slave 246

PUBLIC AND PRIVATE ECONOMY.

CHAPTER I.

THE VALUE AND USES OF PROPERTY.

SEC. 1. THE object of this Book is to show the value of property, or wealth, and how it may be acquired. I shall use the words property and wealth in the same sense. It would be a poor task indeed to spend time in showing how property is to be gained and preserved, unless with a design, that a noble use should be made of it.

Wealth has been said to be "well being;" but this does not give a full and accurate idea of it. God has given man the earth, the sea, and the elements, out of which alone he derives all material things that supply his wants, and adorn his condition; all that enables him to do good to himself, or to others. Whatever these be, the greater part must be obtained by labour; to make labour profitable therefore, must always be an important study. Most of what we get, must be through pains, toil, and anxiety; it is therefore worth our while to labour with skill; to make the most of what we have; to understand the principles by which property is increased. Shall we then waste, or burn and destroy by mobs and riots, our property, our substance, our living, our earnings, without some moderate portion of which we are beggars?

14   THE VALUE AND USES OF PROPERTY.

2. The following are some of the blessings and advantages of property.

First, Property is our *Power*, or a great portion of it; it is the power to do good, or to do evil; if then there be property in the oppressor to do evil, there should be property in the virtuous and the oppressed to counteract it, and to do good. We show our sense of the power of property when we say—"that he is rich and powerful; that he is wealthy, and can do as he pleases; that he has money, and great influence over the conduct, votes, and opinions, of his connexions, friends, and neighbours; provided he chooses to exert it; and we know, that most men do choose to exert the influence of wealth, if they have it.

It is a common saying, that Knowledge is *power*, but it would be more proper to say, that *wealth* is power. The farmers of the United States possess a great portion of the wealth here, they own nearly all the land, and every one knows, or ought to know, how great their power is. Knowledge and education generally, though not always, enable men to obtain good wages, and in other ways to acquire property; and in this sense they may be said to be the cause of power. It is likewise true, that knowledge and education once obtained are often powerful without the aid of property; so too are they often quite helpless; but people who have wealth are never so. Besides; it is property only that enables us to get knowledge and education, whether it be by means of our own, or those of the state, or of our friends.

These few hints will show how important property is in one respect.

2. Second, But property is not only power, it is happiness, or the cause of happiness, unless it be abused.

Talents, skill, strength, beauty, and all the possessions of men may be abused, and are so, often as much as their property, but this is no argument against their existence. Why should God have given us the earth, and the talents to make so much out of it, unless it were good for us to have it, and these talents also? It is ill-gotten, *disproportioned* wealth that is most abused; that is, wealth obtained by unfair dealings, by fraud, by oppression, by monopoly, by which I mean *legal privileges given to some, and denied to others.* It is wealth, for the sake of wealth, for sensuality, for pomp, parade, the splendid outside, the elevation it gives over the humble and meritorious, that no more fills the mind with happiness than husks and ashes, if eaten, would give strength to the body. Where then is the mansion of happiness?—It is in the mind; and how does it gain an entrance? By doing good deeds; and how can good be done without the means, and what are the means, *generally*, but our substance, our property? Is it by doing good then, that we obtain happiness. The savage is a poor man, he cannot do the good that is in the power of a civilized man to do. Civilization then may be said to be property, or to proceed from it.

If a man be happy, let him, at that moment ask himself, "Why am I happy?" And he will find, that he is then thinking of, or planning, or doing some good; it is something *very often* that his property has enabled him to think of, or perform; it is some act of kindness to his own household, that makes them happier and more comfortable; of charity to the ignorant or to the poor; of benevolence and generosity to his friends and neighbours ; of munificence to the public ; or it is some other good deed ; or perhaps he is some labouring man who is collecting by the daily work of his hands, by toiling late and early, by patience, self-denial, and temperance, the means of doing good in other ways. This is the happiness of the poor man, and very exalted happiness it is, when he labours from day to day, through heat and cold, resisting temptation, fleeing from vice ; at the same time that he sees how stupidly and wickedly many, who call themselves his superiors, live, and consume what fairly seems to belong to him. These are his greatest pleasures ; when he thus goes on strong in his integrity, thankful to God, that he has hands and arms to labour and gather together the little property that is to feed and sustain his wife and children. This is the wealth of the poor man; it may be very small, it may be a house not twenty feet square, if he lives in the country ; or a room or two, if in a city, with very small household comforts ; clothing just enough to make him and his family decent; food only sufficient to supply the wants of nature, but not a crumb to waste upon a dog or cat, which he cannot afford himself the pleasure of possessing.

3. This is the beginning of the means of the poor man to do good; they may seem very insignificant in the eyes of some, but a great good it is for a common labouring man to go on manfully and nobly in the exercise of the faculties which God has given him, thus rendering himself a good neighbour and respectable citizen ; thus procuring a reasonable livelihood, enough to pay his rent and taxes, and give a decent education to his children, and this too, often in the midst of embar-

rassments, which tend to harden the heart, and break down the resolution of the labouring man.

4. To do good, then, with the property which we have gained or saved by our honesty, economy, temperance, and industry is *one* great end of our existence; it is the perfection of the Christian character, and should be the first lesson in all education. The selfish and hard-hearted, who strive by monopoly and every unfair advantage to obtain unequal privileges, to get all they can, to accept all that is given, and to give nothing, never dream of that, which is so true, that the giver is the happiest man. But to enable us to give we must have something, and this again shows us the value of property. Those who have nothing may be kind-hearted, generous, and naturally noble-minded; they may forever be thinking to do good, and hoping that the time will come, when they shall be able to bring something about; but very little comparatively is ever in their power. It is too plain, then, to be denied, that, base as are the uses to which property is so often put, the good we can get, or do without, is generally very small.

5. Third, Let us here take a more particular view of some of the uses of our property, by way of introduction of the subject of economy. It provides for the body, clothes and feeds us; it builds our houses; supplies them with furniture; provides all the tools for our work on our farms, and every where else; and settles our wild lands, for a poor man cannot even move from the old to the new States unless he has made some provision for that purpose. Property builds the manufactories, supplies them with stock, and pays the wages of the hands. If indigent people come to us from Europe,

18   THE VALUE AND USES OF PROPERTY.

there must be more property than just enough for us to live upon, or we cannot set them to work, and they must starve. If the destitute English, Scotch, and Irish were to emigrate to the poor countries of Europe, they would perish ; they, therefore, are as much interested in increasing the property of this country, as we natives are. It is the increasing property of the United States, which is now employing these poor people in the building of canals and rail roads.— Nothing but our *superfluous* wealth can feed the hungry, or clothe the naked.

6. All progress and improvement in the arts, in the engines, tools, and labour-saving machines of the mechanic, farmer, and manufacturer, are to be attributed mainly to the increasing property of the people. People can neither make nor buy new tools and engines, unless they have something more than a bare living ; and this is the reason why poor farmers and mechanics suffer so much for the want of labour-saving instruments. Men cannot spend their time upon new experiments without property to do it; and this also is the reason why poor men, who are entitled to valuable patents for their genius and skill, so often lose the benefit of their labours, by being obliged to surrender the advantages of them to their richer neighbours.

7. Fourth, It is not the body only, but the mind, which demands many enjoyments which property alone gives, and is never satisfied without. And what are some of these pleasures and possessions of the mind that are appropriate, not to a favoured few alone, but to mankind ? The pleasures of knowledge, and of being able to impart it to the ignorant and helpless,—the rational enjoyments of hospitality—of society among friends— of education for our children—of reasonable rest from

THE VALUE AND USES OF PROPERTY. 19

labour,—of pleasing recreations, such as travelling, which forms so respectable a portion of the refined pleasures of the American people. To these are to be added the delights we experience in music, pictures, statues,—in cultivated farms, gardens, beautiful domestic animals,—and in the graceful fabrics that adorn our houses and persons. These are natural pleasures, not to the rich only, but to the great human family. Beauty is a legitimate object to every labouring man in the world (according to his means,) which is a very different thing from finery and fashion. If all these enjoyments are mainly procured by our property, and not without, it is worth every man's attention to learn how to obtain it, and how to use it, which is true economy.

8. As these are the peculiar enjoyments of civilized life, it is plain, then, that it is by means of our property that we advance from the condition of savages to that of citizens. This shows, too, that through every progressive stage of civilization, there is an increase of enjoyment corresponding with the increased wealth of the people. To say that there is more wealth, and not more happiness, in a free country, where wealth must be fairly distributed as soon as the people come to understand the true principles of public economy,—is to say that more well-cultivated farms, more good houses, good clothes, and good food, are not best for the people. To show that a people have not ships, manufactories, trade, agriculture, gardens, useful domestic animals, or the most important of these, is to prove that they are a horde of barbarians, selfish, unsocial, and vicious. They cannot have the pleasures of the mind which come from finding beauty, purity, and comfort about our houses and homes. One of the greatest distinctions among

men is between those who are just, patient, industrious, and economical in the acquisition of property, and those who are not. These are the qualities that constitute the true dignity, happiness, and safety of the cultivators of the earth, and of all the working men of the world.

9. There is so much loose instruction about the abuses of property, that weak minds are confounded. Men and women desert their natural duties, and pass lives of miserable sloth, lest the real good things of life should corrupt and destroy them. Even great names have lent their influence to spread the delusion. Milton gravely assures us, that "riches are needless;" and again admonishes us to

"Extol not riches, the toil of fools—
The wise man's cumbrance."

It is essential, therefore, that the subject be well understood. Let us then borrow the words of another poet:—

"The sense to value riches, with the art
T'enjoy them, and the virtue to impart—
To balance fortune by a just expense,
Join with economy, magnificence."

The love of property is called a natural appetite; our children soon show it.[*] The universal passions—those that belong to all men—are good: God has implanted none in the mind of man that has not its uses; and he has shown us the true value of property by making the virtues of order, diligence, and temperance, essential to the acquisition of it, and by elevating the industrious nations above all the people of the earth. If men are

[*] Lord Kames' Sketches of the History of Man.

active and industrious, it must mainly be in the acquisition of property, for there is little else to employ them about. It cannot be supposed that God intended, that after getting good things together, man should scatter as fast as he gathers,—that he should collect with one hand, while he is destroying with the other,—that, having satisfied his appetite, he should, like a brute, trample under foot his remaining food, as men now do. In this way there would be no increase of property; one generation would be as poor as another. The reason why such multitudes are so miserably indigent now, is that they do waste and destroy their property in the manner stated, as will be plainly shown.

10. Fifth, The next great blessing and advantage of a moderate property, and which is well worthy the attention of a free people, who can only hope to support their institutions by their virtues, is, that a reasonable independence is the greatest security to these virtues that can be thought of. One of the first prayers of a good man is, not to be led into temptation. And what can so effectually secure us against temptation as an adequate provision for our wants—a comfortable property? What poor man can say that he will not rob, steal, and defraud, when his wife and children want bread and every comfort? The peculiar crime of the very poor is an invasion of the rights of property, which are at least as important to them as the rich; for, where property is not respected, none are so oppressed as the poor.

11. Independence is secured by our property; and to whom can this consideration be recommended with greater effect than to the American citizen? We have gained our *political* independence; but there is another,

and that is independence of mind: how unspeakable a blessing, when a man is called upon to vote this way or that, or in any way to surrender his liberty as an independent man, to be able to say, "No!" What a blessing to have secured ourselves, by labour and economy, from cringing and currying favour—from asking for wages from masters and employers who have no fellow-feeling for us, and in a business, perhaps, which corrupts all that are engaged in it. One of the first objects of a labouring man should be, to secure himself against the necessity of working for wages in an immoral business; for, though it may be profitable often to the employer, it is certainly injurious, in the long run, to the great body of labourers.

What a blessing it is, then, to be independent in our conduct and opinions, and not to be obliged to follow the multitude in their political follies, and other wild extravagancies in the towns, communities, or states, where we live, because our living, our offices, are in their power. What a miserable life to be dependent in one party or another upon an office for a living! how it narrows the mind,—what mental slavery it is! It is certain that a much greater portion of our people than at present, and a much greater here than in any other part of the world, with pure and noble tastes, and a just knowledge of economy, and of what they should work for, may have these blessings and pleasures. I mean to show that an immense amount of what people now work for is not *property*, in the sense that it answers any of these purposes; and that the present degree of poverty in the United States even, is disgraceful, shocking, and wholly unnecssary.

12. The Christian religion lies at the foundation of

all wholesome and permanent increase of wealth. Political economy professes to point out *all* the principles by which wealth is gained: the surest of all is the observance of the Christian precepts. The divine rule of doing to others as we would be done by, forbids all oppression, all cruelty to the poor, all unlawful taxes to support the pride, vanity, and luxury of the rich. Nothing is more striking in the Christian religion than the constant condemnation of all injustice to, and robbery of the poor, who are the labourers for small wages. The Christian religion equally forbids, on the part of the poor, all hatred of the rich—all wanton destruction of property. There always have been rich and poor— there must be rich and poor. The people have been most miserable in those countries where there are no rich.

The first duty of the rich to the poor, then, is, not to give them bread—for it is better that they should earn it—but the same legal advantages of getting bread that they themselves have. He who is under the influence of this divine religion will be the friend of free government, and endeavour to introduce it wherever the people are fit for liberty: and he will, from the same spirit of justice and love of happiness, oppose monopolies and unequal laws, though he himself derive advantage from them. If all this be true, to attempt to teach economy without reference to our religious duty, is like taking the picture of a man from a corpse. Those political economists who have passed by this, have kept out of sight the greatest instrument of wealth. No man earns so much as he who is contented and happy, from being justly treated.

13. What say the Christian precepts, then, which

have been so often misunderstood, and misinterpreted, as to the uses and value of wealth or property? "For the *love* of money is the root of all evil."—"Lay not up for yourselves treasures upon earth, where moth and rust doth corrupt, and where thieves break through and steal; but lay up for yourselves treasures in heaven," &c. What is this but a rebuke of the miser, of the covetous man, who makes a god of his riches, and is therefore an idolater? It is not said that *money* is the root of all evil, but the *love* of money, meaning for riches' sake, to gratify pride, lust, and selfishness.

The following passages will show that the scriptures have left us in no doubt as to what are our duties upon this subject: "He who provides not for his own household, is worse than an infidel."—"Use this world, as not abusing it."—"Let every man labour, working with his own hands the thing which is good, that he may have to give to him that needeth."—"Be not slothful in business, for if a man will not work, neither shall he eat." What can be plainer, then, than that we are, with diligence and economy, to *make* riches, wealth, property, or whatever else we choose to call the product of our labour, that we may do all the good in our power, and thus "lay up treasures in heaven?"

14. The denunciations in the scriptures are against overgrown, ill-gotten, and abused riches; against those who "grind the face of the poor;" who establish monopolies and unrighteous privileges. Such was the character of the rich, generally, in the days when these scriptures were written; when the poor man was often obliged to hide his bread from the oppressor; and when, as has been said, "there was no people." Suppose the scriptures had told us that the great mass of mankind were

doomed never to rise according to their merits, but to remain "mere hewers of wood and drawers of water;" that it was indifferent whether we were slothful or industrious; that the idler was as happy as the diligent; that it was only a toil and a vexation to exert our genius upon the materials of this world, because we could carry nothing to heaven with us. Suppose they had taught, that it was of no moment to men who could live only seventy or eighty years at best, whether they lived in good houses or in hovels; nor whether the poor worked for high or low wages; whether they saved a proper portion of them; nor whether the farmer ran in debt, and then loaded his farm with mortgages; and that it was of no consequence, also, whether people lived within their incomes, made a decent provision for their families, and laid by something for the poor, for sickness, and the calamities of life. I say, that if this had been the language of the scriptures, we should have turned a deaf ear to them. It is plain then, that there can be no contradiction upon the subject of *true* economy between religion and common sense.

So true is it, that property in the great body of the people, is essential to liberty and happiness, that it will be shown, that we, of the United States especially, owe our freedom to our property.

15. Do the people of the United States desire to bring forth the magnificent riches which are to be found in the natural advantages of their country and free government; to elevate themselves to an eminence which nations have yet never thought of; do they long for the pleasures and glories of science; the delights of charity to their own poor and uninstructed, and to the wretched of other countries; a better and more equal education

for their children; to increase their hospitality and social pleasures; to save their paternal houses and estates from a decay and ruin so common and so disgraceful in the old States; do those whose interest it is to emigrate to the new, wish for the means of making such a delightful change; do the men, women, and children, many of whom now work beyond their strength, desire more rest and time for a proper improvement of their minds; do all the hard-working people wish a more equal distribution of property. Then, both rich and poor, must first combine, discard their jealousies and feuds; get what good they can out of the old world; turn their backs upon the stupid fashions and follies imported by nearly every packet, and study the proper economy of their own country—of this new world. Those, especially, who live upon wages, as journeymen mechanics, labourers in factories, and day labourers of every description, must learn to save their wages, and thus preserve property, which is the true and common sense way of changing their condition for the better, and which can never be done, as long as they are the slaves of fashion.

CHAPTER II.

WHAT POLITICAL ECONOMY IS.

16. IF property, then, be as important as has been represented, even so much so, that little good can be done without it; it is desirable that we should possess the science, or art, by which it is obtained. This, so far as the public, the state, the nation, is concerned, is called *Political Economy;* being the economy of the public, the state, the nation, and it is but another name for *public economy.* The word economy is derived from *Oikos,* a house, and *nomos,* a law, which means the law of the household.* As every one knows something of the domestic rules and habits which secure prosperity to his own household; so ought he in this country to know something of the rules and regulations which belong to the public household, and cause prosperity in that also. By the law and constitution of this country, nearly every man is in part the master of this household; he is compelled to pay a part of its expenses; and whether he be well or ill-provided for, depends in a great measure upon the economy with which it is regulated. Political economy then of which we hear so much in books, or public economy, which, as I have said, is the same thing, instead of being the appropriate study of scholars, philosophers, and statesmen only, becomes, or ought to become to the farmers, mechanics, and la-

---

* Say's Political Economy—Introduction, Note.

bourers, in the United States, one of the first objects of study and attention.

The following are some of the illustrations or definitions of political economy, which will hereafter be called *Public Economy*. That it always proposes some increase of the happiness of the people. It does not teach for the benefit of any particular class of nobles or clergy, or any privileged order, but for the whole nation, and the whole world. It is said to be, "the science of wealth, trade, and population." Its object is to show how industry may be employed to the best advantage, and how, with the least labour and least waste of materials, the greatest quantity of enjoyment may be procured.* Now this is the best thing that a man can do in his own affairs; that is, do all that is to be done with the least labour and the least waste of materials. It is plain then, that it is a science for the whole people to study. Again :—"Political economy is the science of the laws which regulate the production, distribution, and consumption of those material products which have exchangeable value, and which are either necessary, useful, or agreeable to man."† By exchangeable value is meant, the value that belongs to things, sold and bought, in opposition to those things which are common to all mankind, as air and water. Political economy here, is that science which teaches the people how to manage their concerns most profitably, in their several towns, counties, states, and in the United States. For instance, it is as much the part of political economy, to teach the

---

* Edinburgh Review, No. 85.

† Outlines of Political Economy, by J. R. M'Cullock, with very valuable Notes, by Professor M'Vickar. Part 1st.

people of Massachusetts, and of other states, upon what principle they shall take care of the poor, and make and repair their roads, as it is in England to regulate the subject of emigration, tithes, or the corn laws.

The subject of education is introduced into nearly all the books of political economy, for we admit that nothing so much affects the wealth of people as their education; and this is particularly true in the United States, where a good education is said to be better than an inheritance. It is plain, then, that political economy embraces a great portion of those subjects that are most interesting to the people, and certainly to that class of American labourers, whose humble fortunes render every kind of economy indispensable.

Political economy has been called the science which teaches people "how to make wealth;" and it is said, "that he who can make a clock, can make wealth;" so can he who digs a ditch for a road or canal. This fact of being able to make wealth out of clocks is well known to the people of Connecticut, who, it is said, have heretofore produced in this article, a million of dollars annually. Political economy, however, does not teach the people of Connecticut how to make a clock, for that belongs to mechanics; but it does teach them whether it be most profitable to turn their labour to the making of clocks, or to the production of wheat, corn, and wool.

17. Public economy then is a beautiful science; and how can it be otherwise, when it teaches us so to manage our public affairs as to diffuse happiness by spreading plenty among the whole people?

Aurengzebe, the great Mogul, said, that he would so instruct his people that there should be no hospitals in his empire. It is the design of all true economy, to save as far as possible the poor from hospitals, by turning all labour to the best account, so that there may be something for all. A little, a very little only, is indispensable to keep man or woman from those public asylums, where they drink the very dregs from the cup of misery.

18. Public economy teaches, that all the wealth in the nation is divided into one great heap, which is the public wealth, and many smaller heaps, which is the private wealth. The public heap is that which belongs to the nation; as in the United States, the public lands, the public stores, the money, and every other kind of public property. This is for the support of the army, the navy, the officers of government, and all the public institutions. The private heaps are those which belong to private individuals exclusively, as a man's farm, cattle, &c. Public economy teaches, that in the public stock, all are partners, rich and poor, and that no man has a right to take a farthing without the public consent duly obtained. That all the wealth of a nation, public and private, may be supposed to be gathered into one great store-house, which is divided into public and private apartments; that the common stock is stored in the public rooms; that every industrious man has a private apartment, under the same roof, which is under his own lock and key. That as the public apartments are filled from the private, the better supplied the latter, the richer will be the stores of the nation. That if a man set fire to, or in any way destroy those parts of this building, where the public property is stored, he is a loser of course, because he is a partner in it, though the flames do not reach his own apartment; and if, through heedlessness, spite, or malice, he kindles a blaze in one of the

private apartments, he then destroys one of those heaps, out of which the great public store-house is furnished.

From this we see, that in all true economy, property, belong to whom it may, to the nation or to individuals, to rich or poor, is sacred on account of the good it does— that it is very base and stupid for men, or mobs made up of men, to waste, burn, or destroy any property, which is little better than a man's breaking the windows of his own house, or putting fire to a city where he is the owner of stores and houses. It is the characteristic of a brute to waste and defile the food which he will need to-morrow. Property, then. is the life of the people, and it is suicide wantonly to destroy it.

19. What then is the difference between good laws and good public economy?—None—because all good laws tend to the production and just distribution of wealth; all good laws are good economy. But there is a difference between the science of law, and the science of public economy. The former teaches what the law is, which it is the business of the lawyer to learn; the latter teaches what law should be, which is the business of the public economist, or legislator to learn. The people of the United States therefore will be poor legislators, unless their minds are imbued with a knowledge of the economy of the country. The public economy of a country is clearly indicated by its laws; if the laws are good, the public economy is likely to be, and as the people get more and more power and knowledge, new laws will follow of course for the purpose of introducing economical reform.

20. As private economy differs in different countries, so does public economy; no two nations have the same system of laws, morals, or religion, though many of

the general principles of each are alike in both,—It is the same with public economy. In China, the emperor every year goes through the ceremony of holding a plough as an example of industry to his people, and this, there, may be an excellent regulation.* It probably is so, in a country where the emperor is looked upon more like a god than a man. So much so is this the case that he would not suffer the British minister to be introduced to his presence till he had performed the usual *Ko-Lean*, which consists, in nine prostrations of the body, the forehead striking the floor at each time. So also he ordered all the presents made by the king of England upon that occasion, to be placed in one line, that in viewing them, he might not be compelled to turn his head to the right or to the left.† It is not probable that many additional ploughs would be stirred in the United States, should the president annually perform this Chinese ceremony, on the heights of Washington. So in China, they have a wall about fifteen hundred miles long, the stone work of which is raised about two feet above the ground, and the brick-work twenty-five feet higher, which is said to have been built three centuries before Christ. This wall was built to keep out the Tartar hordes, and it may possibly be an important question of public economy there, since it is no longer wanted for that purpose, whether or not it shall be kept in repair.

21. In various parts of Europe, if the repair of a bridge or a new road be required in a town or village, permission must be obtained from the king, the prince, or supreme power. The villages or towns have no authority to tax the inhabitants for that purpose, and if they

---

* Staunton's embassy. † Ibid.

had such a power, it would be of no avail; because so degraded and ignorant are the people in the more wretched parts of Europe, that they would not know how to apportion such a tax equitably.—It is, no doubt, true, that there are towns and villages, where those who are called the people here do not know enough in arithmetic of the rule of three to ascertain the share of each man's tax. Such a people, therefore, upon the happening of every occasion of this kind, must put themselves to the expense of applying to the government, and it is as if the people of one of the towns in Massachusetts were compelled to send to congress, or to the president in order to get a new road laid out, or a bridge built. Here in Massashusetts on the contrary, the towns have by law the right to tax themselves to any amount for such an object. To this extent, and for certain other purposes, their power is absolute and unlimited. This illustrates the true principle of republican government, which is self-government. If the people of the towns in Massachusetts have the competent knowledge to regulate their local affairs, there is no reason why the government, or supreme power, should do it. The government, or supreme power, must act through their agents, and these agents cannot, if the people are well informed, know as well as the people themselves, how and when their roads and bridges ought to be made and repaired.

22. In the same way, every country has its own peculiar public economy, arising from its having habits, institutions, and modes of government peculiar to itself. No country has a federal government, and state governments, for instance, exactly like those which we have. The public economy of England differs from ours, and from that of every other country. England has her

king, lords, commons, and clergy; in regard to each of these she has an economy of her own. In England it is thought good economy to support the clergy by law, and therefore the people are taxed for this purpose in some way or other. But this is not the case in the United States. In England it is said that about an eighth part of the people are supported in whole or in part as paupers; and it is, therefore, there, a great question what shall be done with so many poor people. A great change has lately taken place in the law in regard to this subject. Some are for abolishing the law altogether; some for enabling these poor people, or a portion of them, to emigrate, at the public expense, to Canada, to New Holland, to the United States, and to other parts of the world. On the contrary, we in the old States have too few people; if we had more we should be richer and more prosperous. We do not, therefore, propose that our people shall emigrate, and no one thinks of raising, as a matter of good economy, a public fund to enable any portion of them to leave us.

In England it is thought that the corn crop (wheat) is not equal to the consumption of the people, though various opinions have been entertained upon this point at different periods.* The English government, to favour, as they suppose, their own agriculture, have imposed heavy duties upon the importation of foreign wheat: the laws regulating this subject, which embraces other grains besides wheat, are called the *Corn Laws*, concerning the propriety of which there has been a long discussion carried on by the people of England.

---

* Report of Committee of House of Commons.—Morning Chronicle, 10th October, 1833.

This is, there, a great question of public economy. The reform which is now going on in England, in the representation, in the army, the navy, in reducing the expenses of government, in diminishing legal expenses, by simplifying the laws,—is an economical reform. All these subjects present questions in public economy.

23. This brings us to the public economy of the United States. The people of this country, upon the establishment of their government, had no books upon their own public economy, and still they were obliged to consider and decide upon the economy of every regulation: the very nature of their general government, what powers should be entrusted to congress, what to the state legislatures, and what should be reserved to the people at large. Again, in the formation of their state governments, what powers the governor should have, what the legislature, what the counties, what the towns; how the poor should be provided for; upon what principle the roads should be made and repaired. These, and many others, were questions in public economy. So of the public debt, if a blessing, as some have alleged; so of the taxes, whether they should be indirect, and laid exclusively, as at present, upon foreign merchandize, in the shape of duties; or direct also, as upon lands, houses, &c., which was the case during the last war: these, also, all present questions in economy.

At present, the great questions about free trade, tariff, and protection; (more important than most others) those concerning internal improvements, banks, and paper money; whether private banking shall be allowed; State banks; the United States' bank, and, especially, whether this shall be re-chartered,—are all of great moment to the people of the United States. These, or the more important of them, as the people well know, cause the political discussions of the present times; and this, again, shows how far good laws, and good public economy, are the same thing. It is plain, then, that all these subjects must be well considered, and thoroughly studied by the people, who are to decide upon them; and, if it be true that they are above the comprehension of the people, and that we may as well refer the decision to chance as to them,—then it is certain that they are not fit for a free government. As, however, they have chosen this government, it becomes their solemn duty, and highest interest, to make themselves thoroughly acquainted with, and to teach to their children all that they can learn and teach in regard to the public economy of the country.

Of all people on earth, then, it is incumbent upon those of the United States to understand the nature and value of property—something of the history of it—and how far they owe their very liberties to the enjoyment of it. Persecution drove our ancestors from their native land: there they were obliged to suffer from, and to submit to it, because they were poor. People who are independent, and who possess property, have power, have friends, arms for defence, or can procure them; and though they may not be as numerous as their persecutors, still they generally enjoy the means of maintaining their liberties and possessions.

24. Though it be true, then, that every country has an economy peculiar to itself, are there no general principles in this science, as well as in others, which are applicable to all countries? Certainly there are; many of these principles are perfectly open to the comprehension of intelligent labouring people. It is not true that they

cannot comprehend them,—it is only true that they have not been called upon to think about them. As long as education was a monopoly confined to the privileged few, it was a very natural ignorance to think that these few only could understand the mysteries, as they were thought to be, contained in books.

Some of the most important subjects treated of in books of political economy are, *wages, division of labour, machinery,* &c. ; and who can understand these subjects if *labourers* cannot? One of the best chapters in Smith's "Wealth of Nations," is on wages; and it has often been said that Smith discovered the great principle of the wealth of nations in the division of labour. The farmers, who say that even a wood-chopper does more work, and better, now, than he did before the Revolution, understand the principle that establishes the value of the division of labour, though they never heard of Smith or the words "division of labour." They know that a labourer does anything better for devoting his time to one thing alone; and therefore, as they know that the business of chopping wood is now comparatively a separate business, and followed exclusively, or nearly so, in some parts of the country, they are prepared to understand everything that can be said about the division of labour. They have long been taught the wise proverbs, that "practice makes perfect;" that "a Jack-at-all-trades is good at none;" they therefore know, as well as learned writers, that when a man, in the early settlement of a country, and before there are regular tradesmen, is obliged to be a farmer, carpenter, joiner, and shoemaker, he can do the business neither of a farmer, carpenter, joiner, nor shoemaker, as well as if he were devoted to one of these occupations alone.

25. *Wages*, also, is a great subject in political economy. None, certainly can be more important to men who work with their hands,—none has been treated of more largely by political economists.

This may be said to be one of the first principles in regard to wages,—*that the rate of wages depends upon the number of labourers, compared with the business to be done.* Labour is bought and sold like other articles: if there be a great deal of it, compared with what is wanted, it will be cheap; if little, it will be dear. The farmers here can understand this principle perfectly, when they see, that if there were no emigration of labourers to Ohio, Michigan, &c., there would be more labourers, and cheaper wages; and that if there were half-a-dozen more blacksmiths in every town, there would then be too many for the work to be done, and, of course, that the wages of blacksmiths must fall as long as this state of things should continue. So, also, every mechanic and manufacturer can see the same thing, who knows that wages in his line would fall, in consequence of the influx of foreigners, if the mechanic and manufacturing business did not increase in about the same proportion with this influx: summer, winter, and harvest wages, also, exemplify the same truth. In winter, with us, we have the same number of labourers, or nearly so as in summer; but there is less work to be done, and, of course, wages are lower; in harvest there is more work to be done than in the other seasons, but the labourers are not in proportion, and therefore harvest wages are the best in the year. These truths can never be mysteries to men of business: so far from not being intelligible to labouring people, they are prepared, by their previous habits of mind, in many most important respects, to understand them better than scholars, statesmen, and professed writers. Truth, upon these subjects, is a deduction from the facts which we witness in our daily business; it, therefore, does not require what is called a scholar or philosopher to understand them; on the contrary, it is a great delusion to suppose, that most of our common people cannot comprehend them. The main difficulty at present is, that our books are not written for the common people, but exclusively for scholars, gentlemen, philosophers, and statesmen.

CHAPTER III.

HISTORY OF PROPERTY.

26. A complete history of property would be the history of mankind, and all that can be done here is to mention some important facts in regard to it.

History is the best teacher of economy; it is not made up of theory, and speculation, but it shows exactly what has been the condition of the great body of farmers, mechanics, and other labourers, where they have been destitute of property.

To study economy rightly, it is first necessary to know the true value of property, to be satisfied that it is designed for noble purposes, and to know, that the great body of the people for whom the principal provisions of Heaven are undoubtedly intended, are wretched and degraded without some reasonable portion of it. Scarcely a page of history can be opened without reading this fact. It is in history that the people will learn, how nearly their education, their liberty, their improvement in arts, in sciences, and in the comforts of life have kept pace with their acquisitions in property; and how certain it is, that when their wealth has decayed, these other blessings have disappeared also. They will see, to be sure, that in some countries a few have possessed great wealth and thus been able to fare sumptuously every day, but still if the great body of those who labour with their hands, have been without land or other reasonable possessions, they have either been slaves, or nearly as wretched as slaves; that their houses have been hovels of mud and clay; their minds as low as their habitations; their apparel disgusting; their food of the coarsest materials, and such as is fit only for brutes.—Such a state of things God cannot desire to see continued, and therefore every thing noble in man is called upon to counteract it. This wickedness in mankind cannot prosper. This then is a cardinal point in all true economy; to teach how property may be more equally destributed. The principles of freedom which secure a just distribution of property among farmers, mechanics, and all labourers will increase the power of producing it a hundred, or may be a thousand fold, as we are now proving in the United States. The great riches of our people, small as they are, compared with what they ought to be, will soon shame the civilized world out of their despotic principles.

27. Of all property, *land* is the most important; out of this we are mainly fed and clothed from the cradle to the grave, and nearly every fabric that is beautiful or useful is formed from it. In our law, property in land is called *Real Estate,* or *real property*; the definition of which is "something not fictitious, not imaginary; true, genuine." The desire for this kind of property on account of the power and stability attached to it, is nearly universal. The *owners* of the earth have been the legislators of mankind; whether few or many, whether landlords, as in Europe, or farmers, as in the United States, they have been the principal governors of the world. Land is desired on account of the certainty and durability of the possession; it is not liable to the hazards to which our crops, household furniture, domestic animals, merchandise, and personal property of every kind are

subject; of these we may be deprived by fire, flood, fraud, and robbery: nor to depreciation, and great and sudden changes in value, as bank, insurance, canal, and other stocks are.

The earth is capable of making an immense number of people happy, that are now very miserable; even a quarter of an acre in a village will make a pretty garden and furnish a poor family with many articles that are called luxuries by the rich; in some countries, as in Naples and Tuscany, many farms do not exceed five, ten, fifteen, or twenty acres. On Connecticut river a farm of fifteen or twenty acres is not very uncommon. The poor and prudent labouring people in our cities, and especially foreigners of this description, who have emigrated from countries, where they have witnessed the power, wealth, and dignity of the owners of the earth, are well aware of the superior value of *real estate*, and therefore their first investments, from their little earnings of perhaps not more than a dollar a-day, are often judiciously made in a house-lot not more then twenty-five feet front, and a hundred feet in depth. This is property they think, which will not take wings, and fly away.

28. There are different interests in land. One man has the absolute ownership, which in our law is called the *fee* of the land, this is an estate which a man has to himself and his heirs forever. If the owner die without will, leaving children, it passes, in the United States, to them; and if he makes a will, he has a right to give the estate to whom he pleases. There is another interest in land; it is that of the tenant, whose interest may be for life, or for a given number of years, or he may be tenant from year to year, which is equivalent to being tenant at will. By the ancient English law every man

held his land of the king, and to this day every owner of land is said to be a tenant [from the latin word *teneo,* to hold] as tenant in fee, for life, and so on.

There is another and very important distinction in the history of land, and this is, as to the terms upon which the tenants hold their lands of the absolute owners of it, in respect to the *kind of rents paid, and manner of paying them.*

29. God gave man the earth, commanding him to " replenish " it ; but he did not give it to any small number of men, or privileged class Notwithstanding this beneficence of the Creator, by which he designs, no doubt, to establish those general rules, by which the earth, and all other possessions, ought to be given to the patient, hard-working, orderly, diligent, and virtuous members of the human family, these rules have been most shamefully disregarded,—the earth, and all other possessions, have been monopolized by a handful of men, by means of unequal laws and privileges established by these few, who have been far from possessing any merit corresponding with this great distinction. The earth is properly the people's farm, and still how few have owned any portion of it ; the greater number have been hirelings on their own inheritance ! The people of the United States are the only people who, as a nation upon a great scale, have adopted and practised anything like just principles in the distribution of land and other property. It is by no means intended here to be asserted, however, that these principles have been, in the United States, as yet either fully understood or established.

We may now very briefly proceed to consider how much the civilization of men, their power, their liberty, have depended upon the terms upon which they have cultivated the earth; upon the interest they have had in it; and the kind of rents they have paid where they have been tenants, and not lords of the soil, or landlords. It will every where be seen that property, and especially the greater or less interest which the mass of the people have in the land, mainly decides their condition.

30. It is in Asia that they have no parliaments or congresses, no free constitutions, no elections, no free trade, nor schools, as we have, for all the people; and it is there, too, that the people have no property that they can call their own. In Asia are to be found many of the most abject and miserable of mankind; they are men-worshippers, and the worshippers of false gods. There they have famines; diseases, such as plague and leprosy, that have long since been banished from our more civilized parts of the world: and so stupid are the people, that they shut out Europeans and Americans, who would go among them to introduce commerce and the arts, by which religion and so many good things are spread among men.

31. In Asia, under the Eastern despotisms, the principle is, that the earth belongs absolutely to the sovereign; he is entitled to all, the people have nothing but by his will; he is heir of all his subjects, there is a universal dependence of all upon him.* This is absolute power; these are strictly Eastern despotisms, and very different from the governments of Europe, where, even in the worst, the people have some few privileges, and the nobles many, secured either by law or long-continued custom.

* Mill's British India, book 3, ch. 5.—Jones on the Distribution of Wealth, book 1, ch. 1. sect. 1.

Under the Mahomedan law, there are no nobles, the great distinction being in the offices and power granted by the sovereign to his subjects.* By such superstitions as the following, are these despotisms sustained — for all despotism has its foundation in the ignorant and superstitious mind of the people; this ignorance, however, never exists where there is property, and a fair distribution of it among them :—

" A king, (say the laws of Menu,) is formed of particles from the chief guardian deities, and consequently surpasses all mortals in glory; like the sun, he burns eyes and hearts, nor can any human creature on earth gaze on him; he (is) fire and air: he, the god of criminal justice; he, the genius of wealth; he, the regent of waters; he, the lord of the firmament; a king, even though a child, must not be treated lightly, from the idea that he is a mere mortal. No, he is a powerful divinity, who appears in human shape; in his anger (is) death; he, who shows hatred of the king, through delusion of mind, will certainly perish, for speedily will the king apply his heart to that man's destruction."† The Hindoo law represents the king as created for the guardianship of all, a divinity in human form, to inflict punishment according to the Shaster.‡ The king of Persia is addressed as " the point of adoration of the world ;" and his throne is called " the threshold of the world's glory." It is easy to account for the extreme misery of the people in these eastern countries, where such superstitions as these, getting into their minds, induce them to yield the earth and

* The same.
† Mill's India, book 2d, chap. 3d.
‡ The same.

all their possessions to a single mortal, perhaps, too, the most vicious of his kind.

32. Among many savage people, despotism of the like kind prevails. In the Sandwich Islands, the people have no higher interest in the land, than in the eastern countries generally. The government there, is a despotism also; all rights of property are in the throne, and the will of the sovereign is law.* The condition of the people, and of the kings and princes corresponds with these established principles, that is, all the comforts that property can give beyond a mere existence, fall to the latter. The queen's dowager, of that savage country, contrive, like our civilized queens, to waste the substance of the people by the most stupid ostentation. One of them is represented upon a certain occasion, "as wearing seventy-two yards of kerseymere, of double fold, the one half being scarlet and the other orange; it was wrapped around her figure till her arms were supported horizontally by the bulk, and the remainder was formed into a train, supported by persons appointed for the purpose." The sovereign has a body guard of fifty or sixty persons, though they are dressed as might be expected in such a country, like beggars. He is supported by an annual tribute, which consists of hogs, fish, fowl, potatoes, taro, bananas, melons: and of manufactured articles, as canoes, fishing nets, tapa, mats, &c. The nobles, who, with the king and royal family, monopolize all the good food, are a distinct race in size, often excessively corpulent, while the common people are quite inferior. The immense bulk of some of these nobles is attributed to their

---

* Stewart's Residence at the Sandwich Islands.

nutritious food, and to the extreme care taken of them in their infancy. Every chief has from thirty to a hundred personal attendants, who are always at his heels; one is a pipe lighter; another, a spit-box carrier; a third, a cahile bearer; occupations not a whit more dignified or profitable to the people than some that I shall endeavour to point out, hereafter, a little nearer home. The author, says, that he has seen "a young chief, apparently not three years old, walking the streets of Honoruru, as naked as when born, with the exception of a pair of green morocco shoes on his feet, followed by ten or twelve stout men, and as many boys, carrying umbrellas, and cahiles, and spit-boxes, and fans, and the various trappings of chieftainship.* The whole population of this group of islands is represented to be one hundred and fifty thousand; one hundred and forty-nine thousand of whom are the common people, the remainder are the princes and nobles. These common people are of course abject in the lowest degree, their greatest wealth consisting of a mat on which to sleep, a few folds of tapa, (a cloth made of the inner bark of a tree,) a calabash for water, and another for poe. These are the possessions of the people—these are the occupations of the people, and how can they but be poor?

33. One of the great divisions of mankind is into landlords and tenants; and I have said and shall now proceed to show by other proof, that one of the leading circumstances in determining the condition of a people, *is the title or interest they have in the earth; and especially the kind of rents that are paid where the relation of landlord and tenant exists.*

* The same.

The great division of rents is into—first, labour rents—second, metayer rents—third, ryot rents—fourth, money rents.* These money rents, as applied to the people of Ireland, are called cottier rents. In some of the more enslaved parts of the earth where these labour rents prevail, they are called also serf rents, which is only another name for slave.

The labour rent takes place in this way. "The proprietor of one or more villages accordingly grants to each of his peasants, a house, a fixed quantity of land sufficient to keep him and his family in bread, a right of pasture on his common, and of firewood in his forests. The peasant pays no rent for these concessions, but in his turn is obliged to work with his team the three first days of the week for his master, the three last he is to work for himself."†

34. These labour rents exist in Russia to the greatest extent, and may be traced, in greater or less degree, through Hungary, Livonia, Poland, Prussia, and Germany, to the river Rhine, where they disappear.‡ Labour rents, in Russia, have made the serf the complete slave of the lord. Of these serfs, ten millions and a half, in the year one thousand seven hundred and eighty two, belonged to the crown. The serf is so far attached to the soil, that he cannot leave his village without a special license. The Russian monarchs having manufactures conducted on their own account, the serfs are liable to be taken from their homes and employed on them.*

---

* Jones' on the Distribution of Wealth, book 1, chap. 1, sect. 2.
† Lessons of Experience on the Emancipation of Slaves, by Sismondi.
‡ Jones, book 1, chap. 2, sect. 1.
§ The same, book, chap. 2, sect. 2.

It is found all over the world as a general rule, that freemen, and men possessing property, labour more effectually, and with greater skill, than those who have none, and this accounts in a great degree for the extraordinary prosperity of many of the United States. The capacity of these Russian slaves to labour, comports with their state of degradation; and it is said, that two Middlesex mowers, in England, will mow as much in a day as six of them; and it is said, also, that even considering the dearness of provisions in England, and their cheapness in Russia, that labour is cheapest in England, so much so, that it is asserted, that the labour of a serf is doubly as expensive as that of a labourer in England. It is asserted, also, that, in Austria, the labour of a serf is only equal to one-third part of that of a free labourer.* Another consequence follows in those countries: as serf, or slave labour, degrades all labour and makes it dishonourable, so, of course, it destroys the character of free labour.

35. This is the condition of the poor Poles who are tenants under labour rents. When a young peasant marries, his lord assigns him a certain quantity of land, a few cattle, a cow or two, and steers to plough his land; a cottage, and implements of husbandry. The peasant works three days for himself, and three days for his master. If the cattle die, the master must supply the loss, which, of course, makes the peasant indifferent to their preservation. If an estate be sold, the peasants are transferred, of course, to the new master with the land. The Poles are, therefore, still slaves; they cannot quit the soil, unless they flee to the forest; they cannot sell their

* Jones, book 1, chap. 2, sect. 8.

labour freely to those who will pay the highest price for it, as every man ought to have the right to do. As might be expected of such miserable beings, desiring to drown their miseries in intoxication, they drink to excess. These boors are found about every lordly mansion, where they are employed in the most menial services; having no beds, they sleep like dogs in any hole or corner, their diet is scanty, their best food is milk and poor cheese, the principal article is a coarse rye bread, which the American people could not be induced to swallow. " If met in a winter snow, they appear more like herds of savage beasts, than like men; their coarse mantles, their shrunk and squalid forms, their dirty matted hair, their dull moping looks, and lifeless movements, all combine to form an image which sickens humanity."* Such is a faithful account probably of one nation at least of indigent people. It cannot be wondered at that the Russians have enslaved them, for what means of resistance have they?

36. *Metayer* rents are where the tenant pays one half of the produce to the landlord; the landlord finding the articles necessary to carry on the farm, as cattle, tools, &c.—The word "Metayer" is French, and signifies the half. This kind of rent is well known in the United States, where the tenant is said to take the land "to the halves" or "on shares." In the town of Stockbridge, in the State of Massachusetts, and probably in the northern States generally, the following are the common rules, with occasional diversities, as to this mode of letting. The landlord finds stock and tools. The profits of the

* Jones, Appendix 4, from Burnet's view of the present state of Poland.

farm, which are the produce, and the growth of the stock, [the latter being settled by a rule agreed upon between the parties] are equally divided between them, and the produce which can be measured is delivered to the landlord "in the half bushel," as is usually said. The risk of the stock generally falls upon the tenant.— In some cases the landlord finds half the stock, the tenant the other, the landlord pays half the taxes, the tenant the other.

The Metayer is of course superior to the serf; he has the absolute possession of the land, while he is on it; to his judgment is committed the superintendence of the various modes of farming to be carried on; he has charge also of the cattle and tools, and he is not liable to be called upon for labour away from his farm, as the serf is. Wherever this rent is paid in Europe, there may be found a great advance in civilization generally, compared with the countries where labour rents exist. It is in the western parts of Europe, in Italy, France, Spain, that this system prevails. In Tuscany, this kind of tenancy appears to the best advantage, and an American farmer may well admire a cultivation, where a family usually lives on from six to ten acres of land. The circumstance which makes this kind of possession so interesting in Tuscany is, that by the common custom of the country, these possessions pass from father to son; the farmers therefore feel an interest in them, they ornament them with flowers, and cultivate them as their own.—It is the fact, that the possessions of the American farmer are his own, that makes his condition envied by the whole world, and he will remember, that it is his peculiar lot to be able to transmit them to his children, with the enjoyment not of half only, but of all the fruits of the earth.

Metayers are supposed to cultivate the half of France,* their condition is still far from that of independent cultivators of the earth. In Naples, the metayer farms do not exceed five acres, and the tenants there pay two-thirds of the produce. The extraordinary climate and soil of that country enable them to do this; the climate exempting the farmer from paying for a great many necessaries essential in colder regions, and the soil producing eight crops in five years.†

37. After all, what a wretched mode is this of cultivating the earth compared with that where the farmer is the absolute owner of it! As the landlord advances the capital, he must entrust his buildings, his cattle, and his tools to the care of perhaps a negligent or fraudulent tenant, it is his interest therefore to do this at as little risk as possible, and the tenant will, of course, generally be provided with a wretched habitation, with miserable cattle, and implements of husbandry. On the other hand, the tenant whose possession is uncertain, dare not encounter the hazards of improvements and experiments so necessary to the progress of every art; having no lasting property in the land, all that he does will be calculated to subserve his own short-lived interest in it. It is for these reasons, that in the United States indigent farmers only, with few exceptions, ever cultivate the earth upon these terms.

38. The third species of rents are ryot rents, which, with a few exceptions, are peculiar to Asia.‡ The Asiatic

* Jones, Book 1, Ch. 3, Sec. 4, cites Foreign Quarterly.
† The same, Sect. 5.
‡ Jones, book 1, ch. 4, sect. 1.

sovereigns, as is stated in sect. 31, still continue to be the absolute masters and owners of the earth in that portion of it; and it is in Asia that men remain in the same state of debasement, in which they have been for thousands of years. Ryot rents are a portion of the produce paid by the tenant for leave to cultivate the land. In India the laws fix this portion at a sixth;* but a provision so reasonable, is, of course, disregarded; the tyranny, selfishness, and ignorance of the sovereign and his officers, will determine the amount of exaction, to which the poor cultivator must submit.

39. The fourth species of rent is that which is paid in money. In this case the landlord furnishes the land and buildings, and the tenant, generally, provides the stock, tools, and everything necessary to carry on the farm. In Ireland these rents are called cottier rents,† Ireland being generally divided into small farms, or patches of a few acres only, which are cultivated by the indigent and miserable cottagers of that country. The lords of the soil in Ireland are the gentry and nobility. A portion of these have little or no knowledge of, or connection with their tenants; they do not even reside in the country, but most unworthily in other countries, far from their duties and natural homes: they are called *absentees*. They neglect the education of their tenants, and wring from them the last farthing that they can pay, through a class of persons called "middlemen," who are the plunderers of Ireland. Ireland has long been one of the poorest countries in the world, and wretched in proportion to her poverty. England can

* Jones, book 1, ch. 4, sect. 2.
† The same, book 1, ch. 5.

oppress her because she is poor—for all poor people are for ever liable to oppression.

40. In England, also, money-rents are paid, but under very different circumstances from those of Ireland. England is a country of great wealth, and though it be distributed, by legislation and privileges, very unrighteously and unequally, still the common people of England, the merchants, farmers, manufacturers, mechanics, and labourers of every description, have, by means of the acquisition of property, attained to a degree of independence unknown in any other part of Europe. When we speak of an American farmer, we generally mean one who is the absolute owner of the land, and everything on it. In England, by that appellation they designate a tenant who cultivates a farm belonging to some gentleman or nobleman; nearly all the lands in England being the property of this class. The farmer of England is not, like other farmers generally in Europe, a poor man, but he is a capitalist to the amount, perhaps, of a thousand pounds sterling, and often even a much larger sum. He pays a money-rent, and owns the stock and implements of husbandry used on the farm, which is often leased from year to year, sometimes for seven years, for fourteen, twenty-one, or for life, or lives. The most common lease, perhaps, is for seven years. The farmers of England do not work, generally, as our farmers do, with their hired men, but they are rather superintendents and managers of the farm. Forty, fifty, or sixty years ago, there were many small farms of twenty, thirty, and forty acres; then the farmer worked on the land, as our farmers do, with his hired men. It is not very uncommon for a farm, which

is leased from year to year, to descend in that way from father to son for generations. This will often take place in a country like England, where there are many humane and enlightened landlords who see that their true policy lies in giving their tenants a lasting interest in the soil.

41. The wealth and grandeur of the owners of the land in England are exceedingly great. An individual has a rent of twenty thousand pounds sterling from his estates in a single county; (others may, perhaps, have much greater); the farm in his own occupation consists of two thousand acres, those of some of his tenants of twelve hundred; and he has been known, on the renewal of many of his leases, to make presents to his favourite tenants of houses, which are even ornaments to the country.* Though the cultivators of the land in England are often men of property, the absolute ownership of it by the farmers is preferable. All men must prefer certain to uncertain possessions, and this, in the long-run will be for the greatest benefit of the whole people. The history which is here given of the manner in which the earth is owned, shows how the welfare of mankind, their greater or less poverty or riches, depends upon the certain or uncertain interest which the cultivators have in the soil. Where the farmers are prosperous, there the people are great.

42. There is no subject upon which our opinions have changed so much as upon that of property. As we are of English origin, our ideas of poverty and property are English, far beyond what we are ready to acknowledge. A whole people, like families and indivi-

* Holkam and its Agriculture, &c., by Edward Rigby; 3d edition; being an account of Mr. Coke's farm in the county of Norfolk, England.

duals, derive their sentiments and habits of thinking from their ancestors, and often retain them after they cease to have any just foundation. I shall endeavour to show hereafter how far this fashion in thinking still influences the people of the United States. At present I shall only refer very briefly to the early history of property in land under the feudal law, which was the law of our English ancestors.

43. The Northern nations of Europe overran the Roman empire. These nations had laws in regard to the ownership and cultivation of land peculiar to themselves. They were a martial people, and generally at war. The chieftains and principal characters of these warlike people, as they had the power, so, like all other men in such cases, they resolutely exercised it. They claimed, as the protectors of their followers, a supreme title to the soil, which they allotted, upon their conquests, to the inferior officers and soldiers as rewards for their services. These allotments were called " fœda, feuds, fiefs, or fees," the latter word signifying a reward, hence the name feudal law. Every receiver of lands, or feudatory, was bound to defend his lord and the land which he had received, and the lord was bound to defend his tenant. William the Conqueror of England introduced the feudal law, a main principle of which was, "that the king is the universal lord, and original proprietor of all the lands in his kingdom; and that no man doth or can possess any part of it but what has mediately or immediately been derived as a gift from him, to be held upon feudal services."*

44. This was the oath of fealty: "The freeholder

---

* 2d vol. Black. Com., c. 4.

HISTORY OF PROPERTY. 57

laying his right hand on a book, shall say, 'Know ye this, my lord, that I shall be faithful and true unto you, and faith unto you shall bear, for the lands which I claim and hold of you, and that I shall lawfully do the customs and services which I ought to do at the times assigned. So help me God and the saints.'"* Besides this oath, the vassal, by which word we now signify a slave, did homage to his lord thus: "openly and humbly kneeling, being ungirt, uncovered, and holding up his hands together between those of the lord, who sate before him, and there professing that he did become his man, from that day forth, of life and limb, and earthly honour."

45. The king having established the principle, that he was lord paramount in the English law, and proprietor of all the lands in the kingdom, the slavery of the people, who had nothing that they could call their own, followed of course, and these were some of the principles of this feudal slavery. The tenant was bound to afford aid in money when the lord stood in need—as when he married his daughter, or when he made his son a knight. Also to pay a relief to the lord when his ancestor died, and he succeeded to the inheritance. If the tenant was under age, the lord, as guardian, had a right to dispose of him in marriage. If the tenant died without a son capable of performing the feudal services, the lands returned to the king, which is called "escheating."† The right of the first-born to the inheritance of land, or of *primogeniture*, as it is called in our law-books, and the preference of males, was a consequence of the feudal

* 3d vol. Kent's Com., p. 390, "Of the History of the Law of Tenure."
† Kent's Commentaries.

system, because there must be a vassal capable of going to war, and of doing service, which could not be done by an infant or woman.* How completely, then, have the people of the United States reversed the ancient maxims of property! In France, the maxim under the feudal law was, "*nulle terre sans seigneur,*"—no land without a lord.†

* Kent.
† Robertson's History of Charles V., vol. 1., note, 8., Appendix.

CHAPTER IV

HISTORY OF PROPERTY, CONTINUED.

46. Of all people, it is most incumbent upon those of the United States to understand the nature and value of property; something of the history of it, and how far they owe their very liberty to the possession of it. Persecution drove our ancestors from their native land; they yielded to it in flight, only because they were poor. It is the poor, and not the rich, that history generally shows to have been the victims of oppression. People, who are independent, who have property, have power; they can protect themselves, they have friends, or can procure them, and arms for defence, and though perhaps less numerous than their persecutors, they usually are able to maintain their liberties and possessions.

47. At the period of the discovery of America, in the year one thousand four hundred and ninety-two, the great mass of the common people of Europe were little better than slaves; of that which we now call liberty, they scarcely knew the name. They had no absolute property in the land as we have seen in a former chapter; besides they were so wretchedly indigent as to have little property of any kind. Their political privileges corresponded with this state of their property; they had no elections, and of course, no votes; officers from the highest to the lowest were placed over them.

Those who then cultivated the earth were—first, slaves. These slaves were generally some portion of a conquered nation, not coloured people, but white, like ourselves. Second, villeins, who were said to be fixed to the soil, and were transferred with the land. It has been shown in a former chapter, that large portions of Europe are still in this condition. Third, there were a small number of freemen who held property absolutely as their own. But such was the wretched condition of the times, and such the violence and outrage to which men were exposed in those barbarous ages, that this latter class made a formal surrender of this independent property, and became slaves, that they might enjoy the protection of the lords.* The first dawn of liberty among the slaves arose, not from the influence of religion and and philanthropy alone, as might be expected, but from the fact, *that many of the slave peasants were enabled by their economy and wise savings, to purchase their liberty.* As their property procured them liberty, liberty made them profitable labourers to their former masters, whose revenues were thereby so much augmented, and the value of their lands so much increased, and so many saw the advantages accruing to themselves from the liberty of their slaves, that innumerable serfs were every where enfranchised.† In the progress of time and of public improvement, charters of manumission were granted, as related by the historian, Robertson. These concessions were—first, that the right of sale of the person should be relinquished; second, power was given to convey property by will or deed; third, the taxes and services, which before were at the will of the lord, were now rendered certain and fixed; fourth, marriage was allow-

---

* Robertson's History of Charles V., vol. 1, note 9, Appendix.

† Sismondi's Lessons of Experience on the Emancipation of Slaves.

ed without the lord's permission. Little do we think of the condition of our English ancestors, when we look back to a period long after the discovery of this continent, and find Queen Elizabeth, in the year, one thousand five hundred and seventy-four, granting manumission of certain slaves of her own.*

48. The tyranny exercised over the labouring people, in the times of which a brief view has been given, corresponded with their miserable indigence. They were governed and legislated for more like animals than human beings; what they should eat, what they should wear, and what they should earn, being prescribed by law. Even the dress of merchants and artificers, who were very inferior to the great lords and landholders, was provided for by law. By the statute of apparel, passed in thirty-seventh Edward III, those of this class, who had five hundred **pounds** value in goods, might use the same dress as **squires of a** hundred pounds a year.† Of all injustice, **none could** be more gross or stupid, as respected the **interests of a** nation, than the regulation by law of the wages of labourers. A poor man has nothing to sell but his labour, and he has as much right to sell this high, as his richer neighbour has to part with his merchandize at a great price; *besides the natural wages of men, which means nothing more than what a man earns, are as different as their minds and bodies.* One man, at the same work, in the same time, will earn twice as much as another, or more. By the statute of labourers, passed in the year one thousand three hundred and fifty, the wages of reapers in the harvest are

* Robertson, note 20, Appendix.
† Hallam's Middle Ages, vol. 2, part 2.

fixed at three pence a day, without diet.* If we go back to the times of our Saxon ancestors, it is said that two-thirds of the people were either absolute slaves, or in an intermediate state of bondage.† They might be put in bonds and whipped, they might be branded; and are spoken of as being yoked like cattle. "Let every man know his team of men, of horses, and oxen."‡ In the year eleven hundred and two, it was declared, in the great council of the nation, held at Westminster, unlawful for any man to sell slaves openly in the market, which before had been the common custom of the country.§ The statute passed in the year one thousand three hundred and sixty-three, regulating diet and apparel, provides that artificers and servants shall be found once a day with meat and fish, or the waste of other victuals, as milk and cheese, according to their station, and that they should wear cloth of which the whole piece did not cost more than twelve pence per yard. The cloth of yeomen and tradesmen was not to cost more than one shilling and six pence per yard.‖ In studying the history of economy, the people of the United States will see that it runs along side at equal pace with the history of liberty; and that the more laws there have been regulating the wages, the business, the diet, the religion, the morals, of the people, the more slavery there has been, and that freedom and the prosperity of the people have advanced, as these laws have been abrogated. It would

* The same.
† History of the Middle and Working Classes, by Jno. Wade.
‡ The same.
§ The same.
‖ The same.

have been by far more proper, that the poor should have regulated the dress of the affluent, than that their own should be prescribed, because plainly, the expensive ostentation of rich spendthrifts is more pernicious to the public, than the humble pride and vanity of the poor can be.

49. Such is a brief view of the condition of our English ancestors. Having no independent property they possessed no political rights; they were not merchants because they had neither goods nor ships; nor manufactures, for these never flourish among a poor enslaved people; nor did they cultivate the earth except to earn a bare subsistence; and this accounts for the scantiness of food which produced the disease and famine of which we read so much in those days.

We consider education one of the great blessings of life; we obtain our books, our teachers, our leisure for study for ourselves, and our children, by means of our surplus wealth; that is, the portion, which is over and above, what we demand for more necessary things. But the greater part of our ancestors had no property to enable them to buy these blessings, for they are always bought, and often at a great price. It was not till the eleventh century, that the art of making paper was known. In those dark ages, the price of books was so high, that persons of moderate fortune could not afford to buy them.* A certain countess of Anjou, paid for the homilies of Haimon, two hundred sheep, five quarters of wheat, and the same quantity of rye and millet. When a person made a present of a book to a church or monastery, in which were the only libraries in those days; he gave it

* Robertson's Charles V., Vol. 1, Note X.

for the salvation of his soul. In that poverty-stricken age, it was usual for persons who could not write their names, to make the sign of the cross. Even, at this day, illiterate people, who cannot write, sign deeds and other papers, by making two strokes with the pen in the form of a cross, and we say of a man who does this, that "he does not write his name but makes his cross." People now, who can buy education, always learn to write; but in those days, and as late as the fourteenth century, Du Guesclin, constable of France, and the greatest man in the state, could not write his name.[*]

50. Such was the state of things, when, or shortly before the new world was discovered; here our ancestors cam as freemen; here were neither kings, nor lords, masters nor slaves, landlords nor tenants, and here for the first time have many of the true principles of economy, been either understood or established. The lands which they came to enjoy were granted to them by charters from the crown of England, freed from all the slavish tenures heretofore mentioned. In the language of the law they were held in "free and common socage?" and though nominally they were held under the crown, still to every valuable purpose our ancestors ackowledged no superior, but were lords of the soil;[†] nor did they become tenants or dependants in any way.

Common tenancies and rents arise in this manner: they only commence when some portions of the land being taken up and settled, these become so valuable by the increase of population, and the building of cities and villages, that many prefer to pay rent rather than

---

[*] The same.

[†] Story's Commentaries, vol. 1, book 1, ch. 17.

HISTORY OF PROPERTY. 65

go to the wilderness, and some are so poor that they are not able to emigrate. When our ancestors came here, the whole country was a wilderness, and every man could have land by taking possession of it, or paying some trifling sum for it. This is the present state of much of our western territory, and if we except a small number of flourishing places, a very few tenants paying rent can be found in that territory. If we go to our great cities, however, and to the more settled parts, we find tenants and rents, and the reason is, that in these there is not land enough to enable every man to obtain a portion. The rich in such cases buy the land, and lease it to their poorer neighbours; if these, however, were able and willing to emigrate to Michigan, or other unsettled parts of the country, (where land can be obtained at the government price of a dollar and a quarter an acre) they would of course be relieved from paying rents.

51. From these causes, and from that strong love of independence which has always marked our people, there were in the early settlement of the country a few cases only of manors and tenancies. Some of these were found in the State of New-York; in New England there were a few cases only of lands paying rent.* In New England the principle was established upon the first settlement of the country of the equal division of real estate among all the heirs, except that to the oldest son there was given a double portion. At the period of the revolution this exception even was abolished. In New-York and the southern colonies, the rule of the English common law, of *primogeniture* prevailed. † This prin-

* Story's Commentaries, vol. 1, book 1, ch. 17.
† The same.

ciple of the equal partition of land among heirs has now become the universal law of all the States,* and in this uniform recognition of it, they have shown how important an ingredient they consider it in their institutions.

52. These reflections bring us to the American revolution; which could not have taken place when it did, unless the people had been in some measure prepared for it, by a long course of industry and successful commerce. Property was, to the people of the colonies from the beginning, the foundation of their education and liberal views, the country was filled with a race of men prepared to be free, and they knew well that poverty and freedom could not go hand in hand together. How different would have been the condition of the colonies upon the breaking out of the war, if the country had been taken possession of by a few great lords and speculators from Europe, and the people had been slaves, villeins, serfs, as in Poland and Russia, tenants paying labour rents, or cultivating the lands upon shares, instead of enjoying the whole fruits of the earth? When the struggle began, we had already made great advances in trade and commercial enterprise. Mr. Burke one of the greatest and best friends of our liberty, speaking in the house of commons of the wealth, which the people of New England had drawn from their fisheries, pronounced that eulogium upon their genius and enterprise, which should be indelibly engraven upon the memory of every New England youth in honour of his father-land.

In speaking of the manner in which the whale-fishery had been carried on, he says—"and pray, sir, what in the world is equal to it?—pass by the other parts, and

* Story.

look at the manner in which the people of New England have of late carried on the whale-fishery. Whilst we follow them among the tumbling mountains of ice, and behold them penetrating into the deepest frozen recesses of Hudson's Bay and Davis' Straits; whilst we are looking for them beneath the arctic circle, we hear that they have pierced into the opposite region of polar cold; that they are at the antipodes, and engaged under the frozen serpent of the south. Falkland Island, which seemed too remote and romantic an object for the grasp of national ambition, is but a stage, and resting-place in the progress of their victorious industry. Nor is the equinoctial heat more discouraging to them, than the accumulated winter of both the poles. We know that whilst some of them draw the line, and strike the harpoon on the coast of Africa, others run the longitude, and pursue the gigantic game along the coast of Brazil.

No sea but what is vexed by their fisheries, no climate that is not witness to their toils. Neither the perseverance of Holland, nor the activity of France, nor the dexterous and firm sagacity of English enterprise ever carried this most perilous mode of hard industry, to the extent to which it has been pushed by this recent people, a people who are still, as it were, but in the gristle, and not yet hardened into the bone of manhood."

53. When the war of the Revolution began, though the poverty of the people was great, compared with their present riches; still they were rich compared with most other labourers in the world. If their houses had been hovels of mud and clay, their garments like those of half savage people, their farms a few acres only, their cattle a cow and a few pigs, their principal food potatoes, their arms nothing better than clubs, pitchforks, and

pikes, as has been the condition of the poor Irish, it is probable, that like them, we should now be in subjection. Though miserably prepared for a contest with a great, and affluent people, still they had the first element of war, arms, to which they had long been accustomed.

In this part of the country, as soon as the war broke out, all regular government ceased, and the whole power fell into the hands of organized Committees of safety. One of the first acts of the whigs in some places was, to disarm the tories. The practice was for half a dozen men to go to their houses, and demand their arms. In some towns it being understood very soon after the battle of Lexington, that the tories were a minority, their arms were demanded and when they refused, the delinquents were imprisoned in the common jail. In others, the whigs formed volunteer companies of fifty each, who previous to, and after the battle of Lexington, assembled every day in the week, except Sunday, for military exercise. When the weather was foul they met in barns : all had guns, for they met for the purpose of a regular drill, though many of them were in bad order, and without bayonets. After the battle of Lexington, men were drafted by lot for the army, and those upon whom the lot fell were allowed to find substitutes; in such cases the substitutes were paid forty dollars for six months, which was common agricultural wages in this part of the country.

One of the first acts of Congress was to emit bills of credit to the amount of three millions of dollars, and though all paper money afterwards became worthless, the public then had credit.* When Washington esta-

---

* Marshall's Life of Washington, ch. 3, vol. 2.

blished his head quarters at Cambridge, in Massachusetts, in the year 1775, he found himself at the head of about 14,500 men.* Though the people were thus enabled to make a stand against British aggression, it was owing to their poverty, that they were compelled to struggle through an eight years' war. Our numbers then were about one quarter part of our present population, and had we possessed this proportion, compared with our present means of ships, guns, bayonets, powder, ball, clothes, food, and *money* to pay the wages of soldiers, the war would have ended with a single campaign, for " money is a good soldier, it will on." We know that this was not the case, for upon the assembling of the army at Cambridge, it was discovered that there were but nine cartridges to a man, a great want of bayonets, of blankets and other clothes. For the want of money, which has been truly said to be the " sinews of war," soldiers were enlisted only for a year, and so destitute were the people, that soldiers were obliged to find their own arms, or to pay six shillings for the use of those furnished to them.†

The knowledge of the devastation that was made, the blood that was shed, the miseries that were endured in that war for the want of resources, to feed, clothe, arm, and pay soldiers enough, (for men enough there were to drive the British into their ships, or the sea, in a single year) furnishes one of the highest incitements the American people can have to become independent freemen, and their best lesson upon economy, and the value and power of property.

* Marshall, ch. 4. † The same, ch. 4.

54. What further lesson do we derive from this brief history of property?

1st, It is plain, that the earth, and the greater part of its possessions, have been held and enjoyed in every country by a very small number of families, compared with the whole number of the people, including kings, nobles, gentry, and a few favoured persons. That the rest of the people have been slaves, retainers, tenants, servants, with little or no property of their own.

That, as all property comes from labour, and as these few favoured persons, with small exceptions, have not been labourers, neither merchants, farmers, mechanics, manufacturers, or professional men, that their property has been derived from other sources, than their own industry. That these other sources have been unequal laws in their own favour, which is monopoly.

2d, We see here the great value of property to every man, and especially the importance of land, or *real estate*. That this is stable property, that while the owner lives there is something to be improved, ornamented, beautified, and when he dies, a home for his wife and children. That this blessing is particularly important to an American citizen, because from the cheapness of land here, it is generally within his reach. In our cities we find, that those mechanics, are most prosperous who own houses and lots, rather than personal property, which is liable to various accidents. There is no sufficient cause, why so many day labourers, mechanics and manufacturers in the United States, where land is so cheap, should be destitute of it. Every child here should be educated, so as to have his eye directed to a permanent home, to look upon land, or a house and lot, as a natural proper possession for a hard workingman; not that every man can have it, nor that it is best for every man to have it. The interests and circumstances of some forbid their owning real estate, other property may be preferable in their situation.

It is, in a great measure, because there have been so many poor people, in other parts of the world, that we have so many poor here. Multitudes are so poor from the habit of thinking that there must be just so many poor people, and not because there is any necessity for them to be so poor. Unnecessary poverty should ever be looked upon as hateful and disgusting. The labouring people must awake from this stupor.

3d, The history of property, then, shows, that the great body of the people are nothing without it; that without it, they cannot have liberty, nor independence of mind or body. Is it pretended, then, that property is better than virtue, knowledge, and education? Certainly not. But that it is the means of obtaining all these.

CHAPTER V.

HISTORY AND MARKS OF POVERTY.

55. To write the history of poverty would be to write the history of nine-tenths, or, perhaps, a much greater portion of mankind from the beginning of the world. It is not difficult to show that nine-tenths of the world are actually poor, but it would be to establish, that nine-tenths of the world *need be poor—must be poor;* that they cannot, with all their labour and skill, extract from the earth, and the materials which it yields, enough, if properly *divided and distributed,* to furnish them with a reasonable portion of the comforts of life, such as God has given man tastes and appetites to enjoy. To be without these is to be poor. As other evils incident to man have disappeared by degrees, so will poverty,—we may be sure of that.

56. It has been common to say, that the world has been divided between the governors and the governed. The reason is plain,—the governors have been the rich, and the governed the poor. It has followed, then, as we might suppose, that the world has been divided between the governors and the poor labourers. But this is not all, for the peculiar hardship of the poor has been, not that they have laboured—for labour, *skilful, productive* labour, makes a great portion of the happiness of every man,—but that they have laboured disadvantageously, unproductively, to themselves; that others have received the profits of their labour. In this state

of things, labourers have been a degraded class, never intermixing, by marriage or otherwise, with the higher classes. In many countries they have been slaves; but whether slaves or not, mere "hewers of wood, and drawers of water." Thus the principal producers of all the dainties, luxuries, and beauties, have had nothing assigned to them but mean clothes, poor food, and wretched habitations.

57. So long did this state of things continue, that it was thought to be a natural order established by Providence, and therefore inevitable; and it was not till the period of the American Revolution that different ideas arose. By our *declaration* of independence, it was asserted, " that all men were born free and equal." This put the axe to the root of unequal privileges, and we are now bound to follow out this noble, beneficent, and religious principle, lead where it may.

58. Having in a former chapter attempted to give a brief history of property, which, in fact, was a history of the poverty of the people in the times alluded to, I shall in the present only refer to a few facts, to show the *present* poverty of some of the *richest parts of the world*, and how extremely destitute a great portion of God's creatures are. That such excessive poverty is not necessary,—that no law or design of God requires it,— and that it is owing much to the ignorance and wickedness of man, which may, in a great measure, be corrected, there can be no doubt. That there is a disgraceful and unnecessary poverty in the world, has long been fully believed by some of the greatest men, and by those, too, who have by no means entertained the most favourable opinions of the capacity of mankind for happiness. Doctor Johnson was one of these.

He says, that he does not think it impossible to exempt the *lower* classes of mankind from poverty; that though it be true that there must be rich and poor, and that he that has less than another is comparatively poor; still that he does not see any necessity why many should be without the indispensable conveniences of life; and that he is inclined to imagine, that, casual calamities excepted, there might, by universal prudence, be procured a universal exemption from want.* At the conclusion of the number, he hints, in a few such maxims as the following, at what he means by universal prudence;— "A penny saved, is twopence got." "A man's voluntary expenses should not exceed his income." "Let no man live upon uncertain profits."—"Let no man squander against his inclination," and he might have added, through the dread of fools. This last is what Doctor Franklin calls "seeing with other people's eyes." What part of our merchants, farmers, mechanics, manufacturers, and other labourers, realize that an immense portion of them are doomed to labour; and not only how becoming it is, therefore, but how indispensable, to live up to this kind of wisdom and prudence that Franklin and Johnson recommend—they must decide. It must be remembered here, however, that no prudence in the people can secure them from want, as long as bad government, and monopoly laws, give to a few the property which is created by the many.

59. Many definitions have been given to discriminate between man and the brute. It has been said that man is a reasoning animal, and has a soul; but we know that the brute also is a reasoning animal; but whether

* Johnson's Rambler, No. 57.

he has what we call a soul, we cannot know. Plato is said to have defined man to be a two-legged animal, without feathers. Diogenes plucked the feathers from a cock, threw him into a room, exclaiming, "Behold Plato's man!" By some, man has been called a laughing animal; by others, a cooking animal.

60. There are clear distinctions between the man and the brute. As to most brutes, it may be strictly said, that Providence provides for them; but as to man, he must provide for himself by his *labour*. God has given him an occupation, he must follow it; he has no option of labouring or not labouring; and in this the Supreme Being has shown, that labour is designed to render him useful and happy. As to the brute, God gives him his garments; and for nutriment many graze upon the face of the earth; but men in most climates, without covering of their own procuring, would perish, and, as for food, it must come from the labour of their hands.

61. One of the great distinctions, then, between man and the inferior creatures is, that man supplies his wants by his labour,—so may it be said doth the bee and the ant. There is, then, a still greater distinction: man labours not merely for the present, but for the *future;* he labours, as a *social being*, for his wife, children, and neighbours,—for generations to come,—for successive ages; and the more he has regard to the permanency of his labours, the more skilful a labourer, generally, he will be. Man labours much for things that are intended to endure and be useful for hundreds of years. Such are, the improvements of the earth, by planting trees; building walls and drains, and by every kind of durable cultivation. It is in this way that men lay up a store for future use. This is done by economy, and it can be

done in no other way. Without this economy every generation would be equally poor, and equally miserable; and this shows how great a benefactor an economical man is,—he does good to generations unborn, as well as to his family and neighbours.

62. There is still another distinction between man and the lower orders of beings, and this is the greatest of all, that he labours for the *mind*, and thus while he is laying up treasures on earth, he may by a right use of them, "lay up treasures in heaven" also. Man labours for things that are beautiful to the eye and the ear, as gardens, flowers, pictures, statues, music, and for all that permanently adorns his condition; he labours to lay up stores for benevolence, for charity, for hospitality, and to endow his children when he dies with the products of his love. In proportion as he thinks little of of gluttony, of eating, of drinking, "faring sumptuously every day," of his *animal* appetites, and much of his *intellectual*, in that degree is he a truly economical man. It is this that makes economy a religious and moral science, that sanctifies it, and recommends it, to all mankind, high and low, rich and poor.

This then is one of the great parts of the science of public and private economy; to point out what kind of industry, and what description of labour, is most useful, advantageous, and profitable to man. To show the difference between the labour which does, and which does not, leave something behind it. If a labouring man wants to know any thing, he wants to know this. A drunkard or glutton, who, on the second day, eats or drinks all that he earned by his labour on the first, will, on the third, remain just where he began.

Neither the drunkard, nor the world, can advance an inch by this kind of labour.

63. As it is intended hereafter to give a general outline of the condition of some large portions of the people of the United States, I shall here merely state some facts to show the present condition of poverty in the world, and set down some of those melancholy marks by which the poor may be known in every country. It is unnecessary to give any definition of the poor; for this is a word of comparison, and there are all degrees of rich and poor, from Dives to Lazarus.

64. First, This then is the first mark of the poor that will be mentioned, *excessive labour;* that degree of it, which, exhausting the body and mind, wear out both prematurely; so that a man may be said not to live out his appointed days. The manufacturing population of New England, taking summer and winter, and exclusive of the time occupied in meals, work upon an average not less than twelve hours out of the twenty-four. In many establishments they work a longer time. Many mechanics and day labourers, even in the United States, labour not less than fourteen hours out of the twenty-four. It must be remembered, that the labour here taken into consideration, is that only which the manufacturer or mechanic performs in the service of his employer. There is more labour still for a large class. These are compelled before their working hours begin in the morning, or after they are over at night, to provide conveniences for their wives and children; to do the chores of the family; and they find that this additional work bears upon them with great severity. Some are obliged to walk miles to their tasks in the morning and

to their homes in the evening, and this is the hardest of all their labours.

65. The following petition to Parliament, presented in the year eighteen hundred and thirty-one, of people employed in the Bleachfields, in the counties of Lanark, Renfrew, and Dumbarton, (Scotland,) will show the state of the labouring people there.

"First, Your petitioners are exposed in all seasons, to the extremes of heat and cold, a portion of them being employed, sometimes from five in the morning till eight or nine o'clock in the evening, in rooms heated by stoves, from one hundred to one hundred and thirty degrees. Second, The stuffs and materials which pass through their hands emit effluvia injurious to the human constitution; and, third, the length of time in which they are employed daily, extending generally to *sixteen* hours out of the twenty-four, with only half an hour to breakfast and dinner, leaves no leisure for the young to attend to wholesome instruction or recreation, nor the old for enjoying seasonable relaxation or watching over the religious or moral welfare of their unhappy offspring. That a period of such daily and incessant toil is calculated to reduce your petitioners and their families to the lowest scale of animal existence, and being kept in such a degraded state, thus perpetuates within society a race of beings, incapable of understanding their moral and political obligations, miserable to themselves, and dangerous to the rest of the community."

We may, therefore, fairly set down the average period of labour of large numbers, both in Europe and in the United States, at twelve or fourteen hours out of the twenty-four; and of not an inconsiderable number, still higher.

66. Second, The second mark which distinguishes the condition of the poor is, that, many of them being thus doomed to work twelve, fourteen, or more hours in a day, have no leisure either for the proper improvement of the mind or for those recreations which are indispensable to recruit the wasted and exhausted strength of the body. They can procure neither education nor books, which ought in due proportion to be considered indispensable articles of life to all men. Their ignorance, therefore, is deplorable; they can neither add a row of figures, nor read the signs over the shop-doors, nor the names on the door-plates.

67. Third, Bad and insufficient food is another of the melancholy marks of the poor. Many, to whom the study of economy is proposed, turn a deaf ear, because they think that nothing but pinching, and starving, and miserly habits, are recommended; whereas, one of its first designs is to enable the poor, especially, to live better, and spend more than they have ever done. It is impossible that the good Being who governs us, should have given such a pleasing variety of agreeable and nutritious articles, without designing them for the great body of his rational creatures; to all of whom he has given tastes by which they may be enjoyed. There is no reason to believe that he can have designed these healthful, nutritious things, for only a tenth, a twentieth, or a hundredth part. What means this profusion of flesh and fish, of fruits and vegetables, but that the great family of mankind, having respect to their local situation, their tastes, their wants, and their division into rich and poor, should partake of them in due degree? But it is not only an insufficient supply to which the poor are doomed, but also to *bad, adulterated, unwholesome*

food. This is a disgraceful provision for a human being. He who adulterates food or drink, who poisons them, or makes them less healthful than they are by nature, belongs to one class of murderers.

68. The subject of adulterated food ought not to be passed over here, as the greatest share of it falls of course to the poor, who are obliged for the want of a little money, a little store laid up, to buy what are called the cheapest articles, but which in fact are the dearest and the worst. Wholesome food is indispensable to health and to successful labour, and to contaminate it by the admixture of base articles, is to infuse poison into our daily bread. It is a peculiar wickedness in a country in which nearly all are obliged to labour, for one labourer to inflict this misery upon his fellow-labourer.

69. It is said, in England, to be difficult to mention a single article of food that is not adulterated; and that there are some substances, which are hardly ever to be found genuine.* *Medicines* are adulterated; peruvian bark is mixed with mahogany saw-dust, and oak wood; rhubarb is adulterated; the quantity of medical preparations thus injured is said to exceed belief. Alum is used in flour to make white bread; tea is mixed with sloe, ash, and elder leaves; ground coffee is adulterated by peas and beans; cheese is adulterated; so are pepper, pickles, vinegar and confectionary.† Wines also are adulterated there extensively.‡ Alum is said to be used to give a bright colour to some wines; Brazil wood to give a proper colour to pale port. Astringency is given.

---

* Accum on adulteration.
† The same.
‡ Redding on Wines, Ch. 15.

HISTORY AND MARKS OF POVERTY.

to immature red wines, by oak wood, saw-dust, and husks of filberts.

It is notorious, that wines and other liquors are adulterated also in the United States. Chocolate is adulterated here by mixing with it buck-wheat flour; ginger by adding indian meal; bread by mixing sweet, with sour and damaged flour. It is not these impure articles only that fall in a great measure to the lot of the poor, but all kinds of unsightly, uncleanly, and unwholesome food. It is that which is left after all others have picked and chosen. In New-York putrid hams are sometimes sold to the poor at six pence a pound, and in some cases by honest grocers, who sell with a full knowledge on the part of the buyers of the state of the article. There is a class of poor, who, it is said, do not revolt from this kind of putrid meat; but it is probable, that it is oftener, that "their poverty, than that their will consents!"

Much of the cholera in New-York was attributed to the use, by the poor, of stale and damaged articles.

70. Dupin, a living author of reputation in France, says—"That two-thirds of the French nation are wholly deprived of animal food, and that they live on chesnuts, or maize, [indian corn] or potatoes.* France, and many of the finest parts of Europe are overrun with beggars, and travellers assure us, that in France, at nearly every public-house where the diligences, which are the public stages of that country, stop, these miserable beings beset them crying out—"Charité, mes brave messieurs, charité;"—Charity, my noble gentlemen, charity.

Mc Cullock, one of the most distinguished economists of England, says—" Comparatively speaking, says Mr.

* See Results of Machinery, p. 23. London, 1831.

82 HISTORY AND MARKS OF POVERTY.

Newenham, a very small quantity of animal food is consumed in Ireland, a very great one in England. Much of that sort of food is saved there by religious fasts, and a very trifling quantity here. By the lowest class in England, it is generally eaten once a week, by the lowest class, in Ireland never. In England, that most numerous class next above the lowest, eat flesh meat three times, or at least twice a week. In Ireland, the same class which is in proportion more numerous, than in England, do not eat it more than once a month. A great majority of that class do not eat it oftener than six times in the year. Substantial farmers and country artificers in England live chiefly on animal food; the same description of persons in most parts of Ireland, live chiefly on potatoes and milk. Manufacturers in England subsist for the most part on flesh meat and bread; manufacturers in Ireland subsist for the most part on potatoes, oatmeal, and bread, consuming a very trifling portion of animal food."*

In England, about an eighth part of the people live, as I have before stated, more or less upon public charity. This is one of the richest countries in the world, if not the richest, (some have thought Holland richer, according to its population). It is a country in which there is much to admire, and much to deplore. England having lost sight of the just principles by which wealth is distributed, and heaped it up in the laps of a few, has become a country of surfeit and of famine, of palaces and of hovels, of purple and fine linen, and of beggars' clothes. The poor rate returns for the year 1832, state, that 7,036,968*l.* sterling were expended in that year for

* Mc Cullock's edition of Smith's Wealth of Nations, Note 5.

HISTORY AND MARKS OF POVERTY. 83

the relief of the poor. So desperate is the state of pauperism in England, so numerous are the people often out of employment, that in many parts of it relief has been given to the "able-bodied" population, who could not, or would not (the law supposed that they could not) earn a living by their work. The sums thus allowed varied in different parishes. In some a man and his wife were allowed five shillings sterling a-week, a single man three shillings and sixpence, and one shilling and sixpence a-head for every child.* There are cases in England, in which the poor rate has swallowed up every species of property, "the landlords having given up their rents, the farmers their tenancies, and the clergyman his glebe and his tithes.† As the poor of England, like the poor of every other country, must be supported in some way or other, the farmers employ the paupers, in order to lessen their poor rates, and this consequence follows; that industrious men, of good character, who have got together a little property, a cottage, a cow or two, and a few pigs, can no longer find employment; and, they say, that they must hide their property, or waste it, and drink it up, and thus reduce themselves to beggary, before they can expect to be employed. The poor law commissioners represent this state of the pauperized districts as ending in the greatest prodigality and wickedness of the hitherto industrious poor. What a misery —what a stain upon the character of a country, that the virtues of hard-working people should be a curse to them! One good principle in the United States, of nature's equality, which gives men property according to

* Report of the Poor Law Commissioners, p. 34—36. London, 1834.
† The same, p. 64—65.

their talents, and industry, and economy; which allows a free competition to all, and secures to the working man the recompense of his toil, is worth all the splendour of England.

71. The wretchedness of the poor of Ireland is more or less known to the whole population of the United States. But the subject of poverty cannot be too well understood by them. M'Cullock, in speaking of the fact of the poor of Ireland subsisting, as they generally do, upon potatoes, describes the condition of those unhappy misgoverned people as follows:—

"Their cabins continue to be in no respect superior, perhaps not equal, to the wigwams of the American Indians; they are destitute of chimneys, and of anything that can be called furniture; many families are without either beds or bed-clothes; and the children, generally in rags, are often absolutely naked. The number of persons soliciting employment, compared with the demand for their labour, and with the means of remunerating it, is so great, that very many are altogether unemployed, and reduced to the lowest sum that can purchase the smallest supply of the coarsest and cheapest species of food by which mere animal existence may be sustained. Under these circumstances, it is not surprising, that when the potatoe crop becomes in a slight degree deficient, the scourge of famine and disease should be felt in every corner of the country. Mr. Maurice Fitzgerald informed the committee on the employment of the Irish poor, that he had known the peasantry of Kerry quit their houses in search of employment, offering to work for the merest subsistence that could be obtained,— for *twopence* a-day,—in short, for anything that would purchase food enough to keep them alive for the next twenty-four hours!" Mr. Tighe mentions, "that the number of persons in Ireland supported by charity, is quite inconceivable; they must be supported by charity or by pillage and plunder. To the want of employment I attribute everything that afflicts or disgraces the country." M'Cullock then gives the following extract from the evidence of Dr. Doyle, the Catholic Bishop of Leighlin:—" The population is immediately increased, as every one must perceive, by improvident marriages; but those marriages themselves, in my opinion, result in a great measure from the extreme poverty of the people; for that poverty has paralized their energies —it has prevented them taking such an interest in creating a respectable situation for themselves in life as men possessed of some property always feel; for those wretched people say, that their situation cannot be worse, when married, than before, and hence they go together; their depression throws them together like savages in a wood. It is a frightful state of society, and, when it is considered, it fills me with so much pain and horror, that I have frequently prayed to God, if it were his will, rather to take me out of life, than to leave me to witness such evils." These sickening accounts of poor people are taken from the richest parts of the world.

72. Fourth, The habitation of the poor man, which is alike destitute of much that makes life either healthful or desirable, is another mark of his miserable condition.

73. Fifth, Deficient and bad fuel is another mark of the poor, and in cold countries one of great moment. It is said that in Normandy, in France, even at this day, lace work is made by people who are destitute of

fuel, and are warmed by the animal heat of cattle in stables.*

These people sleep in the day time. But we need not go from our own shores to witness these miseries of the poor; when we see them gathering chips and splinters in the ship-yards, and from the gutters in our own cities; buying green wood by the back load, and coals by the peck or half peck.

74. Sixth, And here is another of the indelible marks of poverty, which we find both in town and country, and among farmers, mechanics, and labourers of every description ; that is, that the poor are obliged to buy on credit, or for cash, in very small quantities. The poor, having no store on hand, nothing laid up, are compelled to purchase in this way. This is the reason why we see them in country stores, buying a single dried cod-fish, or pickled mackerel, or a few pounds of flour, when their richer neighbours purchase by the barrel or half barrel. As the poor buy in small quantities, they pay large profits; for the grocer or store-keeper can afford to sell a barrel of flour or firkin of butter cheaper when he sells in the lump than when he is compelled to weigh it out in small parcels. In this case, his time, which is his labour, makes a part of the price. This is the reason why the rate of profits of the wholesale grocer are comparatively small, and those of the retail grocer large. The poor, in the cities especially, pay an average profit, beyond what is paid by the rich, of not less than twenty-five or thirty per cent., and often, much more. It is for the want of a *little money* laid by, (and for the want of

* Results of Machinery.

cellars under their wretched habitations,) that they are often compelled to pay for potatoes, (an article of great importance to them,) seventy-five cents in the spring, when in the autumn they may be bought for half that price, or less. *When the poor buy on credit,* they purchase still more disadvantageously: in this case, they have nothing but their labour to buy with, and this is labour *promised,* which is to *mortgage* it. A farmer, who is in debt and wants money, mortgages his farm, and thus, too often, hangs a mill-stone about his neck; a labourer, who wants bread and meat, and has no money, mortgages his labour, which is his farm. As the dealer, who supplies such a labourer, cannot know that he shall get the labour that is promised, he makes up for the risk in an enormous price for his articles.

75. Seventh, This leads to the seventh mark of the poor, which I shall notice, and which is produced by a combination of all the causes mentioned; that is, *the greater mortality of the poor.* Their rigorous labours, through every exposure to heat and cold, and often, when sick; without leisure to recruit body or mind; their want of education, and knowledge of the arts of health; their scanty, adulterated, and often, poisoned food; their cold and cheerless habitations; their scanty fuel; and wretched garments; cause so many of the children of the poor to come into the world with diseased constitutions, and so many of their parents to be sent out of it long before their natural time. Among the other miseries of the poor man, then, is, that he cannot live as long as his richer neighbour. It is stated, in Europe, that notwithstanding the baneful luxuries in which the rich there, (and every where,) indulge, that the duration of their lives exceeds about ten years that

of their inferiors.* It is said, also, that it is a fact, well established there, "that out of an equal number of children of wealthy and of indigent parents, at least, twice as many of the latter die in infancy as of the former."† A carpenter, in London, and in some other places, is not supposed to last in his utmost vigour above eight years.‡ It is notorious, that the cholera, and all epidemic diseases, fall with redoubled fury upon the poor.

76. Eighth, There is still another sign of the poor, and the worst of all; I mean, of the neglected, abandoned poor; and this is the mark of vice and infamy. This part of the poor make a great portion of the tenants of the poor-houses, jails, and state prisons. It is a universal experience, that the virtuous are most distinguished from the vicious poor, by frugality, thrift, and the desire to obtain property.

77. Ninth, Alas! after all, this is not a perfect description or account of the poor, nor can any be given. But there is one class of sufferers that ought not to be passed over. I mean a portion of the well born; that is, the well born in the *highest sense*, born of honourable and honest parents. These are those, whose pride and deep sense of independence, cover up the outside appearances of wretchedness, but within there is a worm that never dies. They are not called indigent people, but still they are poor compared with those who are well off. Their wants are few, and pure, and simple, but they cannot gratify them; they are not even comfortable. Many of them are compelled to work at under prices,

---

* Staunton's Embassy to China, vol. 2, chap. 5.
† Say's Political Economy, book 2, chap. 11.
‡ Smith's Wealth of Nations, book 1, chap. 8.

and to submit to a thousand oppressive actions, from their purse-proud, over-bearing employers, and task-masters. Even the common wants of some are not supplied as they have been accustomed to live; their houses are cold—their garments are not suited to the extremities of the seasons; they cannot indulge in the pleasures of society and hospitality to which they have been accustomed in their youth; nor can they send their children to such schools as they themselves have enjoyed the benefit of Their rents are often in arrear, their little family estates perhaps mortgaged, and so they pass on forever pinched with poverty through a life which is a perpetual struggle, and all for the want of a little property, which others have wasted by the most stupid profusion; it is little, but this little is indispensable; as much as the life-boat to the ship in distress, without which all is wretchedness and despair.

78. First, One of the first reflections that arises from this brief account of the poor, is, the fact of the immense number of poor people in many countries compared with that to be found in the United States. In Europe, the great care is to *cure* poverty; here it should be to *prevent* it; the prevention of disease is easier than its cure; and this shows the difference between the economy of Europe and of the United States. If our people had at their tongues' end all that has been written by Say, Malthus, Ricardo, and all the other political economists of Europe, they would still know little of the economy of their own country.

79. Second, There can be little satisfactory knowledge of economy, without understanding the condition of the poor; and, alas! how great is our ignorance of them.

There are thousands, and some of them very virtuous people, who being well provided for themselves, are not educated to think upon such subjects. They live in the world to be sure, but it is not that portion of it where the poor live; they hear of the poor, and sometimes see them walking in the streets; many of them have benevolent dispositions, and when called upon, give liberally; but still they know almost as little of these poor people; what sort of trades they follow; what wages they get; how many hours they work : what sort of tyranny is practised upon them; where they live; in what sort of houses or homes; what kind of food they eat; what they drink; what diseases they have; what medicines they resort to; as if there were no such beings in the world.

This may be said to be the benevolent part of the science of economy, and by far the most important part of it.

80. Third, When we came to know what wretchedness there is among these necessitous people, we shall realize at once what a blessing a little property is, and what a virtue it is to know and practise all we can of economy.

It is said there must be poverty in the world, and that it is a very ridiculous kind of enthusiasm to spend time and money in preventing it; and so it would be, if it were attempted to get rid of poverty altogether, and make angels of men. The scriptures say, "the poor ye shall have with you always," but it is not said, how many poor there shall be, but on the contrary, it is said, "feed the hungry, and clothe the naked."— So there must be storms, and for this reason it is our duty to build houses, and to seek shelter when the storm rages. So there must be disease, but it is not said how much.

HISTORY AND MARKS OF POVERTY. 91

We know that there is less disease than there was in former ages; that in the civilized parts of the world, there is less of leprosy, scurvy, small-pox, plague, yellow fever, and some other disorders; that these diseases have been lessened by the skill of man, and not by any miraculous interposition of Providence; and we know, too, that in consequence of this diminution of disease in the same parts of the world, life has been prolonged; not the life of every man, woman, and child, but the *average duration of life*. Of this fact there seems to be the most conclusive evidence.* Erasmus attributed the plague in the reign of Henry the 8th, to the "nastiness" of the streets and houses in London. Speaking of the English he says—"their floors are commonly of clay, strewed with rushes, under which lie unmolested, a collection of beer, grease, fragments, bones, spittle, excrements of dogs and cats, and of every thing that is nauseous." It is said that the *presence-chamber* of his daughter Queen Elizabeth was strewed with hay for the want of carpets. It is then one of the greatest prerogatives of man, to ward off, or to cure the natural evils of his condition; this makes a great portion of his business in the world. Experience shows that there is no natural or moral evil which men cannot do much to ward off, or diminish, but to do this, we must have the means, and the means are generally our property, some new invention, some

---

* Combe on the Constitution of Man—Appendix, note 3; a book that ought to be understood by every rich and by every poor man in the United States.—Senior's Lectures on Wages. The Working Man's Companion, the rights of industry, capital, and labour, p. 110,--Results of Machinery, London edition, 1831, p. 153—J. R. M'Cullock's edition of Adam Smith's Wealth of Nations, vol. 4, note 4, Population.

discovery, some improvement, some combination of useful matter. Without this increase of our property, there can generally be no improvement whatever. It has been stated that our lives are growing longer, and how is this to be accounted for? It is that men are better fed, clothed and housed than they were, and it has been shown how poverty shortens life. By the increase of property then, in many parts of the world men have actually gained an increase of life!

81. Fourth, From these considerations it follows, that the poor of all men are most interested in those principles by which property is increased. If the rights to property are not as sacred as those of life, they are next to those in sacredness, because property actually gives life, or may be said to be the cause of it; for where there is the greatest increase of property, as in the United States, there also is, the greatest increase of life, of population; besides, if property does not actually give life, it sustains it; and the poor know, how many of their class perish for the want of good wholesome comforts every year; and we likewise know that some barbarous nations kill a portion of their offspring, because they have not food to sustain them.

82. Fifth, Degradation is the inevitable portion of that part of the poor, who having no regard to economy consume one-half or more of their wages in unnecessary eating, drinking, and wearing, and thus subject themselves to the necessity of mean and disgusting clothes, food, and habitations. It is impossible to respect a man who will not respect himself, he shows that he is not fit for liberty. There is not a meaner object in nature, than a man who willingly crawls into a filthy bed, is

indifferent whether he lives in a hovel, or a comfortable habitation; whose food a decent man revolts from; who treats his wife like a slave; and suffers his children to roam abroad like wild animals, without care or education. These are the slaves of all countries.

CHAPTER VI.

POVERTY IN THE UNITED STATES.

83. HAVING in the last chapter shown some of the general marks of poverty, and given a very brief account of it in a few of the richest parts of the world, I shall, in this, make some statements of what it is in the United States. By poverty here, will be meant, the being destitute of those comforts and conveniences, or many of them, which will be particularly stated in this chapter.

In presenting the subject of poverty in the United States, I shall not give an account of poor-houses, of hospitals, of the great numbers of poor supported by cities and towns, with the sums of money paid for their maintenance: this would be a history of beggars rather than of poor people. Nor is it intended to compare the poverty of the United States with that of many other nations; for it is no excuse to us, for unnecessary poverty, that other people are poorer than we are. The people of the United States are the freest, and, if they continue so, they will be the richest in the world.

84. The design, then, is, that the people of the United States may compare their poverty, not with that of the miserably-taxed and enslaved people of many parts of Europe, but rather that they may understand the subject of poverty; that they may know what it is to be poor; that, especially, they may compare their present poverty with what it need be—their little

miserable pittances of property which so many of them possess, with what they might, and ought to possess.

The people of the United States escaped from the poverty of Europe : now it is high time to inquire how they can, as far as may be, escape from their own poverty. Let it, then, constantly be kept in mind, that the object is to show, how the rich, if they will spend their money nobly, instead of running over Europe to find out how they shall squander it, may increase riches ; how the farmer, manufacturer, mechanic, and day-labourer, can earn more, lay up more, and still spend more, and live better than they do at present. It is to show what the people may become, if they will have the heart and soul to long for a real independence, instead of hankering for fashion, for finery, for dainties, for strong drink, and a thousand indulgences, that now consume so much of their substance.

85. In a brief notice of the condition of poor people, I shall begin with the lowest description, and that is, day-labourers. In the city, we mean by day-labourers, not mechanics, or artizans of any description, but, generally, those who perform the manual and out-door labour of the city, such, as in New-York (1834) usually earn a dollar, or eighty-seven and a half cents in a day ; such as work in cleaning the streets, on the docks, &c., and generally all those who work for day's wages, and not those who work by the week, month, or year.

86. In the country are included in this class, principally, agricultural labourers, who live by day's work ; those who are employed by the public on canals and rail-roads, though these latter generally hire by the month.

This is that portion of mankind, both in the United

States and everywhere else, whose bodily labours are severest, whose privations are greatest, and who, therefore, are entitled to the most considerate regard of the higher and more fortunate classes. Their very name of day labourers implies, at present, that they have little or nothing. They generally own no portion of the earth, that God gave to man for an inheritance; and often no more of its productions than to enable them to live from day to day—indeed, they are said "to live from hand to mouth." If they fall sick in this situation, the city, neighbourhood, or village, takes care of them, unless they are helped by the more fortunate of their own class, (which is often the case,) for they are kinder to each other than their richer neighbours are to them; and the amount of charity which they administer among themselves, if the amount of labour and time be computed, is probably ten times as great as that which they receive from the wealthier classes. This class has one lesson to learn, in common with all poor people, and that is, if they expect to improve their condition, they must put their own shoulders to the wheel. Men will continue like the clods of the valley, unless their souls be lifted up.

87. As to these day-labourers, their relative education and character in different countries, varies as much as that of other classes in different countries. The same may be stated of them in different ages of the world. It is said that the great Charlemagne could not read or write. Day-labourers in New England can nearly all read and write. Nearly all vote, and their political privileges have given them an importance, which enables them to protect themselves against oppression. This class in England, generally has no political power.

It is one of the main points in all economy, to understand the condition of those that perform the heaviest labours in producing the riches of all mankind.

88. *Day-Labourers in the Cities.*—New-York is the most populous and flourishing city in the United States. The ordinary house-lot there is one hundred feet in depth, by twenty-five feet in front. There is probably not one day-labourer in a hundred, in that city, that owns such a lot. It is impossible to make any exact statement upon the subject.

It must not be supposed, that in a city where land is so dear, and the population so great, that every day-labourer can earn such a piece of property. Many more, however, may than do. Even now, hundreds, who work for seven or eight shillings a-day, are most wisely constantly laying aside a part even of these small earnings, to invest in a house-lot.

89. The following is a just account of a large number of that portion of the population of our cities which comprises the day-labourers :—The houses which many inhabit are erected for the express object of being rented to poor day-labourers, to journeymen mechanics, and other classes of poor people. Many of these habitations have no other accommodations than what are dictated by the selfishness of the owners; the first object with some of them being to build cheap, and to get the greatest rent possible for tenements that are cold in winter, hot in summer, without ventilation, or cellars to enable the tenants to economize in the storing of provisions; without drains, of course damp and unhealthful; sometimes without cisterns, or pumps in the yards, or a drop of rain-water for cleanliness. These buildings are often leased to jobbers, who underlet and become what are

called in Ireland "middlemen," which means generally robbers of the poor, who live by the most screwing bargains that can be made.

Bad as these habitations are, the poor are *crowded* in them; they have not room enough for health and comfort. Many are compelled to live under one roof. In these houses there is often but one entrance to a dozen apartments; and these are filled with as many families, perhaps, and, what is worse, there are sometimes many families in one apartment. Thus the virtuous and vicious are huddled together, and the most tender parents are compelled to shut up their emaciated little children in these dens, from month to month, even in summer, without a breath of pure air, because they dare not trust them to the pollution which is outside of their doors.

90. The household conveniences of many of these poor people correspond with their habitations,— they amount to nothing; all would sell at auction for a few dollars, perhaps ten, twenty, fifty, or sometimes a little more. In some there is a single bed or two, for a large family; these are often on the floor; the covering is filthy,—there are no linen or cotton sheets, the blankets are made of rags and old clothes. There is no sufficient cooking apparatus, perhaps not a tea-kettle, water being boiled for tea in a tin pan or skillet. In some houses there is not even a stove in winter, or a kitchen furnace, that indispensable article in the kitchen economy of a poor man, some sizes of which may be bought for a dollar, or a dollar and a half. This furnace is worth, in any kitchen, ten times what it costs. In some of these houses you may see a mother preparing a breakfast for half-a-dozen children with shavings for fuel; in others, children lying in bed all

day to keep warm, because there is no fire in the house. Some are nearly naked; there are infants with cotton frocks, and some with flannel, only just covering their knees. Some are without any flannel or woollen covering of any kind, and with no other garment, perhaps, than the remnant of the last summer's finery; for, let the misery be what it may in the United States, there must be finery! Children are often without hats or shoes, and their mothers, perhaps poor washerwomen, go abroad to their daily work, in the inclement seasons, too, so wretchedly clad, that toothache, colds, fever, and rheumatism, follow of course. Let it not be supposed that this is meant for a description of all the poor people in our cities, but of many such. It is disgraceful to the people that there should be so many such; for there need not be, and would not be, if we created property as we might, and then applied it as we ought.

91. *Fuel* has already been mentioned. It is one of the most expensive articles of living; it costs many families, even in the country, twice as much as their bread. In New-York, a load of oak wood, about a third of a cord, costs, upon an average, two dollars and fifty cents. In Paris, it is said to be seven or eight times as dear as at New-York. In the winter of 1832, there was a man living in the neighbourhood of Five-points (New-York,) and not more than a quarter of a mile in a straight line from the City Hall, who kept a junk shop. In these places, old iron, brass, old keys, tin-pots, and kettles, broken glass, old chains, &c., &c., are sold, indeed nearly everything that seems to us in the country quite useless. This man lived in a room about twelve feet square, and sold green wood to his neighbours, which was piled in his room. While I stood at the door, a man came up,

and bought a back-load. The sticks were counted; there were twenty of green oak for ten cents. These sticks were two feet long, and about the thickness of common country oven wood, perhaps an inch and a half through. The same man bought two additional loads of the same size at the same time, and said "that he thought he had a bargain!" This is the way in which some very poor people in the cities live; they make up a large class of citizens, and voters in the United States!

92. *Day-Labourers in the Country.*—Day-labourers in the country are those generally residing in the villages, who are usually engaged in agricultural labour, or garden-work, or other common work, in building, repairing, &c., and who receive day's wages. Mechanics also, in the country, work often by the day, but they are not called day-labourers. Farmers' hired men, who work by the year or month, are not called day-labourers.

93. Not, perhaps, more than one in eight, or ten, of even these country day-labourers own a foot of land; many hire by the month, but they generally hire by the year. Having no steady home to which to be attached, many wander about from one part of the country to another, thus contracting the common vice of vagrant people—intemperance.

A large part, perhaps the half, or it may be greater, do not even own a cow. A cow is the most valuable of all possessions to a poor man; her milk is not only food, but, like the spices so much used by the rich, it makes savoury many kinds of food. It is said, in England, in some agricultural works, that a cow, to a day-labourer there, after deducting the price of her keep, is sometimes worth twelve pounds sterling a year. This seems a very large sum; but it may be. A cow is so valuable, that no one in the country here, who is well off, and has a family of children, or hired people, any more thinks of living without such an animal, than of building a house without a cellar.

94. As these labourers generally own neither houses nor lots, a garden, which is at once a great economy to the labourer's family, and an appropriate ornament of the country, is seldom any part of his possessions. Or if there be a garden, it is usually a miserable patch, where you may see a few only of the most common vegetables, as potatoes, corn, cabbages, beets, &c., and these far out of season. For many excellent fruits, and fine flowers, which grow and flourish with so little labour that they are evidently intended for all mankind, it is in vain to look in these gardens. It is, indeed, a wonder that both rich and poor do not at once rise up in rebellion against the stupid habits both of using and destroying property, which keep men in this state of poverty.

95. The house of this labourer in the country is in substance the same thing already described as being the lot of his fellow-labourer in the city. It is inconvenient, half-glazed, cold in winter, often without a cellar, cistern, or well. The landlords knowing how uncertain their rent is from this class of tenants, think it a poor outlay to put expense upon these buildings. There probably is not in the northern States, a model of a cheap, commodious, and proper dwelling for a day labourer. Agricultural societies give premiums for many rural productions, but I never heard of one for this, though when we consider the wants, the sufferings, and severe labours of the day-labourers, and that many of these are strictly the poor; we might suppose, that to provide such a

model, combining cheapness, taste, and all suitable accommodations, would be giving a proper direction to some of our *superfluous* wealth.

96. *Clothing.*—These day-labourers are miserably clad. It is not meant to compare their insufficient garments with the tatters and rags of multitudes in other countries; nor to say, that they do not often appear abroad with as much gaudy finery as their richer neighbours.—But to contrast their clothing with what that of men should be who are part owners of such a country as this, and they, the producers too of a large part of what may be called for so young a country—prodigious riches, compared with the rest of the world! These day-labourers have no sufficient stock of good durable attire, of cotton, woollen and silk; of hats, boots, shoes, &c., adapted to summer and winter, such as are at once economical and honourable to a hard-working man. Many of their children are deterred from a proper observance of the Sunday, because their parents are ashamed to let them go abroad, and many are kept f om school, because they are destitute of great coats, cloaks, boots, shoes, &c.

97. *Intellectual pleasures of day-labourers.* To give an account of these, is a meagre task indeed, and may soon be despatched. And what are intellectual pleasures? In presenting an answer to this question, we see the true value of property, and the leanness and meanness of poverty. Intellectual pleasure is that of the mind and soul, or the heart; it is that which we enjoy other than as mere animals. The social pleasures, those which we possess in the society of friends and neighbours, make a large portion of these pleasures of the mind and soul. Intellectual pleasure is found in the

grace and beauty of life, in charity, in hospitality, in the luxury of spending our money, so as to do the greatest good with it. It is in a good, comfortable, well-furnished house, a well-ordered farm, in the flower, the garden; in observing neatness and order prevail in our abodes; and in seeing our children neatly and fitly clad. It is, or would be every where, if men would buy it with the money which they can and do earn. So simple and cheaply purchased is much of this kind of pleasure, that those who are not rich can have it as well as the opulent; and when the people come to care for, and to work in earnest mainly for these things, there will be an end of mobs and riots to avenge their wrongs, real or supposed, by the destruction of property. They will then see how mean and stupid it is to waste that wealth which is the source of their greatest blessings, how like children to destroy the hen that lays the golden eggs.

98. The most solid, intellectual pleasure to the day-labourer, and his child, should be their education. This, compared with his other expenses at present, is small indeed. The common schools of the town of Stockbridge,* (besides these there are several private schools,) the expense of which for several years have averaged about six hundred dollars a year, are probably at least as good as those of New England generally. There being in Stockbridge between fifteen and sixteen hundred people, (by the census of 1830,) the average expense for each man, woman, and child, is little more

* As there will be frequent occasion to mention this place in reference to the condition of the people, &c., I must here state, that it is the residence of the author, that it lies in the State of Massachusetts, about thirty miles from the Hudson River, and is nearly in the latitude of Boston and Albany, about forty-two.

than the third of a dollar. The children of day-labourers resort to these schools as well as others, but the parents of some are so poor, that the child is often compelled to stay at home to do necessary work, or to take care of the younger children; their clothes are such that they are ashamed to appear in school; their attendance is late, irregular, and unsatisfactory to the teacher, who, of course, becomes indifferent to their improvement. This accounts in part for the facts which are stated in several of the states of the immense number of children who do not attend school at all. The children of many day-labourers have no proper supply of books; they borrow books in the schools; they read in those that are defaced and half-destroyed.

At home, there is no supply of useful books for either parent or child. Probably, not one-half of the fathers of these children, take a country newspaper; the usual expense of which in New England is two dollars a year; and of those who do, a very small portion pay punctually for their papers. Wherever neighbours associate together, there is generally some sort of hospitality that creates expense. But this expense, these labourers cannot afford, unless it be that of intoxicating liquors, the pleasure of which makes up a great portion of their social enjoyments. They have been beyond all others the drinking people of the United States, but the bad example of their superiors renders these hard-working men the least guilty of the two.

Why all this meanness in the enjoyments of so considerable a portion of a *free* people? Who can give any good reason why so many in the United States, as to the real comforts or life, should remain in a half-barbarous state? No man can.

99. *Poverty of farmers in the United States!* The reader will smile at the very mention of the name of poverty among our farmers, after seeing how superior their condition is, to that of the cultivators of the earth in any other portion of it. Let it be remembered, then, that the inquiry here is, not about comparative poverty, but real poverty. And what is meant by real poverty among the farmers? This is meant: that many, and most of them, are destitute of solid comforts and enjoyments, which they might and ought to have.

The property, dignity, and comfort of a farmer, will be found, if any where, in his house, out-houses, farm, garden, cattle, tools, and the education of his children.

First, *Education.* The common district schools, where a large portion of the children of farmers in New England receive their education, are kept generally by men in the winter, and by women in the summer. The men's schools, in the town of Stockbridge, average about four months in the year, which is probably about the average of other towns in New England, and this is all the instruction that many farmer's sons get from male instructors, till they are about sixteen years of age, when they generally leave the schools altogether, for the farm, for trades, or business of some kind or other. In some parts of the country, private schools are now growing up, which being supported by subscription, are very superior to the common district schools, and are attended by the children of the more intelligent class of farmers. The common schools are generally kept in small, cold, and inconvenient buildings, where thirty, forty, and sometimes a much larger number, are huddled together, and taught by one master. The masters are often young men, many of them yet students in the colleges, not more than eighteen or twenty years of age. The average wages in these schools are about twelve or fourteen dollars a month, besides board, &c., which is a little more than farmers' hired men get, and less than mechanics receive. These masters are too young and inexperienced to be qualified for their tasks; and this, then, is one of the most melancholy marks of the poverty of large numbers of Am rican farmers: that their children are wretchedly educated.

100. *Farmers' houses and out-houses.* It has already been stated, that we have few or no proper models of a day labourer's habitation, and the same may be said of that of the farmer, contrived, as it should be, with skill, and taste; at once, consulting durability and economical accommodation from the garret to the cellar.

The old houses of the northern States having generally been built of wood are many of them greatly out of repair, and comfortless. Even in the richer parts of the State of New-York, which have not been settled more than forty or fifty years, there are many houses and out-houses in a state of shameful decay, from mere neglect and want of economy. While so many of the wives and daughters of the farmers, are running to the stores for fashionable gewgaws, and prefer fine ribbons, to fine farms, the principle of affection for, and pride in the paternal estate, remains uncherished among us,— and this is the reason why many farmers after having so long neglected their farms and buildings are obliged finally to sell them for half the price they ought to bring, and then move to the new States in a beggarly condition. In too many of the farmers' barns, stables, and out-houses, there are the same unhappy marks of the poverty of the owner—few, or no contrivances by shelter and otherwise to save manure, or economize in any way, all of which cost money; and this is the farmer's excuse—"that he is too poor to afford such labour-saving improvements." It is the opinion of some farmers at the north, that the produce of their towns might be doubled in ten years, by the proper use of plaster of Paris, and clover-seed ; of many, that it might be greatly increased; but they say that they are too poor to afford the first cost of plaster, which is here, if ground, ten or eleven dollars the ton. This shows the use of property, of capital, of having something on hand that can be laid out for the purpose of making more property, which is the great design of capital.

A good garden is one of the best parts of the economy of a farm, and that which most highly adorns the farmer's condition.—But it is a very rare possession among our farmers, and they give no other reason for their destitution in this particular, than that they are too poor to have such a possession. The average size of the farms of Massachusetts has been said to be eighty or a hundred acres. Of these acres the farmer devotes perhaps a quarter, a half, and often not an eighth part of an acre to his garden. There will not be found in one in twenty in New England, a *head* of lettuce, nor any sweet corn, which is so much more healthful for early use than the common corn, nor a cauliflower, or brocoli, nor any variety of peas, beans, &c., suited to the different seasons. As to fruits ; there is not a strawberry, raspberry, gooseberry, and often not a tolerable supply of that invaluable fruit the currant.—For any variety of flowers you may look in vain.

His farm and cattle.—Here also is too fatal a proof of the poverty of the farmer. An expense of even a few hundred dollars upon many of these farms would entirely charge their aspect. The diligence of the farmer should entitle him to fine breeds of cattle, but how few such do we see!—In the United States, the farmers own nearly all the land; in this sense, they may be said to own the country. In England, as we have seen heretofore, a few rich gentleman own the country; and their riches have enabled them to carry refinement in the breed of cattle to a great height. A bull has been sold there for a thousand guineas, and a cow for four hundred. The value of the cattle, sheep, and swine of England has been estimated at one hundred and twenty millions sterling.*

Some gentlemen in the valley of the Scioto river in the state of Ohio, not long since sent *farmers* to England to purchase cattle. It is said that they brought home ten thousand dollars worth of the finest breeds. One cow is reported to have cost seven hundred dollars. Such poverty as we see, would not long dwell among a race of farmers animated by such a spirit; fine cattle to them are worth more than fine cap s to their coats. Good breeds of cattle cannot be looked for in a country, where it is still a pretty general practice of the farmer (as in New England) to keep his young horned cattle so poorly fed in the winter, that they are turned to grass in the spring in a starving condition. Any one who will look at them, may see that.—Nothing but the plea of poverty can justify this apparent inhumanity on the part of the farmer. Some few allege, that this practice is good economy in reference to our long winters; but humanity revolts from such treatment of useful animals.

* Library of Useful Knowledge.—Farmers' series, No. 42.

101. The above is a slight sketch of the condition of many farmers in large portions of the United States. To this might be added many other particulars, such as that considerable numbers are deeply in debt to store-keepers, and others, and that, in too many cases, their farms are fatally mortgaged to banks, insurance offices, &c. The only object of these statements is to show, how the farmers may become more prosperous, and still farther elevate their useful class; their condition in the United States is rapidly improving, and if they can do thus much, they can do more.

102. *Poverty of the manufacturing class.*—There is something shocking and disgusting in contemplating the degree of suffering existing in the most prosperous parts of a world teeming with natural abundance; even in the United States, too, where the people are working upon a virgin soil, which requires so much less labour and expense for a crop, than old worn-out lands. Is it not shocking to see so many good hard-working people in the United States, who do not own even an acre of land, where land is so cheap, who have not a house, or home, or even fifty dollars with which to help themselves, in case of sickness, or misfortune? Wherever the eye rests, there is something that may be converted into riches for the use of man, so that we may be assured, that there will not continue to be the same degree of poverty, that we now see, when the people at large shall have acquired any just ideas of economy, and of the true value of riches. Every one may see, who attends to the subject, that the hard-working people of the United States are now finding out, that their condition is capable of prodigious improvement, and that when they see this

clearly, it will be like a new revelation to them. We may be certain, therefore, that an immense simultaneous effort for their improvement such as the world has never witnessed, is at hand.

103. A considerable portion of the manufacturing population in the northern States is supplied in the following way.—Many poor broken-down people with large families of children, and especially poor widows, who have been brought into this state by the intemperance of their husbands, resort to the manufactories as the most expedient way of obtaining a living for themselves and their children. In many such cases, the parents place their children in the factories, they keeping boarding-houses. In some parts of the country, there are many children in these factories, under ten years of age; these are sometimes wholly without education, and universally without such an education as they ought to have. These children often work the same number of hours that are allotted to grown-up people. The manufacturing population are almost universally destitute of houses and lots, of gardens, of cows, or any useful domestic animal. As the houses which they occupy generally in the country belong to the owners of the factories; it is plain, that they must live to a great disadvantage in regard to the rent they pay. In these houses, they are so huddled together, that as many as half-a-dozen, and often many more sleep in one chamber, and this, too, without any proper ventilation. As pure air is essential to life and health, and especially when we sleep to recruit our exhausted bodies, this accounts in a great measure for the pale faces, sunken eyes, and emaciated figures of so many of the manufacturing people.

POVERTY IN THE UNITED STATES. 111

104. At Lowell, in Massachusetts, which is by far the most important manufacturing place in the United States, the people appeared (1833) to great advantage. Very few children were then employed in the factories, in some scarcely any. The working hours were twelve or twelve and a quarter. Even there the people were crowded together in such a way as none but poor people will ever live. There were (1833) some ranges of wooden houses each about forty-two feet front, and thirty two in depth, under one roof, but divided into two *tenements*. In each of these *tenements* were boarded at that time, about thirty persons, some rooms contained two or three beds, and sometimes three girls slept in a bed.

105. The following, among many others, is a striking proof of the melancholy poverty of large numbers of the manufacturing people.—They receive their wages in "store-pay" in whole or in part. By this is meant, that the owners of the factories, are also owners of stores of goods, such as the manufacturers generally want. The owner of the goods receives of course a profit upon them, sometimes greater, sometimes smaller; and this profit is regulated by a variety of circumstances. Sometimes by contract; by the integrity of the owner; the poverty of the labourer; the advantageous, or disadvantageous way in which the goods have been bought. In some cases the contract is in terms, that the labourer shall take store-pay in whole or in part; in others the wages being paid monthly, quarterly, or at the end of six months, and the labourer being often necessitous and in debt; the effect upon him is the same as though he had contracted for store-pay.

This store pay system, which is such a dead weight upon poor people, and all for the want of having a very few dollars in advance of their immediate wants, is called, in England, the "truck system;" a miserable system it is, and might much better be called the truckling system.* To the honour of the proprietors and manufacturing people, at Lowell, this system is not known there. (1833.)

106. So miserably poor are some of these manufacturing people, that many of them, not only buy their store goods, such as clothing, groceries, &c., of their employers, but nearly every necessary article. In this way, meat, potatoes, and all kinds of common vegetables, are sold by the quantity: first by the farmer to the manufacturer, and by him retailed to the labourer. And why? Because, too often, the labourer has not the cash wherewith to buy. In these cases, the labourer has not often money enough to buy his dinner.

107. *Poverty of journeymen mechanics.* Here is another numerous class of poor people. In the large cities, there is not probably one in fifty who owns a house and lot, nor more than one in eight or ten who lays up a farthing from one year to another. It is not meant here to state the precise proportions, but to present the facts as to the poverty of these indigent people, as accurately as may be, after a great deal of inquiry.

The city of Pittsburgh, in the state of Pennsylvania, presents to the eye of a stranger a scene of the most beautiful and extraordinary industry. It is said that

---

* Babbage on "The Economy of Machinery and Manfactures," sect. 287;—a book that ought to be read by every manufacturing labourer in the United States.

the mechanics and other labouring people own there the lots on which they live, to a much greater extent, than is common in the United States. It is said even to be the fashion! This is a fashion of the rich worth following, and better than running after capes, feathers, ribbons, flounces, and ten thousand gew-gaws, which consume the substance of so many poor people. What are these, with a reasoning being, compared with a house and home?

108. It would be a wanton aggravation of the miseries of poor people, thus to expose their poverty, if there was no help for it. There is a help for the greater portion of them. But they must put their own shoulders to the wheel; they must work out their own salvation; there is something to be done. And what is to be done? *This is one of the first things to be done,*—a large portion of the people of the United states who work for wages, and especially of the unmarried, can and must lay up yearly *one-half of their wages at least.* That they can do this, I shall show hereafter in the most satisfactory manner. When this is done, their independence will be secured, and the political improvements which they desire, will be in their power, but not before.

109. There is another large portion of the people whose poverty is worthy of particular attention in a country where so few are exempt from labour.

This is not a particular class, as mechanics or professional men, but it embraces some of every class, from the highest to the lowest. By this class is meant the *fashionable, expensive poor,* or those who are made poor mainly by following the fashions, not the good and useful fashions, but the absurd and wasteful ones. By *fashionable* people, generally, is meant, that portion of the rich, and those who associate with the rich, that adopt expensive and fashionable modes of living at their tables, in their furniture, dress, equipage, &c. By *fashionable and expensive poor*, here, is intended all those, whether merchants, farmers, mechanics, day-labourers, &c., that live in the imitation of expensive fashions, without any proper regard to their wages or fortunes. This class, in the United States, embraces a larger proportion of the people than in any other country whatever. In other words, travellers and strangers agree, that the people of the United States, are, in many particulars, the most wasteful of all civilized people on earth.

110. Many of these fashionable, expensive poor, instead of having lived upon their incomes, and making the two ends of the year meet, have spent so much more than their incomes, that they have been compelled to see their substance waste from day to day, as a consumptive man sees the flesh depart from his bones. Of these fashionable, expensive poor, a large number even of those that belong to the higher classes, are among the poorest people in the United States. If there were weights and scales to weigh human misery by the ounce and pound, it would be found, that these unhappy people suffer more in mind from embarrassments, duns, mortification, offended pride, and conscious meanness and wickedness, at the thought that they are spending the property of their friends, and of honest, hard-working mechanics and others, than many very poor people do in body, for the want of sufficient clothing, fuel, and food. Striving to be something, which their property will not allow, they are in a perpetual conflict in the worst war in the world—a war with themselves. They do not live by any rule of their own, according to what

God has given them, and what it is, therefore, only allowable for them to spend, but they live after a rule set by the fashion of rich people, and thus they see with other people's eyes, whose eyes are their ruin. Instead of having their clothes made in the most economical way, in their own houses, by their wives, daughters, and servants, they run to the fashionable milliners and tailors, at the same time that they are suffering for good, substantial, seasonable garments. Their whole wardrobe often, setting aside the finery, would hardly pay for an auction; they would be ashamed to show it; to have it exposed to day-light, to have their under garments seen.

111. Their domestic condition is equally mean. Some of them in the cities live in expensive houses, and promise to pay large rents, perhaps five hundred dollars a year, and often, much more. This rent is often paid by their richer relatives, and often not at all. Their parlours and drawing-rooms are full of what they call splendour, that is, finery; if they have valuable pictures, it is ten to one, that these are put in the shade in order to show their fine curtains to better advantage.

If you go out of this region of splendour and magnificence, the real barrenness of the territory, in good, useful things, appears. In the kitchen, and other apartments, there is not a decent sufficiency of proper cooking utensils, tubs, kettles, dishes, carpets, and other conveniences for health, comfort, and cleanliness. Nothing is so mean, as the real poverty of these people, but their pride.

CHAPTER VII.

POVERTY IN THE UNITED STATES, CONTINUED.

112. There is still another class of poor people in the United States, who deserve particular attention, and these are settlers on new lands, or emigrants from the old states. It is not meant, that all emigrants are poor people, but that many of them are, and of those who are poor, many are very poor, and great sufferers for the want of a little property, to secure the common comforts of life, in their passage from the old to the new states, and in their new residences.

113. Many of these emigrants are so poor, that their journey is a scene of constant trial and suffering. That portion who go from the northern states, and take a passage by water across the lakes, are exposed to many of the miseries of a sea-voyage. In some of the steamboats (1835) from Buffalo, in New-York, to Detroit, in Michigan territory, the steerage-passengers pay only three dollars for their passages, whilst the cabin-passengers pay eight. These cabin-passengers have each a good berth, some the luxury of double mattresses; their meals being included in the sum mentioned, they often sit down to sumptuous repasts, and enjoy every comfort of which such a condition admits. At the same time, the decks are crowded, night and day, with the poor emigrants. These boats are often so crowded, that even in the worst storms neither men, women, nor children, have room to lie down. Infants are placed sometimes

POVERTY IN THE UNITED STATES. 117

on the head of a barrel, sometimes in the lid of an open trunk, the mother standing all night watching by its side. In one place may be seen a man and his wife in the midst of barrels, trunks, and bales of goods, with no other pillow than a cable or block of wood; and then, again, others without any pillow at all. Sometimes the boats are so crowded, that few or none can sleep in any way. These steerage-passengers find their own food, and often without any "privilege" of the fire or kitchen, which it is impossible to grant to so many. They are often not even allowed, in such cases, the comfort of hot water, to enable them to make a cup of tea or coffee. Indeed, few situations are attended with greater difficulties than those of these poor people. Storms, crowded vessels, and the heats of summer, expose the women and children especially to disease, when, without nurses, physicians, or help of any kind, they are sometimes obliged to remain, from day to day, in the midst of their own filth, *created by the calls of nature!* Now, it is plain, that a very few dollars more than they have would save these indigent people from many of these miseries. A very small additional sum would secure them a comfortable passage. The prudent see every day how moderate a sum it is that generally procures the simple means of health and comfort, and what great evils are suffered by the poor in being destitute of these very limited supplies.

114. Some of these emigrants travel by land, in their own carriages, through the states of New-York, Pennsylvania, and Ohio, perhaps into the territory of Michigan, and even as far as the state of Illinois. The hardships of the land-passage are often as great, or greater, than that by water. The roads in these new states, in

the wet season, are nearly impassable. In Illinois, five yoke of oxen are often attached to a load that here is drawn with ease by two, and even then it is sometimes impossible to get through the "slews," as they are called by the people of that state. These slews are the miry places in the low prairie. In many cases, a bridge, that would not cost ten dollars, might avoid the difficulty. But ten dollars is not to be found for such a purpose; there are other wants more pressing for every ten dollars that the new settler has. In the midst of these wet places, men, women, and children, are sometimes obliged, in order to relieve the carriage of its burthen, to wade through the mire; the goods are then often carried by hand to the dry land, and the carriage is drawn out by extra teams. These hindrances are costly, and attended by great exposure of the health. Disease often follows in the course of such hardships; the journey is protracted, and much more expensive than the emigrant had calculated. Cold, heat, and exposure, bring on evils not looked for,—such as women becoming mothers before their time, and this, perhaps, exhausts the little stock of money remaining. These are a few of the evils that beset the poor wayfaring emigrant.

115. This, however, is but the beginning of his difficulties. We will now suppose that he has arrived at the end of his journey,—at the "promised land,"—at the beautiful prairies of Illinois. These fertile prairies, so easy of cultivation, seem to present the most ample natural provision that a bountiful parent ever provided on this earth for his children. Here are grander beauties, in the rich grasses, variegated flowers, in the skirting woods, and "rolling prairie," than are to be found in the lawns, parks, pleasure-grounds, and palaces of many of

the great nobles of the earth. This beauty is so unlike any other kind of beauty, that no pen can adequately describe it.

The poor emigrant, so far from having prepared a palace for his residence, has often not been able to provide before-hand even a log-house for his abode. In this case he often hires board with some other poor emigrant for weeks or months, when the families of both are sometimes crowded into one room. This house is soon, however, generally put up by the aid of his neighbours. The whole cost of a log-house does not generally exceed twenty-five, thirty, or forty dollars. Many have no cellars or chambers; there is, therefore, but one room, in which the family sleeps, and where all the household work is carried on. Sometimes there is not even a floor to these houses, in which case the family sleeps on the ground.

The life of the poor emigrant is often one of incessant toil. Where there are so few people, he cannot obtain hired help, even if he had the money to pay for it; all his heavy work, therefore, as well as his chores, fall upon himself. There are other evils: new countries are peculiarly afflicted with fever and ague, and bilious fevers; these are not sharp disorders, quick over, but long-protracted, wearing the flesh to the bone, and happening generally in the summer and autumn—that season so precious to the farmer.

It is in the nature, also, of fever and ague, after having once made its attacks, to continue them from year to year, so that the life of the poor emigrant and his family is often one of long conflict with disease and death. A great portion of these diseases in the new countries is attributable to the want of good food, warm garments, houses sufficient to keep out storms and musquitoes, and especially to the want of cleanliness. People in the new states say, that they are too poor to keep clean, and it is true enough.

It is seldom that the poor emigrant can obtain medical assistance, and this is one of his hardships. In the new states physicians reside principally in the villages, and if a poor man in the woods or remote prairies needs aid, to set a broken arm or leg, he is compelled to send, perhaps, twenty or thirty miles to obtain it. Even if there be medical or surgical assistance at hand, the indigent emigrant postpones obtaining it as long as he can, for he has not a dollar to spare for such a purpose. It is one of the hardest things in the lot of the very poor man, and especially of the emigrant, that he is obliged to work on, after disease has given him notice of its approach, when a few dollars expended in nursing and lying-by might save him from a long fit of sickness. A man who has not a bushel of grain in his house, cannot think of lying down whilst he is able to put one foot before another.

116. Reflecting people see clearly, how small a sum of the millions, fooled away yearly both by rich and poor, would if saved by each individual, ward off many of the evils here mentioned. It must be remembered that this is an account of *poor* emigrants, and that there are many new settlers whose property provides them with the means of escaping from the greater part of these miseries. Here we see again, that property is not the *end*, but the *means* of doing good, and getting good, and that without the property, the good cannot be got.

117. There is another circumstance in the life of a large class of the very poor emigrants, that shows their

indigence in a still more painful and striking light. It is, that, not being able to buy even cheap government land, they take possession of that which does not belong to them.

118. The United States have an immense body of wild land, which is now sold for a dollar and a quarter an acre cash, no credit being allowed, as was formerly the case. Great portions of these lands are not surpassed in beauty and fertility. A part is covered with wood, this is called *timber* land; another part is prairie land, which has this peculiarity, that there are millions of acres of continued, open *meadow* [prairie being the French word for meadow] upon great parts of which, there is not a tree, nor scarcely a shrub. There are however frequent woods, but so sparse generally, as to seem to be a sort of fringe or skirt to these open prairies. The best prairie land is that which is skirted by a due proportion of wood, which the settler at present considers essential to his farm. There is in many parts of the prairie a great deficiency of wood, indispensable for fuel and the fencing of the farm. This deficiency on the open unwooded prairie, which often extends for many miles, will, it is supposed, be hereafter supplied by planting young trees for fencing and fuel; by hedges, and terraces. It is very certain, that the industry and ingenuity of the people will overcome every difficulty that stands in the way of the cultivation of this garden land.

119. Besides the wild lands belonging to the people of the United States, there are other large tracts of wild lands belonging to individuals, most of which have been purchased from the United States or individual States.

It is this public and private land, that many poor emigrants, in wandering over the country, set themselves down upon, without a shadow of title, in which case, they are called *squatters*. The law, after a certain lapse of time, gives to these squatters a right to the land, which is called a title by possession. It is however generally a title founded in injustice, for no good and honest man will seize upon property which belongs to another. The most favoured lands in the United States, in which every American citizen has an interest, those where there is the finest prairie, the best water, with a due proportion of wood, are every day thus seized upon by squatters.

These squatters are now often called in some of the western states *claimants*. Having taken up the best lands; in order to confirm their title, they erect a log house, and make some slight improvements, but generally no substantial ones worthy of good farmers and citizens of the state, for as yet they are not certain of gaining a valid title to lands thus occupied. These claimants often sell these claims, with the inconsiderable improvements they have made, and then move on farther west to take possession of some other favoured spot belonging to the people of the United States. A portion of these claimants, after having made some trifling improvements, that may give them a colour of equity as new settlers, wait till the government sales take place, in order that they may buy at the government price, and thus confirm their ill-gotten titles. At the public sales, the lands are put up for sale to the highest bidder, but though the claimants have taken possession of the best lands, they insist upon having them at the least price, that is the minimum price of one dollar and a quarter the acre ; and to effect their object, by combination and threats of violence against all that would bid above them, they defeat the policy of the law, and obtain the lands at their own price.*

120. There is something even worse that takes place in regard to the government lands and these poor claimants, which is this: that many of them are so destitute that they cannot buy even at the government prices when the sales take place; in which case they sell their claims, very often, for some trifling sum to land speculators. The land, in such cases, to save appearances, is bid for in the name of the claimant, (against whom no man dare bid,) but for the benefit of the speculator.

Again, these claimants are sent forward as mere catspaws by land speculators to make claims to the finest lands, but they being men of straw, the lands are finally bid off for the benefit of the speculator as before. In many other ways the poor claimants and squatters become the mere instruments and victims of the land speculator, as all very destitute people are liable to be of capitalists and rich people.

121. Thus we see the natural effects of extreme poverty in the settlement of a new country, and how bad principles and bad practices are perpetuated among the people, though it is certain that all these disreputable proceedings are not attributable to that cause.

The United States possess in their new lands the most ample provision for the poorer and least fortunate portion of the people, as well as for public objects, that exists on the face of the earth. For these objects should they be, as far as possible, protected from the grasp of speculators. As the condition of the nation changes, their

---

* It is well known, that at the last summer sales, at Chicago, (1835,) scenes, in the highest degree disgraceful to the people and dishonourable to the United States, were exhibited.

policy should change. Most of the Indians being removed, or in the course of removal, the frontier man has little to dread from them. Many of the indulgences, therefore, heretofore granted to induce him to settle a new country, are not now necessary. Let the lands, then, of the United States be as sacred as any other property, and disposed of only by the will of the people expressed in their laws. Injustice is a poor foundation for the fortune of an American farmer and citizen. What so noble sentiment can there be in his mind, as that his possessions are the reward of his virtue and industry! What worse lesson can the people suffer to be taught by their government, than that of fraud in obtaining a title to a portion of the earth, which, if honestly acquired and industriously cultivated, is the source of so much virtue and happiness.

122. This account of the poor squatter and claimant is not intended to include all new settlers. Far from it. Many of them are among the most virtuous, economical, and thriving of our people. We have seen how, in other countries, the monopolizer and rich capitalist may, if he will, bring the poor man down to nothing, and we see here how it is done by the land speculator, in the case of the indigent squatter and land claimant. And all for what? For the want of a little independence, a little fortune, perhaps a small sum of money, a thousand dollars, or five hundred, or even a much less sum, such a sum as almost any of our young manufacturers, mechanics', or farmers' sons may lay up in a very few years; such a sum, as with prudence, might be within the reach of nearly every grown-up man in the nation; a sum which has been foolishly drunk, or eaten, or consumed, by some sensual indulgence, or fooled away for gew-

gaws or finery, that the fashionable have introduced among the common people, and which all despise after six months' use.

123. There is nothing so important to mankind, and especially to the poorer part of mankind, as that the people of the United States should continue to prosper—that they should banish mobs, riots, violence, every kind of injustice, as well as all stupid indulgences that consume and destroy property—that they should continue to show how good principles will make it increase, so that it may be distributed more equally than it has been, and so that every poor man may enjoy greatly more than his present portion.

124. There is little that is more interesting in the history of mankind, than the enterprise, industry, and unconquerable resolution of those who, in the face of poverty, disease, and savage enemies, subdue and settle a new country. These were the virtues of our ancestors in the old states, and in our day have been the virtues of our western brethren. These new republics should scorn to take any example from us that is not worth following. They must examine for themselves the reason, sense, and utility of things.

125. The city of Detroit is the capital of Michigan Territory, and is situated on that beautiful strait that connects Lake Erie with the great waters beyond. Detroit is said now to contain about six thousand people. There are in the immediate rear of it, extensive wet prairies and forests of timber land, over which, and within twenty miles of the city, wolves and deer, are now roaming. Such is the vigour of the people of this fertile territory, that they are already (1835) constructing one rail-road, surveying for another, and speaking

confidently of extending a third within a few years over the whole breadth of the territory, (about two hundred miles,) from Detroit to the mouth of the river St. Joseph, on the eastern side of Lake Michigan, which is in the direct route of Illinois, and the still farther Great Western Territory.

126. From Detroit there departs in midsummer daily (1835) a steam-boat for Buffalo. At some other seasons of the year two, one in the morning, and one in the evening. Many of these boats are noble vessels, and seem to be equal to any others in the United States. Steam-boats constitute a large item of our wealth; and it has been seen already how important they have become to all, poor as well as rich people.

127. One of the striking follies of the people of the United States, is the *excessive* use of expensive wines, and particularly of champagne. In the United States it has become the height of gentility and fashion to drink champagne. Not only men and women, but boys, that is, merchants' clerks, young mechanics, &c., drink it, without any reference to the money they are able to pay for it. In the boats which have been spoken of, champagne is drank very much in the same way. The people in the interior of Illinois and Michigan have caught the contagion of fashion in this particular, as in many others; for there is hardly a little village of forty houses where it may not be found. The most scandalous adulteration is detected at once in some of this wine. Would it not be more wise for the people of Michigan and Illinois first to apply their money to the cultivation of their farms and gardens, to the building of good houses, steam-boats, &c.?

It is despicable in the people of the United States, because the English drink to *excess* port, champagne, claret, &c., and that, too, when their country is overwhelmed with debt, and many of their good people are living upon crumbs, to follow their ruinous example.

128. All the fine wines, doubtless, have their proper uses; champagne is one of the most admirable of these wines. In some cases it is said to be highly medicinal, which may well be. Great disputes existed once in France, in the schools of medicine, about the quality of different wines. This wine is made in France alone, and the French show their high estimate of it by this anecdote: " When Vincesilaus, King of Bohemia, and the Romans, on coming to France, to negotiate a treaty with Charles VI., arrived at Rheims, having tasted the wine of Champagne, it is to be presumed, for the first time, spun out his diplomatic errand to the longest possible moment, and then gave up all that was required of him in order to prolong his stay, getting drunk on champagne daily before dinner." Champagne is a very dear wine in the United States, costing at retail in our hotels generally two dollars the bottle. In France it costs, in medium years, when sold by the merchant to the consumer, three francs fifty centimes, about 66 cents.* Some of the vine-lands in France have been sold as high as 500*l.* sterling the acre, which have yielded 750 bottles the acre.† This shows what land may become worth in bringing forth some of the most valuable and rarest productions of the earth.

* Redding on Wines, p. 78. London, 1833.
† The same.

129. This subject of the poverty of the people of the United States deserves a brief recapitulation.

Though all the nations of the earth were ten times poorer than we are, this is poverty,—that is, the people of the United States are shamefully poor, when we consider how much richer they might be, that is, really rich in comforts—in those good, graceful, and beautiful things which all men want, or should want.

130. First, It has been shown how destitute many day-labourers are of small pieces of land, even enough for a garden, a quarter of an acre, perhaps; of good clothes, of a variety of healthful food, even some of the most healthful of all food, common cheap fruits; of household comforts, of domestic animals, including the cow, which is the life of the poor man. What wretched houses they live in, often without cellars, and wells, or cisterns in their yards. How destitute their children are also of good hats, boots, coats, &c., to enable them to attend church and school decently. Then, as to intellectual pleasures, such as those of education, good books, hospitality to friends and neighbours, gardens, flowers, and other beautiful creations, how miserably poor they are!

131. Second, *Farmers.*—That in some of these particulars, the condition of many farmers is not much better. It has been shown how deficient they are in good education for their children. How mean many of their houses, barns, stables, &c., are, compared with what they might be. That many are in debt at the stores, and banks, and that their farms are hopelessly mortgaged.

132. Third, *The manufacturing class.*—That many in this class are poor widows and children quite broken down, who resort to the manufactories as a forlorn hope. That as to houses, lands, gardens, &c.,

many are as destitute as day-labourers. That they are huddled together in their houses much like people in a jail. That many of them have not even a dollar on hand, and that the proof is, that they live on "store-pay," and even buy beef, pork, potatoes, cabbage, &c., on credit. That in consequence of this extreme poverty they are compelled to work excessively, and more hours than is good for them, and that their little children do the same.

133. Fourth, *Journeymen mechanics.*—Without going over the particulars, it has been shown, that in many things, these are as poor and helpless as any other class.

134. Fifth, *The fashionable, expensive poor.*—That this includes some in all classes, from the richest to the poorest, and that taking into consideration all things, these are more destitute of the real happiness which property may be made to impart, than any other people in the United States.

135. Sixth, *Poor emigrants.*—That these are too poor to buy a comfortable passage by land or water; to pay for regular meals on board the boats; or even a clean place in which to sleep, and a "privilege" to cook their food, to make good roads, to build comfortable houses, such as will exclude storms, and fever and ague; or even to keep clean such as they have. Above all, that many being too poor to buy even cheap government land, which costs only one hundred dollars for eighty acres, are compelled to begin their career in the new world by an act of dishonesty in seizing upon lands not their own.

This, after all, is one of the greatest miseries of the poor, that they cannot enjoy the happiness of conscious uprightness, as those do who have laid up a little stock of independence, though it be very small.

136. Let not those who read this account of the misery and poverty of the people, suppose that their condition is not growing better. Quite the contrary. The minds of every class are brightening; their temperance is increasing; they practise more economy compared with their incomes than they did, and of course their property is growing. This is especially true of the farmers of the United States, whose ways of living are more important to the rest of the people than those of any other class.

137. What are the practical lessons which we are to learn from this account of the condition of large portions of the people? What does it teach in regard to the science of economy?

First, The object in giving this account of the poverty of the people, is, to show their real indigence, their destitution in useful things, in things that are good for human nature, for all men, rich and poor. That this is true, notwithstanding all our boasting and exalted ideas about our wonderful riches.

Second, To prove that the first objects for the labour of the people should be the *useful things*.

Third, That as the independent people of the United States can work for what they please, in other words, spend their money for what they choose; to point out some of those valuable things for which they ought to labour and spend their money.

Fourth, To show how many more manufacturers, mechanics, and labourers, of all descriptions, might be employed in supplying the people with those objects, which it has been proved that they are now destitute of.

That, therefore, it is impossible, as some political economists have supposed, that there should not be useful labour enough to employ all the people.

Fifth, To show capitalists that they might employ all their capital, and a thousand times as much, if they would employ labourers in producing what they, the labourers, most want, and what it is best for them to have.

Sixth, To refute the opinions of those political economists, who say, that the people must waste their property, as they now do, in order to give them employment and keep them out of idleness.

Seventh, That to produce property, such as tools, cattle, gardens, productive farms, and good houses, is the immediate cause of creating still more property, and is like putting out money at compound interest.

Eighth, To show the poor how much interested they are in making property grow, whether it belongs to them or another; and that it is much better that rich men should lay out their money in building neat, comfortable houses for them, even though they pay a rent, than to spend it in gluttony and fashionable folly.

Ninth, To prove how unworthy it is in a working people, how despicable in the people of the United States, while they are destitute of so many useful things, to spend so large a portion of their property and wages, as they now do, upon gew-gaws and short-lived finery, which disgrace their houses and persons, upon low sensuality, such as expensive eating and drinking, that now so often either enfeeble or destroy their working faculties.

CHAPTER VIII.

WHAT IS WEALTH?

138. It is time that we should give a more particular description of what we are in quest of. Wealth has already been spoken of as "well-being," or the cause of well-being. As it is that which mainly causes civilization, and is, in fact, a great portion of it; that which most distinguishes a savage from a cultivated man; that which enables us to improve the earth to the greatest advantage; it is proper that a more precise account of it be given. The nature and character of wealth is a great branch of *political economy*.

139. What, then, is wealth? By one, it is said "to consist of all that man desires as useful or delightful to him."* But we do not ordinarily speak of air, water, and the other elements, as wealth in themselves, though they may become private wealth by being appropriated to private use. So, in a large and general sense, the Hudson river may be said to be a portion of the wealth of the state of New-York. In the dry and sandy parts of Asia and Africa, it is as common to sell water as many other things; but the spontaneous gifts of Nature, that are enjoyed in common, are not generally spoken of as wealth.

By another, wealth is defined to be "those material

* Lord Lauderdale's Inquiry into the Nature and Origin of Public Wealth, ch. 2.

WHAT IS WEALTH? 133

objects which are necessary, useful, or agreeable to mankind."*

The same observations may be made upon this as upon the former definition.

140. Wealth is said " to consist, not in matter, but the value of matter;"† that is, when matter is put into such a form as that it may be said to have value, then it is wealth. The common and popular idea of wealth, or of property, is that of something which is bought and sold, or that which is said to have " exchangeable value," as it is called, which, of course, is something agreeable or useful to man. This is commonly something that is obtained by *labour*. Labour, then, is the great ingredient of wealth, and gives the true stamp of value. But a precious stone may be found by *chance*, and still it is valuable. The earth, the desert, in those countries where there is no regular government, and where the wild lands are open to the savage, to be taken possession of when he chooses, —is not yet wealth, because any one may have it who chooses; but, when possessed and cultivated, then it becomes valuable, becomes private property, and wealth.

141. An examination of the principal items of wealth will give a better idea of it than definitions can; all the definitions in the world cannot give us so perfect a notion of a peach, as to see, feel, and taste it.

These principal items of wealth are,—

1. Land, with its improvements, by ploughing, fencing, draining, manuring, &c., including the buildings on the land, such as houses, churches, shops, stores, manu-

---

* Malthus' Principles of Political Economy, ch. 1. sec. 1.
† Say's Political Economy, book 1, ch. 2.

factories, barns, stables, &c. This also embraces roads, canals, &c.

2. Implements of agriculture and all tools of trade, engines, and machinery.

3. Stock in the produce of the soil, as all kinds of grain and vegetables.

4. Stock in domestic animals.

5. Household furniture, including books, plate, jewels, statues, pictures, &c.

6. Public property, or that which belongs to the state or nation; as, lands, wild and cultivated; forts, dry-docks, ships, armories, guns, &c.

7. Money.

8. Lastly, as a general enumeration of what is not particularly mentioned above, all of what is generally called merchandize, namely, raw materials of cotton, silk, and wool, and goods manufactured out of these, and, generally, all that may be bought and sold, or " that has value in exchange for other things."*

142. As to *money*, it demands some comment here, for it is difficult to understand or explain many particulars in the science of economy without some just ideas of money. Many are as much puzzled to understand it, as others are puzzled in being without it.

By some, in serious discourse, it is called "vulgar pelf," " filth lucre," " vile dross," " little worthless pieces of white and yellow metal." Shakspeare says—" He who steals my purse, steals trash; 'twas mine—'tis his, and has been slave to thousands," &c.

After all, common sense, in defiance of declaimers, as

* Smith's Wealth of Nations, p. 1, note.

well as of the greatest poets, will maintain its empire; and however much men may, in other respects, differ about their ideas of money, all agree that it is a very *useful* thing.

143. By money here is meant gold and silver, which, by way of eminence, are called the *precious metals*, because they are the most valuable, compared with labour, or with things that are bought and sold, of all common metals. These metals were in use in the time of Abraham,* and are everywhere now in use in the more civilized parts of the world. One of the strongest marks to distinguish savage from civilized life, is the use of money. Money being employed as a medium of exchange, for the purpose of buying and selling merchandize, and savages having little to buy and sell, there is no necessity among them for money, their little trade being carried on by barter, which is the exchange of one kind of common merchandize for another. The savage exchanges with the ships that resort to his shores for supplies, pigs and poultry, for beads, knives, tobacco, &c. Wherever there is much trade, and civilized society, there gold and silver find their way, for "irresistible reasons,"† namely, the necessity there is for gold and silver to buy all things, which gold and silver alone will do.

In rude ages, other articles besides the precious metals were used as money. In the time of Homer, cattle were so used; in Sparta, iron; in Abyssinia, salt is said to be the common instrument of exchange; a species of shells, called cowries, are employed as money in some parts of

---

* Gen. ch. 23, v. 16, and ch. 24, v. 22.—Jacob on the Precious Metals, Introduction, p. 4.

† Smith, book 1, ch. 4.

India.* So in our own times and country, other things besides gold and silver have been made use of as money. During the Revolution, or before it, tobacco was a legal tender in Virginia for a debt. After the Continental *paper*-money became worthless, during our Revolution, in consequence of the inability of the people, from poverty, to make good their promises to pay, in which consisted this paper-money, there occurred instances, in some of the larger towns, of men going to market with indigo, and weights and scales, to make their daily purchases.

It was said by Mr. Locke, who was one of the best and wisest of mankind, that the value of money was *"imaginary;"* and this shows, that common people, have sounder ideas upon many of these subjects now, than philosophers had two hundred years ago.

So it is said,—" The value which is thus given to the precious metals, is derived from the *common consent of mankind*, and is not founded in any real value otherwise existing in the metals themselves." But this is not the cause of the value of money, for there has been no such consent, any more than there has been a consent, that iron, or the load-stone, or wool on a sheep's back should be valuable.— Nor is the value of money *"imaginary,"* in the language of Mr. Locke; nor can gold and silver pieces be called " counters" in the language of Doctor Franklin ; for pebbles and knotches on a stick by which boys keep their game, will answer as counters, but gold and silver pieces will od much more.

144. What then is the foundation of the value of

* Smith's Wealth of Nations.

WHAT IS WEALTH? 137

money, or the precious metals? It is that God has been pleased to give them to man, to answer a valuable use, just that purpose that was necessary and which could not be accomplished, so far as we know at present, without them. This purpose was to obtain some medium by which all things might be valued, that were to be bought and sold.

But there is another fact that is all-important as to their value, and that is, that though God has mingled gold and silver with the earth, these must be extracted from it by *labour*. Gold is said to be found, sometimes, in a virgin state, silver never. The labour of obtaining these metals in the mines in the earth, where they are mostly found, is immense. *Labour*, then, is the criterion of the value of gold and silver, as much as it is of iron, or wool, or silk, or any other article. The reason why they are more valuable than iron is, that the labour of obtaining them is as much greater than that of obtaining iron, as they are more valuable than iron.*

Money, in one respect, is like all merchandize, it is bought and sold as other merchandize is bought and sold, though inexperienced people who never saw it bought and sold, can hardly comprehend this. In the cities, dollars are bought, though less frequently now than formerly, to send to China for tea, and other things.

But though money is merchandize, it is in one respect better than any merchandize; because though it is bought and sold, it buys and sells all things, which is not true of any other merchandize.

145. The common language of a country often gives

---

* M'Cullock's Edition of Smith's "Wealth of Nations," vol. 4, note 3.

us the best ideas upon subjects such as these. Our farmers when they apply for a loan of money, often say, that they want to "*hire*" money, as they would say, they want to *hire* a horse, or any other thing. To *hire* money is to borrow it for a recompense, which the man who loans is as much entitled to, and for the same reasons, that he would be entitled to a recompense for the loan of his horse. He who hires a horse can make money from the labour of the horse, and he who hires money, may exchange his money for a horse, and thus make more money. Some of the ancient philosophers said that money was barren, and did not breed money, and that therefore it was a crime to take interest for the loan of money, and a few people in our own country have adopted the same ideas. But let us see how reasonable this is. Money is got by labour; and why should not the possessor obtain a recompense for the loan of it as well as for other things that are obtained by labour? Besides, money does breed money, and is not barren.

Do not people who borrow it, trade with it, work with it, and thus make more money? When a man lends a dollar, he may be said to lend a bushel of wheat, if that be the price of wheat; as then, the dollar may be exchanged for a bushel of wheat, and as this may be put in the ground and produce more wheat, why should he not receive his dollar again *with use?* This is the real reason why it is absurd to regulate the interest of money by law, and make it the same at all times and places, because a bushel of wheat and a dollar, and every thing else may be more valuable, by being made to earn more in the hands of the borrower at one time and place, than another, But the subject of *interest*, is not intended to be discussed here.

WHAT IS WEALTH? 139

146. From hence it follows, that gold and silver are precious metals; a species of merchandize, like all other merchandize; that they are valuable because they are obtained with labour; because they answer a purpose which nothing else will; and that they are valuable in proportion to the labour expended in obtaining them. Though gold and silver are at present immensely useful to mankind, and even essential, still it is by no means impossible, that such changes may take place, that something better than gold and silver may be used for the same purpose, and that we may thus be saved from the immense expenditure of labour, that we are now put to, in obtaining these metals. There was a time when nearly all the people of Europe were clothed in skins for the want of cloth. Immense additions are constantly made to the stock of human knowledge and comfort.

These brief explanations upon the subject of money seemed to be necessary here. It will be re-considered, together with that of *paper money*, which is of great moment to us in the United States.

147. We hear a great deal of capital, of the merchant's capital, the manufacturer's capital; and what is capital? It is a portion of the wealth enumerated, and consists of that part upon which men trade and carry on business.*

We speak of the merchant's capital or stock in trade, meaning his warehouse, goods in store, money on hand, debts due, &c., but we do not mean his wild lands, horses, cattle, coaches, &c. So we speak of the farmer's capital, meaning his cattle, tools, hay, grain, &c., but we do not mean his household furniture, because, strictly, this

* M'Cullock's Outlines of Political Economy, part 2, sect. 2.

is not one of the instruments by which he carries on his business, though it may be true that he cannot do without it. Jewels, coaches, laces, are capital to those that sell them, but not to those that ride in them for pleasure, or wear them.

148. Capital, like nearly all other wealth, proceeds from labour, as we have seen, for there is no other means given under heaven by which it can be obtained, and a capital thing it is. Labour procures it; economy, which is saving, increases it. As money breeds money, so may every species of capital, it being that part of a man's property which he works with. As every year it may become greater and greater, it is said to be "accumulated labour," "hoarded labour," "labour laid up;" in this sense, it is old labour, it is what a man worked for last year, or the year before, perhaps, as his ox, or his horse, or it is what his father worked for before him, such as his improved farms, his stock of cattle, his fences, walls, drains, tools, &c.* A poor man's capital may be said to consist of his education, his skill, his capacity to do business; this is his stock in trade; upon this, and this alone, he lives and supports his family; to hamper him, therefore, by restraining his freedom, and directing him where, when, how, and for what wages, he shall labour, is as cruel and unjust, as to seize, by violence, the iron chest of the rich man.

149. The design of capital being to produce wealth, let us see how this is effected.

First, It enables us to do that which cannot be done without it. A farmer's oxen and ploughs are a part of

---

* Ganilh's Political Economy, translated from the French of D. Boileau. This is a work of good sense, and full of noble sentiments.

WHAT IS WEALTH?

his capital. With these, he can break up a piece of land in a week, which probably could not be done by an American Indian in a year, and perhaps never.

Second, Capital saves labour, for allowing that the Indian could, with his imperfect instruments, accomplish at all, what the farmer does in a week, with an iron plough and four oxen, there is no reason to believe that he could do it in less than a year, or probably, even in a much longer time.

Third, Capital procures better work than can be done without it;* for the Indian, with all his toil, sweat, and scratching, of the ground, will never turn out a neat, clean furrow of twelve inches in depth, in a stiff clay, as an American farmer can with his improved iron plough. The plough and the oxen will stand for all the tools, implements, engines, factory machinery, and every thing else, which enables us to save time and labour, and to do work which cannot be done without them.

Fourth, As capital is that which enables us to labour to advantage, it is that also which enables us to employ labourers. If a farmer saves a hundred dollars this year, and as many the next, and so on, till he has accumulated a sufficient sum to buy a new farm, he immediately sets about to get labourers to work it; and if a merchant builds a new ship, there must be more sailors employed to man and sail it. Labourers, therefore, are always interested in saving and increasing capital, by which alone their wages are paid.

150. Fifth, Capital being that portion of a man's property with which he trades or does business, it is the great means of employing poor people, of paying wages

* M'Cullock's Outlines, part 2, sect. 2.

in the establishment, and carrying on of manufactories, the building of cities and villages, and the forwarding of every improvement. He, who lends his capital, enables others to do the same thing. But, if a man has *money*, and puts it by in his iron chest, then he *hoards* it, and this is the true idea of *hoarding*. This is *dead capital*; this is "a talent buried in a napkin."

151. That portion of the wealth of a country, which is composed of capital, is divided into fixed and circulating capital.

Fixed capital is that which remains stationary; such as, cotton-mills, machinery in mills, shops, warehouses, improvements of the land, by clearing, draining, fencing, &c.

Circulating capital is that which changes hands: as, first, money, by which all property may be circulated, or bought and sold, and by which wages are generally paid. Second, the stock of provisions on hand, such as grain, meat, vegetables, &c., which are daily sold by the farmer, butcher, &c. Third, the materials which are in the course of being worked up and prepared for market, as wool, hemp, cotton, &c. Fourth, goods in the hands of the merchant, manufacturer, and tradesman, which are worked up and ready to be sold.* These are not all the items that may be named, but they are sufficient to give an adequate idea of circulating capital.

* Smith's Wealth of Nations, book 2, chap. 1.

CHAPTER IX.

HOW IS WEALTH OBTAINED?

152. The answer to this question was necessarily anticipated in the last chapter. In showing what wealth is, and the different kinds of it, and the nature of capital as a part of wealth, it was impossible not to state the fact, that wealth is the result of labour, and saving, or economy. This then is the answer: labour and economy are the sources of wealth, of the grand and beautiful changes which the world is undergoing, and of the sublime destiny which it is certainly unfolding. As these, then, are the sources from which are to flow man's most important treasures, whether for body or mind, the subject deserves still further illustration.

153. All that God ever gave of earthly things, he gave at the creation of the world. In giving the earth, he said: "Be fruitful, and multiply, and replenish the earth, and subdue it."* God, also, gave man "dominion over the fish of the sea, and over the fowl of the air, and over the cattle, and over all the earth, and over every creeping thing that creepeth upon the earth."† This included, of course, all the domestic animals; their labour, therefore, belongs to man. God did not give man garments for clothing, for Adam and Eve had nothing but fig-leaves for a covering; nor food, except that he gave

* Gen., ch. 1, v. 28.
† Same, v. 26.

the natural fruits of the earth, which, without cultivation, we know, even now, generally, to be very small in quantity, and miserable in quality; he did not build cities and villages for him, nor construct roads and canals for his accommodation, nor give him arts and manufactures, by which the immense variety of his comforts was to be supplied, nor did he make any provision for the neverending wants of his mind, except that he supplied him with the materials out of which they might be satisfied. In this situation, man was cast upon the earth, destitute and naked, having nothing before him but a desert, with no other limit than the boundaries of the world. This might seem a frightful prospect, but it was not, for the genius of labour appeared before him, telling him that perseverance would conquer all things, if he would obey God's commands, and "be fruitful, and multiply, and *replenish* the earth, and *subdue* it." Adam's condition was more helpless than that of the native savage of North America, though he is forever roaming over a great desert to get food and drink, and the coarest garments. The wild Indian has scarcely any stores, very little laid up for the future, he can do little for his fellow-man, he cannot help him, for he has nothing to help him with; and this is the grand distinction between the selfish, unsocial, and miserable condition of the savage and the civilized man. The savage has few of those arts by which the natural evils of life are removed or alleviated. Tanner, in his account of the North American Indians, describes one who was injured in his arm by the bursting of a gun. There were no surgeons among these poor Indians, and of course no surgical instruments. This Indian determined to cut off his own arm, "and taking two knives, the edge of one of which he had hacked into a sort of saw; he, with his right arm and hand, cut off his left, and threw it from him as far as he could."

Of all the property that is laid up, of all the capital that is used, that is among the most valuable which is employed in alleviating human disease. But, how few of our houses, villages, or towns, have even the common conveniences of bathing, which are so important, not only in warding off, but in curing disease.

154. God, in giving man the earth and in ordering him to subdue it, commanded him to labour; to clear the land, to plough, harrow, and sow seed. But he was not to stop here. He was to *multiply;* he was to sow more seed than he could consume the product of, that he might have enough to raise up a family of children. It is known to be a fact, that an abundance of food is essential to the great multiplication of man, as well as of all the inferior animals. We have seen already how many of the poor perish for the want of a sufficiency of healthful food. Man was not to subdue the earth, and to multiply and thus produce a race of miserable, half starved beings, like the poor people of Ireland, but he was commanded to *replenish* it; that is, to *fill* it with good things, such as God had given him tastes and appetites to enjoy, and then he was to *provide suitable furniture* for this beautiful world in all the forms of grace and usefulness, and thus make it a magnificent mansion, instead of a common poor-house. This is to "*replenish*" the world. Man was, therefore, to improve his condition forever; to be adding constantly to his stores; to have something more this year than the last, something for the mind and something for the

body, but a great deal more for the mind than the body; in proportion as that is superior.

155. Adam and Eve, as they came out of the garden of Eden, though they were in full possession of the earth, and all that was on the face of it, were poorer than our savages. They had no tools nor engines, which are our great instruments, both for increasing the power of labour and for saving labour; they had neither knife, spade, shovel, plough, nor an arrow, for the destruction of a wild beast, nor a fish-hook, nor canoe to enable them to get a living from the sea and the rivers. From this state of nakedness and destitution in which Adam and Eve were, we have advanced to that condition of the world which we now see. But we have approached no nearer the end of what labour and economy will do, than when we first began, so far as any one can point out, for no one can imagine a limit to man's worldly possessions any more than he can to those of his mind. Each multiplies the other, and they will doubtless go on together to the end of all time. This is a conclusive proof of the moral improvement of the world, which is as certain as that the world exists. We see the improvement; all our senses testify to it.

156. Now let us reverse this case: suppose that Adam and Eve, at the end of the first year, and every successive generation after them, had suffered their garments, provisions, tools, and stores of every kind, to wear out, mould, rust, decay, beyond the natural wear, tear, and destruction; it is plain, that they would have been compelled to begin anew, just as spendthrifts do now-a-days; that they could not have advanced one inch. If the same thing had taken place with Adam and Eve every

year, they would have been as poor when they died, as at the first moment of their existence, and so it would have been with every generation to this moment, had not economy saved the world from such universal poverty.

CHAPTER X.

LABOUR DETERMINES THE VALUE OF THINGS.

157. IN other words, the amount of labour put upon a thing determines its value, compared with other things; and this must be true, when we have already seen that labour procures nearly all things. Labour, therefore, is said to be the regulator of value, " and the first price of all things." In other words, "the cost of production regulates the exchangeable value of commodities."* This is true, with certain qualifications, which will be stated. In what sense, then, is it true, "that labour is the first price of all things"

When a poor man wants food or drink, and must have it, the first thing he does is to work; this is the price he pays, and at night he receives his recompense in a bushel of wheat, or rye, or money, or some other thing. The reason why he must pay in his own labour immediately, is, that he has no labour stored or laid up; in other words, he has none of the products of labour, such as money, or other property. But, suppose a good farmer, whose farm is not mortgaged, and whose cattle and goods are neither pledged for debt, nor under a sheriff's execution, desires to buy; he also pays in labour; but it is not the labour of that day, but of some former period; he has been a man of prudence, he has stored up labour, which now consists of wheat, corn, rye

---

* Elements of Political Economy, by James Mill, ch. 3, sec. 2.

cattle, &c., these are the things that he worked for last year; these he exchanges for what he wants. Now, imagine a rich man, one who is supposed to live upon his money, inherited, perhaps, from his father or grandfather, and who never worked a day in his life, wants to buy. He may not have wheat, corn, or rye, with which to pay; but he has money, which is as completely labour laid up as the farmer's stores. It is not the result of his own labour, but that of his father, grandfather, or some other industrious man. Some one has given labour for it; for there is no other way, as an almost universal rule, by which money can be obtained, in the first instance, but by being worked for. It is obtained from the mines by labour, as before stated; and the labourer who gets it is paid for his work, as all other labourers are. The merit of this rich man, then, is, that he has saved, and not foolishly thrown away, his hoarded labour—that which he is sure has cost the sweat and toil of industrious people.

158. As labour, then, is the first price of all things, a man's fortune may be computed in the things that he has laid up, or that others have laid up for him. If, therefore, he has a vessel or a house which he values at a thousand dollars, he may say that he is worth two thousand days' labour, computing the price of labour at fifty cents the day, for somebody must have worked two thousand days, to enable him to obtain the property mentioned.

159. All trade, all buying and selling, consists, *finally*, in the exchange of one article for another, all of which have cost labour. In the first instance, however, we often take money in exchange for the articles we sell, because that will buy the thing we want. When a

farmer sells his grain, and takes his pay in money, he means to exchange his money for something else, perhaps another farm, perhaps to stock the farm he has.

In the early settlement of a country, and in those parts which are remote from market, there is little money, and nearly all trade consists in the exchange of one article for another, which is *barter*, and which will be more fully explained hereafter. Let us now attend to the principle of this exchange, which will show that "labour is the first price of all things," or the regulator of their value. In other words, in the exchange of one thing for another, that which has cost two days' labour, is twice as valuable as that which has cost only one. A hatter makes hats alone, and wants shoes,—a shoemaker makes shoes alone, and wants hats; it costs three days' labour, perhaps, to make a hat, and one day's labour to make a pair of shoes; in this case the shoemaker will be obliged to give three pair of shoes for one hat; or he gives one pair of shoes, and makes up the difference in money or some other thing. The hatter says to the shoemaker, "it cost me three days' work to make a hat, and you one to make a pair of shoes, then, plainly, I am entitled to three pair of shoes for one of my hats." The common sense of this reasoning no one can deny. The same thing has been illustrated in this way: Suppose two savages go out, the one to fish, and the other to catch game; that it costs each of them a day's labour, one day with another, to kill a deer and to take a salmon; the deer and the fish will be equal in value, and may be exchanged, one for the other. This, then, is the *general principle* which determines things to be cheap or dear, compared one with another, namely, the more or less labour that is expended upon one or the other.

160. But there are qualifications, or exceptions, to this principle: First, The price of a thing may depend upon its *scarcity*. Suppose that a savage, in roaming over the desert for game, should pick up a diamond, as large as the *Pitt diamond*, and has knowledge enough to make as good a market of it, as a New-York jeweller would. In that case he would send it to London, and there, from its being a precious stone, and very rare, from its great size, it would be worth thousands of pounds, though it has cost nothing, the finding being a thing of accident. It is the scarcity, therefore, in a great measure, which gives an extraordinary value to such things as large diamonds, choice wines, and rare pictures.* Suppose a man should dig or bore for water, and find a spring like that of the Congress Spring at Saratoga; the labour might be small, but the value would be immense. It is a strange principle of our law, that so munificent a gift of God to man, as such a medicinal water, should be appropriated to private use. Some writers on natural law have thought very properly, that *medicinal waters* ought never to be monopolized by private appropriation.† In such case, however, if the public claim the property, they should pay for the labour which has been expended in obtaining it, and remunerate the owner for any injury to which he is exposed by the public use of it.

161. Though we say, then, that things are valuable in proportion to the labour they cost, still there is no per-

---

* Ricardo on the Principles of Political Economy and Taxation, p. 1, 2.
† Paley's Moral Philosophy.

fect standard of value, not in the sense in which we consider a half-bushel and a yard stick as the standards of measure, or weights and scales the standard of weight, because, for most practical purposes, these may be considered to be perfect standards. Labour is not a perfect standard, for several reasons:

1st, Because, though labour be the general standard, the cost of a thing will depend upon the *supply and demand*, which is only another way of explaining the effect of *scarcity* already stated.

Thus, apples, during the year 1833, were plenty and cheap in Stockbridge, that is, they cost about 33 cents a bushel,(two shillings) for the best winter apples, but during the last year (1834), in consequence of an extraordinary frost in the month of May of that year, which nearly cut off every kind of fruit here, apples were very scarce, and very dear ; indeed we sent to New-York for the few we had, and paid three or four times as much as they cost the year before, and still the labour of producing, gathering, and bringing apples to market is about the same every year. The *demand* in the year 1834 was as great as in the year 1833, but the *supply* was smaller. In other words, there was a scarcity in 1834, which was the cause of the high price of apples in that year in Stockbridge.

2d, Again, labour is not a perfect standard of value for practical purposes. 1st, Because labour in one period of the world is more valuable than in another, in consequence of the superior education, knowledge and ingenuity of one age over another. A day's labour with an iron plough now, is worth more than a day's labour with a wooden plough forty years ago. 2d, Because even at the same period in different countries, the labour of

THE VALUE OF THINGS.   153

one man in a given time is in consequence of the same causes, more valuable than that of another. And even in the same country, all know that the labour of one man will produce more than that of another. This fact gives rise *in part* to the variety of wages that men receive for their labour.

After all, labour is the great regulator of the value of things, and we say that a thing is cheap, because it costs little labour, and dear, because it costs much. For this reason peaches in Stockbridge are dearer than apples, because Stockbridge, being in a cold climate, the cost of producing peaches here is greater than that of producing apples. The same cause makes a coach dearer than a cart, a house than a barn, a fine cloth than a coarse one.

162. What now are the conclusions from these three last chapters upon wealth, the modes of obtaining it, and the nature of labour?

1st, These subjects are no longer mysteries, when people give their thoughts to them, and become familiar with the words wealth, economy, capital, labour, cost of production, &c. Common people are more puzzled about words than things; they are often acquainted with the things, but they do not understand the signs; they do not understand the words. If learned writers would use the words, or any thing like them, that the common man employs to express his ideas upon these subjects, the mystery would disappear like the fog of the morning. It is very easy to puzzle a plain, common mind with definitions, and a multitude of words, and learned explanations, when men of education write only for each other, or for a few hundreds or thousands. This is one of the reasons why the common people have been so long kept in ignorance. There is aristocracy in governments, in manners, modes of living, laws; there is also the aristocracy of learning. But, surely, if there be any benefaction which one poor suffering fellow-creature is entitled to from another, it is knowledge. Franklin wrote for all mankind, and so may other men upon most subjects; and, if this were the case, learning would be diffused every where, and like the dew fertilize the field of the poor, as well as the rich man.

163. These subjects are not like those of mathematics, astronomy, and some other sciences, which common people generally cannot understand well, plainly because they have not time, and a few only understand them of any class. On the contrary, the subject of economy is interwoven with the daily business of a working man, and especially in the United States where he is called upon so frequently to discuss it, and to vote upon it. In some way or other the subject of the economy and profit of labour is ever before his eyes. The common people have supposed that it was impossible for them to understand what the learned seemed to be so much puzzled about; for the learned dispute and refine more than common people do; common people, therefore, have supposed that there must be mystery where there was so much darkness. This is *one* of the reasons why little has been understood of the science of economy, but there is *a greater*, and that is because little has been practised. The waste of the people's property has been horrible, and that has been reason enough why rulers have been willing that their subjects should remain in ignorance of their true interests. There is still a farther reason; things have been put wrong end foremost; that which should be first taught has been taught last; even now many are

THE VALUE OF THINGS. 155

learning Latin and Greek, who would be much better employed in fitting themselves for the common business of life.

2d, It is plain, that as wealth is created by labour, it can only be increased by saving and economy. By the same means that one man becomes independent a hundred, and a thousand do, and the same is true of a nation; that is, by keeping on hand for future use, what has already been acquired, or some portion of it; *because all cannot be preserved ; a part must be daily eaten, drunk, worn out, or consumed in some way or other*, which will appear more particularly in its proper place.

3d, *It is in the nature of wealth to increase,* and this is plainly proved by showing what the uses of capital are. One animal breeds many, one seed produces a hundred, or a thousand ; a good tool does more work than a poor one ; a saw mill-may produce a hundred or a thousand times more wealth in the same time than human hands could at the same kind of business; so that we may truly say, that there is no limit to wealth, nor can there be. So far as appears, we are as distant from that limit as when our first parents were placed on the earth. The only question is whether the people will be prompted by the only motive worthy of them, that of doing good, to go on and get all the wealth they can. Our own experience in our country, shows an increase of wealth beyond what the world ever saw under the like circumstances and commands us to go forward. We see every year new sources of wealth opened, labour-saving machines invented; new substances or combinations of them brought to light, and turned to some useful account never before thought of. Steam, gas-light, granite, anthracite coal, india rubber, soap-stone, rail-roads, canals, &c., furnish new employments, and of course increased wealth to thousands who but a few years since did not dream of deriving advantage from any of them, and perhaps did not know of their existence.

164. If these things, then, are the means by which people are fed and clothed, and get good farms and houses and cattle, and after obtaining a reasonable independence for themselves, are able, out of their *superfluous* riches, to get leisure and money to enable them to carry light, knowledge, and comfort to their poorer neighbours, and to the miserable nations, how unwise and unthinking to declaim against the increase of wealth! It would be as childish to talk against too much good land, too many good houses, too many fine cattle. It is the perversion of wealth from the uses that God designed it for, that we have to deplore; it is the heaping up of our meagre stores by monoply and every kind of oppression, in the laps of a few, thus causing poverty and universal nakedness among the multitude, that the world ought to be ashamed of. It is the vanity, pride, selfishness, gluttony, intemperance of both rich and poor that we are to withstand. Wealth can never be an evil but by being turned to unnatural purposes, and an ancient philosopher says with truth, "that it is not the liquor but the vessel which is corrupted."

CHAPTER XI.

CONSUMPTION;

OR, WHAT MUST BE CONSUMED, AND WHAT CAN OR CANNOT BE SAVED OR LAID UP.

165. The Liberia Herald, of the seventh day of October, eighteen hundred and thirty-three, gives the following account of the death and burial of the African king, Tom Bassa, who died in July of that year.

Two bullocks were slain; one put at the head, one at the foot of the grave; into which were put two large chests of dry-goods, in the same position; one high post bedstead and mattress, a present from a slaver; then the corpse, dressed after a civilized mode, with a hat, two umbrellas, and shoes; then a kettle of rice; two large pots of rice, one at the head, one at the foot; two large looking glasses, in the same position; coral beads, pipes, tobacco, mugs, decanters, wash-hand basins, swords, cutlasses, and one hundred native mats. Outside the grave was placed a large pot to receive donations from the pious.

It is easy to account for the poverty of the world, when we see property consumed in this way, which might be laid up and turned to some useful purpose; civilized kings spend the money of their subjects, in many kinds of self-glorification, quite as ridiculous; and instead of asking for "donations from the pious," they insist upon loans and taxes, and call national debts, blessings. The people of the United State would think it a stigma upon their reputation, if it could be proved that they spend a great deal of their labour with as little sense or propriety; and we shall see hereafter, whether they are, or are not, liable to such a change.

166. Having established, as a general rule, that wealth can be obtained only by labour, and increased by economy and saving, it becomes important to show what can, and what cannot, be saved; how far our property must be consumed by eating, drinking, and the natural wear and tear of nature; and how far, when consumed, it returns to us again in some new form.

There are two kinds of consumption, *productive* and *unproductive* consumption.* It is productive consumption, when a farmer consumes his food, and wears out his clothes in ploughing, sowing, reaping, &c. The food which he eats, and the clothes which he wears out, are consumed; the seed which he puts into the ground also perishes; but his food, his clothes, and his seed, reappear in a new crop. It is unproductive consumption, when foolish kings, like Tom Bassa, order their property to be buried in the same graves with their lifeless and useless bodies; or, when an idler or a drunkard consumes his food and wears out his clothes. It must be remembered that nothing, strictly, can be destroyed, or put out of existence, " for we can no more destroy matter than we can create it."

167. It is of great importance to be able to obtain just ideas of what we must consume, and how far we can lay up and save; to know to what extent we can preserve something for ourselves, our friends, for society, for our children, and remote posterity.

* Say's Political Economy, book 3, chap. 1 to chap. 6, inclusive. These chapters are invaluable.

CONSUMPTION.

In common language, a man is said to consume his food and drink, and to wear out his clothes. But here arises the distinction before stated, one consumes his drink and food, and wears out his clothes, and whilst he is doing so, he is cultivating some grain, or rearing some animal, that will produce him more food, drink, and clothes. This is *reproduction* of something that supplies the place of what is eaten, drank, and worn out. It does more; it not only replaces what has been consumed, but with good management, much more. This surplus is the profit of business; this is the source of the riches of people; this is what they earn more than they spend. If a man sows a single grain of wheat, he does not expect a product of a single grain only, but twenty, forty, fifty-fold, or more, according to the fertility of his land. This is the state of the industrious man. That of the idle man in one respect is the same, that is, he eats, drinks, and wears, but he produces nothing; his is *unproductive consumption*. He does nothing for reproduction. The industrious man eats, drinks, and wears, too, though by no means commonly so much as the other, but while he is consuming, his hand is on the plough, and he leaves a furrow behind, which prepares the ground for the seed, which is also consumed, but which in perishing produces a new crop, thus furnishing the means of food, drink, and clothes hereafter. The idle man is said "to be born to consume the fruits of the earth;" he does not produce them; the industrious man is the author of all these fruits, and of all the wealth of the world. The one is said to be a *producer*, and the other a *consumer*. From what has been said, it must not be thought that the farmers, manufacturers, day-labourers, and all those who are usually called manual labourers, are the only producers. There are other large classes, who are producers also, and who often work as laboriously, worthily, and effectually in producing wealth, as any manual labourers. Some of these work late and early, exhaust their strength, and perish in their labours. Washington and Franklin were among the greatest producers of wealth in the world.

168. Strange as it may seem, there is a large number of people, and some very respectable writers, who think that one portion of the world must be idle in order to keep the rest at work; in other words, that there must be a great many to eat, drink, and wear, and do nothing, that the residue may be kept out of idleness and mischief; they say, that if all worked industriously, the world would be overloaded with good things; that every market would be glutted; that there would be more sellers than buyers, more houses than tenants, more horses than riders; that the kitchens would be filled with pots and kettles, and the parlours crammed with carpets, tables, chairs, &c. They admit, however, that if all wanted and sought for comfortable things, such as good farms, houses, clothes, &c., that of course there could never be more than enough.

Not thinking this possible, or anything like it, they believe that there must be spending kings, like Tom Bassa, though they may not recommend exactly the same kind of expense. They believe, that as men have always spent their money like children, they will continue to do so; that the public must support a body of idle sailors, soldiers, &c., and maintain a national debt, which in this way they consider a national blessing, in order to keep any part of the people well at work; in a word, that it is quite fanciful to imagine, that men will ever be wiser than to spend their money, in other words, their labour, very much as they do at present, which, to be sure, is acknowledged to be very stupid.*

169. But all history is against these opinions; for it is as certain that men spend their money more wisely than they did, as that they now have more liberty than they had, or better governments, or less superstition, and a better religion, or better houses, ships, ploughs, or anything else. It is by this wiser way of spending their money that all these things have been improved; indeed, it is this wiser, more dignified, Christian-like, and enriching way of laying out labour, that is the great improvement which is now going on, and which we in the United States approve of as *reform*. Nothing can arrest it; and it will advance just as fast as, and no faster than, the common people are well-informed upon the subject. All great reforms are, and must be, carried on by the common people; they are interested in having reform;—those who live upon their ignorance, in having abuses.

It is this low, irreligious opinion of the capacity of men to understand their own interests, and the designs of the Supreme Being in regard to them, that ever has been, and still is, one of the greatest evils in the world. It is from this that common people derive their ideas, when they think that it is well for the rich to waste and destroy their property by every kind of folly and extrava-

---

* This section is a fair interpretation of Malthus's opinions in ch. 7, sec. 9, of his work on Political Economy, and particularly of the summing up of that chapter, in the last page of it. Malthus is said to have been one of the best of men; and, though the people of the United States cannot agree with much that he has written, there is a great deal in his works that is worthy of all praise.

gance, in order to keep the poor at work, and to furnish the industrious with the means of living. How common is it for them to say, " why do you toil, you are rich enough; if I was as rich as you, I would take the comfort of it. Why not scatter your money so that poor people can get it?" They never think, that the laws of nature, which make men labour, are the laws of happiness; and that the more good things that are got into the world, the better it is, of course, for the whole people; and that this is not done by their kind of scattering.

170. Let us now look at some of those laws of nature which show that a constant consumption is going on, and which doom men to labour. The Supreme Being has shown what a scope there is for the industry of man, and for all his powers, in forming nature of such materials that everything is constantly going to decay. From much of this decay, to be sure, there arises a new principle: the seed dies, and perishes for ever; but there spring from it new plants and other seeds. In the fertile parts of the earth, nature makes a soil by the deposit of leaves, &c.; but after a few years, with small exceptions, the vital principle is exhausted and dies, and the land becomes barren, unless by manure and cultivation we supply new life. Let us see how extensive this principle of destruction is, and how it forces men, in every successive generation, to continued labour.

171. Of all the monuments of former times, the most ancient are the Pyramids.* From all the industry of that wonderful people, the Egyptians, we have little

* Sir Humphrey Davy's "Consolations in Travel," dialogue 6,— "Pola, or Time."

more important left than these useless piles, and the mummies. None of the roofs of ancient buildings more than one thousand years old remain, unless there be some constructed of stone, as those of the Pantheon of Rome, and the tomb of Theodoric of Ravenna, the cupola of which is composed of a single block of marble.* The principle of gravitation is one of the great causes of this decay: vapour is taken up, the rain descends, and we know that a continued drop will, in the end, wear out adamant. Rain flowing down the sides of a building, carries with it sand and dust, which the wind has deposited there, and finally destroys it. Seeds take root in the decayed parts of stone and brick-buildings, and finally destroy them also; thus we see ivy and other creeping plants about old walls. Water, also, entering into the crevices of rocks, &c., when formed into ice, obtains an expansive power, which forces its way against all resistance. " The fox burrows amidst ruins; bats and birds nestle in the cavities in walls; the snake and the lizard make them their habitation; the ant, by establishing her colony, and forming her magazines, often saps the foundation of the strongest buildings; and the most insignificant creatures triumph, as it were, over the grandest works of man."

172. Time has left us nothing, scarcely, that belonged to the ancients but their writings, and a few specimens of the fine arts. There is hardly a bridge, temple, road, aqueduct, or anything that is useful to the people, that exists as they formed it. Not a dwelling-house of all those that sheltered one million two hundred thousand

---

* The same.

inhabitants of Rome, (by the computation of Gibbon)* has survived. The same process of decay is still going on in our habitations, garments, tools, walls, fences, &c., and shows us too plainly that we need not look in vain for useful work. We build of stone, brick, and mortar, in a way that would seem to set time and destruction at defiance; but the fabric is hardly completed before the elements have begun their work, and there is something to be repaired. In the sandy loam of the village of Stockbridge, a chesnut post in the ground, six inches square, will last twelve or fifteen years only. A large portion of New England has been settled less than two hundred years, and appears now to be an old country; many of the houses looking old and shabby, the fences and out-houses being in a state of rapid decay. A cultivated field, highly tilled and manured, must be renovated generally at the end of every three or four years, or it will run to waste. Our garments may endure half a year, some of them, perhaps, a little longer; our household-furniture and tools generally a few years; the house itself a hundred or more; a ship ten or twenty; domestic animals a few years, according to their natural lives, which are usually shorter than ours;—all that the public owns, such as roads, canals, guns, ships, fortresses, is in constant decay, and requires an immense sum for annual repairs.

173. There is another principle, that shows that there is *useful* work enough to employ all the industry and power that man has, and it is this: he is not like the brute, at a stand at the end of a single generation, but

* Gibbon's Rome, vol. 4, ch. 31.

has the capacity of advancing forever. He has not only the power, but he is advancing, and has been from the beginning of the world; not every individual or generation, or nation, but man; the human race, human nature, civilization, improvement, these are always moving forward. Man admires new forms of beauty, grace, and elegance, not the favoured and educated man alone, but all men, rich and poor, they love improvement; God has formed their minds for it; this love is an instinct, and it can no more be eradicated, than their desire for pure air, and good meat and drink. The exercise of man's ingenuity in procuring new and useful things is a pleasure; when exerted successfully, it affords him property, this gives him power, and power is gratifying, and may be useful to all men. Man, therefore, is ever in search of something which shall be an advance beyond that which he now possesses. The beginning of civilization (says Sir Humphrey Davy) is in the discovery of somê useful arts, by which men acquire property, comforts, and luxuries. Man first begins to till the earth with some rude instrument like a pointed stone, he then invents a hoe or something like it, then a spade, shovel, or plough, but it is a wooden plough pointed only with iron, then it is an iron plough altogether, which latter has been in use only twenty or thirty years.

174. This succession of improvements is one kind of consumption, and is as inevitable as that of our daily bread. Old tools must be laid aside after a few years, and such is the ingenuity of *our* countrymen, that a farmer is afraid to buy a new one, lest it should perish in his hands through some new invention. Thus the old is superceded by the new, and we every day see tools, engines, household furniture, thrown by, because better have been

invented or introduced; and he who supposes, that we shall hoe, dig, plough, build, or sail a hundred years hence, or even twenty, as we now do, shows that he knows little as to what is going on in a single year, much less in a century.

This is the progress of knowledge, and if the farmer, mechanic, and manufacturer insist upon using old tools and machinery, instead of the improved, they are ruined by their folly. Upon the whole it is pretty certain that the world is far from having too many good things in it; that there are poor men who would be very glad to obtain one good coat or shirt, and say nothing about a dozen; their puzzle being rather to get what they want, than to rid themselves of what they have, and still we go on scattering, wasting, throwing away our little insignificant heaps, for fear that they will fall down and bury us in the ruins. Children, when they obtain a little money, amuse themselves with buying gunpowder, putting it in a train, and producing an explosion; grown-up people do the same thing, except that they make a greater noise, and produce a greater blaze.

175. Let us now see what can be saved or laid up— It is common to hear people say, that such a one has so much money laid up; that he saves so much money every year, &c. If you go to a hundred such men you may not find, that they have more than a few dollars perhaps on hand. Ask one of them where is all the money that he has laid up, and he will tell you that he has exchanged his money for land, or cattl, or that he has built a barn, or that he has lent his money, and taken a note for it.

The note stands for his money, he has the promise of another to repay him with interest, and his security lies in the property of the borrower. No wise man hoards his money, that is, permits it to lie idle in his chest, or buries it in his cellar, but he lends it, puts it in a Saving's Bank, or trades with it in some way or other. The story goes, that an old miser kept a tame jackdaw, that used to steal pieces of money, and hide them in a hole, which the cat observing, asked, "why he hoarded up those round things, that he could make no use of,"— "why," said the jackdaw, "my master has a whole chest full, and makes no more use of them than I do." What is saved and laid up is the surplus of men's income over their yearly expenditures, and consists of all those things, which are the result of man's labour. It must be remembered, however, though these useful things may be laid up for future use, that as we have seen before, this can only take place for a limited time.

176. These are some of the most important savings!

First, Improvements of the natural state of the earth by clearing, fencing, manuring, draining, irrigating, &c. This is increased capital to the working man, it enables him to work to more advantage than he did before, and is the same thing to him, as though he had a present of more strength, or of another arm and leg. These improvements often last for many years, they compose an important part of a farmer's savings, of his *hoarded labour*, it is to this that he looks for support in his old age, when his strength is exhausted and he can work no longer. It is by these improvements, that the government land which cost him a dollar and a quarter the acre, may become, in his own life-time, worth twenty, forty, and fifty.

177. Secondly, Our habitations are a part of our property saved and laid up. A stone or brick house will last for

centuries, if taken care of, and so will a wooden house, if kept covered and in good repair. There are wooden houses now in the town of Stockbridge which number a hundred years.

178. Thirdly, Some articles of household furniture will endure for a long time ; a carpet in a spare room perhaps for ten or twelve years; tables, bedsteads, mahogany furniture, for centuries with prudent use. Those wasteful people who consider it beneath their dignity to count sixpences, or to provide for the future, would be astonished at the piles of bed linen and some other kinds of furniture, which the Dutch, who are noted for this kind of economy, lay up, and which descend from generation to generation, as regularly as houses and lands. Some portion of this kind of saving might not be considered as the best economy, unless it were, on account of the formation of the habit of it.

179. Fourthly, There are many articles of wearing apparel, suited to the various seasons of the year, which with prudent people last for a considerable period. Some are the better for age, as boots, shoes, &c., and to a certain extent the increased value exceeds by far the interest lost in keeping the thing on hand. A labouring man should never feel at ease, till he has obtained good and seasonable garments.

180. Fifthly, There is another large class of savings of a different character, and many of them of the most enduring kind—this is that wealth, those collections, which are got together, for the education, the instruction, the refinement of the people. These are the peculiar possessions of the mind, and show their superiority, in their longer duration than that of many of those which are designed for the body only. The food of the body

perishes in the using, not so, that of the mind. This ennobling portion of the wealth of the people consists *in part :—*

First, Of books and libraries, which may endure for thousands of years, and which are the depositories of the facts, the sciences, arts, inventions, discoveries, which have given knowledge, wealth, and power to the people. A people can no more get freedom without the knowledge there is in books being spread among them, than in the present state of the world, they can remain free, without fire-arms and gunpowder.

181. Second, The second portion of this kind of wealth, consists of all those philosophical collections and specimens which are gathered together in our colleges, schools, and useful institutions, to illustrate and aid the sciences, natural philosophy, chemistry, botany, geology, &c. The working-men, for the same cause, are equally interested in this kind of knowledge. Simple, as the labours of many of them are, their prosperity depends upon the progress of science. In those countries where science does not exist, they are the most miserable of all men. But much science, without much wealth, is an impossibility.

Third, The third portion of this kind of wealth, consists in the products of the fine arts : music, architecture, painting, statuary, &c. These are among the most enduring possessions, and they are calculated to give pleasure to all mankind. Instead, however, of being possessions enjoyed by the people, rich and poor, for the improvement of their common nature, they have been monopolized by those who have engrossed every other kind of wealth. In Boston, there is in the State House, a beautiful statute of " him, who was first in peace, first in war, and first in the hearts of his countrymen," which was a noble and patriotic gift to the people, by an association of gentlemen in that city; and Congress have ordered another to be executed, by our countryman, Greenough, in Italy, at an estimated expense of twenty-five thousand dollars, to be deposited in the Capitol, at Washington.*

It is designed, hereafter, to attempt to show in what manner the people of the United States may, safely and wisely, under their democratic government, become the patrons of the *fine arts*. They will, however, very wisely determine that the useful arts shall come first. The *vulgar arts*, which now swallow up so much of the labour of the people in every country, in an abject and slavish imitation of the fashionable and great, must first cease before either the fine or the useful can prosper, as they are destined.

182. Fourth, In addition to the above items of savings, belonging to individuals and institutions, there are many that appertain to the public at large, such as fortresses, ships, military roads, munitions of war, canals, railroads, common roads, literary establishments, &c. The New-York canals will soon be paid for, and are a great property laid up; such evidence of the sagacity and forethought of a people, afford the best evidence that they are destined to be great. It is a melancholy reflection, to consider how much of the property of the public commonly consists in superfluous masses of the implements

---

* When the statue was first exposed to public view, in Boston, multitudes flocked to see it, rich and poor, common people of every description, and among the rest, many a bare-footed boy. It is a very unhappy and false judgment and feeling of those rich people who suppose that the poor and uneducated have no relish for such enjoyments.

of destruction, piled up year after year, without reference to the military wants of the country.

183. What we consume, how we consume, how consumption may be productive or unproductive, what we save, and how we save, will appear in the brief history of a settler, on the wild lands, in the western states.

In the year seventeen hundred and ninety, the population of the United States amounted to 3,884,635, in the year eighteen hundred and thirty, the population of the States and Territories was 12,859,194.* This is a prodigious rate of increase in forty years, and in a few instances only, has been known to take place in any other part of the world. This increase cannot take place in new countries without a corresponding increase of property. All, or a greater part of the new settlers, must save something, or there would be no provision for other new settlers. New settlers would never resort to a country of which they had heard, that it had made no progress, that after twenty or thirty years, it was as much a wilderness as ever. It is the increase of property that enables a people to multiply, just as it is an abundance of food that increases the number of animals; food is the only property, generally, that the brute needs; it makes an inconsiderable portion of that of a civilized man. If we wish, then, to see the world peopled with beings, who have comfortable food, drink, clothes, and places in which to sleep, and something more with which to help, instruct, and delight each other, we must inculcate the duty of economy, of saving *over* and *above* what we earn. This is not the duty of every man, for upon some, (though very few,) there are such claims, that they

* Hayward's Tables.

are bound to spend more than their incomes; but it is the duty of most men to increase their stores, otherwise the world would be at a stand.

184. The young settler, to whom we have referred, is a man of twenty-five years of age, who, having laid up a little property each year, for six or eight years, is now worth three or four hundred dollars. His parent, to be sure, is strictly entitled to his earnings during his minority, but this makes no difference as to the amount of them, which often, in the United States, in the period mentioned, equal or exceed, beyond his support, the sum mentioned. What a contrast between his condition and that of the miserable, young man of Europe, who abandons home and all that is dear to him, in search of *food*, and what an exhortation to gratitude, to wisdom, to prudence, and a due preservation of the good things of life! Our settler first purchases eighty acres of land, at one dollar and a quarter the acre; he marries: his prudence has secured him that right, as he does not live in a country where marriage and pauperism, among the common people, are pretty much the same thing. He goes out perhaps in the spring, builds a log-house, in which his neighbours assist him; he begins a clearing, buys seed-wheat, puts it in the ground, and now after a summer and autumn of hard work, the winter is at hand. His clothes are worn out, in part at least, some of his tools wholly, and some partly, his seed-wheat has disappeared, he has spent some of his money for provisions which are eaten up, and some for hired help. Indeed, the small store with which he emigrated is considerably diminished.

185. Thus far we have nothing but consumption; and if things were to remain in this state, the settler

would be on the high road to destruction. But that is not the case; the succeeding summer brings forward the result of his labour in a crop of wheat; if it be abundant, he keeps a part and sells the residue for provisions, clothes, &c., and if there be still a surplus, he buys cattle, perhaps, to stock his farm. Thus far he is as well off in every particular as when he began; and besides, he has saved something; what he has laid up is his house, the improvements on his land, his cattle, and probably a number of household comforts. This is so much of *reproduction;* his hopes as a man and a citizen now brighten, he has begun to let in the light upon his dark spot on the earth, and the sunny side of his little hill looks bright and pleasant. He now goes on as he began, earning more than he spends, his protecting genius being always at his side, whispering in his ear, "prudence, perseverance." This is the beginning of his fortune in the wilderness. He still presses forward; his family increases; he has enough for them too; his earnings exceed his expenditures; he every year grows more and more grain, and adds to his stock of every kind; and at the end of twenty or thirty years, he becomes a great and prosperous farmer. This is the end of labour and saving. The reverse of this case would show the fate of an unthinking, spending settler, who, like a fool, eats and drinks up all his substance; he toils, but he preserves nothing; he produces, but he consumes all; he earns good wages, but his wages bring him no wealth; in the midst of abundance, he is in poverty. These two men stand as representatives of the whole world. A man grows rich who lays up a little every year; if he spends all that he makes, he ends where he began; if more, his store is soon exhausted, when neglect and contempt await him.

Upon the whole, it is plain, that the prosperity of a people will depend greatly upon the way in which they consume what they work for and earn.

CHAPTER XII.

CAUSES OF POVERTY.

186. Having in former chapters given a brief history of property and poverty in different ages, and some account of the present poverty in the world in this and in other countries; and having subsequently in the chapters upon wealth, labour, and consumption, attempted to show how wealth is obtained, how it is consumed, and what part of it must be consumed, some satisfactory statements can now more easily be made as to the *causes* of poverty.—As we know that the products of the earth may, take the whole of it together, be immensely increased, we may be sure, that the fault or dificiency lies in man somewhere.

187. Every poor man may give, in a great measure, a true account of his own poverty, though he may be puzzled to tell, why there are so many poor. People like to seem ingenious, and to resolve all that they see into some grand general principles, of which they suppose themselves to be the discoverers. The great discovery of Mr. Malthus was, that the earth was overpeopled, that the number of people was out of proportion to the amount of property. The question that naturally arises, is, how comes the population to be out of proportion to the property?

This suggests the reflection that there are many causes of poverty, and not one alone; which is the truth. For instance, if a man become intemperate, it is almost

CAUSES OF POVERTY.

certain, that sooner or later, he will come to poverty; and the reason is, that he does not work steadily and skilfully as he did in his sober days, and thus *produce* the means of living. *One* of the great causes of poverty, then, plainly is, that there are so many who do not *produce* the *means of living*. If Mr. Malthus had pursued this subject as he should have done, he would have found that this is a most prolific cause of poverty in his own country.

188. But as has been said, there are many causes of poverty; there is a natural and necessary poverty, and an unnatural and unnecessary poverty. We say, with truth, that one makes himself poor by idleness, and another rich by industry. A great many made themselves poor in the United States, before the temperance reform, who are now making themselves rich. Nature did not make them rich or poor, she left them to do good or evil as they chose.

189. This temperance reform in the United States, of which more will be said hereafter, is the greatest moral and intellectual reformation that ever took place in the same time in the world. In the *country* we know the fact to be so; in the cities the same progress has not been made, nor do they ever keep pace with the moral improvement of the country. This reform will stand as a monument of the divine spirit of benevolence that has furthered it, and of the genius of a free people who have set about to inquire into the causes of their own happiness. Not only the temperance societies, but a great body of excellent citizens who have never joined them, have contributed to this reform. All have seen the necessity of it. It will do more to enable the people to see what true economy is, how it may be practised,

and what it will bring about, than perhaps any other, and all other causes whatever. It is the temperance reform, that is one great cause of the present unparalleled increase in the wealth of the country, and which people are so much at a loss to account for. It will lead the people on to think about all their immoral and wasteful habits.

190. We know that the laws of nature make some poor; and that it is for this cause, that Christ says:— "The poor ye shall have with you always." Some are born in a state of infirmity; they are deformed, they are diseased, they are idiotic, or their powers of body and mind are feeble. As, however, it is certain that a large amount of disease both of body and mind is *inherited*; we must take care that we do not attribute to nature that portion of the evil and cause of poverty, which is very great, and which our advances in knowledge are constantly showing to be greater and greater, and to proceed from the vices of parents. The child is generally what the progenitors were, and we see a certain constitution, healthy or unhealthy, running through whole generations.

191. There is another kind of poverty, and this proceeds from what we call inevitable evil; it is that which men cannot from their imperfect nature, and imperfect knowledge, avoid, or guard themselves against. Some portion of this proceeds from storms, lightning, fires, shipwreck, &c. If men knew when the storms would rage, the lightnings fly, the fire burst out, and where the hidden rocks and quicksands were, they might protect themselves, and their property against ruin.

192. Some ascribe poverty to a bad religion, to false religion, to superstition; and no doubt, a pure and un-

defiled religion practised through the world, would change the face of it. Some assert that the evil lies in bad forms of government, as where there is a king, nobility, and priesthood to be supported at the expense of the people. Others affirm, that it is of no great moment, what the form of government may be, if we can only get rid of restrictions upon trade and monopolies, which they say, with truth, must be unfavourable to the poor, and the creation of wealth. Then again, as suggested before, there is a large class, with Mr. Malthus at their head, who assert; that the grand cause of poverty, in most parts of the world, is an overgrown population; that things are out of proportion; that there are too many people for the property which there is to support them; that man may propagate faster, than it is possible to create food for his sustenance; that it is impossible for all the children that may be born to bring farms along with them; in fine, that nature provides so many dishes, and that if more come for food than there are dishes, she bids them to be gone, and drives them into the regions of poverty and despair.

193. After all, the question returns upon us,—How comes it that false religion, superstition, bad government, restrictions upon trade, monopolies, produce poverty and prevent the people from growing in wealth? How comes it that there is an overgrown population, and more people than can get food? These are important questions, and worthy of an answer, if one can be given. As it is plain, that the causes of poverty are as numerous as the follies and vices of men, I shall only take notice of what seems most prominent.

194. It appears, from what has already been proved, that *labour* is the cause of all the wealth in the world,

or nearly all. It is admitted, and every one knows, from common observation, that in most parts of the earth, *labour* may be made to produce more than it does at present. We know, *that it is possible* to turn the whole earth that can be cultivated, into garden ground. It is plain, then, that the great reason why there is not more wealth, and why, in such large portions of the world, the people are wretched, and not comfortable, is, either the *want of labour, or the right sort of labour.*

Either then, 1st, The people are idle, or they do not work as hard as they might; or, 2d, They work unskilfully, with poor tools, and in a bad manner, as savages do; or, 3d, Their labour is wholly, or in part, misapplied—that is, they work at the wrong things, and their labour, therefore, brings little or nothing to pass; in other words, their labour is in a great measure unproductive, yielding little or nothing of UTILITY, of real good to the great body of the people; it produces neither food, nor drink, nor clothes for the body, nor any real, delightful, desirable pleasure to the mind, compared with what it might produce. As was suggested before, there are thousands and thousands that do not produce the means of living. On the contrary, some of these, in the way in which they live, consume all that thousands produce. It is plain, that here are causes enough for poverty; because, if people do not work to produce what they want, and what it is best for them to have, how can they avoid being poor and miserable? It is this unprofitable labour, that brings nothing or little to pass, that I shall principally here consider.

195. This, then, solves the whole mystery, if there be any mystery about the matter, why bad government, bad religion, superstition, monopoly, make the people

poor and miserable; and it is that where these exist the people work to a disadvantage. They are compelled to labour for the king, for the nobility, for the priesthood, for the great men who have the monopolies, in ten thousand contemptible, frivolous, and unprofitable occupations, which are attended with little or no real permanent good to the labourers. This explains the unexampled prosperity, riches, and *happiness* of large portions of the United States, compared with other countries, that is, that the labourers here are permitted to work for their own benefit, to work for *property*, at such occupations as are useful to themselves, and thus to enjoy the produce of their labours. Happiness, then, is one great cause of labour and wealth, as surely as that misery, discontent, and despair are causes of idleness and poverty. And this is the reason why the slave is such a miserable labourer compared with the white man.

196. The prosperity of individuals depends in a great measure upon the *utility* of their occupations, and as individuals make up nations, those nations will be the richest and happiest where the *useful occupations prevail*. One of the great reasons, then, why there is so little property in the world, and why there are so many poor people, and why those who are not absolutely poor are far less well off than they might be, is, that so many men, women, and children, labour without bringing anything to pass, or anything compared with what they might bring to pass. Many work to no more advantage, so far as regards the prosperity of the whole, than if they laboured at digging ditches and filling them up again, or in pumping water out of one cistern into another, and so back again for ever. Now, it is certain, that when a poor man is hired to disgrace himself and

his employer, by such a disgusting waste of his time as this, though the poor man may thereby earn a dollar, he does not in any way, in the long-run, help the condition of other poor men like himself, by *increasing property* for the general good. It is true that he may help himself by gaining a dollar in wages; but it is as true that another man loses one. Between them both they have created nothing new or useful, of course nothing remains more than there was before. About thirty years ago, nearly every man wore a little silk tassel at the top of his boot, in front. The boot was property, but the tassel was a contemptible appendage of a man. Poor people who work for small wages, can find something better to lay out their money upon; it is for their interest to create PROPERTY.

197. It is by labouring and earning, or producing something that can be laid up, and added to the general heap, out of which the whole nation is fed and clothed, that a man can increase the wealth of the people, and thus improve the condition of poor people in future. Every child has seen a soap-bubble; it is a pretty toy. As it escapes from the pipe through which it is blown, it presents the appearance, though not regular in its movements, of a little world sent into the air by the breath; it dances about for an instant, and then bursts, and disappears for ever, showing that it is but a bubble! An immense amount of labour, even in the United States, is spent upon what is no better than soap-bubbles. But wheat, and rye, and cotton, and corn, fertile farms, beautiful cities, and villages, do not spring from soap-bubbles. We see every day some of the poorest of the people, who are often without bread, or meat, or comfortable clothes, occupied in manufacturing the soap, or the pipes, or in performing some of the operations of this

ignoble soap-bubble business. It is plain, that these poor people had better be making shoes, hats, and coats; for it is certain, that the more of these there are in the world, the more will fall to each man's share; unless it be true, as Mr. Malthus says, that there must be more heads than hats, more backs than coats, more guests than dishes, *which is denied.*

198. The ends of Providence in regard to man cannot be answered in his present disgraceful state of poverty, and this is perfectly true even in the United States, the happiest portion of the world. The great body of the labourers cannot look for any substantial improvement of their condition, till they have learned to lay up their wages, to increase their substance; and thus to obtain the means of a little rest and leisure for the improvement of their minds.

199. In proportion as people are easy and independent, and have made some little provision for the future by laying up their wages and earnings, *are they able to work at what occupations are most for their advantage.* When people have the option it is generally found that they work at the *useful occupations,* and this accounts (as was said before) for a great portion of the present wonderful prosperity of the United States, compared with that of most portions of the world. Not wonderful, however, compared with what it might be or will be. The power of labouring where we will, and how we will, is our independence! If we have this power in the United States, why is there not more brought to pass, why are there not more useful productions, why are there so many contemptible, frivolous ones, that no wise man cares anything about; why is there so much poverty, why so many that are removed only a hair's breadth from poverty?

This is one great, and a very important reason. The labouring people do not know their own power; they have never seen it in other countries, and have never been taught it here. The great body of those who labour with their hands, make this grand mistake: they think that they are compelled by their condition, to spend their time in blowing up soap-bubbles, if the rich, who, as they say, have all the wealth, prefer this; that, as they live upon wages, they must live according to the will of others; that if the rich man, the capitalist, chooses to carry on a vicious, and of course to them, ruinous business, they have no option in the matter. Many of them, however, see and admit, that it must make an immense difference in the comfort of the whole people, whether a proportion of them are employed in ploughing, sowing, reaping, &c., another in fashioning those beautiful products that administer to the rational pleasures of all, another in healing the sick, instructing the ignorant, and spreading knowledge in the world, and so on, or whether they are occupied in blowing up soap-bubbles, in which case it is plain that these must be supported at the expense of the rest. All idle lackeys, servants, and retainers, ought in this industrious country to be called the soap-bubble blowers;—and all their employers, the idle sons of rich men, all the expensive fashionable people *who do nothing*; all the lottery people; all the gentlemen (to the honour of the country there are but few) who spend their lives in breeding and training horses to game with, indeed, all idlers, rich or poor ought to have the exclusive honour of carrying on the soap-bubble business.

200. This then is the grand distinction of a free nation, and by far the most important.—That the people

have the power of producing what they choose, in other words, of using their labour as they choose, and then of spending their money, which is the product of their labour, as they choose; and it is because so much depends upon this being rightly understood, that I shall hereafter attempt to prove and illustrate it in the fullest manner.

201. In England great personages sometimes hire three stout, full-grown men as footmen, to stand behind their carriages. These are clothed in rich liveries, with laced coats and hats, and receive wages for their services. The hard-working people must, of course, earn the money that pays these wages, and for the laced coats and hats. In the present condition of England it may be necessary for a portion of the poor people to get a living in this way. But this would be a contemptible employment for three able-bodied men in the United States, where there are so many productive employments, by which labourers may *increase property*. This is a specimen of the worthless occupations which consume the labour, and cause the poverty of the people.

So different is the condition of the United States from that of the greater part of the civilized world, that the labourers here are the arbiters of their own destiny, and of that of the country; they and they alone, have the power to decide what occupations there shall be, how men shall labour, in what trades, at what arts. When I say they have the power, I do not mean the power to pass laws for that purpose; but a much higher and better power, the power of becoming independent, after which men may work as they choose. I shall attempt

CAUSES OF POVERTY. 185

to show hereafter how this power may be exercised in the United States.

202. There is a large class of vicious employments, these do not simply leave the world where it was, but make its condition worse. Some of these have already been alluded to. Men who are employed in keeping and fighting game cocks, or in training horses to game with, or who spend their time in manufacturing and selling little pieces of red or blue paper, which they call lottery tickets, are engaged in occupations, that are at once contemptible and vicious. These do not add to the general store by which the wealth of the world is increased, but they lessen it, by corrupting themselves and their fellow-citizens, and thus taking away their working faculties. The working-men who follow at the heels of these horses and their gaming owners, do not understand what they are about; they have not studied their own interests.

203. There is another large class of employments that may be called *the frivolous employments.* It cannot be said, that the labourers in them produce nothing, but that they produce nothing of substantial value.

These labourers are not idle, that is not the difficulty; no, many of them work like slaves, late and early, and in the most unwholesome occupations. The singularity of this kind of labour is, that though the labourers earn wages, and often very high wages, still that they do not produce any thing of substantial utility, nothing that increases the general wealth, and thereby enables other labourers to fare the better for the work they do. The labour here meant is that immense amount of labour consumed in the *fashions.*

Fashion, fashion, this is the only tyrant left to exercise an uncontrolled sway over the labour of the people of the United States. It is a prodigious passion for finery and fashion, that makes poor and keeps poor very many among us. The rich employ the poor in this kind of ostentation to gratify their love of expense, and to keep up their superiority of appearance, and those who work for small wages do not know that there is any other mode of getting a living. The rich have not been taught any nobler manner of spending their money, nor the poor that there is any way of getting rid of this kind of degradation. There are in every country a given number that want good food, clothes, houses, domestic animals, gardens, and other proper accommodations and enjoyments, but they cannot have them unless they will work to produce them. At present, instead of employing our capital in setting people to work for what they want, or rather should desire, we employ them in fabricating what they do not want, and should not desire. The evil, in respect to these frivolous occupations, is, that neither rich nor poor procure, with their labour or money, the best enjoyments in their power, but like children, cover their bodies, and fill their houses, with baubles, playthings, and trinkets. These playthings, baubles, and trinkets, are not worked for because they possess true beauty, taste, and elegance, nor are they even thought to possess them. Elegance and beauty, always, in due proportion to his ability, are proper objects for the labour of man, rich or poor; and one of the great causes of poverty at present, is, that the poor are not trained to admire, and of course, to labour for them. Much of this beauty is so cheap, and so easily obtained, that the poor would find in it a full indemnity, and more than an indemnity for all their imagined deprivations of the pleasures of the vain and sensual. But this is not our education; on the contrary, the country is deluged with gew-gaws; there is an immense expenditure upon the most frivolous products, in and out of doors, upon our dress, furniture, equipage, &c., for no better reason, than that it is the *fashion*.

204. And what is fashion? The story is: " That one Calthorp purged John Drakes, the shoe-maker of Norwich, (England,) in the time of King Henry the Eighth, of the proud honour which our people have to be of *the gentleman's cut.* The knight bought some fine cloth and sent it to the tailor's to be made. John Drakes, the shoe-maker, seeing the cloth, told the tailor to make him one of the same, and the same fashion. In came the knight, and seeing the shoe-maker's cloth, asked whose it was. The tailor told him, it was the shoe-maker's, and that he wanted a coat after the fashion of the knight's. 'So be it,' said the knight, 'cut mine as full of gashes with your shears as you can.' The shoe-maker could get no time to go to the tailor's till Christmas. Seeing his coat cut full of gashes he began to swear. 'But,' said the tailor, 'I have done nothing but what you bid me, for as Sir Philip's garment is, so is yours.' 'By my latchet,' says John Drakes, ' I will never wear gentlemen's fashions again.' "

205. I shall, for the present, mention one instance only of the expenditure of the *public* money for fashion sake, and that is in the dress of a midshipman in the American navy. When he enters, as midshipman, he must be fourteen years of age, and is, perhaps, the son

of a poor mechanic, farmer, or clergyman. His annual pay, (including rations,) amounted to three hundred and eighteen dollars, previous to the last winter, (1835,) when it was increased by act of Congress.

206. In the year eighteen hundred and thirty, the then Secretary of the Navy, issued an order, regulating the costume of several of the officers; accompanying these orders, were patterns of the dresses required, of the swords, &c. The midshipman's coat, (full dress,) is particularly prescribed; it must be an *embroidered* coat. It is proper that those who pay the expense should know what is meant by an embroidered coat. It is made by working a profusion of silk braid upon the sleeves and other parts of it. This coat cost at the shop of a fashionable tailor, in New-York, in the year eighteen hundred and thirty-two, fifty dollars; the embroidery on it, as a part of that fifty, fifteen. It was said, at that time, that the entire full dress cost one hundred dollars.

Here is a boy, then, that cannot be known as the servant of his country, without an embroidered coat, which is not worn by the president, or any member of Congress, or any private gentleman in the country. Neither is it worn by any member of the House of Commons, or of the House of Lords, upon ordinary occasions. These are declared to be the most simple, well-dressed gentlemen, in England. The first lesson taught to this boy is a lesson of profusion, to spend what he never earned, and more than he ever spent before, and for no better reason, than that this is the warlike fashion; and still the sensible gentlemen of the navy despise this finery, and object to it for the same reason that a farmer or mechanic should. The money that a country pays its public officers should be mainly for good work and no-

CAUSES OF POVERTY. 189

ble deeds; these are always entitled to good wages. Little do the people know of the immense amount of their money paid by government in follies of this kind.

207. Fashion does not mean a good fashion; so far from it, that it is true, that there are admirable articles, such as particular kinds of cloths, and other things, of the most excellent and durable workmanship, that are thrown by, even by those who earn their daily bread, and never resumed, because the fashionable part of the public have abandoned them. Thus, the labourers do not bury their talents merely, but throw them into the sea; they voluntarily give up a power which feeds them and clothes them, which they have gained by their own ingenuity, and hard work, and surrender to vanity and pride the charter of their freedom.

Fashion, therefore, does not imply any thing solidly useful, substantial, or beautiful, (for good and useful fashions should be adopted of course,) nor that it is better than a former, more fit or graceful, but only, generally, that it has been introduced by some insignificant people in London or Paris, and thence transplanted into this country by merchants and traders, to turn the heads and empty the pockets of the people into their own. Besides, there are thousands, not only in London and Paris, but in our own country, whose sole business and trade, is, to get up these fashions, to establish them, to set them afloat in the world. It is by thus following the fashion, not on account of intemperance, or any other vice, not on account of pauper wages, and the necessity, as they think, of turn-outs, that many of our respectable mechanics and labourers, in the factories and elsewhere, sacrifice their independence for a bauble; that our upright and otherwise high-minded farmers, load their estates with mortgages, and finally reduce themselves to beggary; that the very poorest of the people sacrifice their last shilling in some tawdry decoration of the person or fashionable sensuality, who have not sound shoes, or stockings, or a whole flannel garment.

208. In this way the utmost skill and ingenuity of the mechanic and manufacturer are called forth, to keep up the folly, to vary the mode, to change the stripes, to make the thing large or small, round or square, black or white, short or long, or in some other form, or of some other colour than it was before, for it matters not what form or colour, only that the thing be changed. Change, change, is the eternal, clamorous cry of fashion! Much finery is made in Paris and in other parts of France, principally for our market alone, in the same way as we buy and make beads and other trinkets, to send to savage nations. These worthless things first appear among the extravagant people of the cities; the refuse and sweepings are afterwards sent to filch the money of our plain country people. Their life is short, however, perhaps six months, or a year, in town or country, at the end of which time they are discarded; for nothing is so disgusting to the camelion eyes of fashion as old finery —and then it may be seen on the backs of servants, as presents from silly masters and mistresses, who are for ever complaining of bad service, and who thus debauch the morals and tastes of the people whom they hire, by the use of that which is entirely unsuitable to their condition. Another part of this finery is doled out by hard-hearted and dishonest employers, to the very poorest of the people, in pay for *under-price wages;* for none work for ever so little a pittance that some cannot be

CAUSES OF POVERTY. 191

found to work for a less, and thus these miserable people, by their vanity and pride, and running at the heels of the rich, are kept ground into the very dust. If those who call themselves the working-people, would "cut" the fashionable world, they would create a new world for themselves; this would be better than a thousand turn-outs.

209. Of all the ways of spending money, few can be thought of more contemptible than to load the head, neck, ears, body, fingers, feet, with a mass of finery and trumpery, created only by immense labour, and to be discarded for ever upon the first turn in the fashions: if done by the rich, it is extreme folly—if by the poor, certain ruin. The silly people who do not know what their money is worth, or stands for, ought to have a coin of their own, stamped with the figures of houses, horses, family utensils, loaves of bread, &c., to show them that these are the things that they are wasting and destroying. Nothing belittles the mind more than the employment of it upon mere fashion—perhaps an embroidered coat, or a button on it, or a shoe-string, or ribbon, the height of a hat or cap, or something equally insignificant. One of the first objects of those who set on foot ostentatious fashions, is to keep themselves as far off as possible from the common people; for, the moment that these fashions descend to them, the bubble bursts,—there is an end of the fashion for ever!

It is this ostentatious tyrant, fashion, that breaks up families, by setting a barrier between the rich and poorer members of them; it is this same tyrant that destroys that sympathy, and intermingling of different classes at once so benevolent and so necessary in a great republican country; it is this tyrant that severs the bonds of love. Let the whole nation, therefore, cast off "these hair-devices, adulterous trinkets, and monuments of their shame!"—let the labouring people of the United States rise in their might, and proclaim to the world their regeneration!

210. As I intend hereafter to give some account of the fashion trade, I will here make but one statement in regard to it.

It has been supposed that in England, at the present day, "the quantity of gold and silver in actual existence, including utensils, ornaments, jewellery, trinkets, and watches, is three or four times as great as the value of those metals which exists in the form of money."*

What proportion of this immense amount is consumed in baubles, trinkets, useless gilding, and plating, sham ornaments, &c., it is impossible to say. It is certainly not intended to include so useful an article as a watch, the wearing of which has, within a few years, been discarded by a certain portion of fashionable females, and for no better reason than that the common people now wear watches.

211. If the rich only purchased these baubles and trinkets, the evil would not be so great as it is, though that would be bad enough; for every rich man's money may be well employed, not only for his own advantage, but for that of the poor also, and a thousand times as much if he had it. It is impossible that so many human beings should consent to be employed in ministering to each other's vanity, in fabricating trash for their mutual use, did they not suppose that it must be so—that it is best that it should be so. Yes, they believe this to be

* Jacob on the Precious Metals, vol. 1, ch. 9.

CAUSES OF POVERTY. 193

true political economy; and they show some of the greatest teachers to be on their side. Therefore we are taught to waste, destroy, consume, that the poor may find employment. They say, that if the rich did not scatter, the poor would starve; whereas the fact is, that the more wasteful the rich are, the more poor people they create. They say, also, that if the rich did not spend their money like children, they would hoard it like misers. The way, then, to satisfy all men, both rich and poor, that is not for their comfort and happiness to spend any part of their money, or labour, which is the same thing, in the many wicked and stupid ways pointed out in this chapter, is to prove to them that there are a great many *better* ways. The way in which a nation spends its money, will *generally greatly depend* upon what they have produced—upon what they have created by their work, and this will decide what occupations, arts, and trades there shall be. The *useful arts and trades* are those by which alone the great mass of men can prosper. It is plain, then, that the wealth, the comfort, the independence, the respectability, of a people will much depend upon the amount not only, but the kind of productions that their labour creates. The great reformation at present in the world is, that the people are more usefully and virtuously employed than they were, for this produces improvement in all things. These virtuous labours are the foundation of civilization—of our Christian civilization—of the civilization of the present times; not Roman civilization, where the rich hired the poor, at their private social parties, to kill each other in gladiatorial combat, for the entertainment of the company. If, then, there be now an improvement in the labours of the people, in what they are hired to do, it may be greater still, if they labour now more to their own advantage than they once did, they can go on in the same good course. Let this, then, be a cardinal American maxim, that there can never be a limit to the good things which the heart of the people can conceive and execute!

CHAPTER XIII.

BRIEF HISTORY OF LABOUR.

212. As in the last chapter it was stated, that poverty was the natural consequence of the want of labour, of unskilful labour, of the abuse or misapplication of labour, I shall, in this, present some memorable cases from history, to confirm what was then said.

213. By the history of labour is meant, what labourers have been employed in, what they have made, produced, manufactured, or brought about by their labour. This will show whether they have been well or ill-employed; this will prove whether their occupations have been most useful to themselves and to their employers.

214. A beautiful picture, that is intended to improve the heart and the mind, is an object of admiration to all men. It is not meat and drink for the body, but it is one of the best kinds of food for the mind, and the labourer who produces it, or contributes to its production, is worthily employed.

I have seen exposed to public sale in a shop, in New-York, and by a woman, too, the most obscene and vulgar pictures. To make and sell such pictures are detestable occupations for a labouring man; both makers and venders are enemies of all labouring men; their occupations are nuisances. The moment that you see a labouring man, broken down, and an outcast, running about from one shop to another, and begging for employment, you may trace his ruin, in nine times out of ten, to the influence of some such cause upon his passions. The working man, the producer of a great proportion of what is beautiful, elegant, graceful, and ennobling in the world, should hold his head and hands above so mean and impoverishing an employment of his talents. It is he that makes poor people; it is against this employment that the working people must combine.

215. History is the best teacher of economy, as has been said, for it shows that the world is improving, and how it has been improved; it shows how labour has been employed, and how many better things are now done with it, and may still be done with it. It is a great thing to be satisfied that the world is improving; this is one of the most important of all truths in political economy.

216. The religious sentiments of Gibbon, the historian, were not such as to give him the most favourable opinions of human nature, and still he says,—" We may therefore acquiesce in the pleasing conclusion, that every age of the world has increased, and still increases, the real wealth, the *happiness*, the knowledge, and, *perhaps*, the *virtue*, of the human race." He need not have said " perhaps the *virtue*," while he admits that the wealth, the *happiness*, and knowledge, of men have increased.

The Christian system commands us " to use the world, as not abusing it ;" and still how true it is, that in using the world, men have abused each other more than they have the brutes! It is now certain where the great reform lies, and the people of the United States will take care that it is carried on.

217. It is a *labour reform*: It consists, 1st, In ren-

dering it the duty of all men, rich and poor, to be busy and active in some useful, religious, virtuous way, with the head, or hands, or both, according to their talents. One of the greatest abuses of human nature has been, in suffering the rich to be idle; and one of the greatest follies to think, that it is best for them to be idle, in order that their money may be scattered among the poor. If the rich are not employed in working for themselves, they may be in working for others. 2d, In the people working not the many for the few, but the many for the many; in labourers working for themselves, and other labourers. 3d, In working to produce things, that are *property;* things that are useful, good, comfortable, innocent, ennobling to the labouring man, and to all men; that are healthful to the body that improve the mind and heart. Things that make drunkards, gluttons, idlers, which pamper the lust, pride, vanity, and devouring rage for fashion, do not produce these happy results. There is a labour which makes poor, and a labour which makes rich, the labouring people cannot doubt which to choose.

218. The following quotation from Mr. Paley contains a useful lesson that ought to be well considered by the people of the United States. "If you should see a flock of pigeons in a field of corn, and (if, instead of each picking where, and what he liked, taking just as much as it wanted and no more) you should see ninety-and-nine of them gathering all they got into a heap, reserving nothing for themselves, but the *chaff* and the *refuse*, keeping this heap for one and that perhaps the weakest pigeon of the flock, sitting round and looking on, all the winter, whilst this one was devouring, throwing about, and wasting it, and if a pigeon, more hardy and hungry

than the rest, touched a grain of the hoard, all the others instantly flying upon it, and tearing it to pieces; if you should see this, you would see what is every day practised and established among men—among men you see the ninety-and-nine toiling and scraping together a heap of superfluities for one (and this one too, oftentimes the feeblest and worst of the whole set, a child, a woman, a madman, or a fool,) getting nothing for themselves all the while, but a little of the coarsest of the provision, which their own industry produces, looking quietly on, while they see the fruits of all their labours, spent or spoiled, and if one of the number touch, or take a particle of the hoard, the others joining against him, and hanging him for the theft."

219. Let us now see what have been the labours of former times. One of the most signal and ancient proofs of the waste of human labour is found in the Pyramids of Egypt. Of these there are many, but the most remarkable are the three Pyramids of Memphis. The height of the largest is said to be six hundred feet, and the length of its base seven hundred feet. There are said to be in this pyramid cubic feet enough of solid stone, to build a wall of four hundred and fifty miles in extent, three feet high and five inches in thickness; these pyramids are four miles from Cairo. Pliny says that in the building of the largest three hundred and sixty-six thousand men were employed for twenty years.* It is said also, that it covers eleven English acres, and something more.† Pliny said that the pyramids were built from ostentation, and to keep an idle people employed—but we know that people are not idle, who are permitted to

* Beloe's Herodotus, vol. 2, p. 404,—note.
† London Quarterly Review, No. LXVII.

work for themselves, their wives and children, instead of working for the "chaff and the refuse." If the poor people, who worked at these pyramids, had been suffered to labour on their own farms, as the farmers of the United States do, it is not very probable that they would have employed themselves for twenty years, in piling up such enormous stones one upon another. The people of Egypt had good notions of economy, if it be true as Herodotus says, that they "*hated* " the memory of those kings who compelled them to build the pyramids. It is said to have been recorded on one them that the onions, radishes, and garlic, which the labourers consumed in erecting it, cost sixteen hundred talents of silver. This is wretched food, to be sure, for a labouring man employed in laying up such masses of stone, but all labourers must remember that none fare so miserably, as where much of this wretched sort of work is going on, and that if they will build pyramids, or spend their labour about things as useless, they must expect sooner or later to come to no better food, than onions, radishes, and garlic. If the rulers of Egypt instead of giving an account in *money* of the amount which the pyramids cost, had been compelled to set down the number of cart loads, wagon and ship loads of onions, radishes, garlic, and other things, which were eaten and consumed by the labourers, we should have a much more perfect idea of the prodigious destruction of property that took place. The same would be true now of our own destruction of property : people are lost when they count millions in a labyrinth of figures; but if they could see the loads and piles of bread, meat, butter, clothes, &c., that are wasted, defiled, thrown away, moth-eaten, moulded, it would very much change their ideas of the value of economy.

220. And what, after all, was the *use* of the pyramids? They were not erected as temples of religion, as seats of justice, nor as halls of science, but as tombs for dead kings (this is the popular opinion,) who, in Egypt were embalmed and turned into mummies!—the end, then, of all this toil is a mummy!—what disgraceful, ignoble, worthless labours, what a cruelty to force them upon poor suffering men! Though we do not waste our labour in the United States upon so great a scale, we spend no very small part of it, to as little purpose, as the poor Egyptians did, and all the excuse we can make for ourselves is, that it is not so much in the kind of folly, as in the degree that the difference lies.

221. As the Romans were the greatest of all the ancient nations, and as their example is so much held up for our instruction, a few illustrations from their history cannot be unprofitable.

The object, then, is to show, what the Romans brought about by much of their labour, *what it pr duced*, what good it effected, especially to the labourers. To show, then, what the people produced by that portion of their labour, of which a particular account will be given, it will be necessary to exhibit the manners and customs of the people, and to state what kind of government they had.

In the early ages of the Roman people, there was great simplicity in diet, dress, and furniture, but after the people had lost their liberties, they were made the slaves of the pride, lust, and every other degrading passion of the emperors their masters;*—under these masters, the people were compelled to labour, as all other slaves do,

---

* Domestic Manners of the Romans, ch. 7.

that is as the masters order. These labours I shall divide into :

222. First, Those which ministered to the pomp, pride, and vanity of the emperors and great personages. The Emperor " Nero had saloons in the golden palace wainscotted with ivory ; the panels turned on pivots, and showered down flowers and perfumes on the guests, from the reservoirs behind them. The most splendid of those apartments was circular, and its vaulted roof was so constructed, as to imitate the movement of the spheres, which represented a different season of the year as each course was on the table. The supper rooms of Heliogabulus were hung with cloth of gold and silver enriched with jewelry ; the frames of the couches were of massive silver, with mattresses covered with the richest embroidery, and the *tables* and table-services were of pure gold."* This is the prince of whom it is related, that he ordered that all the spiders and mice in Rome should be collected, and that the quantity of the former amounted to ten thousand pounds weight, but that the mice not being very easy to catch, only 11,000 were taken.

223. Second, The labour which was expended in sensuality, in gluttony, drunkenness, &c. The author cited says, "that the cook who had formerly been considered as the meanest of the slaves, became the most important officer of the household, and his art, which before was held in contempt, rose to the rank of a science, the professors of which were so valued, that Pliny says, that the expense of a cook, was equal to that of a

*The same. As this is a cheap and useful book, it can be recommended to every reader, and I refer to it rather, than to more learned authorities.

triumph, and no mortal was so much valued, as the slave who was expert in ruining his master.* Sumptuary laws (that is, laws regulating expense) were passed forbidding these excesses, and the same kind of laws have been continued down nearly to the present day, but without avail, and they are an admonition to the people, that their own virtuous opinion and example are better than all the sumptuary laws in the world.

"At length," says the author, "epicurism reached to such a sickly pitch of refinement, that viands were only esteemed according to their cost."

" Thus, Maltese cranes, and rare singing birds, though hardly eatable, were esteemed great delicacies, and their tongues and brains still greater ; oysters from the coast of Britain were more prized than those taken on their own shore, though the former could never have been eaten fresh : and we are told of a single sur-mullet, (a kind of fish esteemed in proportion to its size) which had reached a size somewhat larger than common, having been sold for a sum equivalent to fifty guineas. Nor was this all, gluttony kept pace with epicurism, and was indulged to such disgusting excess, that emetics were used to enable the stomach already gorged with a full meal, to bear a further load."† It is said of Julius Cæsar, that he vomited after supper, that he might immediately enjoy a repetition of the same pleasure.

" The table of Heliogabulus was regularly served with ragouts of the livers and brains of small birds, the heads of parrots and pheasants, and the tongues of peacocks and nightingales, the carcasses were given to the

* The same.   † The same.

beasts in his menagerie. But our astonishment at the absurdity of this extravagance in a monarch will be lessened, if we reflect upon that of the celebrated Apicius and of Esop, the famous tragic actor, the latter of whom served up a dish filled with birds, which had each been taught either to sing or to speak, and dissolved pearls in the wine which his company drank."*

224. Gluttony, in Rome, appropriated to itself dainties unknown to us. "Snails, and a species of white maggot, found in old timber, were fattened with peculiar care, and served only at the best tables. Fricasseed, sucking puppies, and water-rats, were in great request." "Fish was sometimes brought to table alive, and weighed in the presence of the company, that they might ascertain its value, and enjoy in anticipation the pleasure of feasting on it, when dressed. When any very rare dish was served, the slaves who bore it were decorated with flowers; it was announced with great ceremony, ushered in with music, and received with the joyous acclamations of the expectant guests."†

225. The author, in the thirteenth chapter of his book, says, "That the ancient sobriety of the Romans ceased as soon as the grape became abundant; and excess in wine became so prevalent in Rome, that Pliny speaks of men in polite society, who, after having drunk to repletion, took goblet after goblet, until they regorged it; then re-commenced, and repeated this disgusting essay of their powers several times, at the same sitting."

226. Third, Fashion came in for its portion of the labour of the people of Rome. A woman's toilet and ornaments were called "her world," and it is plain

---

* The same.   † The same.

enough, that the same planet still belongs to our system. Poppæ, the wife of Nero, invented a sort of pomatum or ointment, to preserve her beauty, called from her name, Poppænum, made of asses' milk, in which she used also to bathe. Five hundred asses are said to have been milked daily for this purpose. The ladies, then, wore ear-rings, and necklaces of pearl, and other precious gems, set in gold, as our ladies do.

227. Fourth, The sports and amusements of a country, whether for gratification or indispensable recreation, necessarily and very properly, consume a good deal of the labour of the people. But, those of Rome were cruel, debasing, and wasteful, to the last degree.

Of all these sports, the gladiatorial combats were the greatest delight of the people. They were exhibited in amphitheatres; the largest, was the Colisseum, being five hundred and fifty feet in length, four hundred and seventy feet in breadth, and one hundred and sixty feet in height.* It is supposed to have been able to contain upwards of eighty thousand persons. "a multitude that would stagger belief, did not the vast ruins of the antique fabric still sufficiently attest the accuracy of the calculation."

"The gladiators were originally chosen from among the captives or malefactors; then slaves were trained to the profession; and when the encouragement, which it afterwards received, rendered it lucrative, it was adopted by many free persons."

"When a gladiator was only wounded, he lowered his sword in token of submission, and his doom then depended upon the will of the spectators, who pressed down

* The same, chap. 14.

the thumbs, if they chose to save him; but held them up, if it was their pleasure that he should be slain."

" When killed, or even mortally wounded, he was dragged with a hook from the arena, and thrown into a common receptacle for the carcasses of the miserable beings who were thus slaughtered."

" Nor, let it be supposed, that these brutal exhibitions were confined to the rabble of Rome; the most distinguished among the knights and patricians; the very magistrates and consuls; the emperors themselves, and even senators of rank, sanctioned, by their presence, and joined in the cruel signal of destruction."

" At length, they constituted so material a portion of those festivities, that ten thousand gladiators are said to have fought in Rome alone, during the celebration of Trajan's triumph over the Dacians; and such was the waste of human life, occasioned by these barbarous shows throughout the provinces, that in Europe only, upwards of twenty thousand men have perished by them, in one month."

228. History will show, that where a few have had all the property, it has been abused, of course, that where a few have wallowed in ill-gotten riches, the people have been poor, their employments have been wretched, and vicious too. In such cases, living as they do upon low wages, and these wages not being husbanded, but squandered—they have no option in their employments—they must work, as their masters order, whether *nominal* slaves or not. Then, like the people of Rome, they become a vile rabble, equally pitiable and hateful to all good men; and then, too, not having education and character enough to control the powerful, all are ruined together. Under the head of *wages*, such as

they are in the United States, I hope to be able, hereafter, to present this subject in a useful light.

229. What then was the fate of Rome? Gibbon, the historian, describes her latter end. He says, "that some of the richest of the Roman senators, at the time that Rome was beseiged by the Goths, received from their estates, an annual income of above one hundred and sixty thousand pounds sterling, without computing the stated provision of corn and wine, which had they been sold, might have equalled one-third of the money."*

" That there were many side-boards, in the time of Pliny, which contained more solid silver, than had been transported, by Scipio, from vanquished Carthage;" and still, he says, truly: " That a plenty of glass and linen has diffused more real comfort among the modern nations of Europe, than the senators of Rome could derive from all their refinements of pompous and sensual luxury." " That the coaches of the Romans were often of solid silver, curiously carved and engraved, and the trappings of the mules and horses often embossed with gold. Yet, *pomp and luxury* are often well exchanged for convenience, and a plain, modern coach, that is hung on springs, is much preferable to the silver or gold *carts* of antiquity."

230. Gibbon gives from the pen of a Roman historian, (Ammianus Marcellinus,) an account of the manners of the Roman nobles, just previous to their final destruction.

" Their long robes of silk and purple float in the wind, and as they are agitated by art or accident, they occa-

---

* Gibbon's Roman History, vol. 4, chap. 3.

sionally discover the under garments: the rich tunics with the figures of various animals." " That as soon as these nobles have bathed, they resume their *rings*. They have a contemptuous indifference for the rest of the human species; when they call for warm water, if the slave is tardy, he is chastised with three hundred lashes. At the tables, the birds, and squirrels, and fish, are nicely weighed, and the weight attested by notaries, as an important matter."

From this brief history of the habits and customs of the Romans, who are so often placed in many respects b fore our eyes as an example, we may derive a useful lesson. It is not necessary, that the people of the United States should read all the systems of public economy, in order to understand the subject. The history of the world will give us the best ideas as to the mis-spending of our money or labour, and all who can get a decent education may know something of that.

231. First, It appears plainly, then, that the condition of the people must depend mainly upon what they labour for, whether their labours are of the *useful* class or not, and this truth is to be seen in every country, but no where more clearly, than in the history of the Romans. That great body of labourers whose time was spent in administering to the pride and sensuality of the great men of Rome could of course do nothing for themselves; they laboured for others. They were not farmers, nor mechanics, nor manufacturers in the production of things necessary, useful, healthful, and ornamental to human nature. What they produced was not what the people most wanted; such as good houses, cultivated farms, clothes, education for their children, &c.; the working men who provided the flowers, the perfumes, the cloth

of gold and silver, the rich embroidery, the gold tables, the rare singing birds for pies, who fed the five hundred asses that supplied the milk for the wife of Nero to bathe in, may have been paid wages for their work. Miserable wages, no doubt!—but this was only paying back to the working men, what they themselves had earned, and been robbed of. It was only paying them their own money, for it is plain that Nero, and the great men of Rome whose lives have been described were not working men; they consumed what others produced, they earned nothing themselves. Gladiators, prize-fighters, cock-fighters, gamblers, did not *produce* their own bread, or anything that might be sold for bread. Their bread was produced by the hard-working farmers in the country, or obtained by plunder, which was a great resource to the Roman people, and ever must be to many who will not work. For instance, when Julius Cæsar returned from his African victories, he told the people, that he had subdued a country (in other words plundered it,) that would bring into the public stores two hundred thousand attic measures of wheat, and three millions pounds of oil. The people gave him a triumph, which was followed on his part, with large donations to the soldiers, and diversions for the people. He entertained them at twenty-two thousand tables, and presented them with a numerous show of gladiators and naval fights in honour of his daughter Julia, who had long been dead.*

232. Second, The poverty of the labourers in Rome was just what we might expect, where the people were so miserably employed. In the first place a large portion of these labourers were the poorest of all people, for they

---

* Plutarch's Life of Julius Cæsar.

were slaves. There was scarcely any *middle class* of farmers, mechanics, and manufacturers, who have now become so important and are every day, not only gaining more and more of the property of the world, but increasing the total amount of it. Those who had all the power then were members of the rich patrician families. Such was the poverty of the people, that according to Cicero, there were not two thousand in his day, when the city, and its immediate suburbs are estimated to have contained one million two hundred inhabitants, *who possessed property.** The plebians were oppressed with debt and usury; all property was monopolized by the nobles. Nothing shows more completely what a gulf there was between the rich and poor people of Rome, than the *donations* bestowed upon the latter by the former. Augustus made them many royal presents; upon one occasion he gave four shillings and ten-pence three farthings to the whole populace, not omitting the children; though on former occasions it had not been customary to include any under eleven years of age;† and in his will he left to each of the common men two pounds eight shillings and five pence sterling. There are frequent instances of donations of the like kind from different emperors. What would be the condition of the people of the United States, if the President and other great men were able to make these Roman compliments, and they were degraded enough to receive them? Suppose that the President should, as a parting legacy, bestow upon every man, woman, and child, fifty cents!

* Jacob on the " precious metals " vol. 1 ch. 9—cites Cicero de Officiis, II., 21.
† The same.

In presenting this account of the manner in which the people of Rome were deprived of the benefit of their own labours, it must not be supposed that any thing like a complete view is intended to be given of the economical condition of the Romans. Some of those facts only which are most notorious, most certainly to be relied on, and which can be most easily understood have been stated.

233. *War* is one of the great gulfs in which the property of the people is constantly swallowed up, and this was true in Rome beyond almost all other countries. But it was *slavery* that, among the Romans, was, above all other things, the cause of the abominations that have been mentioned: of the destruction of the property of the people, and finally of the extinction of the Roman name and power.

234. I shall, at present, give but one more specimen and that from modern history, of the manner in which the labour of the people is wasted upon a great scale, in those countries in which they are not their own masters. It is from the history of Louis the fourteenth of France, which is more particularly interesting to the people of the United States, from the relation in which the French revolution stands to ours. Louis the fourteenth died in the year 1715, aged 77 years. His expensive follies and destructive wars, in connection with those of his successor, Louis the fifteenth, paved the way for the French revolution. The first great step of it was taken in the reign of the decapitated monarch, Louis the sixteenth, in calling together the *notables*, and this was caused by the disorder of the finances, which meant nothing more, than that the country was insolvent, and that the people were oppressed with taxes, caused

BRIEF HISTORY OF LABOUR. 211

by the wanton uses which had been made of their labour and property.

235. Voltaire, in his history of the reign of Louis the the fourteenth, gives an account of the fête of Versailles, then a royal palace about twelve miles from Paris. This palace (a portion of which is now used as a gallery for pictures) with its appendages, cost *nine hundred millions of francs ;* * about one hundred and eighty millions of dollars, and thus the people had, for so much worth of their labour, a chateau; the greater part of which is now deserted. This fête was got up by Louis, in the year 1664, in honour of his young mistress, Mademoiselle de la Vallière.

236. The following is the statement of the historian. On the fifth day of May of that year, the king came to Versailles with all the court, composed of six hundred persons, whose expenses with that of all their attendants were defrayed. "The cavalcade was followed by a gilded chariot ten feet high, five feet wide, and twenty four feet long representing the chariot of the sun ; the four ages of gold, silver, brass and iron, the celestial signs, the seasons, the hours following the chariot. Every thing was personified. Shepherds carried pieces of the list, which they adjusted to the sound of trumpets; to which succeeded, at intervals, the music of pipes and violins. Some persons, who followed the car of Apollo, recited to the queens, verses suitable to the place, the time, the king, the ladies. This course being finished, and the night arriving, four thousand torches illuminated the place where the fête was held. The tables were served by two hundred personages who (after the

* Say's Political Economy, book 3d, chap. 6, note.

heathen mythology) represented the seasons, the gods of the country, and the forest; the nymphs of the woods, the shepherds, those who harvest the grapes, and the reapers.

Pan and Diana advanced upon a moving mountain, and then descended in order to place upon the tables, the greatest delicacies of the country and the forest. Behind the tables, in a semicircle arose suddenly a theatre filled with those who had charge of the concert. The arcades which surrounded the tables, and the theatre, were ornamented with five hundred green chandeliers of silver, which bore wax candles. A gilded balustrade surrounded the whole. This fete lasted seven days." *

237. Such a use of the labour of the people ended, as might have been expected, in their misery and the bankruptcy of the king. He ordered all the plate to be melted, tables, knives, forks, spoons, chandeliers, &c., he setting the example. The plate had cost *ten* millions, but, when melted, it brought only *three*, upon a sale. † *The labour expended upon the plate* made the difference, which was lost to the people forever. Louis, in order to extricate himself from his difficulties, altered the nominal price of money, as if the United States were to pass a law declaring that half a dollar should pass for a dollar. Louis must have supposed that a king could make money, but by the decree of heaven it is ordered, that those only who employ their faculties usefully shall have that honour. Louis died in disgrace, and Voltaire, the historian, says, that in the three last years of his life, every thing that was memo-

* The Age of Louis the fourteenth, by Voltaire, chap. 18.
† The same.

rable about him was obliterated from the minds of the greater part of his subjects. This should be the fate of every public man in the world, here and every where, whose example or conduct shall tend in any way to bring upon the great body of the people, that unnatural and unnecessary curse, poverty. Public spendthrifts are a scourge to any country. Let the eyes of the people be upon them! for those who will not take care of themselves must be poor stewards for the public.

238. And what is the lesson that we are to learn from this brief history? It is, that multitudes of labourers have been employed in all ages, and still are, in a way best calculated to keep them in poverty; for it is certain, that labourers cannot grow rich, unless riches grow; they alone *grow* riches A greater number of them cannot live in good comfortable houses this year than the last, unless a greater number of good houses be built. If they desire good clothes, they must first make good cloth. All the plate that Louis melted, while used as plate, will neither feed them nor clothe them. Labourers can never expect to improve their condition, unless their labour be mainly expended upon those useful things which they themselves want. The more there are of comforts, such as are useful to human nature, the greater portion will every man get.

239. When we see labourers in that state of poverty to which Louis reduced his subjects, there is nothing loathsome, mean, or wicked, which may not be found among them. So great a number having employed their time, in the service of the rich, in their stables, kitchens, and halls, and not for their own benefit or improvement, their habitations are hovels, their garments

like those of beggars, their manners vulgar and odious, their persons disgusting; and then arise those unfeeling and contemptuous opinions of labour, and the labouring man, which are a disgrace to human nature, and they will continue till the labourers shall, through a just understanding of their interests, rise to that state of dignity and self-respect which of right belongs to the producers of wealth.

CHAPTER XIV.

LABOUR IN THE UNITED STATES.

240. In all inquiries concerning economy, labour stands foremost as the subject of the greatest importance; and it is for this reason that I have, throughout, attempted to show how criminal and senseless it is for the people to spend much of their labour as they do at present; and how certain it is, that when they come to reflect upon the subject, they will in some very important particulars turn it to a better account.

Who does not see, that he spends his labour for much that he does not want; for things that are not to his taste; or that are not becoming his condition, education, property; and that this is because he is a slave of fashion, because he looks with other people's eyes, or for some no better cause? Who can take a view of his own house, or garden, or farm; or cast a glance into his city, village, or town, and not see how many useful and perhaps admirable things are wanting, which people really suffer from not possessing? For instance, what a blessing an abundance of pure water would be in the great metropolis of our country, New-York; that should supply cheaply, not only the ordinary wants of the people, who are now so destitute of that essential article, that some boarding-houses pay annually more than a hundred dollars for water drawn in carts!—but should also furnish those invaluable blessings, *public baths*, to the great body of the citizens. How much more worthy and noble an expenditure of some of the wealth of that prosperous city would this be, than so many others which we are compelled to witness. Let any man or citizen then compare the things that are wanting, that he begs, or borrows, or rationally longs for, with the things that he has, with many that he daily uses, eats, drinks, wears; this will bring him to some just reflections upon economy, if any thing will. Let him place his debts on one side (if he has any), and his finery, and baby-house parlour furniture on the other; compare his insignificant expenses, with his useful ones. Let him put his segars, tobacco, snuff, champagne, expensive food, wines, and strong drink, *an immense proportion of which, as they are now used,* are poison to his health; I say, let him put these into one scale, and his independence, peace of mind, and true dignity, as a labourer in the other, and then see which will kick the beam. These considerations are worthy the attention of workingmen, if any are. If anything deserves to be reflected upon deeply and dispassionately by the industrious people of the United States, it is *labour*. It is for this reason, that I have endeavoured constantly to keep the subject of labour before the reader. It is well worth the attention of the people of the United States to know how to live with a dignity becoming their free institutions, and the sacrifices they have made to gain them, which can be done only by a thorough knowledge of the subject of *labour;* how they shall labour; what they shall labour to obtain; who must labour; what kind of labour the great multitude, the people, the many, are destined to, in the United States.

241. As this is a young country, and we are just beginning the world, the people will not fail to look into

other countries, and see how they, by the most wretched laws, monopolies, usages, and fashions, have been deprived of a large portion of nature's natural bounties; so that, in a world teeming with abundance to such a degree, that taking one acre with another, cultivated and uncultivated, the earth may produce a hundred or a thousand times as much as at present, (as has been stated before,) still so wretched are the majority, so poor, so little do they know or care what their labour goes for, and so little have those the power at present of escaping from the slavery under which they lie, that do know or care; that perhaps not one in ten of this vast multitude can afford to give a loaf of bread. One of the first lessons, then, to be taught in economy is, that the *existing* state of poverty throughout the world is wholly unnecessary?

242. Nothing but the practice of a true economy on the part of those who understand it, and the gaining of a just knowledge of it, by those who do not, can secure to them, not their *lost* rights, for these rights have never been found, but their natural rights, the rights and plenty which God intended for them. How, then, may the working men keep clear, not altogether, but of the miserable *degree* of poverty to which they are subject? *So far as the utility of labour is concerned in the question*, that has every where been inculcated in this book. It is by labouring for what they ought, that is, for what they want or ought to want, and then expending the produce of their labour for what they want, or ought to want; which implies that they should lay up a proper portion of their wages. No one, who knows anything of the habits of the working people, does not know that this is not the case at present. In its proper

place hereafter, I intend to compare wages with expenses, such as they are, or ought to be.

243. If the people of middling property ask how they came to have the power and influence in the United States which we all see they have, they will find the answer to be very easy; it is because they have the wealth or a great portion of it; this being diffused among the farmers, mechanics and other labouring people with a degree of equality unknown in any other civilized country. To such a degree have they the power, that in the free States, universal suffrage, or what amounts nearly to the same thing is adopted. But in Great Britain and Ireland, and in France, notwithstanding the great reforms that have taken place in these countries; there are in the former with a population of 24,271,763* but about 800,000 voters and in the latter with 32,000,000 about 170,000 voters. The state of New-York with a population of 1,919,132, by the census of 1830, gave, at the govenor's election in 1832, 323,082 votes.†

244. In France, the payment of a tax of two hundred francs of direct taxes, or about forty dollars, is a necessary qualification for a voter for a member of the chamber of deputies; such a qualification here would exclude nearly all the farmers of the United States from voting for members of congress. No working people on earth ever gained and maintained the right of voting, till they had first gained a large portion of the property of the country. The liberties of Europe have gone on hand in hand to this moment with the successful labour of the

---

* Population returns for 1831.—Marshall's Digest of Population, &c. London, 1833. † William's Register.

LABOUR IN THE UNITED STATES. 219

people. The more property the people get, the more votes they will have, and deserve to have; and the reason why reform is going on at present in England is, that, miserable as numbers of the working people are in that country, they possess ten times, and perhaps a greater proportion of all the property of the country, than belonged to them five centuries ago.

It has been stated, that, in England, in the middle ages, seven-tenths of the whole kingdom were in the hands of the clergy.*

245. Labour is a different thing in the United States, from what it is in most other countries. What is this difference, and what is the cause of it?

Let us now see then what is meant in the United States by the words "labouring people," "working people," "labouring classes;" in other words, which are the "labouring classes," who are the "working men," in the United States? This will, of course, create an inquiry into the subject of different kinds of labour, as mental labour, manual labour, &c.

The following definition has been given of one portion of the labouring people. It is said,—" That the people of a nation fall under some one of these classes. First, those who live by *muscular exertion or simple labour*, whose time is their fortune, and who may be said to sell their time, or to exert their bodily powers in a certain way, for one or more hours, days, months, or years, and who are to be paid therefor an agreed sum, under the name of *wages*. This last, part with nothing in the nature of property, they receive property, that is money, or its equivalent, for the service which they render to other

---

* Wade's History of the Middle and Working Classes, ch. 4.

persons, or for the time and labour which they expend on the property of others. This class of persons is a large one throughout the world, in proportion more numerous in the old world, than in America. It is divisible into other classes, but the distinction which includes all and separates all from other classes, *is that they dispose of time for wages.*"—" The second class, are those who use bodily powers by means of mechanical instruments, in changing the materials which come from the hand of Nature into such forms and fitness for use as the wants of mankind require," &c.—" This class includes all who are engaged in the mechanic arts,"* &c. &c.

The definition given is neither an accurate nor favourable one of any labouring man in the world, much less of labouring people in the United States. This account of the labouring man is intended, no doubt, to include mainly day-labourers (though strictly it answers to none) and servants; for these, *less* than most others, " use mechanical instruments in changing the materials which come from the hand of Nature, into such forms and fitness for use, as the wants of mankind require."

246. In speaking of those who live by muscular exertion, or simple labour, it is said, " But the distinction which includes all, and separates all from other classes, is, that they dispose of time for wages."

It is important that we should understand what wages are, and who live by wages. Wages, in its common acceptation, *is pay for service*; it is pay for labour and

---

* Political Class-Book, by Wm. Sullivan, ch. 27, sect. 345-6. This is the production of an accomplished, excellent man who is the Author of very useful books, and a lover of his fellow-creatures, whether labouring men or not.

time expended in the business of another, and generally under the direction of that other. It is what a hired man receives; it is what any labourer receives when he exchanges mental and bodily labour for money, or other recompense. In this sense a man's wages are his earnings; in this sense clergymen, lawyers, and physicians, *live by wages*, as labourers. They not only live by wages, or by what they earn by their labour, but they are obliged to get their living by earnings, in the business of others, and *under their control and direction*, so that they may strictly be said to be *hired* men. Those who are included in these professions, therefore, will be compelled to realize, that, in the United States, they take rank with labourers, though it be undoubtedly true that one class of labourers is higher than another.

To show what the Christian sense of labour and wages was, it is said in the scriptures, that when Christ sent forth his disciples to preach the gospel, it was declared "that the labourer was worthy of his hire." It is true, then, in the best and strictest sense, that the great body of the people of the United States are *working people*. If a man must work to get his living, if he must live by effort and anxiety of mind, and toil of body, it makes no difference as to his being called a working man, whether he earns one or ten dollars a-day, whether he be a domestic servant, with ten dollar monthly wages, or the superintendent of a factory, with a yearly salary of three thousand dollars. The latter may, and sometimes does, work much the hardest of the two.

247. *Farmers* make up the greatest class of labourers in the United States, who cannot be said to work for *wages*. They are, in the highest and best sense, inde-

pendent labourers; they are not hirelings, as all may be said to be who are employed by others, to exchange labour and time for wages or money.

The moral and intellectual condition of the farmer in the United States is peculiar, and worthy of the most serious consideration. He is not obliged to get a living under the eye, direction, or control of another; to eat, to get up, and to lie down at the ring of a factory bell; nor is he called upon to perform this or that hard, disgusting, or immoral action, at the beck of clients, patients, and parishioners, as lawyers, physicians, and clergymen, sometimes are. It is this, which gives the farmer a real independence, a noble courage and fearlessness in being frank and above-board, in saying and doing what is right, without first looking to this or that great man for his opinion, that those alone understand who have lived among them; it is this that gives him a heart and mind corresponding in strength with the stability of his possessions. One of the first prayers is, "lead us not into temptation:" they have fewer temptations than men generally have who live by traffic, their business operations being usually confined to a few articles sold periodically, the price of which is well known.

Although all classes have their peculiar virtues and vices, still it is as true that some are more virtuous than others, as that some have better opportunities for education, and fewer temptations than others. This is the farmer's distinction; both philosophy and common sense have assented to the fact of the superior virtue of the independent cultivator of the earth; of him whose life is spent in the midst of its bounties and beauties.

Lawyers, physicians, merchants, manufacturers, are richer, upon an average, than farmers in the United States;

but the benign power which springs from the superior morals and intelligence that flow from the regular tilling of the earth by the owner of it, is constantly increasing here, and the farmer will take care that it shall never be less.

248. Let us now go back to the definition given of a portion of the labouring people. It is said of a part, that they live by "muscular exertion, or simple labour." This is not true even of the slave; it is true only of the brute. One of the most important distinctions among labourers arises from the *difference in their wages;* which difference proceeds by far more from the difference there is in the intelligence and fidelity of one man and another, than from the superior bodily strength, or muscular exertion, which one man has over another. Virtue and intelligence not only give one man better wages than another, but they also give greater wages in one country than another.

249. As to the humbler classes of labourers, it is true that they all have something more to exchange for their wages than " muscular strength, simple labour, and time ;" and this is true of sailors, soldiers, farmers' hired men, servants, and all day-labourers of every description. With many of these, individual virtues and talents are the regulators of wages. Fortunately for labourers, these are articles that bear a high price in the labour-market. What would become of us if we could not trust to the integrity, affection, truth, and fidelity of these labouring men, many of whom are at once our servants and fellow-citizens, and whom the proudest of us are compelled to pronounce our equals by nature?

250. *Servants.*—One of the humblest class of labourers known in the United States is that of domestic

servants. This is a class that exists in every civilized country in the world, and always will exist. This is a real distinction, founded in nature, as soon as the different kinds of business that flourish in a great country spring up. Civilization is nature—it is natural that men should be divided into different professions and employments. This is one form of nature; in the Indian wigwam we see another—there are no domestic servants there. It is idle, then, for the people of the United States to revolt against what is natural and proper—they must submit to it. It is as certain that there must be higher and lower classes, as that there are hills and valleys, small trees and great ones. If one man gets more knowledge than another, he will be greater, he will be more powerful; he will get more property, and property is power; common sense teaches that, and no one will deny it. Common sense teaches, that the time of the President of the United States ought not to be spent in boiling his tea-kettle; and that a man, whose business it is to administer justice as a judge, or set broken bones as a surgeon, has not the time to clean his own house and stables. Here, then is the foundation of higher and lower classes.

251. As there must be higher and lower classes, it is Providence that assigns us our places in the one or the other; but he does not order us to remain there; on the contrary, he directs us to be careful and diligent to get wisdom and education, so that we may advance. At the same time, the world is so regulated, that very many will remain in that situation in which they were born, and where, devoting themselves to one occupation alone, their labour, for that reason, becomes most productive.

The higher situations in life are meant to be the rewards that shall urge men on to exertion—these are so many prizes to superior virtue, skill, and industry.

252. This, then, is the great consolation in the United States to every working man, that nearly every other man is a labourer also; and that all, without distinction, have many opportunities of elevating themselves, of passing from one business to another, from one class to another. This is the true plan of a free government,—it is, that in the law all are equal, and that there shall be no institutions *by law* that shall make men unequal. To this plan we have not conformed in all things, as will be clearly shown. But still we are conforming, more and more to this perfect liberty, which alone can satisfy the people, and give peace; for experience shows, that one man will not submit quietly to receive the yoke from another, nor will any yield to the principle of unequal privileges.

253. It is the power of *self-elevation*, then, that is one of the grand distinctions of the people of the United States. And in what way does this take place? There is but one *true* way—it is in the acquisition of property, virtue, and education; but it is property that gives the means of education, which, in its turn, creates more property. When industrious, virtuous, young men rise in this country, it is nine times in ten by husbanding their wages, and thus furnishing them with a capital for a higher and larger business.

In the factories of New England, very large numbers may annually lay up half their wages; many much more, and still live in a manner becoming their station. These wages, laid up for a few years, will enable the men, either to settle as farmers in the new states, or to undertake an independent business in the old. In some parts of the country this takes place constantly. A first-rate young man, in Massachusetts, hired to a farmer, earns one hundred and forty or fifty dollars a-year; if he is determined upon success, he will not spend more than fifty or sixty, and he lays up ninety or a hundred. At the end, then, of five or six years, he is amply provided with the means of becoming an independent farmer in the new states, where he buys land at the government price of a dollar and a quarter an acre.

A new world may be provided for labourers in factories, journeymen mechanics, servants, day-labourers, and all who live upon small wages, but they must first know what economy is, and what they *can* do, and then they must work out their own salvation. The house that a man builds for himself is a very different thing from that which another builds for him.

254. In Europe, the common rule is, once a servant, always a servant; once a mechanic, always a mechanic; once a tenant, always a tenant; and is not this an infamous usurpation? Let a man be born in one station or another, let him be rich or poor, does he not desire the power of rising; has not God given him the power of self-elevation; does he not long to advance in the scale of existence; is it not best that he should advance, if he has the talent to change one business for another, to his advantage, shall he not be allowed to do it; is it not best for the whole that he should have this privilege? Is it not a beneficent arrangement in nature, that all should have the opportunity of moving forward? And, if so, is it not a heartless, cruel thing, to keep down a virtuous man, to stifle his ambition, to prostrate his mind, by depriving him of all hope of bettering his con-

dition? Never did a more grovelling policy creep into the world than this of keeping labouring people "in their places," as it is called.

255. What is meant by a *manual* labourer; who are manual labourers in the United States? Strictly speaking, we have seen, that there is no *mere* manual labourer, for no intelligent creature works with his *hands* alone. But, there is *this* distinction: some labourers work more with their *hands* and less with their *minds* than others. A judge, a lawyer, a painter, a sculptor, a musician, *labours* most with his mind, though his business may require that he should use his hands and bodily powers constantly.

A man, therefore, who labours with his hands mainly, whose business requires, *comparatively*, but little mind or education, is said to be a *manual* labourer. The more ideas, the more mind a man has, the better for him: all agree to that; so, also, the more a man *labours* with his mind, which is mental labour, and the less with his hands, which is bodily labour, the higher he is in the scale of labourers: all must agree to that, whether they will or no. This is a real distinction in nature, and can no more be got rid of by laws, constitutions, and form of government, than the complexion of the face, or colour of the eyes. This is a distinction founded upon individual character; it is the most valuable of all distinctions, for it leads men, above all things, to the cultivation of their minds, and impels the people of the United States to a desire for universal education. It is upon this ground, that there ever have been, and ever will be, high and low, rich and poor, masters and servants, officers and their men, masters of ships and their crews, farmers and their labourers, master mechanics and journeymen, manufacturers and their workmen. These are a part of the higher and lower classes in every country.

256. What then is the true principle upon this subject of grades and classes, as to who shall be high and who shall be low? It is that every man should have perfect freedom, unrestrained by monopoly or any unjust privilege, to exert his talents and raise himself to any height that he can. But this is not wholly the case, even in this favoured country, as will be shown hereafter.

257. Let us pursue the subject of labour, and take care that our minds are not filled with ideas that belong to other countries; labour has no where in the world the same ideas attached to it, that it has in the United States. For the want of understanding the subject, there is a good deal of uneasiness, and there are some serious evils. These errors and evils, though slowly, perhaps, will certainly be corrected.

258. Let us, then, go back to the case of the farmer. In a former chapter, there is a brief mention of what farmers are in most other countries. They are but a kind of upper servants on the land; they are tenants, and as they hold at the will of their landlords, they must till their farms as they direct. It is, therefore, the head of the landlord, and the hands of the tenant, that cultivate the earth in those countries. In such countries, it is very natural that such a farmer should be called a *mere* manual labourer; his degradation follows from having no certain possessions, and from being directed by another mind instead of his own. To transfer, then, this idea of *manual* labour to our country is a very unhappy perversion of the truth.

259. Let us now see more particularly what a farmer is in the United States. There are very few in the United States who are usually called gentlemen farmers, which means here, a man who is not obliged to work on his farm. The common farmer of the country is a manual labourer in the sense, that he is a *working* man, with his hands, with all his bodily powers; he works with his hired men, late and early; he does all the kinds of work that hired men do; there is nothing in the way of work on his farm, that some people look upon as dirty and disagreeable, that he is not commonly engaged in; he often does his own chores: work that naturally belongs to children. This is one-half of the farmer, if you please, that is, the *manual labourer;* and now let us look at the *mental labourer.* He is the lord of his own soil, "the monarch of all he surveys" within his own bounds. Every thing on his farm, therefore, is subject to his will; he makes his farm, a grain farm, a sheep farm, a dairy farm, at his pleasure; he, therefore, must count the cost; he must educate himself to be an economical farmer, or he is very certain to be a broken-down farmer. These duties throw upon him the same kind of responsibility that belongs to the greatest man in the country, that of maintaining his rank. It is no shame to any man not to be able to rank as high as a farmer: but it is a deep disgrace to a farmer unnecessarily to lose his rank, to surrender his paternal acres to a speculator, or bank, or insurance office, at half price, and then be driven into the wilderness, because he does not understand farming, and will not economize and live within his earnings.

260. This is the *social* condition of the farmer, and

now what is his *political* condition, for this has much to do with his character as a labourer?

In most of the free States, something approaching very nearly to universal suffrage is adopted; almost every citizen of age votes upon every subject that comes before the people in the towns. These towns are strictly perfect democracies; in their town-meetings the people act in their original democratic character, and not by their representatives; it is here, that the great power and influence of the farmer first appears. To be satisfied of this, it is only necessary to be familiar with these assemblies; the silence, order, decency, and despatch, with which many of them are conducted, ought to put to shame some that claim to be much higher. In these assemblies, in many of the States, the farmers are clothed with more power, (as far as belongs to the towns to confer) than any other class, and probably more than all others. Here the farmer is chosen selectman, supervisor, road-master, surveyor of high-ways, poor-master, school committee-man, assessor and collector of taxes, &c., and a member of the state legislature in those states, in which there is a town representation. In some of the state legislatures, in the northern and western states, the farmers are a much more numerous class than all others. Here then is the foundation of the influence which the farmer exercises over political affairs, and no one should be ignorant how extensive this is! Long may it be exercised in its full vigour!

261. It is the greater or less amount of mind, of ideas, of education, of virtue, that belongs to a trade, art, or business, that constitutes the true foundation of rank, and this is not a rank or degree which a man can alter

by quackery, or by any means, but by his own improvement, nor is it desirable that he should.

Those who pursue the elegant arts, are called artists, such as, sculptors, painters, musicians, &c., they, also, as well as the farmer, work with their hands, but their *labour* is mainly mental. Theirs are some of the best productions of superfluous wealth, after we are supplied with the necessaries and comforts of life; and should take the place of those petty baubles and trinkets, and outside finery, by which so many people think to equalize all things, but they cannot. Many of these artists earn great wages, and it is because their productions are those beautiful creations that are gazed at, and sought for, not by the rich and luxurious alone, but by all mankind. Congress has resolved to pay our young countryman, Greenough, $25,000 for a statue of Washington, as has already been stated. In equalling the anticipations of his countrymen, may it become an imperishable monument of genius and gratitude!

It will be said, that these are high wages, but we must remember, *that one of the great laws of wages is*, that they are regulated by the circumstance of the number who can execute the thing to be done. Besides if it cost a great price, it is expected that it will have a great value, and not be sent to auction after two or three years, as some people now dispose of their fine furniture. These artists, then, are not only labourers, *but producers of wealth*, of what is ennobling to man, whether he works most with his hands or his mind, call him what you will, a manual labourer or not.

262. What then is the great and peculiar distinction that the people of the United States have established by their institutions? What is that here, which is to

found in none of the great nations of the earth; what is that beneficent principle which here is going on to produce all that equality, that fair partition of the bounties of life of which nature admits? It is, that the whole people are compelled to labour, and though a few individuals may become rich by lucky speculation, fortunate trade, or inheritance, there is no *class* that is not compelled to work. There is no king, nobility, or gentry, or favoured class by any other name, that are supported at the public expense. These favoured classes in other countries make up the governing class, the idle class, the spending class. It is shocking to think of the havoc they make of the wealth of the people, living as they do upon dainties, which cost ten or perhaps a hundred times more of the labour of the people, than the most healthful provisions. Still, among all mankind goodness is to be found, and in the aristrocratic or despotic countries, there are individuals in the governing class who labour as worthily and industriously as any others; all diligent, faithful public officers in every country truly belong to the industrious class; they are a part of the working bees; they contribute honourably to the great stock of wealth, of good things. Good government is one of these.

263. The idle class will be in proportion to the riches of the people, and to the numbers of idlers that the people agree to support at the public expense. In England there is a debt of eight hundred million pounds sterling; this, in one way and another, supports a great many idlers. In England there are idlers who pay from two to four thousand pounds sterling for a pack of hounds, a thousand guineas for twenty couple of hounds, and, on

an average, two hundred guineas for hunting horses.* All idlers are, of course, supported at the expense of the industrious.

264. Blackstone in his commentaries gives the following table of precedence, which shows the various ranks and degrees in England.†

TABLE OF PRECEDENCE.

The king's children and grand-chil-	Bishop of Durham.
" brethren. [dren.	Bishop of Winchester.
" uncles.	Bishops.
" nephews.	Secretary of State, if baron.
Archbishop of Canterbury.	Barons.
Lord Chancellor or Keeper, if baron.	Speaker of the House of Commons.
Archbishop of York.	Lords Commissioner of Great Seal.
Lord Treasurer, if baron.	Viscounts' eldest sons.
Lord President of Council, if baron.	Earls' younger sons.
Lord Privy Seal, if baron.	Barons' eldest sons.
Lord Great Chamberlain.	Knights of the Garter.
Lord High Constable.	Privy Counsellors.
Lord Marshal.	Chancellor of the Exchequer.
Lord Admiral.	Chancellor of the Duchy.
Lord Steward of the Household.	Chief Justice of the King's Bench.
Lord Chamberlain of the Household.	Master of the Rolls.
Dukes.	Chief Justice of the Common Pleas.
Marquisses.	Chief Baron of the Exchequer.
Dukes' eldest sons.	Judges and Barons of the Coif.
Earls.	Knights' Bannerets, royal.
Marquisses' eldest sons.	Viscounts' younger sons.
Dukes' younger sons.	Barons' younger sons.
Viscounts.	Bannerets.
Earls' eldest sons.	Knights' Bannerets.
Marquisses' younger sons.	Knights of the Bath.
Secretary of State, if bishop.	Knights' Bachelors.
Bishop of London.	Baronets' eldest sons.

* See an account of Fox-hunting at Melton Mowbray, in England. London Quarterly, 1832, No. XCIII.

† Rights of Persons, chap. 12.

Knights' eldest sons.	Esquires.
Baronets' younger sons.	Gentlemen.
Knights' younger sons.	Yeomen.
Colonels.	Tradesmen.
Sergeants at Law.	Artificers.
Doctors.	Labourers.

Thus, we see, that the yeoman, (farmers,) tradesmen, artificers, and labourers, in this "Corinthian Pillar," as Mr. Burke calls it, are put last; in this unnatural, perverted order, the first, the original, the greatest producers of wealth, are placed beneath many who do nothing for the good of mankind. England must rid herself of such barbarism or sink beneath it. "As for *gentlemen*," says Sir Thomas Smith, "they may be made good, cheap, in this kingdom: for whoever studieth the laws of the realm, who studieth in universities, who professeth the liberal sciences, and (to be short) *who can live idly* and without *manual labour*, and who will bear the port, charge, and countenance of a gentleman, he shall be called master, and shall be taken for a gentleman."* Thus, we see how the idle classes are made up in those countries which yet support them.

265. But, why should there be any idle class, or why should any class be exempted from contributing its share to the public wealth? why should not every class be compelled to work?

The answer, in England and in those countries where the idle classes exist, is,—

"That if all are obliged to work, all will be compelled to work for the *necessaries* of life, all will be brought down to manual labour, to *servile* labour, as it is called;

---

* The same.

none will have leisure to improve their minds, to study, to read, to cultivate the arts, to instruct the ignorant, to become philosophers; to contrive canals, rail-roads, and other improvements; to write good books, to make fine gardens, pictures, statues, &c., &c.

On the contrary, what is the fact? Are not the working people, are not those who have no incomes provided for them, but who are obliged to labour for their daily bread, the people who do most to cultivate their own minds and those of their fellow-men; do not those who have the stimulus of necessity to urge them on, make up that class who study most, read most; are they not the philosophers and inventors; are they not the artists, the architects, sculptors, painters, poets, &c.? There can be but one answer to these questions in any country in the world.

266. There are some people in this country who think that the farmers, mechanics, manufacturers, and others, whom they call labourers, are the only producers of wealth. But, as this is a lamentable error, that creates heart-burnings in different classes, it must be wholly rooted out of the country.

Is not the judge, lawyer, sheriff, constable, who administers the law that protects all working-men from thieves, robbers, and murderers, himself a working man? Is not the surgeon, who sets the broken bones of a working-man, one, also? Is not a physician, who restores a working-man to health, and enables him to go to his work again, the cause of wealth?

There arises here, then, another question: who furnish the funds, who earn the money, that supports these working people that are neither farmers, mechanics, merchants, or manufacturers? The answer is plain: they, the working people, furnish the funds; they earn the money; some of them are the public men, magistrates, lawyers, physicians, surgeons, &c., &c., that no great and prosperous country can live without; some are those who produce those thousands of beautiful things in the arts, that the merchants, farmers, mechanics, and manufacturers cannot produce, but are willing to buy and to pay for, *out of that surplus which they create*. This explains the mystery, if any mystery there be, of the rise and progress of all the arts, which spring up as soon as the merchants, farmers, mechanics, and manufacturers, are supplied with the common conveniences and necessaries of life; that is, after obtaining these, they are willing to work for something more.

Thus, we see, how, in the United States, the working-men are the patrons of the working-men, and that we do not require an idle class, a spending class, of dukes and earls, to hold the purse, first taking out what they choose, and then decreeing the prizes and honours to the labourer. Thus, we see, too, how the working-men, in the United States, *combined*, pay Greenough twenty-five thousand dollars for a statue of Washington; and Irving, and Cooper, many thousand for those beautiful national works that have proceeded from their pens. An abridgement of Irving's History of Columbus, is a school book in the common district schools in the state of New-York.

The greatest lesson which the working men can learn, is, how to *combine*, how to unite their hands and heads, their purses and their influence, in the good works which they should desire to bring about.

CHAPTER XV.

LABOUR IN THE UNITED STATES, CONTINUED.

267. "MAN is, by nature, an active being. He is made to labour; his whole organization, mental and physical, is that of a hard-working being. Of his mental powers we have no conception, but as certain capacities of intellectual action. His corporeal faculties are contrived for the same end, with astonishing variety of adaptation. Who can look at the muscles of the hand, and doubt that man was made to work?"*

268. As man is made for labour, it is clear that much of his happiness flows from the necessity of it. Let us, then inquire what those fortunate institutions are in the United States, which compel most men to labour. Why is no class exempted from labour? What makes the surprising difference which we see between this nation and others?

269. 1st, It is the equal division of property among children, which, in Chapter IV., is stated to be the law in every state of the Union. It must be remembered, that the law of descent, as well as nearly all the laws which regulate the domestic relations of the people, pro-

* This is the beginning of a beautiful lecture, delivered by Edward Everett, at Charlestown, in 1830.

ceed from the state governments, and not from the government of the United States.

The opposite of our law is the English law of *primogeniture.* " The third rule, or canon of descent (says Blackstone*) is this: that where there are two or more males, in equal degree, the eldest only shall inherit, but the females altogether." This is a part of that feudal law established by William the Conqueror of England.† Primogeniture in males anciently obtained only among the Jews, in whose institutions the eldest son had a double portion of the inheritance. The Greeks, Romans, Britons, Saxons, divided their lands equally.‡ " The insolent prerogative (says Gibbon, speaking of the Roman law of inheritance,) of primogeniture, was unknown;‖ the sexes were placed on a just level; all the sons and daughters were entitled to an equal portion of the patrimonial estate." In France, one of the first acts of their first revolution, was to abolish the law of *primogeniture.*

270. 2d, The second great cause, which happily compels so large a portion of the people to work for a living, is their universal education, their equal education, compared with what exists in other countries. Universal education is the greatest distributor of property, because it enables a great many people to obtain property. As the portions, however, of so many are but moderate, labour is necessary to enable them to get what they want. Thus we see, in the United States, how almost univer-

---

* Blackstone's Commentaries, ch. 14., Tit. Descent.
† The same.
‡ The same.
‖ Gibbon's Rome, vol. 5, ch. XLIV.

sal it is, upon the death of parents, for children to be compelled to work.

Ignorance, which is always found in company with poverty among the people, is the fruitful source of their miseries, for who can turn poverty into learning? how small a portion of the people can obtain education where a handful of men have all the property—where it is divided between the tenants of hovels and palaces!

It may be declared, without a moment's hesitation, that it is in New England, that these truths are most completely illustrated. Compared with the riches of the whole people, nowhere is education found to be so universal, or property so equally distributed. It is universal equal education, as far as that can be, that produces equal minds, as far as those can be; and also equal skill, labour, and wages, as far as it is possible for these to exist. Universal education distributes property more equally than all the other contrivances of which man ever conceived.

271. 3d, The third great cause, which compels so large a portion of the people to work for a living, is, their equal political privileges. These also tend to an equality of property; these confer the rights of choosing public officers, and of enacting laws, and, if they be intelligently and virtuously exercised, no laws can be passed to produce an improper distribution of property. Universal suffrage, or what amounts nearly to the same thing, is now engrafted into the political system of each of the free states.

272. 4th, There is another great cause of that wide diffusion of property in the United States. which creates the necessity of universal labour. It is the ease with which we obtain new lands, and the small expense

incurred in moving to them, that enables so many poor people in the old states to improve their condition, by acquiring wealth.

273. It has been the object of this and the last chapter, to show, that nearly all the people in the United States will be compelled to work, not, however, for mere necessaries, not for things to eat, drink, and wear merely, but (if they will have them) for all that is graceful and beautiful—all that makes a nation virtuous and great. The design has been to show, that there cannot be in the United States, an idle, vicious, spending class, supported at the expense of the great body of the people. Facts show this to be the case here; a single glance at the condition of the people will illustrate it.

274. The town of Stockbridge, in the county of Berkshire, has been mentioned. This county has been settled about a hundred years, and is said to be the first or second-best agricultural county in the state. It will, for the present purpose, with sufficient accuracy, represent the old free states. There are not, in each town in this county, more than one or two persons, at most, who may be said to live upon their incomes, and without labour. It is true, that in the cities, and in certain other parts of the country, there is a larger proportion of the people than is here stated that can live without work, but it is not so great as to affect these statements. It is true also, that a few more than have been named in his part of the country could live upon their incomes, and without labour; but to live without some regular employment or industry is not reputable in the United States; and whether men work from necessity or a sense of duty, if they work fairly, is of little moment to the public. The great concern is to get men to work vir-

tuously, and diligently, either for themselves, or for others, and if that were the case, if we had in the county of Berkshire, a hundred times more than at present who could live upon their incomes, so much the better, so much the richer and happier would the people be on that account.

275. We are so far from having an idle class, that it is becoming less and less reputable to be idle, and the sons of the rich are educated for industrious occupations to a much greater extent than they were thirty or forty years ago. In the cities the same is true, with slight differences. In these there is greater wealth, and compared with the population more persons living upon their incomes without labour than in the country; but their number is so small, even in the largest, that the idle are not a class; they do not make up a society; their influence in every way is very insignificant; they are generally those gaming, dissipated people, that nobody cares for. Labour then is the order of the day in the United States, and the labouring people will take care that it shall never cease to be so. They must show their respect for the industrious, whether *rich or poor ;* if the rich be diligent and virtuous, they have a great power to do good, that the poor can never have.

The people of Europe need not wonder at the unexampled prosperity of the United States. It is not a new country, a virgin soil, fine rivers, and great lakes that bring this about; it is universal labour; it is *free* labour; it is not labour for a master, but for a man's own wife and children; it is the combination of the labour of freemen in useful works; it is happy, contented labour; it is labour with the rewards of industry; it is, that men here are beginning (though, it is painful to say, too slowly) to realize, that they are all fellow-labourers; to feel their natural equality, and to treat each other with a degree of love and respect never before exhibited in the world. It is this which travellers remark, when they speak of the superior kindness of the people. These are the causes which have given such wonderful animation to the industry of the people of the United States. This, however, is but the beginning of the good things we shall see, provided the common people shall tear asunder the fetters of fashion, proclaim their independence, and establish over all classes, their empire of economy virtue and reason, as they certainly may.

276. After all that has been said about the influence of our law of descent upon labour, in producing a just distribution of property; it must be remembered, that laws alone will never bring this about. It was not the case among the ancient nations generally; and in Rome, where property upon the death of the parent was divided equally among the children, it has been stated, what a miserable rabble the common people were, how many were slaves who had no property, and to what an extent nearly all the property fell into the hands of a few.

277. Nothing is more common than the undue importance which people ascribe to laws. Laws remedy but a few evils; laws are a dead letter unless they conform to the general habits of the people; to make the laws of avail, the people must be like the laws. We have had laws against sabbath breaking, lotteries, usury, &c., but their influence has been slight, compared with what the law-giver expected from them. The people, then, must mainly look to themselves; they must be "a law unto themselves;" if they can combine to make good laws, so they may often much more effectually

combine to bring about what they wish without any law; if they can combine for one good purpose, they may for another; if they combine for good ends, none can resist them, if for bad, no resistance is wanted, for they will destroy themselves. *Combination*, then, among the labouring people for wise ends, is what they want; they need no other aid, to accomplish what they reasonably desire.

278. The power of the people of middling property, including the labourers for moderate wages, in the United States, will be uncontrollable, if they are guided by virtue and intelligence, and will practise economy. These may be called *the people*, in the sense that they make up nine-tenths of the people ; they have the power, not only to make the laws, but may say what shall be done in all important respects. They may establish the most essential usages and fashions, direct the rich how they shall spend their money, and make property subservient to themselves, as they will. They must not, however, expect to do this by law, but by setting a noble example of what property should do. Wealth is a mere engine to do good or to do evil, as has been said again and again. It is painful, and disgusting to see how insignificant this power of the people is, compared with what it might, and certainly will be.

279. Those who desire a wise and fair distribution of property must conspire to be economical; to save their wages; to produce the most useful kinds of property; to create something that will last, and may be beneficially distributed; instead of working for trash, and where no work is wanted; being servants where no servants are required; grinding where there is nothing to grind; drawing for water, where there is no water.

They must cease to produce or use that immense amount of trinkets, finery, gewgaws, fashionable trifles, dainties, and poisonous drink (poisonous, in the degree in which it is now used) with which our persons are decorated, our groceries, stores, cellars, kitchens, pantries, and houses, are now too often crammed. This is not the kind of property that wise people wish to see distributed; nor is it property at all in their eyes. So far as this kind of property is imported from foreign nations, and paid for by our products, it is certain, that we may substitute the more useful productions of those nations, for this trash.

280. But how can the farmers, mechanics, labourers in manufactories, and other common labourers, help working to produce this kind of property? They say, that they must live; must have employment; must earn wages; and if the rich merchant, capitalist, and manufacturer, chooses to manufacture it, or import it from foreign countries, what means of prevention have they?

The answer is plain. *They can cease to use it, to buy it, to pay their wages and earnings for it, to the rich capitalist and manufacturer.* As they are the consumers of nine-tenths of it, and probably a much greater proportion, they would soon put an end to the production, if they ceased to be customers for it. It is by not combining and using their power in this way, as they certainly can, that they defeat the just distribution of property, and keep themselves down. Thus they make the rich richer than they should be, and the poor poorer than they need be: thus we see the poor playing into the hands of the rich, and throwing their solitary, hard-earned sixpences and shillings into others' heaps, where there are already thousands; thus we see them running about from tavern to tavern, from store to store, emptying their pockets into those of men who are ten times richer than themselves. All the congresses and legislatures in the world cannot prevent this; the people alone can do it.

This power of the people of middling property, and labourers for small wages, by whom is meant the great body of farmers, manufacturers, mechanics, and common labourers, over the most essential customs, and fashions of the country; over the wealth of the rich, and the capital by which it is produced, is a subject so important, that it will be resumed.

CHAPTER XVI.

SLAVERY.

281. It is not intended, in this place, to discuss slavery, any farther than it is connected with the subjects here treated of.

Some of these have been—the progress of liberty; the emancipation of slaves in former times; the effect of this upon the general prosperity and happiness of the people, and especially the poorer people; labour, and how different a thing it is in the United States from most other countries; the labouring people; the working classes; who are working people in the United States; who must work here; the duty of all men, including the rich, to take their chance in performing all useful labours, as Providence orders; the adaptation of man's hands, limbs, and faculties, to work, thereby showing that he is the happier for it; labour, as being the order of the day in the United States; free labour; happy, contented labour, as the cause of our unexampled wealth; farmers, their superiority as men and citizens, how they work with their hands; manual labour, and whose duty it is to perform it; servants, how they rise in the United States, and how it is best for all men to have an opportunity of doing so; the grovelling policy of keeping any working man down, so that he shall never rise.

Above all, this book treats of the economy of the United States; the *free* United States; and especially the value of property, and how it may be best acquired.

It is plain, then, that the mention of slavery, and some

consideration of it, cannot be excluded from a book like this. To write upon the subjects mentioned, and to take no notice of slavery, would be a violation of candour and truth; it would be unintelligible nonsense. By the census of 1830, there were, in the United States, 2,009,043 slaves. Every candid and generous mind, therefore, will confess, that it is impossible to discuss, with truth, the subject of our free government, and particularly the nature of labour under it, without recognizing the fact, and taking some notice of the effects of slavery.

282. But it has been questioned whether this is a subject fit to be discussed in the *free* states. That can never be a serious question with the people, but rather *how* it shall be discussed. One of the first principles inculcated upon the mind of the American citizen, from the beginning, has been, to speak his opinions freely upon every important subject. We have not seen evil, but good, come from this, wherever good was intended. To say that a subject is not to be discussed, and that men's mouths must be closed, shows that the subject will not bear discussion, and that there is in it some hidden mischief, which will not endure the light. If it be best to have slaves, it is best to write and talk about slavery, provided this be properly done; if slavery be a necessary part of the economy of the United States, it ought to be pointed out, and clearly made known to the people. If slavery be useful to the people of the United States, or any part of them, that can be made plain.

283. If it be true economy to perpetuate slavery in the United States, then proper books should be written to show it; it should be made a part of the education of our youth, to understand the advantages of slavery,—

how it benefits agriculture and other arts,—how it produces great cities, commerce, and manufactures,—how it spreads property among the great body of the people,—how it elevates the labouring man, by making labour respectable,—how it redounds to the peace, quiet, and successful industry of the whole country.

284. If it be so, these books should point out every material circumstance, showing how slavery may be rendered useful and economical; such as, what proportion there should be between the slaves and the free people,—how the slaves should be prevented, by exportation, or otherwise, from increasing beyond such just proportion,—how they should be bred, fed, and clothed, —what labour they should perform, and what the whites,—how far they should be taught to read and write,—what kind and degree of Christian knowledge should be communicated to them, and so on. One thing is certain,—if slavery be a bad thing for one-half of the country, it must be for the whole, though not equally. If one-half of the blood of the body politic be corrupted, it is impossible that the other should remain pure. There can be no such thing as extensive political evil existing in one part of a nation, without spreading its influence, in a greater or less degree over the other, any more than there can be a great sore on a particular limb, without affecting the health of the whole body.

285. The history of the world shows, that men have advanced from one degree of knowledge to another—from one degree of improvement in their condition to another—from one degree of liberty to another; just as the human being advances from infancy to manhood. Because slavery has been allowed, that by no means proves that it always is to be; for God placed men here

for the purpose of improving themselves; and if he had not permitted hurtful things to exist, and to try men's virtue, there would have been nothing for them to do. Slavery is a sin to those only who see it to be so; multitudes do not. To impute wickedness, therefore, to this portion of our southern people, is in a high degree unjust and uncharitable.

286. As liberty is the greatest good in the world to nations; as it is that which deprives the wicked of the power to do evil, and gives to the good the power to do good, we may be as certain that there will be more liberty, as that there will be more people. The best part of the history of the world is little else than the story of how men have become free. As far as we can go back, we find that the great struggle has been to knock off fetters and chains. To perpetuate slavery, therefore, in the United States, is impossible; this just democratic government will put an end to slavery, or slavery will put an end to it. People will give freedom, and become free, as fast as they get knowledge, and no faster. One of the greatest trials to which men are ever put, is to give up unreasonable power over their fellow-creatures.

287. Let us now look back for a moment, and see what the experience of the world has been, and what ideas slavery has inculcated, and still does inulcate, as to *labour;* for it is this which will finally put an end, in this free country, to all controversy upon the subject: the labourers cannot, and will not, suffer their class to be dishonoured here, as it has been, and still is, in other parts of the world.

The most eminent of the ancient nations were filled with slaves. The practice of domestic slavery was early established among the nations of antiquity generally,—

the Egyptians, Phœnicians, Jews, Babylonians, Persians, Greeks, and Romans. That a freeman, a gentleman, an orator, or a man fit to vote and govern, should ever degrade himself so much as to perform manual labour,—as to get a living with his hands, as the farmers, mechanics, and manufacturers of the free states here do, never entered the minds of the Greeks, as a thought to be endured. All the household work was committed to slaves. Most, if not all, trades were carried on by slaves, who were also universally employed in the manufacturing business.* "In well-regulated states, (says Aristotle, one of the wisest of the ancients,) the lower orders of mechanics are not admitted to the rights of citizens."—" In Thebes, there was a law, that no one who, within ten years, had been engaged in retail dealings, should be entitled to a magistracy."†

288. Many of the institutions of the Greeks passed to the Romans. Rome, also, was filled with slaves; and there, also, manual or servile labour was equally degrading.‡ The cultivation of the soil, during the flourishing part of the republic, and under the emperors, also, was almost entirely carried on by slaves.‖

Cicero, says: "That the gains of merchants, as well as of those who live by labour and not skill, are mean and illiberal. Their very merchandize is the badge of their slavery. Those persons, also, are to be esteemed sordid, who buy from merchants that they may immediately

---

* Millar on Ranks, chap. 6, sect. 1st.—Reflections on the Politics of Ancient Greece; translated from the German of Arnold H. L. Heeren, by Geo. Bancroft, chap. 10.

† The same.

‡ M'Cullock's Outlines of Political Economy, part I, note.

‖ The same.

SLAVERY. 251

sell again, for their profits can only be made by falsehood. All *workmen* are servilely engaged; nor can the work-shop have anything worthy of a freeman."* A republican government can never be upheld where such sentiments are entertained of the great body of the people.

289. In a former chapter, many facts are stated to show, how universal slavery was, in Europe, after the fall of the Roman empire; how long it continued, and to what degree it exists now, in various parts of Europe. The same cause, which degraded labour and the labouring man in the ancient nations, has produced the like effects in the modern; and from the gradual banishment of slavery, arose the dignity of labour and the wealth and power of the inferior classes. From that epoch, commerce, arts, trades, which are, of course, mainly carried on by the labour of the common people, have attained to an eminence never before known in the world, and these have brought in their train, liberty, education, and property.

290. Two facts, in the history of slavery, will show that it cannot be perpetuated here.

First, The constantly increasing humanity to the slave, is a certain preparation for final emancipation. As nations grow more humane, just, and religious, they will certainly, more and more, loathe slavery.

Second, From this and other causes, freedom to the slave, in the civilized world, has been growing like other kinds of freedom, so that there is but a remnant of slavery remaining.

291. Let us see what the treatment of slaves was in

* Cicero on Morals.

ancient times. There is a story, that a man, by the name of Veddius Pollio, a Roman citizen, fed the fish in his fish-ponds, with the flesh of his own slaves. This may be thought to have been a single act of cruelty. But, it was a general practise to oblige slaves to fight with wild beasts, and this was carried to so prodigious a height, as to be a favourite amusement with men of all ranks.* The custom of exposing old, useless, or sick slaves, in an island of the Tiber, to starve, was common, in Rome. By an edict of the emperor Claudius, it was forbidden to kill any slave merely on account of old age or sickness.† Dungeons, where slaves were forced to work in chains, were common all over Italy. A chained slave, as a porter, was usual in Rome.

Fear, and the dread of revolt and murder, caused the most terrible laws in Rome: for it was decreed, that where a master was murdered, all the slaves under the same roof, or in any place so near the house as to be within the hearing of a man's voice, should, without distinction, be condemned to die.‡

Those who, in this case, sheltered a slave, in order to save him, were punished as murderers. If a master was murdered on a journey, they put to death those who were with him and those who fled.

292. As to the number of slaves among the ancient nations, the accounts differ. By some statements, there were in Athens twenty-one thousand citizens, ten thousand strangers, and four hundred thousand slaves. By others, the free Athenians were eighty-four thousand,

---

* Millar on Ranks, chap. 6, sect. 2.
† Hume's Essays, XI, "Of the Populousness of Ancient Nations."
‡ Montesquieu's Spirit of Laws, book 15, chap. 15.

strangers forty thousand, slaves one hundred and sixty thousand.* So great was the number of slaves at Rome, that in one case it was discovered, that there were some hundred slaves in a single palace, who were all executed for not preventing their master's murder.† It has been asserted, that many Romans possessed ten, and some twenty thousand slaves.

293. The following was the former condition of slavery in Europe.

First, Those who cultivated the earth were slaves. Slaves were composed principally of those who were captives in war.

Second, The masters had absolute dominion over the slaves, and could punish them capitally. Slaves might, also, be put to the torture.

Third, Slaves originally could not marry.

Fourth, All the children of slaves were slaves.

Fifth, Could be sold at pleasure.

Sixth, All the profits of the labour of the slave accrued to the master.

Seventh, As among all the barbarous nations in Europe, long hair was a mark of dignity and freedom, slaves were obliged to shave their heads.‡

It must be remembered that this kind of slavery existed over white men like ourselves. From the more enlightened parts of Europe, as England, Scotland, Ireland, France, Germany, Prussia, Italy, slavery has wholly disappeared.

---

* Hume's Essays, XI.

† Gibbon's Rome, vol. 1, chap. 2.

‡ Robertson's History of Charles V., vol. 1, note 9—Proofs and Illustrations.

Experience, then, is against the possibillity of the long continuance of slavery in this free country: for the experience of all past ages, among civilized people, in such a matter, will be the experience of the future. That ours is slavery over the *coloured* man cannot alter the case.

294. In addition to all these considerations, there are reasons peculiar to the United States, which show that slavery will not be perpetuated here, and that the time has arrived to begin to think how we are to throw it off. Public opinion, both at the south and north, is slowly but surely, undermining its foundations.

Slavery is the natural enemy of every man who performs manual labour, of every working-man in the United States, whether he lives in a slave, or a free state. It degrades him, it puts him upon a level with the slave, in the opinion of a large portion of the people. So indelible is the disgrace of every kind of labour in some of the slave states, that eminent public men there, are compelled to lament the low state of estimation in which even the *merchant* is held. Because, then, a merchant must work for his living, he is not the natural equal of planters and great owners of slaves.

Slavery, whether of the white or black man, has ever poisoned the mind upon the subject of manual labour. When men see all kinds of necessary, useful work, respected and honoured, they will perform it with cheerfulness: if not, they will be disgusted with it and flee from it, as the poor white people of the slave states now do, and as even some, to our disgrace, among us do. It is reserved to the free people of the United States, to put an end to all these revolting ideas of necessary, useful labour.

295. To love and respect the labouring man, to treat

him as a brother and fellow-citizen, as the agent of God in bringing to perfection, the useful, necessary, and elegant productions of nature and art, will alone enable us to enjoy our free institutions, or preserve them. This is the only sure foundation for a free government; there will never be peace and harmony in the country, as long as the manual labourer is thought of, and treated as a creature pursuing only a mean and servile work. The taint of slavery is yet upon the *free states;* its poison still runs in the veins of the people. Slavery has given to the common people those mean names of reproach which have been attached to all who perform the common manual labours. In Rome, the free common labourers, who worked with their hands were called "plebeians," which meant the mob or rabble. In France, the common people were called "canaille," the vile populace, the swinish multitude. In our own country, the poorest classes in the free States, have been sometimes called "white slaves."

296. In the southern states, it is a disgrace to be a poor man, because a poor man must do the work of a slave. The poor white people of the southern states are often more degraded than the slaves; they do not appear, or dress as well; many of them do nothing by which to earn their bread; nobody can tell how they live; and yet they scorn to put their hands to the very earth that bears them. Even the slave himself despises the poor white man, and in some of the southern states, it is common for the slave to call the poor white man, "poor trash."

297. These are the natural effects of slavery; thus, even the tilling of the earth, one of the purest, noblest, and most enlarging to the mind of all employments, is

committed almost exclusively to the lowest of mankind; to those who are not permitted to read and write, or to acquire any just knowledge of the fertility of the earth, of the animals that are sustained upon it; or the plants that spring from it.

298. Some of the fairest portions of the old slave states are exhausted, worn out, and nearly depopulated. In the new states at present appearances are more promising; the soil is new, the crops with little labour are great, the price of cotton is far above the average; all this gives a great value to the slave; but still the poison of slavery is there, and always at work. The earth will not continue to yield her produce to the slave, this is against all experience; she will not long grant her favours but to the man of knowledge, patience, skill, and perseverance; to the real farmer; to him, who like the elder Brutus, acknowledges her to be the universal mother; who delights to nourish her and bring to maturity her beautiful products. What infatuation, what blindness, to think, in these times, and in the United States too, of making a prosperous country where the labourers are not ingenious, skilful, educated, respected, where they are but a little above the brutes!

299. But it is supposed by many that there are good reasons why the black man should be a slave, though there may not be for the slavery of the white man. Let us, therefore, look for a moment at the various races of men.

The human race has been divided into five varieties the European, Asiatic, American, African, and Australian, they have also been called, the Caucasian, Mongolian, American, Ethiopean, and Malay varieties.

1. The Caucasian, or European variety, includes

the ancient and modern Europeans, except the "Laplanders and the rest of the Finnish race;" it includes also some portions of Asia, and Africa.

2. The Mongolian, or Asiatic race, includes the wandering tribes of central and northern Asia; the Chinese, Japanese, and some others.

3. The American. This is said to include all the aboriginal Americans, except the Esquimaux.

4. The Ethiopean or African variety includes the negroes of Africa, and all its other inhabitants, except those mentioned as belonging to Africa in the first variety.

5. The Malay, or Australian variety; which includes the people of New-Holland, Vandieman's-land; those scattered through the southern islands, and some others.*

Though the human race has been divided into these five general varieties, there are numberless shades and divisions of these.

300. If it be proper to perpetuate slavery over the black race, who can say, that it is not equally so to extend it over the other coloured families. Who shall say with what shade of colour or condition slavery shall begin or end? Why not make a slave of the Chinese, the American Indian, or the Laplander?

301. So great are the present differences in these races, that some have supposed, that all could not have proceeded from the same first parents. A far greater number probably are of a different opinion. It is enough for us to know, that the supreme Being has seen fit to separate his people on this earth into various

* Good's Book of Nature, series 2, lecture 3. Lawrence's Lectures, chap. X.

families, and that the *white man* stands at the head of all these families. White people have never been seen in that state of barbarism in which many of the other races have been known to exist. The greatest attainments in the arts and sciences; in morals, religion, and especially in the knowledge and practice of free government have been made by the whites; a republican government of equal laws and just privileges is not known to any of the coloured nations in the world.

302. This is a rank that we are bound to maintain. It is enough for us to know, that the black man, by a long course of degradation, is our inferior. As the white people, then, are at the head of the human families, they are bound to advance, to go forward in the race of civilization, and never backward by amalgamation, intermarriage, or any kind of corruption of their pure blood The interests of humanity, of free government, and of all the labouring people, depend upon the white man's retaining his superiority. The blacks are no longer a natural part of our society, either in the free or slave states; we cannot and ought not to consent to intermarry with them, or to give them equal political privileges ; so far as to make presidents, governors, and magistrates of them. There cannot, then, be a happy union of the black and white people.

303. But, as long as they continue with us, there will be amalgamation, corruption by intermixture, and debasement of the white labourer. There is now a disgusting criminal intercourse between the blacks and whites, both in the free and slave states, which produces the *mulatto*, also, every shade of black and white; and this is an unnatural corruption of pure white blood.

304. In this pernicious intermingling of different

races, we find the greater portion of the free people of colour, perhaps, the most miserable in the United States of all.

Even, in the free states, we give them the name of liberty, but nothing more, though many of them vote; they never vote for a coloured man; the substantial rights of equality are denied them; they are sometimes treated, and particularly have been recently, with a scandalous cruelty. Under the influence of neglect and unkindness, and a deep and universal conviction of their helplessness, the coloured people, in the free states, are becoming torpid and lifeless. While the condition of the white people is every year improving, that of the coloured is becoming more and more hopeless; they are treated with far less consideration than they once were, and with less than they deserve. We do not, even, attempt to assist them and get them along, as we once did. Do not the people see, then, that in the midst of freedom, they are a servile race, and that we have done little more for them than take away the name of slave.

305. It is this debased state of the coloured people in the free states, that here degrades some of the most useful kinds of labour.

Domestic service, through which is taught the *art* of house-keeping, one of the most important to a wife and mother, and which should be held in the highest respect by the working people of the United States, is scorned by a large portion of them. They hate it, that is, this kind of labour, and in a great measure, because it is the work of a servile race; because they cannot bear an association with coloured people in the kitchen; "they cannot bear to eat and drink with negroes." They prefer the society of their equals: and who does not? Who can blame in them that good part of this sentiment which elevates and ennobles all? Thus, we see, how the intermixture of white and coloured, of free and of slave or degraded labourers, and degraded because not admitted to the same privileges with ourselves, is a poison to them and to us. Good persons deplore the existence of this feeling towards the free coloured people, which, in the coarse and hard-hearted, degenerates into cruelty; and they grieve to see any rational portion of God's creatures in their condition. Can any one set any limits to these evils, if slavery is permitted to exist in a country in many parts of which the slave is increasing faster than the white man? This fact, that there are large districts of slave country, where the slave is increasing faster than the free man, demands the most serious deliberation of the people.

306. It is plain, then, that in the course of providence, circumstances are forcing upon us a great revolution, which it would be impious to attempt to resist. This revolution is, the breaking up of the union between the white and coloured men, which, no doubt, Providence has made to answer good and useful purposes, though perhaps to us inscrutable. This revolution is *gradual emancipation* and the *gradual removal* of the coloured people, with as much humanity as is due to an injured race, to such residences as we can find best suited to their tastes and wants.* There will be no occasion for removal by compulsion; when we shall once have

* Mr. Dew has stated, the obstacles which oppose emancipation in any way, with great ingenuity: but he will find, that his noble-minded countrymen, of Virginia, will, sooner or later, prove an over-match for them all.

agreed upon the subject, the coloured people will look at it in the same light as we do, for no people can be willing to see their race, either enslaved or perishing, and disappearing from the earth.

Upon this idea alone of gradual emancipation and removal, can the slave be permitted safely to enjoy the blessings of education. If ever he is to participate in the enjoyments of freedom—real, genuine freedom, he must, like all other men, be prepared for it.

307. The people of the United States have a nobler effort to make for the coloured race than has ever distinguished them since the revolution; but they will make it, and the work will be done. The difficulties are great, but not insuperable, and they will be got over, as soon as the people are united in putting their shoulders to the wheel. The people of the free states will consent to pay a great price for this good work.

Who, then, is to liberate the slave? The southern people,—they will do it nobly and freely, when they come to see the matter in all its lights; and it would be a miracle if they could, as some most unreasonably expect, understand, in the twinkling of an eye, the arguments against slavery, as we do. It is certain, that, if the slave be liberated, it must be done by them. He is not ours, we cannot liberate him: by the law and constitution he is their property. It is not mobs, war, violence, and denunciation that do most to make men free, but reason, humanity, and benevolence. All that we can now do, is to present a fair view of our own happy situation, and show its opposite in slavery. The public opinion of the sound, thinking, benevolent portion of the civilized part of the world, is against slavery, whether of the white or the black man; and this is an argument that will gather strength just as certainly as that men's minds will expand and become nobler.

308. There has been no good cause for alienation, for heartburnings between the northern and southern people; nor for the mobs, violence, injustice, and stupid, abominable violations of law, which have disgraced them and us, and caused the tyrants of the world to chuckle with delight that we, as they suppose, are wallowing in the mire of discord. The opinions of a vast majority of the northern people were never more sound than they now are upon the subject of slavery. They know that they cannot liberate the slave; they do not think of it, nor of intermeddling or interfering, in the least, any farther than their interference shall be constitutional, acceptable, and useful.

The free states, therefore, will not interfere; it is enough for them to know, that the cause of liberty and knowledge is always advancing, and that slavery is bad, both for master and slave. They consider time as the great emancipator; while they know, that what men were once centuries in performing, is now brought about in a much more brief period. The question with them is not, whether the slave is to be free, but *when*, and *how;* and they will wait till the "accepted time," taking care, however, that no concession shall ever be made to the *principle* of slavery.

In the meanwhile, they will present the subject calmly and dispassionately to the nation, knowing that there is no other way, under heaven, by which the people can find out what they are to do, or not to do.

In the meantime, also, they will be prepared with the power of the nation (if that be required) instantaneously to put down insurrection, and prove to the slave, that freedom cannot be had here through revolt, and remorseless murder of men, women, and children, who are of our white blood and family.

In regard to the future, we may safely predict, that when men see their interests, they will pursue them. Their interests lie in free labour. The slave, who has neither country, nor wife, nor child, nor property, that he can call his own, as he labours without hope, inevitably in the end entails poverty upon his master. In looking forward, then, the fact of the superior industry, wealth, content, security, and happiness of the free to the slave countries, cannot be excluded from the mind of any American citizen.

If slavery be what is here represented, who can say that the question of slavery is for the slave states alone, and not for the white man, the labouring man, the American citizen of every state?

THE END OF PART FIRST.

ERRATUM.

In page 249, fourth line from the top, *instead of* "Slavery is a sin to those only who see it to be so; multitudes do not,"—*read*, Slavery is a sin to those only who see it to be so, after having taken due pains to enlighten their minds upon the subject. Multitudes do not see it in this light.

PUBLIC AND PRIVATE ECONOMY

ILLUSTRATED BY OBSERVATIONS MADE
IN ENGLAND IN THE YEAR
1836

BY

THEODORE SEDGWICK

PART SECOND

[1838]

AUGUSTUS M. KELLEY • PUBLISHERS
CLIFTON 1974

First Edition 1838

(*New York:* Harper & Brother, *No. 82, Cliff Street*, 1838)

PUBLIC

AND

PRIVATE ECONOMY.

ILLUSTRATED BY OBSERVATIONS MADE IN ENGLAND
IN THE YEAR 1836.

BY THEODORE SEDGWICK.

PART SECOND.

NEW-YORK:

PUBLISHED BY HARPER & BROTHERS.
No. 82 Cliff-street.

1838.

[Entered, according to Act of Congress, in the year 1838, by
HARPER & BROTHERS,
in the Clerk's Office of the Southern District of New-York.]

PREFACE.

HAVING, during the summer of 1836, in company with a friend, made a voyage to England for the benefit of medical advice to him, and thence a short excursion to France, I have determined to make my journey a vehicle for observations on "*Public and Private Economy*," which will constitute the second part of my work. I am fully aware how very limited my means of information have been in so short a time in those countries. It must be admitted, however, that important knowledge even in so brief a period may be gained. I shall mainly confine myself to those facts which in essentials are too well known to be called in question; and, as to all minor circumstances, shall most scrupulously endeavour to relate them in such a way as not to mislead the reader.

Any one who reads what I have written, and observes the course of my inquiries abroad, will see that I have particularly endeavoured, by plainness and simplicity, to make them useful to the general mass of American citizens. These subjects have usually been treated in such a way as to be thought great mysteries. Certainly they are not; on the contrary, they are as clear to the comprehension of a common labouring man, if plainly treated, as most other topics. The common people have not yet been called to think upon these subjects, but it is high time that they should be.

The present economy of the United States is one thing, and that of Europe is another; at the same time, the great interests of men are the same, because everywhere the people are interested in producing all the property they can, and in doing all the good with it they can, and this is the sum and substance of *public and private* economy. As to the use of property, though generally left entirely out of sight, it is not the least important branch of the subject; for the more good people have it in their hearts to do with their property, the more industrious, ingenious, and animated they are in obtaining it. Economy, therefore, belongs to a man's *duties*.

The labouring man of the United States who may read this book must determine whether I have true ideas of *American* economy, and he will not ask whether I have written according to the authority of this or that great man.

The moment that we of the United States touch

the shores of Europe, we are astonished at the small number of people that have property or hope for it; on the contrary, the people of Europe are astonished here at the great number proportionably that have it, and they see scarcely any without the hope of it. Here lies the wonderful secret of the property-getting power of the people of the United States! All, as a general rule, may obtain property here. This plainly accounts for the prodigious increase of our wealth compared with other nations. Though all can obtain, all do not use it wisely. It is, therefore, the childish, selfish, pernicious use of property which we see in Europe that I have insisted upon so much in this book. An inevitable result of the *privileged system!* The universal, pervading hope among us of property and consideration has given a new character to the people of the United States never known among men, and which the people of Europe cannot understand. *We* cannot believe that the good Being who created this beautiful world designed it mainly for a few favoured thousands.

It is reserved for the people of the United States to carry into practice those principles of equality which they have avowed. But they must first learn the true, religious, unprivileged use of property. It is this godlike plan of conducting towards our fellow-man, so as to make him a sharer in the bounties of Heaven, that will lead the people of the United States to that glory which is designed for them.

One who has seen that great country England cannot but desire that our ancient animosities should be forgotten for ever. In speaking, therefore, very freely of its customs and institutions, I cannot be suspected of ill will. The cause of reform, the true cause of the people in both countries, the interests of humanity, of civilization, of the poor, the unfortunate, the oppressed, depend more upon the continuance of hearty good-will between these two great nations than upon any other circumstance. Causeless war would be to all except a very few, usurers, speculators, spendthrifts, job-seekers, office-holders, contractors, the curse of curses.

CONTENTS.

CHAPTER I.

Passage in the ship St. James for London, May, 1836.—Passage-money.—Paying for Liquors.—Travelling.—Money spent in it.—Importance of cheapness of things of general enjoyment.—Clean Servants, mark of English Civilization.—How servants' wages ought to be regulated.—Clean ship.—Character of Passengers.—Meals on board.—Grog on board of.—Dress of our Pilot.—Pilots, how licensed.—Strawberries, when ripe in England.—Wages of Sailors.—Their Diet.—Rule of Wages.—Degradation of Sailors.—Character of Common Sailors.—Improvement of Condition of Common People.—Servants' wages on board ship, how paid.—Steerage Passengers on board ship.—What they pay.—Their Food.—Accommodations of Cabin Passengers.—Privileged System, what it is.—Examination of Baggage at Portsmouth.—Quarantine Regulations . . . . . Page 13

CHAPTER II.

Portsmouth.—Benefits of Commerce.—Merchants called Unproductive Labourers.—Fresh eggs in England.—Education of Common People there.—Regimental Review at Portsmouth.—Construction of Houses there.—Economy of small Houses.—Numbers of People in England.—Mr. Malthus's Doctrine.—Portsmouth Docks.—Prices in England.—Dearness there.—Cause of.—Monopoly.—Baths, price of at Portsmouth.—In New-York.—Coaches in England.—Rate of Travelling.—Price of.—Condition of Coach-horses.—Abuses of Travelling here.—Coachmen in England.—Dress of.—Character of.—Health of.—Wages of.—Horsing the Coach.—Union of Labourer and Capitalist.—Character of Labourers here.—Cost of Travelling a year in Europe.—Causes of it.—Roads of England.—Cost of.—One of the best modes of distributing Property.—Equalize prices of Land and Products.—Prices in England.—Of Beef in

London and the Country.—Price of Carriage, how far it affects prices of Articles.—Mode of making Turnpike-roads in England.—Acts of Parliament in relation thereto.—Rent of.—Division of Property in United States.—Upon what principles going on here.—True cause of affluence of United States.—Aristocratic privileged wealth, its character . . . . Page 53

CHAPTER III.

London.—St. James's Park.—Duke of York's Statue.—Civil Soldiers, how made so.—Coffee-room.—Hour for Breakfast.—Power of People in regulating fashions here.—Horse Guards, expense of.—Dress of the Men.—Cows in the Park.—Fresh Milk.—Adulteration of.—Time of opening Shops in London.—Forsyth's Tree-plaster.—Trees in St James's Park, how trimmed.—Use of Language by Common People.—Advantage of Paper Circulation.—Character of, when Regulating Medium.—Injustice to the Poor of irresponsible Paper Money.—Advantages of free Banking.—Character of Modern Political Economy.—Old Servant at the door of my Hotel.—Church St. James, Westminster.—Character of the Preaching.—Charity Sermon.—Tailor in the Churchyard.—Wages in London.—Rents of Poor compared with the expenses of Rich.—Moral and Political Improvement.—Character of Coffee-rooms.—Rank in England.—Travellers' Room.—Their Salaries.—Wine they Drink.—Quantity drank in the Hotels.—Wages of Agricultural People in England.—Office in United States, how sought for.—Hospitality of England.—Character of.—Roads near London, how made 89

CHAPTER IV.

Père la Chaise.—Labourers in.—Their Dinner.—Expense of Dinner at Clarendon Hotel.—Causes of Poverty.—What Labour is most productive.—All Labour productive of some good or other.—Adam Smith, his Political Economy.—His idea of what this Government and People were to be.—Incident in his Life.—Ideas of Labour in England.—Flying Hawks.—Falconry.—Character of this Sport.—Two kinds of Property.—Uses to which it has been put.—Characteristics of it.—Prices of some luxurious articles in New-York.—Mr. Malthus's and Mr. Paley's Political Economy concerning Labour.—Bawbles of England.—Rundell and Bridge.—Diamonds, Bracelets, &c.—Pitt Diamond.

—Privileged System, its effect upon the Moral and Intellectual Faculties.—Condition of Labouring People.—How it has affected our ideas concerning Labour.—No sufficient excuse for Poverty here generally.—Pauperism in England, how caused.—Different kinds of Labour.—How they affect Wealth.—All interested in the increase of Wealth.—Character of the most productive Labour . . . . Page 114

CHAPTER V.

Productive and Unproductive Consumption.—Character of Vicious Employments.—Pauperism in England.—Some of the Causes. —Mr. Hume's opinion.—Horse-gaming in the United States. —Newmarket.—Races at.—Jockeys.—Uses of Plate.—Lord Wellington's.—Extent of Horse-gaming in England.—Training grounds at Newmarket.—Racehorses at.—Frauds practised in Horse-racing.—Grooms.—Trotting Horses sent to England. —Mr. Osbaldiston.—Gaming at Cards.—Case of Lord de Ros vs. Cumming.—Consequences of Horse-gaming in England.— Races at Ascot Heath.—King's Plate.—Egham Races.—Effect of Races on character of the People.—Abuses of the Turf.—Intelligence of working-people at Manchester.—Race at Reading. —Mr. Southey's Opinions as to the mode of Improving the People.—Case of injustice at Court of Sessions.—Equal laws for Rich and Poor.—Vices of the Old World.—Gaming.—Intemperance.—Licentiousness between the Sexes.—Turf-gaming in New-England.—Gaming in the Northern States.—Aristocratic Sports 140

CHAPTER VI.

Temperance.—Doctor Franklin.—Anecdote of him.—Division by William the Conqueror of Lands in England.—Intemperance greatest cause of Poverty.—More equal Division of Property, how brought about.—Comparison of Wages with Expenses.— Power of Common People over Prices.—Mobs, character of them in the United States.—Ignorance of people of England as to Temperance in the United States.—Value of Spirituous Liquors consumed in United States.—Effect of on character of People.—Beer, when introduced into England.—Hops, when first made use of.—Peg-tankard of the Anglo-Saxons.—Common use of beer in London.—Beer of different degrees of strength.—Ideas of Common People in England as to Wages.—Wages of Railroad men at Bristol.—Beer they drink.—Beer drank by Coachmen.—Adulteration of it —Merthyr Tydvil.—Beer drank there.—Wages there.—Railroad Iron made there.—Elevation of the Labouring Classes.—Contrast of the Past with the Present.—Temperance the foundation to build on.—Amount of destruction of property in England by the use of Beer.—Barley in England.—Amount of Beer made there.—Use of Gin in England.—Gin Palaces.—Duty on Gin.—Gin Palaces compared with Dram Shops.—American Bar-room.—Improvement in Temperance in England.—Manchester, Intelligent people of.—British Association for Temperance.—Number of Members.—Breweries in London.—Barclay's Brewery.—Lincolnshire Horse.—Conclusion . . . . Page 174

PUBLIC AND PRIVATE ECONOMY.

PART II.

CHAPTER I.

SEC. 1. I LEFT home in May, 1836, accompanied by a labouring man, whom I hired to attend me as far as the Hudson River. We ascended the Nobletown Mountain; and when we had arrived at the summit, which overlooks the broad and beautiful valley that lies between it and the Hudson, he exclaimed, "Heavens, how much land and property, and I have none. What is the reason?" This is an important question to millions in his situation. The inquiry, then, is, why is there so *unequal a distribution?* Is there any good reason, in fact and nature, why a few should possess nearly all the property of the world, doing with it as they choose, leaving to the multitude so little comfort and enjoyment? And there is another inquiry still more important. Why is so little property created or produced, when we know that the earth, with the materials that come from it, might yield a hundred, a thousand, or ten thousand times (we cannot say how much) more than they do at present? Why, then, is there so little property to distribute compared with what there might be?

2. In the first part of this work, the twelfth chapter is on the causes of *poverty*, where some are stated. In this second part, I shall endeavour to illustrate those causes by a reference to such facts as came within my observation, the most important of which are indisputable.

3. In taking passages in the ship St. James, at New-York, for London, for myself and friend, I was required by Messrs. Grinnell & Minturn, the packet agents, to pay one hundred and forty dollars for each, and told that this sum included compensation for *liquors*. To paying for liquors for my friend I objected, on the ground that, as an invalid, he drank none. The answer was, that that made no difference; that the rule was inflexible; that the packets had tried the other plan, but that it had been found very *inconvenient*, and that the passengers even were opposed to it.

4. Travelling has become, to great numbers in the United States, so great a source of pleasure and instruction, that it behooves them to regulate it upon the best principles. In former days it was enjoyed by a few rich people only; now the case is altered; at home and abroad it may have increased in a hundred years a hundred or a thousand fold. It has become one of the refined pleasures of a more civilized age; as an amusement, with many it has taken the place of vicious sports and barbarous modes of wasting property. As a remedy for the invalid, the wisest physicians prescribe it when all others fail; and we know that, in a change of society, exercise,

air, climate, scenery, however inexplicable it may be, new life is given to the constitution.

5. People are not aware, generally, how important travelling is in affording a living to great numbers of labouring people. The more that can travel the better, if there be an adequate object. Allowing that there are fifteen millions of people in the United States, and that, upon an average, they spend, one with another, in travelling at *home*, five dollars a year, we have seventy-five millions of dollars in this one mode of distributing property! And who get the money? Farmers for their produce, mechanics, servants in public houses, railroad men, &c., &c. Travelling also becomes the cause of good roads, good inns, ships, &c.; or, if you please, good roads, inns, ships, promote travelling. They are at once cause and effect.

It is in the United States only that farmers who work with their hands, common people, people in middling circumstances, travel, or can afford to travel, to any extent. If there be abuses, then, in the public conveyances, by far the greater number of people are interested in putting them down. A public abuse in the United States ought to be abated as a public nuisance.

6. In the sum I have mentioned of one hundred and forty dollars, there being no exemption as to paying for liquors, all must pay alike; invalids, ladies, boys over fourteen years of age, and all those who belong to the temperance societies. This is equally against decency and the common usages of

16   PUBLIC AND PRIVATE ECONOMY.

the country, in packets, steamboats, inns, lodging-houses, &c.

7. There are unanswerable moral objections to this practice. As the expense falls upon all alike, there arises, of course, with most, a strong temptation to get their share of what they must pay for. This leads to intemperate drinking. Few who have not witnessed what some people in the garb of gentlemen drink upon these occasions would credit the truth if told. With some a voyage is little better than a long carouse of thirty or forty days. I have been told, and believe it to be true, that a party of Englishmen drank in one of these voyages six bottles each upon an average daily, including liquors of all kinds, cider, beer, porter, wine, brandy, &c.

It must be remembered that youth of all ages travel in these packets; young men just beginning business, and going out as agents, clerks, &c., who are, of course, liable to these excesses. So absurd are these packets in their extravagance, and so far beyond those indulgences in which even the richest generally allow themselves, that they have upon their tables daily Madeira, sherry, port, claret, German wines, beer, cider, porter, and, several times in the week, Champagne without limit. In this way wine and all other liquors flow as profusely as water for all, young and old, rich and poor, and for some who never in their lives drank a bottle of Champagne before.

8. *Women* also travel in these packets, often helpless women, no doubt, who have had their full share of this world's poverty and misery. What a gross

injustice and indelicacy to force this liquor bill upon the most helpless and needy! Many a delicate lady does not participate in these liquors to the amount of a dollar in a whole passage. People who guzzle the whole way ought to be ashamed of such a robbery! Any man of right feelings who will think of it for a moment will see that the practice is inexcusable.

The hardest of all cases is that of the invalid. He who travels to save life, perhaps for the benefit of a helpless wife and children, must pay not less, probably, than fifty dollars, out and in, towards this very *just taxation.*

But let us hear what the owners allege. They say that what we propose has been tried in the New-York packets, and that the passengers objected to the change so strenuously that they were compelled to give it up; that the making a distinction between those who drink and those who do not is inconvenient, &c. Who are those that objected to the change? The truth lies here.

A large portion of those who pass over in these packets are either rich and fashionable people from the cities, who travel in foreign countries; or, what is more common, English and American merchants, agents, &c., who make frequent voyages.

A considerable portion of these are very young men, whose example and opinion in such a matter are entitled to little weight. Be that as it may, the persons mentioned give the tone and set the fashion. Many of these are such good customers that the captains and proprietors feel bound to consult their wishes. And what are their wishes ? Why, certainly, with their habits as to drinking on board ship, this equitable assessment upon the *whole* is very *convenient*. As it only takes about a dozen of Champagne to make up the sum of twenty-five dollars, which all, including women, invalids, boys, &c., must pay for liquors upon the present plan, it is no wonder that any change should be objected to, and particularly by the captains and owners ; for if the plan should be altered, it is probable that not a fourth part of the liquors now drunk would, in that case, be consumed.

No one who has beheld the admirable order, neatness, general propriety, and comfort that prevail on board some of these ships (*not in all alike, however, by any means*) ; the wonderful assiduity with which they are sailed ; the gentlemanly character of the captains ; the sober and steady behaviour of the crews ; and who, at the same time, has a just pride in all the important establishments of the country, can fail to wish abolished a practice so odious and unjust towards the poorer members of the community; so uneconomical in a country where all, or nearly all, must work for a living ; so liable to abuse by young people and so offensive to temperance. The people of the United States will sooner or later be compelled to see that these magnificent ways of eating, drinking, and wasting their property were not designed for them.*

* The substance of these observations was inserted in a New-York paper after the author's return.

9. The happiness of the people of the United States greatly depends upon the *cheapness of things of general enjoyment.* Let it be remembered that these are *American* packets; that it is not all gold that glitters in this country; that poor as well as rich people go as cabin passengers. Great and unnecessary dearness in things of common enjoyment arising from our sensual and selfish modes of living, is like a curse that blasts the common fruits and grain upon which all subsist. Instead, therefore, of contriving travelling establishments as showy, luxurious, and dear as possible, the first aim should be simplicity, economy, and comfort; not that it is expected that all should or can spend the same money upon these common enjoyments. As a general rule in steamboats, packets, hotels, &c., the charge to each will be in proportion to the expense of building, furnishing them, &c. In these packets we have cabins fitted up like palaces, three or four thousand dollars being expended upon them (upon many, more) in ornamental rosewood and mahogany work, &c. How many gentlemen in the United States can or do afford such expense even in their own private apartments? The interest of this money must be paid yearly, and every passenger must contribute his proportion. At best, the packets are very expensive ships, costing, upon an average, not less than about fifty thousand dollars. Several of them have cost much more.

We make a superb outside show with feathers, flounces, and fine colours, leaving behind the weightier matters of respectable living; we begin at the wrong end, with magnificence instead of comfort, with Champagne when very many of us can only afford beer, water, or cider. There is not, after all, a very great proportion of the cabin passengers, if they were brought to the truth, who would like to say that it was quite convenient to them to pay even their proportion of the expenses of this "splendid," gorgeous carving, panelling, and gilding. No man can go to Europe without seeing that the wisest part of the people there are looking very sharply at the Western World, and for examples, wherever they can find them, for their own improvement. They laugh at us, as well they may, when they see so many of our peacock feathers draggling along in the dirt and mud. It must be confessed that, with bilge water below and seasickness in the cabin and on deck, a ship makes but a poor figure dressed out as for an opera!

But, after all, these are small considerations compared with the exclusion from a republican country of a base counterfeit imitation of aristocratic taste, and of the introduction into it of a purer and holier, consisting of such a way of spending our money as shall at once do good to ourselves and our fellow-citizens. There is a meanness and selfishness in making wealth merely instrumental to personal glory and elevation that is unworthy our origin and deeds, and that is every day proving the old truth, that "pride will have a fall."

10. But what would we have in preference to this

exquisite carving, gilding, and panelling, as it seems we cannot pay for both ?

First, clean servants, a feature in English civilization so beautiful and interesting to the traveller! The elegant cabins and luxurious wines afford a poor contrast to the filthy servants whom we sometimes see about the cabins, and even tables, in greasy jackets and tattered shirts that are worn half a voyage. But the captains do not make the servants; they cannot make their waiters decent and cleanly. Yes, they can; and how? By paying proper wages for cleanly waiters; for any quality of men may be had for proper pay for any service. When these ships are in port they are dressed as for a Sunday, in Brussels carpets and silk curtains; but one would think it better to dress the servants decently than the ship luxuriously, if both expenses cannot be afforded, for the servant can suffer from his own disgusting appearance, but the ship is not sensible to her honours; he is a man and a fellow-man. He should be hired upon a strict contract that he will provide himself with clothes suited to his employment; and if things are at all rightly regulated, his wages will be in proportion to this additional expense; and so they should be. Nothing degrades men more in their own estimation than mean and filthy garments; and there are few points of superiority in English civilization to that of the United States more striking than this of wearing appropriate clothing. In every country it is best for all parties that every man should get all the wages he can by his exertions, let people say what they will about making cheap goods by means of poor wages. If servants' wages are high, so much the better; we shall finally teach them to spend their money wisely; and then we shall have the less Champagne to throw out of half-empty bottles in our drunken frolics, lest the servants, after we have left the table, should get drunk also.

Many, to a certain extent, and to a great extent, may regulate their own wages; but, to do this, their habits, manners, persons, and services must correspond with the increased wages which they demand. There is no more justice or propriety in paying all servants alike than all physicians and lawyers alike. None are so much interested in substituting a better taste, in getting rid of this superlative finery, as servants and all descriptions of working people. The more money that is wasted or misapplied, be it public or private, the worse for them. The rich can bear the waste.

11. There are other things in this packet service that we all ought to be willing to pay for, and one is a *clean ship*. A ship at best, to many people, is little better than a jail; the unavoidable privations are so great at sea, that few things are more revolting to most people, and certainly to a seasick man, than a *dirty* ship. To see collections of dirt under the tables and in the corners of the staterooms, which are sometimes not removed for weeks; tablecloths spread day after day besmeared with gravies, sauces,

and overturned glasses of ale, wine, and porter, is enough to send a man out of the cabin sick or well. Let the ships, then, provide themselves with a sufficient supply of table furniture to enable them to spread a clean cloth every day; with pure water, which in some ships we have not, but which, with the aid of proper filters, may be had; with conveniences for bathing, so important to health, which all the packets ought to have; for there is no doubt that perfect cleanliness of the person on board ship would not only greatly mitigate the evils of seasickness, but add to the benefits of a sea voyage. These are some of the substantial comforts and respectable things which we sacrifice for shadows; for "splendour" and dainties!

12. There are other things that require amendment. The dainties and profusion that abound on our tables in these packets are a disgrace to a republican people. Let other people spend as they will, but let us live according to reason and nature; for, till then, we shall never know how much property and how many comforts all may have, and to what extent we can remove poverty from the world.

It is for the interest of the captains and owners to induce the passengers to drink all they can and eat all they can; the more extravagantly the ship is supplied, the better for them, for more profit is made upon a large than a small supply. On board of these ships, where strong and robust men are cooped up for thirty or forty days without exercise, and where simplicity of diet should reign, if ever, every allurement is held out to gluttony, for every dinner is a feast. We have upon our tables not only all the usual viands, but all the ornamental cookery in jellies, whips, &c., that can be got up in the galley, which is a kitchen not more than eight or ten feet square. And who are these passengers? We know who they are.

There is an odd mixture, to be sure, and among them a goodly number to whom this magnificent profusion must present an odd contrast to their daily and more healthful simplicity at home. In addition to our eating twice as much as we ought on board of these packets, we eat twice as often, for we have *four* substantial meals. We breakfast at nine, and at twelve there is a lunch, when there is spread a round of beef, slices of ham, tongue, bread and butter, potted herrings, sardines, &c., or other articles as substantial and seductive. Then comes dinner, and after that tea and coffee, with cold meats, &c. For all this we pay (with the exception of the price of transportation) one hundred and forty dollars over, and one hundred and seventy-five back, which, allowing twenty-two days for the one passage and thirty-four for the other, is equal to about six dollars and a third per day for eating and drinking one way, and a little more than five the other. Nothing reconciles us to such a wanton waste of our property but a long-continued abuse of reason, judgment, and conscience; for there can be no doubt that, with more simplicity and a juster taste, the sublime pleasures of a voyage, and the pure enjoyment of seeing Europe, with all its glories and beauties, might be obtained for one half or two thirds of the money that it costs at present, and with still greater comfort. The reader must decide whether this kind of economy is worth contending for. Of course, it is only a question as to one kind of economy or another, for it is certain that we shall "make trade flourish and our money stir," if we have money; if one description of labourer does not get it, another will. Ten people might visit Europe to one now, if it were not for these vulgar expenses. So the rich and luxurious spend and live, and so we think we all must; and then we cry out that a collar has been put about our necks, and that it chafes, when the fact is, that we are the most extraordinarily willing vassals that ever have been heard of in the world. Let me not be understood as saying that this disgraceful waste of property in drinking and gormandizing is peculiar to the packets; far from it.

With exceptions like these, the packet service is highly honourable to the country. The ship St. James was one of the best-regulated establishments I ever saw of any kind, and for this we were indebted mainly to the admirable character of the principal officers. I never but once during the whole voyage heard a vulgar word from officers or men, not even from sailors to sailors. The comfort of such propriety is inexpressible to the passengers. The quiet, subdued tone in which commands were given seemed contagious among the men; all partook of the same spirit, all were made happy by it.

13. "*No grog*" stood at the head of the shipping articles of this ship; and, though small portions are sometimes smuggled by the men into their chests, they are afraid and ashamed to open them to get at the contraband article. I often talked with the men on board of this ship, and could never perceive from their breath that they had been drinking. Still the captain informed us that he suffered the mate to bring on board a small quantity of liquor, to be given upon emergencies. As soon as the common sailors can be made to respect themselves as they did on board of this ship, there will be an end of half their vice and misery. Temperance, as Lord Mansfield said of obedience in a soldier, should be the first, second, and third law of a ship.*

No officer of a ship ought to be indulged in the habit of drinking ardent spirits, and the less he takes of any spirituous liquors the better. If the officers drink, the men will drink; the contagion of

---

* As I shall often have occasion to speak of the subject of temperance in such a manner as may imply that I am a member of a temperance society, it is proper that I should state that I am not. I can say, however, that my habits of abstinence have long been such, that I should not for a moment be deterred from taking the pledge by any sacrifice it would cost. While, therefore, I have the greatest respect for the conscientiousness of those who take the pledge as an example to others; and while I believe that it is indispensable to the safety of many, I must claim the same indulgence of opinion towards myself in not taking it. The temperance societies have proved a great blessing in the U. States.

the example is too much for them, and why should they not do what their superiors do? If the captain is in the habit of indulgence, the passengers may rely upon it that the mate and inferior officers will sneak down the companion-way at sunrise in the morning, or at some other time, to get at the brandy bottle in the pantry, through the connivance of the steward or servants.

The inferior officers in our ship had nearly the whole responsibility of sailing her when off soundings. The head of the man who has charge of a ship should be as steady as the planets by which it is directed. Men who are placed in responsible business situations ought not to be tolerated in a practice of drinking spirituous liquors of any kind; it is ruinous to all parties concerned; no man can tell when he is safe in the hands of these people; they are generally either in a fog or a gale, and there can be no doubt that a large portion of the losses that are sustained by sea and land, by the overturning of stage coaches, the burning of ships, &c., proceeds from this cause. There is nothing that the owners of these ships can do that will gratify the public so much, or redound more to their honour and advantage, than by putting "no grog" at the head of their shipping articles. A sailor at sea, generally, is no more to be trusted with ardent spirits, than children are with gunpowder. Every temperance ship that carries passengers ought to publish in the papers in the principal towns under what sort of colours she sails. The people of the

United States have begun a temperance reform, the greatest of all reforms, and such as, to the same extent, was never dreamed of in the world; and under God they will carry it on in spite of all opposition. Some people talk of a reaction; there is no reaction; they do not know the facts; they think that the slow progress, slow by comparison, which temperance has made in the cities, or that some little dramshop, or depraved village which they happen to know, shows the condition of the nation.

14. The pilot who took us outside of the Hook was habited in an entire suit of *black*, with a white hat, and still his business was to navigate a little schooner drenched with water from morning to night; a costume about as appropriate as wigs for the coachmen whom I afterward saw in St. James's-street, coming from the queen's drawing-room. It is a pity that the American people should not be able to get rid of the enormous expense which they put themselves to in the mere foppery of dress, when there are so many other things besides trappings for which they are distinguished. Oh, the millions, the millions that we spend, not for good, substantial, graceful garments suited to our condition and means, but for some trumpery or finery, or things outré, inappropriate, and out of proportion.

15. On the 7th day of June, 1836, we arrived off the Bill of Portland and took a pilot. His boat presented a singular contrast to our pilot schooners. This pilotboat was a sloop-rigged vessel, and built like a tub, being about thirty tons burden. In a

conversation with the pilot, he said, "we are all licensed by 'the Trinity,'" meaning "the Trinity House." Here is a fine instance of the infection of example; because the Trinity House appoints pilots, the governor and senate of New-York must do the same!*

This pilot told us that the pilots in England were obliged to serve seven years as apprentices, three as masters, and then they become pilots of the second class, who are allowed to take charge of vessels of only seventeen feet water. After that, according as they have luck and influence, they become pilots of the first class, who take charge of any vessels. This man presented an odd contrast to our American pilot! He was dressed in a coarse roundabout, blue trousers, a tarred hat, and shoes to match. The people of England, notwithstanding the horrible burdens of taxation under which they lie, and the cruel expenses to which they are annually put to support kingly and aristocratic ostentation, are far better and more appropriately dressed, with some exceptions which I shall mention, than the people of the United States; I mean, of course, as far as I could in so short a time observe.

16. I asked our pilot (7th June) whether strawberries were ripe. "Oh no, sir." "When will they be ripe?" said I. "In August or September," replied the pilot. "Strawberries, strawberrries!" I rejoined, in order to avoid the possibility of mis-

* The law has since been altered.

take. "Yes, sir, they come about the time that *nuts* do, in August or September." This is an instance of what my subsequent experience furnished the proof, that the poor people of England know little about the fruits generally; they cannot know, for they do not eat them; they do not eat them, for they cannot buy them; they cannot buy them, because they are too *dear*. Oh the curse of unnecessary dearness to the great body of the people! The fruits, which are at once the most healthful and the most delicious food, are, with the exception of the most common, eaten almost exclusively in England by the great and rich. This subject of cheap and dear is one of the greatest importance to us, and I shall endeavour to illustrate it in every way I can. As the people of the United States are now doing what other nations have done hundreds or thousands of years ago, that is, establishing their own principles of public and private economy, it is of the greatest importance that they should make as few mistakes as possible.

17. We were told that the common wages of the mates on board of these ships was thirty-five dollars per month, but that our mate on board the St. James had forty. This was a poor compensation for a man so estimable, faithful, and intelligent, and out of all just proportion compared with many other services. If things were regulated as they should be, and as they will be some day in the United States, the owners would be compelled to spare a little of the expense now put upon the exquisite carving and

gilding of the cabins, and a little from the sumptuous entertainments that stupify the senses of the passengers, and make them forget the faithful men on deck; and then a portion at least of this little would go to increase the just rewards of some of the best of labourers. Before this can take place, however, the labourers must understand their interests better than they now do.

They must give a right direction to all the property of the country, whether it belong to rich or poor; by showing the vain, luxurious people, by their own example, what a noble use may be made of property; that it is more to the purpose for any man to get a good dinner than to eat one from a silver plate with a silver fork; to this end they must first begin at home, throw their hidden liquor jugs overboard, and then join the temperance societies or the *temperate people*. This is the true road to good wages.

18. The common sailors! What a strange thing is this which we call civilization! Where should we find the Rothchilds; the Girards; the Astors; the four-story granite and marble houses; the sumptuous dinners; the splendid midnight parties; the gorgeous furniture; the rich equipage of the opulent merchants, without the services of these faithful sailors! The common sailors on board the St. James and the St. Andrew received fifteen dollars per month (1836), and the same in 1835. When we find so much improvement in other things, it is pleasing to be able to state that the character of the

common sailors also has improved; and this, we were told, was owing to *their better treatment.* In this there is no great mystery, certainly, for it seems that the sailor has a heart as well as another man. The captain told us on board the St. James that, when he first sailed out of New-York, the sailors had no small stores allowed them, such as tea, coffee, sugar, &c., but that these were now furnished even in the merchant ships; that in Boston, however, they did even formerly allow small stores to the sailors. Now the sailors have many vegetables, such as we have in the cabin. In the St. James they had cocoa every morning; pudding twice a week: on board the St. Andrew they had a sort of broth every day for breakfast, beef and pork for dinner, at evening tea, and twice a week after dinner a pudding called "duff," composed of flour and suet. I do not mean, however, to say that these were all the articles of food which the men had on board of these ships. I had a great deal of conversation with the hands on board of the St. Andrew, and, without an exception, they never failed to express gratitude for their treatment, nor to draw the necessary contrasts between their condition in the packets and in the common merchant ships.

19. Without being able to say exactly what the fare of these hard-working men should be, it is plain that good substantial food, with a sufficient variety for health, strength, and a reasonable enjoyment, is their due. This world is so capable of abundance, that every hard-working man should

have something to thank God for every day of his life. That the fare of these sailors at present is pretty *plain* is *plain* enough, and if the captains and owners would transfer a little of their moderation to the cabins, so much the better; a little fasting there with the feasting would probably be as well for all parties.

20. *Wages.* The following statement is made in part first, chapter second, section twenty-five, in regard to wages.

" *Wages*, also, is a great subject in political economy. None, certainly, can be more important to men who work with their hands; none has been treated of more largely by political economists.

" This may be said to be one of the first principles in regard to wages, *that the rate of wages depends upon the number of labourers compared with the business to be done.* Labour is bought and sold like other articles: if there be a great deal of it compared with what is wanted, it will be cheap; if little, it will be dear. The farmers here can understand this principle perfectly, when they see that, if there were no emigration of labourers to Ohio, Michigan, &c., there would be more labourers and cheaper wages; and that, if there were half a dozen more blacksmiths in every town, there would then be too many for the work to be done, and, of course, that the wages of blacksmiths must fall as long as this state of things should continue. So, also, every mechanic and manufacturer can see the same thing who knows that wages in his line would fall, in consequence of the influx of foreigners, if the mechanic and manufacturing business did not increase in about the same proportion with this influx; summer, winter, and harvest wages, also, exemplify the same truth. In winter, with us, we have the same number of labourers, or nearly so, as in summer; but there is less work to be done, and, of course, wages are lower; in harvest there is more work to be done than in the other seasons, but the labourers are not in proportion, and, therefore, harvest wages are the best in the year. These truths can never be mysteries to men of business: so far from not being intelligible to labouring people, they are prepared, by their previous habits of mind, in many most important respects, to understand them better than scholars, statesmen, and professed writers. Truth, upon these subjects, is a deduction from the facts which we witness in our daily business; it, therefore, does not require what is called a scholar or philosopher to understand them; on the contrary, it is a great delusion to suppose that most of our common people cannot comprehend them. The main difficulty at present is, that our books are not written for the common people, but exclusively for scholars, gentlemen, philosophers, and statesmen."

21. There is another important rule as to wages; that is, they are regulated, in a great measure, by the intelligence, education, good conduct, and independent condition of the labourers. This state of things has ever existed between the employer and

the employed; that is, the employer desires to get wages as cheap as he can, and the employed to get as much as he can. This competition, then, is always going on. But here is the difference: the employer is a man of property; he is a capitalist; he can let his ship or his mill lie idle a while, if necessary, as we know now (1837) to be the case in consequence of the money distress in the country.

Therefore, when things get to the worst, and the parties fall out, the owner lays up his ship and the manufacturer stops his mill, till the labourer can be brought to terms, which, generally, is quickly done; for the labourer has nothing; he has laid up nothing, not even the means of living for a month, and it follows that he is little better than a slave. He is compelled to strike his colours, and this is the condition of the common sailor, whose situation, as to wages, illustrates fully some of the most important parts of the subject of wages. No class of men scarcely is more destitute than that of the common sailor; it is quite rare to find one of them who has laid up a dollar. Still there is no doubt but that their condition is improving; they already begin to make use of the Savings Banks. I repeatedly asked the men on board of our ship (the St. Andrew) this question: "How many men are there on board of our ship who have laid up any money?" They generally laughed in my face when I asked it. And still their wages are such that, in a very few years (not many of them having wives and children), they might lay up enough for a comfortable independence for a few years at least. Their clothes, from the nature of their employment, cost little, and at sea they are at no expense. They are so reckless on shore that, after a few days, their pockets are emptied, and they are as much slaves as ever; so that, though just returned from a long voyage, they are compelled, after a week or two, and some of them in a less time, to ship again, even in the depths of winter. In this way they make themselves slaves, and are, in fact, sometimes called so by their masters. They are slaves in a triple sense. Slaves to their mistresses, slaves to their landlords, a set of harpies that keep sailors' boarding houses, who, by seducing them into deep drinking and other destructive expenses, soon rob them of all that they have, and then they become slaves to the owners of the ships.

22. *There is no reason in the nature of things* why the common sailor on board of these ships should earn fifteen dollars only a month, while the captains earn annually three or four thousand, and the owners sometimes many more. But it is said that the owners and captains earn as capitalists, that is, their money invested in the ship earns interest. Yes, they do. But can anybody give any good reason *in the nature of things* why the property of these different classes should be so disproportioned? If the sailors were as careful to lay up their earnings as the captains and owners are to lay up theirs, the proportion would soon be altered; and then the sailors themselves, instead of being

PUBLIC AND PRIVATE ECONOMY. 37

slaves to poor wages, would be capitalists also; small capitalists, if you please. The present enormous disproportion of property, that leads to such a stupid waste of it on the part of so many, is not inevitable; quite the contrary; and it is certain that an economical improvement is constantly going forward. But this inequality, according to our present ideas, is inevitable. We have seen the common labourers in every country worked so much like brutes, that we have supposed this to be the order of Nature; but Nature is a kind mistress, if we will obey her commands and be kind to each other. At present, the great difficulty of the common labourers as to wages is this: there are so many of them that are living from hand to mouth, that they have no option as to wages; they must take what are offered. When a poor sailor has got to the bottom of his purse, his landlord will compel him to ship again, or kick him out of his house, of course.

23. *In the nature of things*, the wages of sailors on board of these ships are not proportioned to their services. In many respects their characters are far more interesting than is generally thought, and their labours are always so.

On land, the common sailor is intoxicated with pleasure and liquor; at sea, without liquor, he shows much of the true dignity of a man. There he is a grave, serious-looking, reflecting person; the grandeur and uncertainty of the scenes about him make him thoughtful. His exact and arduous duties in the midst of tempests, when, if, through heedlessness, he misses a rope, he may with hundreds be plunged into the fathomless regions of the sea, compel him to think. There is a practice of this kind on board ships, a very good one, and indispensable to safety. The officer gives the command to the man at the helm, and he responds. In hard weather, when lying prostrate with seasickness under the bulwarks, I have heard for half hours together the officer crying out "Luff," when *he*, to show that he understands the word, and that there may be no confusion, answers, " Luff, sir." " Keep her steady ;" " Keep her steady, sir," and so on. I never knew the man to miss the word of command, or to neglect to respond to it.

These men are in situations of great responsibility. After our *Champagne days,* when the senses of many of our passengers are steeped in forgetfulness, and both captain and mate have turned in, you may, at the midnight watch, when the stars can no longer be traced, and the ocean is rolling in its glory, see all committed to the vigilance of two of these faithful men, one at the helm, one at the look-out, with an inferior officer, perhaps a mere stripling, silently pacing the deck. At such a moment, lost in gratitude, you forget all that a sailor is on shore.

24. The common sailor lies under great disadvantages ; he leaves the paternal roof young and without education ; he is then transferred from ship to ship, and never knows home again. He is committed to the charge of that class of men, many of

whom are so coarse and ignorant of all but one kind of human nature, that they despise the wisdom of Nelson and Collingwood, and think that there is but one mode of government, and that this is to be administered with a rope's end. With these opinions of a sailor, of what sort of consequence is it what amount of wages he gets ?

After all, there is a consolation. The labouring part of the world is rising; they begin to be economical; they begin to see what all labourers will at last find out, that is, two things: first, that, let the laws be what they may, without economy and a right use of property, nothing can help them; second, that those who have property are equally bound for the good of society to make a right use of it, instead of squandering it upon unmanly and paltry appetites and indulgences. The common people must help themselves; there is no Hercules to lift them out of the mire. The condition of a sailor is in one respect like that of every other man: if he has nothing, he is nothing; he must work or starve, and he must, too, work whenever he is called upon; so that he cannot say to the rich merchant, "Stay a little; you wish to send your ship to sea, and I want better wages, and when you are ready to pay them, I am your man." At present, a great portion of the common labourers are little better than slaves, for the want of a little property; it is but little, but that little they must have to save themselves from chains. It is, then, the want of economy, of foresight, of temperance, that is one of the great causes of the present bad distribution of property; if we will correct our own follies, we shall soon put government in a good train, for governments are conducted by men. Some people think that they are never learning political economy till some profound principles are announced which are beyond the ken of common men; but, after all, we shall find that the greater part of it is a very common-sense-like affair.

25. *Servants' Wages.* In England they have a practice by which travellers generally pay servants in this way: that is, a shilling to the coachman; the same to the manservant at the hotel; sixpence to the chambermaid, &c., according to circumstances, which I shall mention hereafter. The English practice, so admirably contrived to lower the standard of independence, to degrade the servants by putting them all upon a dead level, has crept into our American ships. In other words, it is the *fashion,* which is as much as to say that it is the law; but there is this difference between this law and many others at least, and that is, that, while some others are made by rich and poor for the benefit of all, this is made by the rich, the fashionable, and by great travellers for their own peculiar benefit.

The matter is managed thus. As we come in sight of the Bill of Portland or the Needles on one side, or the Long Island Lights on the other, some old traveller says to his fellow-passengers, " Gentlemen, it is *customary* in these voyages for the passengers to give the steward a pound (English) each for the benefit of all the servants; whom shall we appoint to collect the money?" To say that it is customary, is only saying that it is the fashion, and fashion in the United States is a grim tyrant; when he orders, every man, woman, and child looks up as they would to a speaking Juggernaut, and, without turning to the right or left, says, "Yes, sir." So we all gather about the collector and pay our pound *alike;* that is, the rich merchant who owns the ship, and half a dozen more; the poor clergyman who is on a voyage for health, and may not be worth a dollar; the young man, a clerk, a mere boy, who goes to England upon a salary of perhaps a hundred pounds, and so on. And then the ladies, rich and poor, and without any reference to the trouble to which one or another has put the servants, pay their pound alike also; though it is no doubt true that some generous people, who have given the servants more trouble than is usual, pay accordingly; but this is in a private way, of course. Now what can be more un-American than this English practice? Why should rich and poor, sick and well, those who give much trouble and those who give little, pay servants alike? And, what is as much to the point, why should servants, good and bad, civil and uncivil, clean and dirty, be *paid alike?* On board of our ship, the St. James, it was said that this money was paid to the steward, and that he divided it into three equal parts, he taking one, and the other servants the residue; but after what rule I know not, nor do I know that a third was the steward's proportion. The English custom of paying servants alike, without reference to their merit, is to reduce them to one standard of inferiority. There is no more reason why these labourers should receive equal wages than many others. No services can be more unequal; and if they are paid by gratuities, these should be the rewards of civility, temperance, skill, and good conduct. There is nothing that debases the lower classes more than placing the individuals in them upon the same footing in esteem and compensation. Every man should be paid, other things being equal, as far as that be possible, *according to what he earns,* as this gives to every man the best chance of rising according to his merit, which is conformable to all just democratic ideas. The opposite practice is one of the worst of those which prevail in England, where servants seldom rise, compared with what is common in the United States, and where the rule is, once a servant, always a servant.

It is this selfish attempt to counteract the laws of God, who has promised rewards to his creatures according to their merit, that has so long kept the lower orders down, and the world in such a miserable state of poverty. Men will not work in earnest unless hope is for ever brightening their prospects. This is the subservience which some people so much admire; and which, as they say, makes the best servants, but which, in the end, will be found to be false; for the best men in every class are those who are treated with the greatest justice and humanity. This is according to the everlasting principles of human nature, and not the slavish laws of custom, fashion, pride, in England, in the United States, or in any other country.

26. But there is another consideration in this matter, of which I shall say more when I come to give an account of English servants; and that is, the less they are paid by *gifts*, so much the better, so much the more independence, so much the less subservience in the bad sense of that word, so much the less underbidding for places, so much the better wages in the end. Why should they receive as a favour, with cap in hand, that to which they have a right? American servants must remember that oft-repeated gifts never returned make slaves; that the labourer is worthy of his hire; that his services cannot be dispensed with; and that *wages* are better than *gifts*. But, after all, the grand argument with the stand-still part of the world is, that the English servants are the best in the world, and this is enough for them, they never dreaming, any more than their grandmothers did, that the world is changing. But let them go to England, and then inquire in the parlours or the kitchens, it is all one which, and they will find that the miseries which we so foolishly suffer in the United States from the joint folly of mas-

ters and servants, but the greater folly of masters, for they have the best means of knowing their duties, are beginning there; that discontent and revolt from the principle of injustice I have mentioned are fermenting, and will sooner or later leaven the whole lump. The truth cannot be disguised; the principles of democracy are growing everywhere; by this I do not intend any mean party thing, but the true thing; that kind of government which produces the greatest love for God and man. We have, however, a great deal yet to learn to make it what it should be, and will be.

27. STEERAGE-PASSENGERS. Economy is a virtue of selection; she saves here in order to spend there; she knows that a man cannot have everything, she therefore chooses the best. Economy is not mean and miserly, saving everything, and starving herself; she does not think it necessary to make a voyage in a floating palace, nor would she, if she could, gormandize every day at the expense of her humbler fellow-citizens; on the contrary, she is generous and noble-minded, and, instead of confining her invitations to that beautiful country England, to a few rich ladies and gentlemen, she would extend them to as many enlightened people as possible of every class, so that all might come home freighted with wisdom for the benefit of that great human family of which she is one of the wisest instructresses.

To drop the metaphor, the false kinds of expense in travelling are equally contemptible and injurious to the character of our people, who will sooner or later discover that fashion and custom do as much, or more, to degrade the great body of the people, as those iron men who rule with the sword. If the common people of the United States are to be anything, they must have a mind of their own, and become their own masters in morals and economy; if these be right, they can give the law to whom they will. But ignorant people will give the law to nobody.

28. We left New-York on the sixteenth day of May, and on the twenty-fifth of that month were about half way across the Atlantic, after nine days of hard, steady westerly winds. On the morning of that day the sea was calm and the scene beautiful; all were well, miseries and sorrows were forgotten. Our lives being now in the present and the future, we began to look about us, and to compare our condition, basking as we were in the sunshine, and surrounded by every luxury, with that of our neighbours the *steerage-passengers*. It is at such a moment, when we remember how wretched we have been, how equal in misery all men may be, how unimportant and even loathsome all the dainties of our table had been to the seasick; it is at such a moment that the heart expands, and we cast an eye through the thin partition that separates the different grades of passengers on board the ship.

The steerage-passengers, of whom there were about thirty-seven on board the St. James, were divided from the cabin-passengers when on deck by a piece of canvass suspended from two spars lying across the ship about midships, a little forward of the mainmast. This canvass formed an impassable barrier between the parties, except that now and then some little brat of a child, who knew not or cared not for the laws of the ship, would play truant, lift the canvass, and overstep the barrier in order to see what sort of creatures the cabin-passengers were. This thin canvass partition, which custom makes a wall of brass, is a fit emblem of many of the fanciful and unreal distinctions of life. The steerage-passengers pay (1837) for their passage from New-York to England eighteen dollars, and from England to New-York five guineas. This difference is produced by the different length of the two voyages, as already stated. They furnish their own stores, which, upon an average, cost them about fifteen or twenty dollars. A pound English, when we left New-York, was worth about four dollars eighty-seven cents, we having bought a few sovereigns at that price. Passengers usually, in addition to their bills on England, or letters of credit, carry a few sovereigns (a sovereign being an English pound), to provide for accidents, such as shipwreck, &c. At this rate, the price of a steerage-passenger over, including passage-money and the cost of provisions, would be equal to, say thirty-six dollars. Travellers, in all general computation as to expense, call a pound English, or a sovereign, five dollars, which the reader will find sufficiently accurate for common calculation. The English pound by our tariff is valued at four dollars forty-four cents. Between the sum of thirty-six dollars which the steerage-passenger pays, and the one hundred and forty dollars which we pay, there is a wide difference, and there is, to be sure, a vast difference in our accommodations. The steerage-passengers put up hams, pilot-bread, dried beef, cheese, butter, tea, coffee, salt, pepper, potatoes, &c., &c., according to their ability and tastes. In the St. James, we had on the dinner-table chickens, ducks, geese, veal, beef, ham, mutton, tongues, pilot-bread, excellent fresh bread baked on board, and at breakfast as good corn-bread as was ever eaten. For our dessert we had pies, puddings, tarts, oranges, figs, prunes, apples. Of wines, we had claret, port, and Madeira every day; Champagne twice or three times a week, but which I do not recollect; brandy and other spirits whenever called for, and soda-water in unlimited quantities.

29. We have for our sleeping apartment a stateroom, which is a nice little chamber with two berths, an upper and an under, sufficient to accommodate two persons. The door that opens into it is made of beautiful mahogany or other expensive wood. In this little chamber we have room enough to hang our greatcoats and cloaks; it is about six feet and a half one way, and about five or five and a half the other. We have in it a small chest of drawers with four divisions, sufficient to accom-

modate two people; a washstand with two bowls and two pitchers. These make up a portion (no doubt many things are omitted) of the luxuries and comforts which we the cabin-passengers have on board these excellent ships.

30. The steerage is that portion of the vessel amidships immediately under the deck and over the hold. Into this space all the steerage-passengers are crowded, the ship sometimes carrying a hundred and more, as is well known. What better accommodations they can have, or whether any, upon the present plan of regulating these matters, for the money they pay, I cannot say, not being familiar with their condition. In justice I must declare, that all the steerage-passengers that I heard say anything upon the subject uniformly spoke well both of our ships and their officers.

At best, the steerage-passengers, if numerous, are in a miserable plight. In the morning they come up to the galley, and fill their tea and coffee pots, which are then carried down into the steerage. During the forenoon, all that choose put meat, vegetables, materials for puddings, &c., into separate bags, which are boiled in one pot for dinner. In the steerage, some have berths made in a coarse way with common boards, some sleep on chests, some on trunks; trunks and chests are sometimes piled one upon another to separate families; sometimes they are separated by a blanket for a curtain; often they have no separation, and are huddled together much like pigs in a sty. In very bad weather, almost every sea that is shipped sweeps over the bows, when the steerage-passengers are, of course, drenched, if on deck ; if the weather is so bad that the hatches must be closed, their discomfort is still greater. No degree of misery can well surpass that of a hundred steerage-passengers in such a situation, some very poor and without adequate provision, some seasick, some ill with other maladies, some women with infants at the breast, and all, sick or well, compelled to administer to their own relief and wants.

Among the steerage-passengers you may plainly observe some delicate and refined individuals, who have evidently seen better days, and who, from their decorous manners, if those alone could give them a right to a place in the cabin, would have as good a claim there as those who now enjoy that privilege. But, then, the sum of one hundred and forty dollars is wanting. And where is it ? " In the Adventures of a Guinea" we may find it perhaps. It may be on some lady's finger, about her neck, or in her ears, or in a luxurious shawl about her shoulders. Some people would rather flourish in a fine shawl than see Europe. (Shawls were sold in New-York at auction, some years since, for a thousand dollars each.) It may be in the exquisite chiselling and gilding of the ship's mahogany-work ; perhaps it is in *Sillery* made in France, or, it may be, brewed in New-Jersey ; or Johannesbergh* man-

---

* See Redding on Wines. It seems that Prince Metternich

ufactured at London or New-York, which some gentlemen would think ungenteel to touch at less than five dollars the bottle, they graduating the quality by the price, as some Southern ladies order their finery from the New-York milliners, saying, in a postscript, "Let it be as dear as possible." Or perhaps causeless war, that aristocratic device contrived to make fat jobs, offices, and poor people, may have swept it from the board, or some political spendthrift like George the Fourth, who thinks more of a ride in a pony chaise to Virginia Water than of all the industrious people who have made England what England is.

Till the great human family is duly considered in the use of property, both by people and government, we shall proceed pretty much as we have hitherto, building cobhouses to be overturned by every gust of "panic," or crushed by every "pressure."

31. These steerage-passengers exhibit many of the true distinctions which we see in the world; these are the common people; these are a portion of that multitude of poor people whom we see around us, and who are made poor and kept poor, not by an invincible necessity of being so, but greatly by the vices, follies, and frauds of those above them, who govern them, and partly by their own follies and vices. Distinctions in riches, in the comforts of travelling, and all other accommo-

is the owner of all the Johannesbergh, of which there is very little.

dations, there must be. But such want, recklessness, and wretchedness on the one side; such vanity, pride, sensuality, and superfluous expense on the other, show that there is something radically vicious and false in our systems, public and private. *We are still living too much under the influence of that privileged system of other countries which, in giving a bounty to vices that destroy property and happiness, is the great social curse.* In pointing out the *effects*, I mean more fully to illustrate the *cause*. It is certain that the rich are richer, comparatively, than they should be, and the poor poorer than they need be. If the people have an interest in anything, they have in right principles of economy, and in understanding them thoroughly. No mortal can conceive of the property there might be in the world, and of the comforts that all, or nearly all, could obtain, if property was not wasted and destroyed in the stupid ways in which it is, both by rich and poor. Voluntary poverty in this free country ought to be despised, hated, and abhorred.

32. What, then, follows from the abuse of property? Not only a horrible inequality of comforts, but a disgusting poverty of supply for the greater part, so that they have neither good food, clothes, houses, gardens, roads, pavements, nor a thousand other common things that might be mentioned: then, again, so costly are pride, vanity, and fashion, that nine tenths of even those who are best off can hardly keep their heads above water; and then

many of those who are called the working-people, being houseless, comfortless, and hopeless, become disgusted with the waste of property which they see in the higher classes, fall into idleness and intemperance, and destroy all the property they can.

33. At Portsmouth our luggage was examined at the custom-house, which was a mere form, for our carpet-bags (I can only speak of ours) were not opened, and the trunks were barely unlocked, a few articles being lifted up and then put down again. While the man was doing this, he said, in a whisper to my friend, "It is usual to give something for despatch." He, in compliance with the vicious custom which is said to exist in these custom-houses, gave two shillings and sixpence for both.

34. Before getting on shore at Portsmouth, we were detained some hours by quarantine regulations. The health officer came alongside of the ship, and asked the captain many questions about our health. After this he sent up a Bible to the captain at the end of a long pole, enclosed in a copper or brass case, from the little boat in which he sat. The captain, being obliged to swear to the statement he had made, kissed the Bible, case and all. The case was for *preservation;* of which principle, as the minds of the people of England are imbued with it, we know little or nothing, and may well learn.

CHAPTER II.

35. *Portsmouth, June,* 1836. Here we are in England! Reader, be you gentleman, farmer, mechanic, or whatever you are, if you be a citizen of the United States, and have money enough after discharging all the debts that folly and fashion fasten upon you; if you have time, and it be consistent with other duties, go to England and see the race from which you sprung; go and see what a nation loaded with a debt of eight hundred millions of pounds has accomplished; look at the palaces, pictures, statues, houses, cottages, roads, horses, sheep, &c.; consider what they might have been, how few paupers, how little of extreme poverty, with a proper economy, and without such a debt; go, and gain the pleasure of giving up your prejudices; go, it will do your mind and heart good.

36. From the moment we touched the shore I felt that I was at home. The outward state of things, to be sure, is far different, and, in most respects, far superior; but the man, his soul, his language, is essentially the same. To say, then, that we respect the English, looks like a sort of national vanity; it is the same thing as to esteem one's self.

37. We had hardly entered our hotel at Portsmouth before we were reminded of home, of the

blessings of commerce, and the free intercourse of nations. We saw the same furniture as in our own parlours and chambers; the same patterns of hanging-paper; the same bamboo chairs; the same green inside window-blinds; the same dimity counterpane upon our beds; washstand, bowls, basins, &c. The merchant is the great and first agent in the intercourse that disseminates the blessings of trade; and still, in the United States, he has been called an *unproductive labourer.* It would be quite as good sense to call the sailors of the St. James unproductive labourers. True political economy is founded in the wants of human nature itself.

38. I asked a friend in the United States who had been travelling a very short time in England, whether he got *fresh* eggs at the hotels. " Oh no," said he; " I understood that the nobility ate all the *fresh* eggs in England." It is true enough that the nobility have the choice in England, but we must confess that we found very good eatables there, sometimes a stale egg, but very rarely. It has often been said that anything may be bought in England for money, and it is generally true enough. This is one of the distinctions of England, good bread, butter, meats, &c., &c., and by far more universally good than in the United States, but there is not the same abundance of them for the great human family. And why not? I shall from time to time give some of the reasons.

At our hotel, I asked the waiter the price of eggs. He told me that he did not know, nor of any marketable article ; meaning, no doubt, of the general provisions for the house. This is the kind of education which the common people of England get, and which is so inferior to that of the United States. These are the antiquated notions which leave a Chinese where he was under Confucius, and an Englishman, in some respects, like his forefathers under the Edwards and the Henrys. This, they say, comes from the nice division of labour and keeping a man to one thing, by which he becomes so much more perfect in that. But why should not a waiter know prices? What is more important to a man who is to get a living? Waiters in England often become landlords ; every man ought to know the prices, as far as he can, of the things he lives upon.

This keeping of useful knowledge out of the heads of people is quite too frequent even in the United States; in that class, especially, who send their daughters to boarding-schools, where they are taught "all the sciences and all the accomplishments," and at twenty-one many do not know the prices of half a dozen common household articles. This is a part of the ignorance in which the poor people of England are brought up; it is a part of that mode of vicious education by which the lower orders there are made and kept underlings from generation to generation. They have a prejudice in England against a man going out of his own narrow circle, for every man has his own, some larger and some smaller ; and if he oversteps it he may tread upon others. The boundaries established for lands and trades in England are equally distinct. If anything distinguishes the people of the United States over other nations, it is that every individual is a part of the whole, and that he is educated to take an interest in, and to know something of all that concerns a human being.

39. Portsmouth is said to be one of the most strongly fortified towns in England. We saw a regimental review by the governor of the town. The soldiers were neatly and well dressed, except that, I suppose, their dress may have cost three times as much as it ought. Some wore huge bearskin caps, some a large (I think leather) hat. Here was a magnificent display of epaulettes and various kinds of military coxcombry, very like what we have in our great army, the militia of the United States. It costs millions; no one knows the cost. The trappings of the horse or man do not make the horse or man. A huge bearskin cap is not needed to distinguish one corps from another; a simple military badge will do that. We underrate the man when we think that we make more of him by putting finery upon him. The more he thinks of his petty ornaments, his feathers, his epaulettes, his laced coat and hat, the less likely are his actions to be noble. Every man of common sense knows that those whose minds are busied with the thoughts of this trumpery are, with few exceptions, not first-rate people in any class. Cuvier was one of these exceptions. He prepared with the care of a pro-

fessional dressmaker the costume of the court under Bonaparte. But this was an idiosyncrasy. All the passions of men are useful in the different stages of society, even vanity, pride, and the rest; but the question is, which *are the most useful?* A poor girl in the United States, who bakes, washes, scrubs, for five or six dollars a month, and is driven on by a passion for a five-dollar cape, had better work for that than not work at all; but it is better still if her ambition be for something substantial, that will serve her in a sick day, or when *panics* and *pressures* come, and the factories stop. This love of finery, which has become so universal among us, from seeming to put the rich and poor upon a footing of equality, but which can never effect that object, may be useful in a half-barbarous state, when there is no other motive sufficient to make people work; but the time has now come when our labour is wanted for things more useful.

40. At Portsmouth I looked in vain to see one wooden-covered house; there may be a shingle in the town, but I doubt it. This construction of the houses in England accounts, in a measure, for the few fires they have compared with our bonfires of churches, stores, houses, &c. There are other causes for fires here not known in England. From what I saw of the careful habits of the people of England, I think there must be ten times as much property destroyed and lost here as there by carelessness and recklessness. It is equally painful and disgusting to see how we waste and squander.

From the top of St. Paul's, which looks down upon some of the most indifferent parts of London, there is not a single wooden roof, partition-fence, stable, outhouse, not even a board or shingle to be seen. All appears to be one mass of stone, brick, and mortar.

41. We are by far too lofty in the United States in all our ideas of expense, that is, compared with our fortunes; there is no *true* economy in anything. Mr. Dewey says, very truly, that the English are never ashamed to count the cost, nor to speak of it. We were witnesses to the fact of not less than eight or ten persons asking for franks to their letters of a member of parliament in his dining-room, they not making the least secret of the matter. I say nothing of the meanness of cheating the government, or rather the people, in this way, which I believe to be quite as common here as in England. We were surprised, in Portsmouth, at the smallness of the houses, even in some of the best parts of the town. In these we saw many good brick houses, two and three stories high, with fronts of not more than fifteen feet, and some, I think, not over twelve or thirteen. It would be very well for large numbers of people in the United States to import this modest fashion. A great soul does not require a large tenement, and a jail is better than a twenty thousand Waverley Place house with a millstone of debt about one's neck.

42. It will be nearly incredible, in a future age, that political economists should have taught the im-

possibility of finding employment for all the people, and wholly so that multitudes should have actually starved for the want of something to do by which they could earn their bread ; and still this is the actual fact in Europe at this moment. But this is nothing strange at present, for a large proportion of the people are, in a great measure, idle, or doing some kind of work that is comparatively useless. Nothing is more striking upon entering an English town of any size, even in a country so industrious as England, than the sight of so many idle people, or of those who seem to have little or nothing to do. In the neighbourhood of our hotel, upon the docks, and about the water, we saw hundreds such, not boatmen alone, who might be waiting to transport passengers, but persons of various descriptions. I asked the boatman why there were so many idle people about. " Oh," he replied, " they have nothing to do; there are too many of us in this country." This language I often heard from the common people. Here appeared to be a true disciple of the Malthusian school. It is quite true that there are too many, and will be as long as so large a portion are set to work in the way they are at present. They will certainly want bread as long as the corn-laws prevent them from buying bread where they can get it cheap, and as long as the people are put to making fine caps and feathers for soldiers instead of manufacturing axes, saws, shovels, spades, &c., wherewith to exchange with those nations that produce the materials of cheap bread. The truth is, that the fashions, systems, and laws which at present regulate labour are so barbarous, and the whole fabric of opinion upon which they are erected so baseless, that Mr. Malthus's opinions, as applied to the actual state of the world, are plausible at least. But that is not sufficient for the American people, nor ought it to be for any people ; for the true question is, not what is, but what ought to be, what may be, and what must be, if we have faith in the goodness of God, and the capacity which he has given to man to move onward, " to go ahead" in the American vocabulary.

At Portsmouth I attempted to get a sight of the docks, which are said to be among the great things of England, and was told that a stranger could not see them ; but that, if I would put myself on the books as from any town in England, there would be no difficulty. Upon getting inside of the gates I was requested, by the person who introduced strangers to the place, to insert my name and place of abode. This I did truly, when he observed that he was very sorry, but that I could not, as a stranger, be allowed to see the docks unless I first sent up to London and obtained the necessary document from our minister. I remonstrated, and told him, with a little enthusiasm, such as cannot but be excited by the view of so glorious a country as England, that I had endured twenty-four days' suffering from that most villanous of all diseases, seasickness, and had come across the ocean to see his country. I cannot suppose that this compliment, so just and so well deserved, was the cause of his kind attentions and effort to obtain for me a sight of the place; for nearly everywhere in England, known or unknown, I received civilities which can never be forgotten, and often those substantial kindnesses which can never be repaid. However severe, therefore, my criticisms may be upon the usages and institutions of the country, they will not be more so than are often bestowed upon my own, and will never be the result of spleen or ill-temper. This man told me that, so far as he had any power, the rule was inflexible; but, if possible, he would get leave from the admiral or commanding officer. He then went to an officer and stated my case, who, not less civil than himself, said promptly, that, if possible, he would get me permission. He went for that purpose, and returned after about twenty minutes, saying that the admiral could not consent to dispense with the rule. Between two great nations everything should be done to facilitate intercourse, and make the inhabitants of each country as kind and agreeable to the other as possible. Besides, in the present state of the world, it would be about as judicious to blind the eyes of strangers lest they should see the gaslights between London and Windsor, as to shut them out of these dockyards.

43. Everybody has heard of the horrible *dearness* of England! The word "*dear*" conveys a very bad idea to the minds of most people, and to

the poor it is often a word of dreadful import. There was a time when we could boast of the cheapness of our own country. I believe it is pretty well understood, at last, that the excessive issue of bank paper for some years past has had much to do with prices, with *cheap* and *dear*. As to *cheap* and *dear*, I shall from time to time give such information as to the relative prices in England and the United States as came under my notice. Few subjects are more important than those embraced in the words *cheap* and *dear*. The causes of cheapness and dearness are well worthy the greatest attention. Dear bread, dear meats, dear fruits, all things dear, are generally found in those countries where monopoly has gathered the blessings into the laps of a few, and sown the curses broadcast among the residue of the people.

At our hotel we paid 3*s*. 6*d*. for a warm bath, that is, 3*s*. for the bath and sixpence to the waiter. The English shilling, at the ordinary rate of exchange, is worth about 22 cents of our money. At this rate we paid 77 cents each for a bath. In turning English shillings into ours, it will be sufficiently accurate for common calculation to consider the English shilling as equal to two shillings New-York currency, or twenty-five cents. Here, then, is nearly a dollar for a little hot water, a place to wash in, a piece of soap, and a clean towel, and, if you please, the attendance of the waiter for five minutes! Now a poor man in England must work a whole week on the land in order to earn ten shillings, or two dollars and a half of our money. What a frightful disproportion! There must be something very wrong and false in the system which produces such a result. I will, however, as to the cause of it, leave the subject here, to be resumed hereafter. In New-York we pay, or did pay, for a bath in Chamber-street, $37\frac{1}{2}$ cents. No poor man can get one for less, that I know of. His bath, then, costs nearly the price of his whole daily living, for many labouring people did not, but a little time since in New-York, pay more than twenty shillings a week for their board and lodging. The consequence is, that no poor man can afford to take a public bath in New-York in winter or summer, except at the docks; and by poor men here I mean as well many of those who associate with rich people, live in their houses, and are their relatives, perhaps, as those who are known to be poor.

44. The expensive comforts and ways of living in all countries mark the gulf between rich and poor. The natural comforts which God designed for all his people have become to many dainties and luxuries; they show the debasement of the people, and that property is not made to do what it ought and might do. Think of a bath costing a poor man in England two or three days' labour! a man, too, who does the hardest part of the drudgery that makes all property.

What should be done by the public, and what by private individuals, so far as property is concerned, I shall consider hereafter. Thus much I will say here with confidence, that public baths ought to be furnished to the poor in our rich cities at little or no expense. If the barbarous spendthrifts of Rome could furnish them to the poor at about a farthing as the price of admission, it would be a pity if we should not be able to do the same thing at some very small expense. *

45. On the 10th day of June, 1836, we took our seats for London in an oldfashioned coach, the "Royal Blue." This deference to royalty in England did not appear to me very much to enlarge the minds of the people. The names of it appear on the coaches, inns, shops, &c. The giving coaches a name is a good plan, because in England there are so many on the same routes that the designation becomes convenient. Ours was what is called in England a *slow* coach. We left Portsmouth at half past 8 A.M., and reached London at about 6 P.M.; $9\frac{1}{2}$ hours, 72 miles. Our stoppages made it slow. We dined at Ripley upon good mutton, the uniform excellence of which in England is very remarkable. We paid two shillings for our dinner, and sixpence to the servant-maid who waited at table. The miserable meats which we get in many of the country parts of the United States show a poor economy. Our coach contained six seats for inside passengers, or, as the English elliptically express it, six "insides." We paid for an inside 16s., and for an outside 11s. Every working-man should remember that all his pleasures must be paid for. As the coaches in England pay a toll at

---

* See Domestic Manners of the Romans, chapter X.

the turnpike gates, the traveller must pay his portion in the price of his fare. Eleven shillings for such a ride, over such roads, and in such a country, was one of the cheapest pleasures that I ever enjoyed. Such pleasures more of us could enjoy if we would renounce our vain and costly trappings, give up our debasing appetites, eat and drink according to reason, and then be just to each other in the distribution of property.

46. The English coach with four insides, the most common coach, so far as I saw, is very much of a humbug; and nearly the only one that I know of in England, so far as the comforts of travelling are concerned. As to the coach, it really is not the thing that it purports to be, heretical as this assertion may be to our friends over the water. The inside is so small that, with four good-sized persons, you are too closely packed; and so low that, with a reasonable height, you are compelled to wear a cap. There is no light except through two little windows; and on the outside, where you have places for fourteen with the coachman, the seats are nothing but bare boards, with the exception of that next to the coachman, which has a cushion. I stated these objections to an Englishman; "Oh," said he, "you can always get a wisp of straw to sit upon." The reader will understand that I only speak of the coaches which I saw; I was never in a mailcoach.

There are in coaches in the country parts many wretched horses; by this I do not mean horses so broken down that they cannot perform their regular routes at nine or ten miles an hour, but horses which, from their bent and often lacerated knees, show the dreadful service to which they are put by such rapid travelling over flinty roads. It is said, in England, that three years is the common life of a horse in a stagecoach. How to reconcile the laws of humanity with the interests of the traveller in this respect, I know not.

47. Here the humbug ends; the coach is clean, the horses are beautifully groomed, the harness is as black as jet, the ear-pieces are sometimes ornamented with roses, sometimes with dahlias; the coachman is one of the best-looking men in the kingdom; his whip does its office faithfully; the long lash is hardly larger than a good-sized twine; the thin-skinned horses feel it so keenly, that it seems only to be necessary to lay it gently across their backs. Nor is there any racing or contending of opposition coaches on the road, that I saw, though I heard of it as not uncommon formerly; nor is there any breaking of thorough braces, and repairing them with rails (I saw no rails); no stopping to tie broken harness with tow strings; no kicking or pounding horses that are unable to perform their routes in the accustomed time; nor did I ever see but one unruly horse in a coach, and that was in travelling from Bristol to Cheltenham. As we came near our stopping-place, not far from this latter town, we passed a groom on a refractory horse. The coachman, who recognised an old ac-

quaintance, cried out, " That horse has no more mooth than a bool." We remonstrated, but the horse was put in, when it appeared, truly enough, that he had no " mooth," for he bolted off from the road, stopped, cramped the wheels, and would have turned us over, but the passengers insisted upon his being taken out, which was done, for the coachman dared not refuse. The abuse of travellers in the United States by the use of refractory horses is common, and is a shameful imposition upon the public. If life is wantonly sacrificed in this way, or by committing the traveller to the charge of a drunken driver, the proprietor, upon every legal principle, is guilty of manslaughter. We shall never be safe in travelling in our stagecoaches in this country till the people unite to make an example of these " stage accidents," nine out of ten of which take place through the wilful inattention, carelessness, or mismanagement of the proprietors or drivers. Every abuse of this kind should be published in the newspapers far and near.

I was told in England that the coaches, or some of them, were owned by the builders; were hired by the coach proprietors, and kept in order by the builders at their expense, and for that purpose frequently inspected. In England they consider it important not only to *make* things, but somewhat so to *preserve* them when made; an art not quite so well understood in the United States.

48. It is a great pity that the working-people in the United States will not at once shake off their

chains, combine, turn their backs upon men and women made by tailors and milliners, set up a taste of their own, and dress *appropriately*, consistently with their means and employment. For this it is not necessary that they should wear a uniform, or discard beauty and taste, or reject anything but tawdry finery and things out of proportion. Dress is a great refinement and ornament. Many of the coachmen whom I saw in England were dressed in a way to delight a stranger, their clothes being of excellent quality, clean, and adapted to their employment; no wigs, no silk stockings, no *white* gloves. Our coachman from Portsmouth to London was not exactly after this pattern; he wore a velvet collar upon a dark greasy green coat, a white vest, dark trousers, fine black leather gloves, a breastpin, and white cravat, with a rose in his buttonhole. The passion for flowers in England is universal, and one of the most beautiful things to be observed there. These are cheap luxuries. This was the only drinking coachman whom we saw that we knew to be such.

49. The coachmen in England who drive the stagecoaches are a very peculiar class, and show how much *wages* will depend upon good character. I heard it said everywhere, that no class had improved more than these coachmen, and especially in temperance. This is the sheet anchor of a labouring man; let him stick to it. The stage-drivers in our country, also, have greatly improved, though there is quite room enough for further im-

provement. An immense proportion of them were hard drinkers; that was at a period when it was a universal opinion that it was hopeless to expect a drunkard would recover; but we now know better from actual experience. The truth is, a man has but a little soul, be he a gentleman or a labourer, who cannot give up his tobacco, brandy, or port, when he finds that they are killing him by inches and filling his house with tears.

50. I travelled about twelve hundred miles in England, and nearly always in stagecoaches, but never saw a drunken coachman, and never one in the least excited by liquor, so far as I could observe, but the man I have named. A drunken stage-driver ought no more to be trusted with the command of a stagecoach than a madman with that of a ship.

The coachmen in England are placed in very responsible situations; they have often sixteen passengers, and are intrusted with valuable packages. They are among the best-looking men you meet; stout, well-made, have an air of cheerfulness and contentment, naturally belonging to men who are well paid and fed; a remarkable freshness in their countenances indicating good health, which, no doubt, proceeds from their regular, temperate life, and constant exposure to fresh air. They have, however, the English mark of malt in their veins, though to a very moderate degree compared with some others. Beer is a god in England; a common man there thinks that his legs would not sustain him a month without beer.

51. As soon as the common people come thoroughly to understand how much their wages, and, of course, prosperity through life, depend upon their intelligence, good manners, fidelity, and especially temperance, they will cease to paddle along in the troubled waters in which they have ever been tugging against wind and tide. These virtues are the qualifications by which the English coachman earns his great wages. Why should a coachman, in the nature of things, earn a thousand dollars a year, when the menservants in the hotels in which I was did not earn over sixteen or eighteen shillings sterling a week? His work is not so hard, and often does not require as much skill as that of the servant. From every inquiry I was able to make, I think that the average receipts of the English coachman are at least £200 a year; many get much more.

52. I was told that a coachman who drove from London to Cambridge, about sixty miles, earned £500 a year; he was said to be the son of a clergyman, a person of excellent character, and a great favourite. As the coachmen are paid by the passengers, their receipts will depend greatly upon this last circumstance. A coachman who drove us from London to Windsor was said to receive at least a pound a day; several passengers paid him a shilling both going and coming. A young man who drove us from Newmarket to Wells, in Norfolk, told us that he earned £200 a year; and this is a road of little travel compared with many others. Two hundred pounds, or one thousand

dollars, is a larger average sum than is earned by all the lawyers and clergymen in the United States; but it must be remembered that many things are upon a very different scale in England from that which we have.

53. Some few broken-down gentlemen in England resort to the coach for a living; I mean broken down by their own folly and extravagance, by far the most common way of breaking down here and everywhere. There is no reason, to be sure, why a coachman should not be in all essentials a gentlemen, but there is reason enough, generally, why he should not be a broken-down gentleman. We met with one instance of a half-pay officer who drove a coach. This man is well known; we first heard of him repeatedly by name, and then saw him on the route from Brighton to London. There are many false gods in England, as there are, no doubt, in all countries. I have mentioned one; rank is another; before this supreme deity a common man falls prostrate. Our coachman was a *baronet*, and, as he approached the coach to take the reins, a man on the box said, in a most deferential whisper, " That's a baronet, that's a baronet." The servants have a customary sign of deference of this kind. For instance: they ask a gentleman, " Will you have your clothes washed to-day ?" or, " Shall I move your trunk to the opposite side of the room ?" The gentleman says yes, and the servant says, " Thankee, sir." This we in the United States think is being thankful for small favours.

Such is the subservient tone of the servants and common people in England, and so painful is it to those who truly delight in the equal condition of things in the United States! Our man of rank was very communicative to the passengers; the coachman being a sort of showman, who points out the various objects of interest on the road to those who set near him. A farmer (he seemed to be a very inferior sort of a farmer) on the same seat with myself asked some person for information about the weather, or some equally indifferent matter; to which the baronet replied, and the farmer said, " Thankee, sir."

54. A coachman, if for anything, should be distinguished by the appropriateness, simplicity, and durability of his dress, and not by its finery. I have seen more than one start from the White-horse Cellar, Piccadilly, in white gloves, waistcoat, and pantaloons; and this is a man who is to drive through rain, dust, and all kinds of weather; he cannot get inside of the coach and save his fine clothes in case of a storm, as the outside passengers may. I have seen, also, from the seventh story at Meurice's in Paris, in the area below, three coachmen at once in white gloves, and, I think, all dressed in *black*. But the coachman says, " I am not an hostler; I do not clean horses, coach, and harness, as your American coachmen do." That is quite true, for his main business is to drive the coach; but, then, he must drive in all weather; and then, again, when passengers get down on the road, or

in entering a town, he must, if there be no guard, which is very common, help them off with their baggage, clean or dirty; so that, after all, his white gloves, waistcoat, and pantaloons, in his situation, are in poor taste. This is one of the very foolish ways in which the common people waste their money. Our baronet was compelled, as we entered London, to leave the box to take off the dirty baggage of several passengers, among others that of two very coarse women, and did not fail to give us the usual recognition of thankfulness in touching his hat upon receiving our shillings. This gentleman wore two diamonds or other precious stones in his checked neckcloth, and had carnations in his horses' headstalls, another *cheap* beauty. This baronet was the only swearing coachman that I heard in England, though I believe that the English, in this elegant accomplishment, are not behind most of their European neighbours.

The baronet told us that he "horsed the coach" a part of the way from Brighton to London, that is, he owned the horses. Our coachman from Portsmouth to London, and from Newmarket to Wells, told us the same thing. This plan of making the coachman interested in the establishment is certainly a good one; it requires him to be a man of property, and gives greater security to the passengers; for every man will take greater care of his own than of what belongs to another. To be at once a partner and a labourer is one thing, to be a labourer only is another. The institutions of the United States present this advantage to the working man in a degree not known in any other country; and it will be for him, in the practice of a wise economy, and thus obtaining the means of becoming a partner, to show how much farther still he may carry out this idea. If a coachman may become a partner upon a small capital, so may thousands of others in various other kinds of business. This union of the labourer and capitalist in one person may be made a new principle here. Many small capitals make a large one. The first stone laid as the foundation of this union will be *character—temperance.*

No man knows what he can do till he has tried, and the same is true of the millions of common people and common labourers. There is no doubt, not the least, but that they are on the highroad to a better lot. In the United States, certainly, there is nothing wanted but education, the will, the determination, the moral force of temperance, industry, and righteousness; the combining together, as all people do who mean to exert their power to any advantage. To expect any great amelioration from caucuses, elections, laws, or political movements, without a corresponding change in these respects, is childish.

55. It is worth years of economical self-denial to see the beauty of England, and still how few can enjoy that pleasure upon the present scale of expense, the whole system of which would seem to be established to depress every portion of the people except the opulent.

It is a common opinion in the United States among gentlemen travellers, I do not say universal, that a gentleman cannot travel a year in Europe for less than about three thousand dollars, that is, comfortably, without meanness and pinching. There must be something very wrong in such a state of society; it results from the privileged system; it is the wretched tyranny of fashion practised against all the poorer members of it; it is inconsistent with pure pleasures and a moral existence; it supposes, in regard to the greater number, a large expenditure for vanity, show, and a sensual life. But if a man will pay as much for his wine as his dinner at a London hotel, when his wine is a curse to him altogether, or when, perhaps, he is better off with one fifth of it, why, then, it must be so; or if he dare not be seen drinking a glass of cold water instead of the wine, why, then, it will be so. Enormous taxation, which makes everything dear, and disgraceful privileges to a few, with the paltry ideas of gentlemanly expense which they have engendered, can alone account for this state of things. The people of the United States, among themselves at least, can put an end to it.

56. Among the greatest wonders of England are her roads! The labour expended in this way is one of the best modes of distributing property; all derive advantage from them, the poor as well as the rich, though not all equally. This, then, I consider one of the first points in all true political economy. *That is:* in regard to *those things of common en-*

joyment which either cannot be accomplished by private individuals, or which naturally belong to the public, like the highways of a country, the people should take care that the property, by that I mean the property of all the people, be first applied to them rather than to suffer it to be squandered *in public or private pomp.* To prevent, as far as possible, the spendthrift part of the people from throwing away their property like children, let good roads be made; pure water brought into the cities; streets properly paved and lighted, as well where the poor live as the rich; above all, *let the youth be well educated.* I say let these and all things like them first be well done, for they produce a wholesome democratic equality, not only giving comfort to all, but enlarging our minds and souls, and knitting us together as brethren of the same family. In a free country these objects can, in a great measure, be accomplished by general taxation; and it is because the poorer voters do not understand their own interests that they have been so neglected. The people must correct these proceedings.

57. It was said, years since, that the highways of England extended twenty-five thousand miles, and that the expense of them was not less than twenty millions sterling.* The Abbé Raynal says of roads, " Let us travel over all the countries of the earth, and wherever we shall find no facility of trading from a city to a town, and from a village to a hamlet, we may pronounce the people to be bar-

* Edinburgh Encyclopedia, tit. Roads and Highways.

barous, and we shall only be deceived respecting the degree of barbarism." I think, if a stranger was asked what is that most perfect thing which England has done for the common enjoyment of her people, he would point to the roads! In other things you can see deficiencies and imperfections; but to us, who are compelled to drag through the mud and mire, and over the stones and ruts of the roads of New-England, which are the best in the United States, the roads of England seem perfect. Not one, but nearly all of the few I saw. I allude to two trifling exceptions, one in Norfolk near Wells, where the road was not a turnpike, and one in Wales from Cardiff to Merthyr Tydvil. To have any just idea of the roads of England, it is indispensable that you should see them, for no description can give any adequate information. People are incredulous upon such a subject. When the people of the United States cease to pay so dearly as at present for their whistles and pretty playthings, more of them will be able to go to England, and see that beautiful country, and those magnificent roads, and then there will be more witnesses to the truth of what I say. All such will get another high pleasure, that of glorying in ancestors whose amazing industry and reliance upon God to relieve them finally from misgovernment, has held out and kept up their courage against some of the most stupid waste of property by their rulers that was ever known among mankind.

58. I have said that the making of good roads is

one of the best modes of distributing property. That is generally the best way of laying out money which produces more money, or, in other words, property; and, when we speak of property, wealth, riches, we do not mean what a miser does when he talks of his bonds, his stocks, his houses, lots, &c., but what rational men mean when they speak of those thousands of good, healthful, beautiful, agreeable things which enable them to enjoy the world and each other. These things are undoubtedly worth getting together; but what a miserable scarcity of them at present in the human family!

59. In laying out our money upon a road, we have a new capital; in doing so, we have paid labourers for making something that is lasting, that enables every man to travel more cheaply than he could before. When the gentlemen of England spend their money in maintaining two or three hundred racehorses at Newmarket yearly, it is quite true that they distribute property (as to improving the breed of horses, that I shall speak of hereafter); that is, the groom, and the groom's lad, and the sadler, &c., get wages, but they *produce* nothing. On the contrary, the man who works on a road not only gets wages, which none but people of some property can pay, but he produces a road which is good for all, rich and poor, to the end of all time, if it be kept in repair. This shows the difference whether labourers work to produce one thing or another, or, in other words, whether labourers are employed merely for the sake of keeping them at

work and giving them wages, or for the purpose of producing *some useful thing as well as earning wages;* a point of the greatest importance in all economy, and which, in my opinion, makes one of the grand differences between the condition of Europe and that of the United States ; a consideration I wish the reader distinctly to keep in mind.

60. I have said, too, that those are the best modes of distributing property which produce the greatest equality of enjoyment, always taking care that nothing be done to injure the rights of property, thereby taking from industry its true reward and stimulus. For what can be the design of the property of this world but to make a great many people happy instead of a few ?

Good roads equalize enjoyments and spread property in many ways. The very making of the road takes so much property as the road costs, in wages, from those who have it, and transfers it to the labourers who make the road, and who have it not. Then, again, a road is not like a coat, good on the back of one man and ragged on that of another, but it is equally good for the poor man and the king.

Good roads, by opening easy communications from the sea and rivers to the remotest parts of the country, enable those who live in those remote parts to bring their products easily to market. This increases the price of their products, and of their lands, of course, and this tends to equality of prices. So that, finally, by the aid of good roads, railroads, canals, and other communications, all parts of a country stand as nearly as may be upon the same footing of equality, instead of being in a half barbarous condition, where all commerce, manufactures, and riches are confined to a few places on the sea or the rivers. This state of things is now advancing very rapidly in the United States. Equality of prices in provisions is very remarkable in England, and much greater than in the United States. For instance, beef sold in the London markets for eightpence a pound when we were there; while in the remote country parts I never found it below sixpence halfpenny, and generally as high as sevenpence. Most other marketable articles are in something like this proportion. But we know that in the United States the difference of prices, where the difference depends upon carriage alone, is much greater. It is the *price of carriage*, then, that produces this great difference in the price of marketable articles. There was a time, before the Erie Canal was made, when wheat in the county of Ontario, about two hundred miles from Albany, at the head of tide water, was not worth more than thirty-seven and a half cents the bushel; whereas, at Albany, wheat has not probably, for fifty years past, been worth less than the double of that price. But it is the great advantages which good roads impart to commerce, trade, manufactures, and agriculture, wherein we see a proper distribution of property, and the immense advance of the common people. It is in those

PUBLIC AND PRIVATE ECONOMY. 81

countries where these do not flourish that, as Sismondi says, " there are no people."

61. The few crossroads that I saw in England were nearly in the same admirable condition with the great highways, but I can speak only of a very few. It is hardly possible that their general condition can be the same.

All the roads in England were originally made very much as our roads generally are in New-England.* By an act passed in the reign of Philip and Mary, surveyors of highroads were provided for, the parishes being compelled to make and repair the roads by a labour assessment. The disadvantage of this labour system was perceived in England, as it is with us; and this led, during the reign of George the Third, to a commutation of the labour contribution for a money tax on land. The sensible people of Massachusetts know that a money, instead of a labour tax, would save us at least one half of our expense on the roads; and still ancient prejudices keep up this imbecile, shiftless, thriftless way of wasting our property.

62. The turnpikes in England are made in the following way. The roads are called trusts. The business of making them is given to commissioners, who are gentlemen of the county or parish where the road is to be made. These gentlemen apply to parliament for leave to make the road, and to be appointed trustees; they are authorized to borrow money to make the roads, for which they give bonds

* M'Cullock's Commercial Dictionary.

that run indefinitely, there being a power in the trustees, however, to take them up if they have funds. When the road is made the trustees put up the tolls at auction to the highest bidder; the tolls paying the interest of the bonds and all other charges; the holders of the bonds having a lien on the gates for their security; so that the roads are, in fact, a pledge for the security of the payment of interest on the bonds. In this sense the roads are private property.

63. In giving the above account of the provisions in the acts of parliament for making roads I do not pretend to entire accuracy, as I have not one of them before me. To a stranger, who is rioting in innocent pleasure at every step in England, the top of a coach on an English road is one of the most enviable situations in life. I have travelled a whole day, that is, one hundred and ten miles in twelve hours, without any fatigue that put me to inconvenience. In many coaches the travelling is more rapid.

64. We were told at Reading that the road from that place to Basingstoke (twelve miles) let for thirteen hundred pounds a year, which sum goes to keep the road and tollhouses in repair. That two gates on the great western road were let for three thousand pounds annually, the whole of which sum was expended yearly to repair the tollhouses and road, and for incidental expenses (nearly fifteen thousand dollars). It shows the magnificent scale upon which affairs are carried on in England. Some of the tollhouses on these roads are among the most graceful

structures in the country. What could not such a people accomplish with a fair field for all!

If the people of the United States would keep the forms of beauty and utility constantly before their eyes, their bills at the milliner's and tailor's would be far more moderate ; nor would they empty their pockets, as they have been accustomed to do, into those of the grocer and tavern-keeper. When we come to add up the amount of money misspent in any important particular, it seems incredible that so much can be wasted in such a way. At present, in New-England, a surveyor of highways would as soon think of providing prussic acid for his men at work on the roads as ardent spirits. It would be a pleasant sight now to see in a pile the money that has been spent in this way upon our highways since the revolution ! Reader, try to make it out, if you can, and see how far it would go to produce those magnificent roads which I saw in England, over which the horses sometimes gallop as easily as they would upon a racecourse. I heard it said that Lord Brougham was in the habit of travelling from London to his country-place in a postchaise at night, he reading all the while by lamplight ! Compare this with the corduroys and wheels up to the hub in mud !

65. I pronounce no opinion as to the most economical mode of making the roads of England ; but it is certain that they are a great ornament to the country and comfort of the people ; that they show

what property might do in other things if there was a wise use and a just distribution of it.

It is certain that a division of property (I do not speak of our laws for the equal division of property among children) is taking place in the United States, such as has never been known among mankind. New principles are at work here; they are yet feebly understood and exerted, but their existence is certain. True equality is that where the law secures to every man the fruits of his labour and skill, but *nothing more*. This better distribution of property is the unavoidable result of our new state of society; it follows from our equal constitutional privileges; from universal education, which tends to a great equality of mind, for it is mind that produces property. These are the consequences: high wages, combinations of small capitalists, where large capital is required; so that the capitalist is at once labourer and capitalist; control of the working people over all property for public purposes; a respect among them for each other; temperance; an innocent and enlightened country population, that overawes the natural vices of the great cities; an unexampled facility to poor people of obtaining land and other property. Above all, the pure principles of the Christian religion are daily gaining ground, and sanctifying, confirming, and establishing this sacred charter of the equal natural rights of mankind, which is entitled to the unbounded love and reverence of the people! In public opinion, other consequences follow.

It is a settled point, that riches can have no such power here as they have in Europe. The rich are beginning slowly to see that labour is the safeguard and honour of their children; that great riches too often spoil them, render them feeble, insignificant, and contemptible in the eyes of their fellow-citizens, and are, what religion has pronounced them to be, a moral impediment, a social evil, what Lord Bacon calls "the baggage of virtue." It is certain, then, that the rich, from affection to their children, will turn their thoughts to nobler and less exclusive uses of their riches.

66. This greater equality, this better distribution, is the great truth to be taught and enforced in our political economy; it is the beginning and the end; it is the true *democratic* doctrine; it is equally consistent with the rights of rich and poor. This equality of property was that which the Declaration of Independence meant when it declared all men "to be born free and equal," and it is what we mean when we inculcate the necessity of universal education; without it the democratic system has no perfection; it is a name and a delusion. This is not the political economy of Europe, but it is of reason, religion, and nature, which will sooner or later establish their empire.

The love of property is a universal passion. It can never have been designed as the blessing of the few. It is through the property passion that men become careful, economical, temperate, and virtuous; it is this that makes them think seriously of the uses of property. It is one of the great supporters of morals. Without this passion men are mere clods of the valley; they are fit for no relation as subjects or citizens; if the bread that they have worked for is snatched out of their mouths, in despair they desert their wives and children; they fly to hovels and ginshops; they lie down in the dirt, and shut their eyes against the sun. Look at the poor people of England; multitudes of them live without motive or hope; they work by day from the dread of starvation, and revel at night; they waste as fast as they create. Read the accounts of Ireland! The idea of so beautiful a world, and so capable of abundance, being enjoyed by a few, is equally revolting to reason and religion. Those who take care of the earth ought to inherit the earth. The careful, conscientious, temperate labourers, who lay up ten dollars this year and twenty the next, are as superior in virtue as they are in industry to their idle oppressors.

67. It is the universal hope of property, of independence, of the dignity that belongs to a man, that is producing the "wonderful affluence of the United States." Let our labourers, then, raise a new banner, and inscribe upon it, in letters of gold as bright as the sun, " A just division of property; the earth and all its glories to the virtuous; no others shall gain them, no others deserve them."

Upon the plan of a noble and generous existence; of equal laws, no monopolies; of giving fair play to all; " of living and letting live;" of getting rid of over eating and drinking; of the ten thousand costly fineries and sensualities that now either swallow up property or prevent its production, one result is certain, and that is, *an immense increase of wealth.*

68. The people of the United States may write and talk against monopolies; they will never be free till they have got rid of the bondage of sensuality, intemperance, and fashion; till they cease to run after the great, the rich, and fashionable, and can gather courage to overthrow the little, contemptible, aristocratic image, with embroidery upon its shoulders, with gold in its ears, around its neck, and upon its fingers, which they now worship; till they seek for independence in the virtue, temperance, simplicity, and economy of their lives. These are the great and natural dividers of property; this is the true *agrarian code.*

69. A monstrous inequality of *aristocratic privileged wealth* has been the great political and social evil; we are yet living unconsciously under its influence; under the influence of a barbarous age, of European fashions and customs. We know not how barbarous we are; the future only will show it. It is the rage for speculation, to live without work, to get rich out of nothing, to be richer than our neighbours, to show off how great and fashionable we are, that has seized so many with an epidemic fury, and brought them to the disgrace and ruin in which they are now involved.

70. Equality of condition, or as much of that as is attainable, with freedom to all to exercise their

genius and industry for their own advantage, must be the law. The *privileged* system is as great a moral blight to man as it is a physical curse to the earth. A privileged rich man, who is under no control from those about him, becomes a brute in caprice and sensuality. It is this equality, compared with what has existed in other countries, that has given to the people of the United States kind tempers and generous hearts; which, in the midst of revolution, have saved them from the bloody massacres which have disgraced other nations. It is not the good things of the earth that hurt a man, but it is having all the good things to one's self that corrupt the soul. At present, the horrible evil is the want among our " brother men" of many of those common, simple good things that are necessary for all, and that God designed for all, while so large a number are in the pursuit of expensive phantoms. Upon this plan there must be white or black slavery, of course; a division " horizontally into up and down," into labourers and capitalists, the owners and the owned. And then we shall be told " that the institution of domestic slavery is an indispensable element in an unmixed representative republic."

In part first I have spoken plainly and freely of slavery, and have since seen no cause to alter my opinions.

As to *agrarianism* in a country where so many have property, and so many can easily acquire it, it is the " shadow of a ghost." People ought to be ashamed to be frightened at it, or even to talk of it.

CHAPTER III.

71. June, 1836. We arrived in London yesterday, and were put down at the Colonnade Hotel, Charles-street, near Pall Mall. Before breakfast (the coffee-room not being prepared), at eight o'clock, I went into St. James's Park, where I saw St. James's Palace, Carlton House, formerly the residence of the Prince of Wales, afterward George the Fourth, and the Duke of Sutherland's princely town-house. At the foot of Regent-street, as you pass into St. James's Park, stands the Duke of York's statue, said to have been erected by the voluntary contributions of the army. As I passed near the statue I overtook four small boys of nearly the same age, the eldest in appearance seemed to be about eight. I asked whose statue it was, but none of them could tell me. If monuments were erected only to the truly great, I think even boys would know them.

72. I was directed by some soldiers on duty in front of the palace how to get into the rear of it, where I found a common passage that conducted me within a very few feet of the kitchens, or some of the offices of this awkward fabric. I was told that these soldiers were gruff and uncivil, but I found them quite the contrary, as I did all the people

of England, with very few exceptions; so that, at last, I have come to think, that, if all people were put into one cage, like John Austin's little sparrows and great birds of prey, his cats, rats, and mice, and taught to be civil to each other, they would soon become so.

73. At nine o'clock I returned for breakfast, which was rather an early hour. At eight o'clock I repeatedly went to the coffee-room for breakfast, when I found the servants dusting the tables, chairs, &c. If the people of the United States suffer the fashionable part of the world to turn day into night, as the people of our cities are beginning to do, and as the people of England have already done, they will have to thank their own folly for it. In the United States the rational class, who are everywhere the labouring people, and by labouring people here I mean all the industrious and hard-working in every class, have the staff in their own hands, and may, to every reasonable extent, decide this matter for themselves; but they must begin early. It is easier to put things into a right train at first, than to get them back when they have for a long time gone wrong.

74. Having understood that the Horseguards were to be in front of the palace at eleven o'clock, I went there at that hour. Their station is called the *Horseguards*. Mr. Bulwer, in giving an account of the king's civil list, sets down three regiments of horseguards, eighty thousand pounds! I saw at this time but about forty, who were re-

lieving guard. The horses were beautiful and noble animals, jet black generally, with long tails; and I have heard that, when the streets are dirty and the flies troublesome, they disperse a mob simply by throwing about these long tails! Such a breed of horses is very much wanted in the United States! The men wore caps, buckskin gloves reaching half way to the elbow, and a steel breastplate. The seat of the saddle was lambskin, or something of the like kind covering the whole saddle, and as white as the driven snow. They wore boots reaching above the knee, and I observed that the toes of one were shod with nails, and I suppose that others may have been, in the same way. It is a general thing for the common people of England to be iron shod, for they are not able to buy more shoes than they want, nor ashamed to wear such as will last. I saw very few *paper* boots in England.

75. On my return through the park I saw five fine cows tied by the head. A milkwoman, who had the care of one or more of them, told me that the cows were milked there; that people came to drink the milk fresh from the cow's udder, and that there was no other place in London where they could get it in this way, or were sure of its being unadulterated. This practice of adulterating food that God gives to man to nourish and strengthen him for his labour is so dishonest and detestable, that one would not credit its existence, or suppose that one labouring man could have the heart to sell

it to another, if these poisonous compounds were not every day detected. In part first, page 80, I have stated, upon the authority of Accum, some of the facts set forth by him, to show the murderous extent to which this business is carried in England. There is not a little of it in the United States. This milk was sold at sixpence a quart, in pint and penny measures. The woman told me that the cows were pastured in St. James's Park, and that she paid for the pasturing of hers.

76. On the — day of June I took the same walk before breakfast at about the same hour, stopping opposite Carlton House, where I saw thousands of sparrows making their nests or tending their young in the fluted columns of this building and in the neighbourhood. They had been up and doing many hours before the people of London, for the shops of London are not open, generally, before half past seven or eight o'clock; a melancholy evidence of the overwork of the lower, and of the little or no work of the higher orders. The morning light in that high latitude, fifty-one, comes earlier than with us, and the evening light departs later. It was said in a London paper when I was there, that, during a short part of the summer, twilight never disappeared wholly.

77. The people of England are humbugged out of their money much easier than those of the United States, though there is a good deal of that facility here. Parliament paid Mr. Forsyth several thousand pounds for his tree plaster, a cement to put

over the wounds of pruned *fruit*-trees, and still the trees in St. James's Park are trimmed in a shameful way; the limbs of some as large as one's leg being cut several feet from the main stem, so that they can never heal. If cut at the main stem, the bark forms over the wound, and the tree is preserved. So it seems that his majesty's pruners have not been very apt scholars; and it exemplifies another thing pretty well understood nowadays, and that is, that nobody's trees are so poorly trimmed, or produce so little shade or fruit, as those of the public.

In the park I fell into conversation with a boy of the common class who was well dressed. I asked him if he had ever heard of America. "Oh yes," said he, "I have heard of a great *conflagration* there" (meaning at New-York), " and that the agriculture is very good." He having, no doubt, heard of our fairy land, the western prairies.

It is well known that the English common people do not treat his majesty's English as well as the people of the United States; they toss about the moods, tenses, and pronouns strangely. The young countrywomen, as they come out to get a place upon the coach, sometimes cry out, " Have you any places for we." I told the boy that we were a very happy people in the United States, and had a great deal of good bread and butter, and much cheaper than in London. This certainly was not true comparing London with New-York at the time I left New-York. But I meant to speak of common prices heretofore in the country generally, and not to include these present mad times.

78. If the common people are interested in anything, they are in purchasing their moderate comforts with as little labour as may be, for labour with them is the only means of buying. The advantages of paper circulation have been so great in the United States, that it will never be dispensed with; and it is to be regretted that many honest people have been deluded by the idea of the possibility of an exclusive metallic currency. When, however, paper money is the *regulating medium*, *wages* do not rise in proportion as *prices* rise, as is notoriously the case at present (1837) in the United States; and then it is that the poor, who have *nothing to sell*, and nearly all who live by *wages*, suffer by a gross injustice. One of the greatest scourges that has fallen upon poor people in modern times is that of irresponsible paper money, which, by some bad management or other, cannot be converted into gold and silver. This inconvertible paper money is one of the great causes to many, not of *nominal* only, but of *real* dearness in those necessary things which the poor must have, which dearness is scarcity with them, and often little better than a famine. Those who are allowed to make any portion of the currency, which becomes a *debt* due from individuals or companies to the people at large, ought to be compelled to give the public the greatest security possible for

its redemption; and this will be best done through a proper system of *free private banking*.

The interests of a large portion of God's creatures, and by this I mean strictly the day labourers, those who live upon wages, the people of small property, are now, in our days, for the first time, considered by political economy. This is the true Christian civilization, the circle of which is growing larger and larger every day.

79. The boy of whom I have spoken told me that he was a pot-boiler in a public-house, and that he earned five shillings a week and his victuals. A boy who was filling water-casks for the purpose of watering the roads in the park told me that he earned twelve shillings a week; that his horses ate three pecks of oats a day, and as much chaff as they chose. This chaff was cut clover hay. This economical practice of cutting hay and straw for horses is extensively in use in England.

— June. This morning, before breakfast, I found at the door of our hotel an old man, who afterward told me that he was there attending upon his master. This man subsequently proved the only companion I found in these London hotels, where people, to be sure, go about with their eyes open, eat, drink, and sleep, but who, for all the purposes of companionship and society, are dead; and all this from a horror of getting out of rank, and of being compelled to know those who are not so rich and fashionable as themselves; as though there could be any other object in sending people into the world but to know each other, speak to each other, and help each other.

80. Yesterday I went to church at St. James's, Westminster, Jermyn-street. I had been often told that there would be no difficulty in obtaining a seat, there being in these churches regular pew-openers for strangers, they expecting, of course, pay for this service. No seat being offered, I crowded in at one of the doors, and took my stand in a back aisle, where I remained till the sermon was about half finished. In this aisle were a good many common people, who seemed, by their dress, to be servants and other persons of the lower classes. Some of these were children, and some grown persons. The pews were so high that many of these people, who were near me in the aisles, could not see the preacher, nor did they attempt it; some, however, were stretching their heads over the high pews for this purpose. Others may think as they will, but these strong lines of separation between high and low, rich and poor, are not to my taste. I would rather see, as in the Catholic churches, the rich and the poor man's knees bent at the same altar. It is a very unchristian-like taste to crowd the servants and poor people in at the doorways, where they are placed in most inconvenient situations for hearing and seeing the preacher, or making their devotions profitable. The sermon was preached for the Burlington school of charity girls, in which it was stated that one hundred and ten were wholly maintained and

educated. It seemed to me that the sermon was a pretty poor comment upon the occasion. A prepared hymn was handed about, in the last stanza of which were the following lines:

> " By thy pattern, in thy name,
> Aid from brother men we claim."

" Brother men !" words of deep import; words that will make a prodigious change in our books of political economy some day or other, how great probably none can divine; words not so well, I think, understood in many things in England as in the United States, nor as well here as they should or will be. What sort of systems would Mr. Paley and Mr. Malthus have proclaimed had they written under William the Norman? That we cannot say. And what would they have written fifty years hence? Neither can we say that; but we may be pretty certain that Mr. Malthus would not then dare to tell the poor people of England that there was " no plate set for them" in that beautiful country, till he had told the rich people that they must first do all in their power to provide plates and food too, before they ventured to charge such barbarity upon nature. Yet the writers whom I have named were among the best of men, and desired to propagate nothing but truth. The radical defect of much of their systems arose from their living in a country in which they were educated to believe that no great change could take place for the benefit of the poorer classes. All true political economy will certainly enlarge its plans for extending more and more the happiness of mankind, and making the words "brother men" not a name only, but a reality.

81. The sermon, so much of it as I heard, was a very indifferent production for a man of high rank; it dealt in many unmeaning generalities, as the importance of instilling into the minds of youth "specific principles, such as were taught in the Church of England," &c., a topic turned over and over, but of which neither young nor old could very well see the force. As this was a charity sermon for the benefit of poor girls who were to be educated, it occurred to me that a plain, intelligible discourse, teaching the high and fashionable people who were partitioned off by closed doors that there were other duties to perform in order to educate these young girls besides that of paying their money to "teach them to read, write, and cast accounts; sew, mark, mend, and make, and do household, kitchen, and laundry work;" that the highest of these was to set to their lowly brother men a personal example of Christian benevolence, temperance, chastity, humility, and industry; knowing that this example of the high teaches the low more than all the homilies and sermons of pope, bishop, or priest. The time for deluding the people in this way has nearly gone by; they draw better distinctions; they know that going to church, saying prayers, and giving money to educate them is but a small part of true religion; that, if a man means to make the peo-

ple holy, holiness must begin in his own household. The greatest mistake which the educated and exalted people are now making is in underrating the understandings of the common people.

82. One ceremony in this service was rather striking. As the preacher ascended the pulpit there followed him a person (I suppose the beadle) habited in what appeared at a distance to be a blue surtout, with a rich livery cape, who went up the pulpit stairs, opened the door, and closed it after the bishop had entered. This appeared to me a low and wasteful service to put a " brother" man to, thus occupying his mind with a frivolous, unnecessary, and, of course, degrading duty; it is but a common way of destroying the lower orders by putting them to perform acts that make them contemptible in their own eyes. It is a sure way of breaking down the spirit of a man. I was certain, before I left England, that I saw at work, in the minds of good people, of whom there are so many, that true Christian principle which will go on slowly but certainly to level those distinctions which pamper the pride of the great and demoralize the lower orders. The true Christian equalizing principle will do it, and nothing else can. Other causes will combine; governments, societies, equal laws; but this principle in the heart is stronger and better than them all by themselves. It is the principle of love towards " brother men," each seeking to extend to others those equal privileges which are followed with equal blessings, so

far as God intended, in this imperfect state, that they should exist. It is the sun shining upon the righteous and the unrighteous. All that the king, lords, and bishops in England can do to arrest the progress of this glorious principle will be like the outstretched arms of children to stop the winds and waves.

83. As I could get no seat, I went into the open area adjoining the church, where I found a man leading a little child; he seemed to have come out to enjoy the pure air and a day of rest. He was reading the inscriptions upon the tombstones in the churchyard. He told me that he was a tailor; that work in London then was much better than usual; that the average wages of journeymen tailors were about 15s. a week; that many got 25s. or even 30s., which account was afterward confirmed by my tailor. In conversation upon rents, he told me that he paid 3s. 6d. in London for a single room, he having a small family. This is the same sum that I paid in Portsmouth for a bath! he paying 3s. 6d. a week for a house and home, and I the same sum for a plunge into warm water for fifteen minutes. These things are out of joint. It is plain that the poor need not be as poor as they are, and that the rich ought not to be as rich as they are, compared with the poor. In other words, the equalizing processes are going on, and will go on, but the people who are in greatest need of the result must carry them on. They must not, however, be deluded by gabble, by idle decla-

rations of pretenders to patriotism, who put the unction of soft words to their souls. Every great amelioration of the laws must be preceded by a moral and intellectual improvement of the people, which gives them independence of mind, property, and power. If a code was sent down from heaven to abolish test-laws, corn-laws, laws to authorize privileged persons to circulate irresponsible paper money, based on no security, and all other monopoly laws, that alone would not be enough; there would still be wanting the moral determination, temperance, prudence; the abandonment of the gluttonous, vicious, dram-drinking practices by which the people waste their property and make themselves slaves; there would still be wanting the virtuous, popular sentiment, to combine, sustain, encourage one another; and without all this they would soon find themselves back again in the old slough. It is by the combination of the working people to live religiously, simply, and nobly, that the world is to be regenerated. Let *combination, combination!* be the watchword!

84. There are, doubtless, a goodly number of humbugs in all countries. The distinctions of rank in England are nowhere observed more scrupulously than in the coffee-rooms, that is, in this respect; as no man knows the rank of his neighbour, he takes care not to let down his own dignity by speaking to his inferior. If this rule were transgressed, a peer might be found in conversation with a tailor; a sad affair, to be sure. This, then, is the

theory of society in England; that is, every man must stand on his own round of the ladder.

85. An English coffee-room in London or a large town is generally a spacious apartment, provided with small tables that will usually accommodate two persons, some more; these are set around the walls of the room, and often in the middle of it. Whenever a guest appears he takes one of these tables; sometimes you see three or four persons who are dining together as friends at the same table. I have called these coffee-rooms regions of the dead, and so they are to a stranger. No man speaks to his neighbour, as a general rule, though the legs of their tables may not be a foot from each other; not even when they sit around the blazing, cheerful fireside, so far as I saw. This is rather tantalizing, after thirty days of seasickness, to one who has come over the water three or four thousand miles to enjoy social pleasures and gain useful knowledge, and all because he may turn out to be a shopkeeper or a tailor; or perhaps it is the tailor or shopkeeper himself that declines the intercourse. This they call in England the etiquette of rank, which prevails to a degree not known in any other country. Some attribute this reserve to the unsocial character of the English, but that is not the case. I did not find it so; but, on the contrary, this barrier of rank out of the way, by a fair introduction, so that they may know who you are, and that you are entitled to their society, they become at once communicative, natural,

and pleasing. Men of knowledge are communicative, of course; they have something to say, and they like to say it. But in these hotels you are chained to your table and muzzled like a bulldog. If all these nice distinctions of rank be so important, it is a pity that so good a people as those of England cannot find out some more pleasing, natural, and useful way of maintaining them. They have a stupid little book in England, which, if I remember right, is said in the title-page to have gone through six editions, entitled "Hints on Etiquette, &c." In this work, which the unfledged newcomers into fashionable society, called in Europe *parvenus* or upstarts, and who are generally the greatest sticklers for rank, read with great attention, there is this very sage rule of manners, " Never make acquaintances in coffee-houses," &c.

After all, coffee-houses must be great levellers in England, for if the shopkeeper can sit in the same room with the great man, eat of the same food, ring the same bell, read the same newspaper, be obeyed as quickly by the same servants, and pay the same sum for his dinner, they cannot be a thousand miles apart. Coffee-houses, railroads, steamboats, and, it seems to me, nearly all the modern improvements, are making up a very pretty little machinery for subverting rank in Europe. It is nature, then, and science, and art, with a pure religion, that are working to bring men into that predicament of mutual love and assistance which eighteen hundred years ago was pointed out as their true condition.

If so, the old prejudices are striving against wind and tide. One would have thought that a two years' residence in the United States might have been sufficient to enable so sensible a man as M. de Tocqueville to come to right conclusions as to the working of this machinery! The people of Europe cannot understand us.

86. I crossed in a steamboat from Dover to Calais with a lady and gentleman who appeared to be of the higher class, but whether lord or lady or not, I cannot say, for I did not see their fingers. I think it is Lord Byron who says that long fingers or delicate hands are a mark of nobility in Europe, which, unfortunately for distinctions, means no more than that short thick fingers are the true hard-working fingers, such as we see generally in the country parts of the United States. I doubt, therefore, very much, whether the shopkeepers and scriveners of London, who use their fingers lightly and gently, as gentle people do, provided their great grandfathers have been shopkeepers and scriveners too, and their great grandmothers milliners and mantuamakers, have not as long and beautiful fingers as the nobility. I saw the Sioux delegation of Indians at Washington last fall (1837), who certainly had *noble* fingers.

The lady and gentleman of whom I spoke were seasick, their servants were sick, and their beautiful little boy being equally so, was taken in lap by a friend of mine who was once a shopkeeper, but is now dignified by the name of merchant, as high a rank as he or any other man will, I think, ever attain in the United States. After all, seasickness, with the other natural infirmities of human nature, and our mutual and irrepressible wants, will finally open our eyes and bring things to about the right position.

87. In most of the English coffee-houses there is no common table as in the United States, but every man breakfasts or dines when he chooses *and upon what he chooses*, which, in regard to time, is a great convenience, and, in respect to economy, a great advantage. Let those who choose to live upon dainties pay for them. A common table, however, must in many other respects be more economical; fewer servants and less work being required to provide for a common table than for guests that call at all hours of the day. Our practice of a common table is adapted to the habits of our country and the equal condition of the people; at the same time, it is well that establishments upon both plans should exist; and this is beginning to be the case in the United States.

88. There is, however, in England a common table at some of the inns; it is in the commercial or travellers' room. These travellers are a class of mercantile agents, who go from town to town for the purpose of obtaining orders for goods from the mercantile and manufacturing houses. I was several times in these commercial rooms, which, I believe, are increasing; they were said in Paris to be increasing in France when we were there.

This is the natural and sure progress towards the intermingling of different classes, which must increase where trade and manufactures, which have social and equalizing tendencies, are advancing. So that it is apparent that those who undertake to keep up the old fabric will have a prodigious deal of work to do in repairs. The frogs are becoming so numerous that it is impossible to prevent them from creeping into kings' houses.

89. I was told that the salaries of these travellers might average about 200 pounds per annum besides expenses, which are calculated at about twenty-one shillings per day. When several of these travellers meet, and particularly on a Sunday, they make a social party at dinner, and I was told that it was common, upon such occasions, to choose a president for the day, and, after drinking a pint of wine each, to put to vote whether the company would drink more. I do not, however, pretend to be well informed as to the particulars of the social life of these travellers. Of one thing, however, I am sure, that such is the fashion in England; that it requires a pretty bold fellow to eat a dinner at a coffee-house without calling for wine or some other liquor; and that Englishmen at the hotels with which I was familiar drank a good deal more wine and liquors of all kinds than we drink in the United States.

If wine be ordered, I think that a pint is the more usual quantity for a single individual. There are a few who begin to think that water was made

PUBLIC AND PRIVATE ECONOMY. 107

for a gentleman to drink, but the number yet is small, and particularly in the hotels. They think in England, as we once did, that it is cheating the landlord not to call for his liquors, and that it is better for a man to poison himself than not to be genteel. Up to a certain extent, the wine a man drinks in an English hotel is a great criterion of a certain amount of rank. It looks so poor for a gentleman to drink nothing but cold water with his dinner, though his wine and beer be killing him by inches, that it requires very strong nerves to do it. To be poor in some parts of the world is nearly as bad as a crime; a crime in the Napoleon code of morals was said not to be as bad as a false step, for that made a man appear ridiculous. With such an iron despotism does this law of the fashion rule in these hotels, that I have seen men drinking their pint when I knew that the wine was a curse, and that their stomachs were already half burned up. Too much wine, as we know, has destroyed, within the last forty years, several of the greatest statesmen in England. I have seen a rich country squire in a hotel in a large town, who gave me an account of the ravages which that genteel disease dyspepsy was then evidently making upon his mortal part, drinking his pint; and upon my taking the liberty to say to him that I thought wine injurious in that disease, he averred that though he could not drink sherry, *port* did not hurt him, at the same time saying that potatoes were indigestible, that even *bread* sometimes gave him a heartburn and pain at the stomach. Such is the madness of people who cannot, or will not, resist the fashions and their appetites!

90. The truth is, that in these matters we are far, very far from any right morality or just thinking. Who are the people that think wine indispensable in these hotels? who are they that lack the courage to let the servants see them drink water? who are they who often pay as much for their rich wines as for the rest of their entertainment? Why, taking the world together, though we may not know the individuals, we do know very well that gold is not drawn up from the mines in buckets; we do know about what proportion of these people can, without mean pinching, afford these luxuries; we do know that a large portion of them are just like the same class in the United States, who at the lodging-houses and hotels, yes, even at the country hotels and in country villages, drink Champagne from goblets! That large numbers at any rate, not all certainly, are those whom pride and poverty are fast leading to ruin, who can even now only just keep their heads above water; some are struggling to pay their notes from day to day, and dread a "panic" as they do a whirlwind; some are living upon the alms of rich friends; some are spending the little pittances that are barely sufficient to sustain, in decent comfort and honourable independence, their fathers, mothers, brothers, and sisters; some live upon borrowing; some are boys at school; some have just left

school at Oxford, or somewhere else, and as yet have not earned a farthing; some are mere striplings and clerks in counting-houses. This passion for doing as the rich do, eating as they eat, drinking as they drink, wearing such finery as they wear, is the same sort of madness as if these people were to sign, seal, and deliver a bond to sell themselves into slavery, and the meanest slavery, too, that can be, that is, slavery to masters who despise them for selling their birthright for a mess of pottage. Bad as things are, however, it is certain that a great economical process is going on both in England and in the United States, by which the people are breaking their chains by slow though sure degrees. Both street beggars and gentlemen beggars are getting out of fashion. It is to this spirit that all great reform is attributable. Property is the great engine of reform, property is the great engine by which nearly every great movement is carried on. As soon as the people of England come to feel that a ten-pound vote is better than a pint of wine a day, or a gallon of beer, they will get to understand the machinery of all good government. Notwithstanding what I have said about these hotels, all classes in England concurred, so far as I heard, in stating that there was a very striking improvement in the wine-drinking habits of the people.

91. It would seem impossible that any one should be alone in the midst of nearly two millions of people, and still that was my condition in these hotels. I had, however, one resource, and that was often a

conversation before breakfast with my old acquaintance at the door. This old servant was generally sitting in the morning watching his master's bell in the hall, which, being one among many, required an accurate attention to its call. He appeared, from his conversation, dress, and manners, a man of respectability, and to understand well the interests that belong to his class, which is to understand a good deal, for these are the interests of human nature. It has been the fashion of the world to call all these low ignorant people; the fashion will change, and the day will come when the test of sense will be the living more or less accórding to the laws of God and nature. He told me that the agricultural people in the neighbourhood of Plymouth were earning 9s. per week, the man finding himself; that the poor people of England were very discontented, that many were going to the United States, to Canada, and other parts.

92. June. I this day called, with my friend, upon one of the most eminent men in England for surgical advice; the interview with whom is of no moment to the reader, except that he confirmed the general statements as to the then great prosperity of England, and gave, as an evidence of it, the fact, that he knew of a vacancy in a steward's place worth 120*l.*, for which there were two or three applications only.

I think that if a vacancy were to occur in an office in the United States worth as much, there would be, upon an average, in the cities certainly, not fewer than twenty applicants for it. A friend in our ship told us that a gentleman, high in office in the United States, informed him that for a foreign consulate, not worth more than $1500 per annum, there were a hundred applicants. So it seems that there is good and evil in every country, and that compensation is for ever going on so as to make things more equal than we are willing to acknowledge. Heaven has not poured all its blessings into the lap of any one nation; and if we travel and find, in some particulars, what we do not like, we shall be sure to find good, if we look for it, in something else. We have not here, therefore, all the perfection that there is in the world, for I doubt whether there be any country on earth in which there is so much office seeking, or in which more mean things are done to obtain office, than in ours; in which opinion I may differ with many others in this particular, perhaps, that they may suppose that it is wholly confined to *one* party in politics, which is far from my way of thinking. As, however, not one in fifty or a hundred of all the people of the United States will ever be able to obtain office, I have no doubt that they will see the danger, and not suffer the trade in politics, which has ruined so many countries, to add this nation to the number of unhappy victims.

93. There is no pretence in the hospitality of England, of which we have heard so much, any more than there is in the roast beef and plum pudding. This hospitality, so pleasing to a stranger,

so benevolent in its character, that opens so many avenues to curiosity and useful knowledge, might be wide spread among all classes, if they would spend their money as rational beings, and not waste their souls in vanity and vexation of spirit; consuming in a single ostentatious feast or rout what would furnish a year's supply to pure and simple tastes.

True hospitality is not sensual or ostentatious; its pleasures lie in society, friendship, and good wholesome cheer; it gathers around its board people of different tastes and religion, and opens a natural, improving, and highly interesting source of knowledge with other countries, and the useful arts that belong to them. This is society and social intercourse in its most advantageous form, so that those that can enjoy it have many of the pleasures of travel at their own fireside; and, if rightly improved, it may be made one of the best means of education to our children. But, alas! with all our fine clothes, diamonds, and other bawbles, our dram-drinking, our overloaded tables, our " splendid" furniture, how few can afford the pleasures of even a simple and economical hospitality? This true kind of hospitality we enjoyed to-day. Neither upon this occasion nor at any other hospitable board did we hear that everlasting gabble about White top, Black top, Eclipse, Lynch, Brahmin, &c., &c., which we have in the United States, and mostly from those who never tasted a glass of good wine till they left their father's humble roofs.

PUBLIC AND PRIVATE ECONOMY. 113

Here we saw specimens of that neatness, order, and propriety in the servants (their costume was very different from that which we see in some of our ship "*palaces*" and "*splendid*" hotels), the furniture, the table, the courtyard, of which there are so many in England, and which are well worthy the labour of the people.

The road upon which we came out from London about six miles seemed as hard as a rock, the wheels of the omnibus not making the least visible impression. A man in the omnibus stated that the top of the road was covered with a stone brought from China as ballast, which statement was repeated to us.

CHAPTER IV.

94. THE people of the United States are fast gaining good ideas upon political economy, and this without any other teacher than their own equal condition. A people doomed to labour will naturally look sharp into the philosophy of it; they will find out, sooner or later, what is productive and what is unproductive labour; what is to them profitable, and what is not. The first aim of the people here should be to obtain *respectable things*, good houses, gardens, clothes, roads, schools, education for their children, &c. It is where these *respectable things* are in most repute that there is the greatest industry and trade. This is true practical equality. It comes from freedom, from entire liberty to every man to exert his genius as he will. If a man, then, desires a larger house than his neighbour, let him have it, but let it be the result of his genius and industry, and not of a legal privilege which is refused to his neighbour. Do not let it proceed from test laws, or corn laws, or bank laws, or any other laws by which one man is able to pay five pounds for his dinner, while another is dining upon a crust of bread. I saw one day in the famous cemetery in Paris, Père la Chaise, fourteen men

who were making a road, twelve of whom were dining in the shade upon *dry bread!* Nor was the five-pound dinner a *very* expensive repast for a party of gentlemen at the Clarendon Hotel, in London, according to their own modest boast. And how many of these gentlemen could afford five pounds for a dinner if the natural equality prevailed; if God's laws, not man's, had the sway? Think of a man's eating and drinking to the amount of twenty-five dollars in an afternoon, even allowing what you choose for his being served from gold and silver, and in a palace, which the Clarendon is not! But the worst of this kind of gluttony is, that it proves that labour is not free; that a man cannot exert himself where he will and about what he will; it is proof positive that there are unequal privileges, for how comes *so extensively* this immense disproportion between the price of one man's dinner and another? The people of the United States ought to be ashamed of this expensive sensuality and abhor the causes which produce it. It literally takes bread from the mouth of labour. If the people of the United States will live simply, naturally, and healthfully, and hate the fruit, they will soon root out the tree which bears it, and then their labour, which is their money, will be spent, first for the necessaries and proprieties, and afterward for that beauty and magnificence which gives fulness and completeness to the enjoyments of the whole. Then, too, the ranks and orders propped up by vanity and pride, the finery, the bawbles, the "*adulterous* trinkets," the expensive gluttony, and ruinous drinking, which now confuse their judgments as to the natural rights of their fellow-men, will fade away from their imaginations for ever. By productive labour, then, I mean the *most productive*, and no working man ought to admit the thought of any other for a moment.

95. In part first of this work, chapter twelve, section one hundred and ninety-four, some of the most prominent causes of poverty are stated; it is said, among other things, that one of the greatest causes of poverty is, that there are so many who do not produce the means of living; that labour is the great cause of the wealth of the world; that it is possible to turn the whole earth, that can be cultivated at all (even Wimbledon Common or the Hampshire Downs), into garden ground. That the reason, then, why so many are wretched or not comfortable, is either the want of labour or the right sort of labour. That the labour of many is wholly, or in part, misapplied; that is, they work at the wrong things (at a Clarendon five-pound dinner, perhaps); their labour, therefore, brings little or nothing to pass: in other words, that their labour is in a great measure unproductive, yielding little or nothing of utility or real good to anybody. That it produces neither food nor drink, nor clothes for the body, nor any real delightful desirable pleasure to the mind, compared with what it might produce. That there are thousands who do not produce the means of living; on the contrary, that some of these

(like, for instance, the gentlemen who dine for five pounds at the Clarendon), in the way in which they do live, wickedly and stupidly consume all that thousands produce. That it is this unprofitable, contemptible labour, which naturally creates so much disgust among the poor, and produces so many idle and vicious people, as is the case among the grooms, pampered servants, and other unhappy classes of people in England.

96. In connexion with the same subject, it is stated in the same chapter, that where bad government, bad religion, and monopolies exist, rendering the people poor and miserable, it is because they work to a disadvantage. That in such cases they are compelled to labour for the king, for the nobility, for the priesthood, for the favoured who enjoy the monopolies, in ten thousand frivolous, contemptible, and unprofitable occupations, which are attended with little or no real good to the labourers. That this explains the unexampled prosperity of the United States compared with other countries, the people here being permitted to work for their own benefit; to work for property at such occupations as are useful to themselves, thus being able to enjoy the produce of their labours. That, as the prosperity of individuals depends upon the utility of their labour, inasmuch as individuals make up nations, those nations will be the richest and happiest where the *useful occupations* prevail. That many work to little more advantage, so far as regards the

prosperity of the whole, than if they laboured at digging ditches and filling them up again, or in pumping water out of one cistern into another, and so back again for ever. That when a poor man is hired to disgrace himself by such a waste of his time, though he may earn a dollar, he does not in any way, in the long run, help the condition of other poor men like himself by increasing property for the general good. That though he earns a dollar in wages, it is as true that another loses a dollar; that as between them both, having created nothing new or useful, nothing exists more than there was before.

97. The design of this second part, as already stated, is more fully to illustrate the truths above summed up, by observations made upon what I saw in England; thus endeavouring to show, by plain illustrations, what kind of labour, in the present state of the world, is *most productive;* for that is the real question, and the mighty dispute about productive and unproductive labour is mostly a dispute about words. All labour, directly or indirectly, is productive of some good to somebody or other, and the only common-sense inquiry is, whether the labour does the most good that it can do. If all labour produces something, the question arises, what that something is, what is it good for, who wants it, or, rather, who ought to want it, or to have it. The journeymen and apprentices who make E O tables, and the grooms who prepare horses for the Jamaica races, earn *wages;* that is getting some good out of labour; but the question with a man who is compelled

to work ten or twelve hours out of twenty-four should be, if that be the only good that can be got out of labour. The people of the United States are teaching the Old World several new lessons. For instance, how much happier every creature is for labour of some kind or another, and, therefore, how much happier the whole must be ; and the difference between one kind of labour and another.

98. Adam Smith saw all this when he foretold what this great democratic empire was to be, though it would not do then to proclaim it as plainly as he foresaw it. His voice has been ringing in the world's ears for sixty years, but it is only now in the United States that he is listened to, reverenced, and followed. He was compelled to write for statesmen and politicians; for the people when he wrote could neither read him nor understand him. As to the thoroughbred politicians and office people, they are the last to look to for any very valuable lessons in economy. There are a few eminent exceptions.*

99. Adam Smith was the father of the science of political economy ; we are now reaping a rich harvest from the seed which he sowed. The first edition of his great work, "The Wealth of Nations," was published in the years 1775, '6. Well might it be called the " Wealth of Nations." Smith's discoveries on the earth were like those of Newton in the heavens. But it is as the friend of American liberties that he is entitled to peculiar love and reverence here.

* This mention of Adam Smith is taken from a newspaper notice of him published by the author heretofore.

120 PUBLIC AND PRIVATE ECONOMY.

In our darkest days, when the people of Stockbridge were leaving their cocks of hay standing in the field, and rushing to the relief of General Stark at Bennington, he predicted that we could not be conquered by force, declaring " that out of shopkeepers, tradesmen, and attorneys, we were making legislators and statesmen, who were forming a government which was likely to become one of the greatest and most formidable that ever was in the world."

100. " A touching incident in the life of this great and good man had wellnigh deprived the world of the benefit of his labours. He had been carried by his mother to Stratheny, on a vist to his uncle, Mr. Douglass, and was one day amusing himself at the door of the house, when he was stolen by a party of that set of vagrants who are known in Scotland by the name of Tinkers. Luckily, he was soon missed by his uncle, who, hearing that some vagrants had passed, pursued them with what assistance he could find, till he overtook them in Leslie Wood, and was the happy instrument of preserving to the world a genius that was destined not only to extend the boundaries of science, but to enlighten and reform the commercial policy of Europe."*

101. We shall never arrive at any thorough-going public or private economy, or know anything of the amount of comfort which this fruitful world is able to yield, till the great class of beings who work mainly with their hands are taken into the account in all our plans; till this class realize that

* Account of the life and writings of Adam Smith.

all property, public or private, may be made to redound to their benefit; till they scorn those contemptible enployments by which they earn wages alone, and do not increase property or enjoyment. This is only to empty one pocket and fill another; they may get along like snails, as they have in Europe, upon this principle, but they will never " go ahead," as the people of the United States design to do. The idea which has crept into the European political economy, that it is sufficient if the labourers earn wages, if they live, if they subsist, if they keep body and soul together, is an outrage upon human nature. Upon this plan, it is sufficient if a man and woman, husband and wife, are employed, get wages enough to feed and clothe them, and bring up two children to take their places when they are dead and gone. Some think they do a mighty fine thing, and very charitable too, when they employ poor people, " and keep the money snug at home," as they call it, let the work be what it may. It was but the other day that there was an account in an English paper of the Duke of St. Albans flying hawks. This was anciently a great sport in England, called falconry. Falconry was making a hawk, after long training, fly at and kill other birds. It seems that the duke, in a joke, was threatened with a prosecution for trespassing upon other people's grounds while flying his hawks. This attack upon the duke excited great indignation (not the trespass, as it ought to have done), and a vote of thanks was passed to the duchess for her *magnificent charities;*

it being stated at the meeting " that each time the duke flew his hawks he spent £500, and that during her stay the duchess weekly expended from forty to fifty pounds among the flymen." It is the multiplicity of these contemptible employments that fills an American with so much disgust. When idle gentlemen spend their money in this way, it only serves to make the poor idle also. It is ten to one that the half of this money is spent upon beer, gaming, and carousing, for there is nothing that sooner leads a labouring man into these courses than the consciousness that he is meanly and worthlessly occupied. But these barbarisms are fast disappearing.

102. After all, the great question is this: What is that labour which most tends to create property? and by this we mean noble enjoyments to the great body of the people being spread here and there, as the dew falls from heaven. Is it in flying hawks? As long as the titled people of England can make a parade about such charities as these, they must in vain expect to keep up with the people of the United States.

Productive labour, then, is the labour for a rational being; it is this which, by equalizing property as far as it can be equalized in a state of freedom, produces the greatest happiness of the greatest number. This is called the " greatest happiness principle;" it is an emanation from God himself; it is the very principle upon which he acts; and though he has suffered evil, sin, and misery to exist in the world, he doubtless designs to bring out of them the greatest happiness possible to his creatures that is consistent with his views of infinite benevolence. Nearly all the plans of happiness devised by the governments of this world have been conceived and carried on for the benefit of a few only, such as kings, princes, masters of slaves, and a small number of rich people. These plans being equally mean and selfish, most of them have failed; the rest are failing. It is from the absence of the true divine principle that people have carried on their work with slaves, instead of using their own hands; and this is the reason why, after six thousand years of labour, so little has been accomplished; why so much of the earth is yet a desert, a jungle, a swamp overgrown with weeds and thorns. This, then, is the reason why the poor agricultural labourer in England is earning only ten shillings a week, while the Duke of Sutherland is said to have an income of a thousand pounds a day. This is a common report in England as to his revenues, though probably a gross exaggeration; still the riches of many of the privileged people in England are prodigious; and the disproportion in riches there is so great and so extensive that it never could exist in a state of freedom.

103. By productive labour, then, I here mean that which results in the greatest amount of virtue and happiness of the people, which, no doubt, will, in the long run, end in their greatest riches. And by riches is meant the true, durable, exalting riches, that of which every man gets his natural share, not that which pampers the pride and sensuality of a few,

but such as give the greatest bodily comfort, and noble, social, intellectual enjoyments to the whole.

104. There are two kinds of property, one for the mind and one for the body; many kinds of property contribute to the wants of both. The spectacles which enable me to read are an unspeakable blessing to my mind, but they do not sustain my body; the garments which I wear are essential to my body, though not to my mind. Riches, when virtuously used, are synonymous with the greatest good of the people. Nothing but the mean uses to which property has been put, as in the five-pound dinners, the covering servants' heads with wigs and their bodies in rich liveries, and so on, could ever have made even the most ignorant of the people enemies to it. It is not the property that they hate, but this disgraceful application of it. Nothing else has ever so much confused their judgments as to the intrinsic value of it. To impute to the poor a general wish to destroy property is a gross libel upon human nature; it is against a man's instincts. The amount of property destroyed by the poor is a drop in the bucket compared with what the rich have destroyed; the poor have been the destroyed, not the destroyers. If the rich expect that the poor will respect property, they must teach them to do so by their own example; for if they rob, who can prevent the poor from stealing? All property ought to contribute to the public good in some way or other; it supports the poor by giving them wages, and the greater the property the greater the wages, other things being

regulated as they should be. After all, it is a most heart-satisfying pleasure to recollect England, the good people who open their doors and spread their hospitable boards for you, and to know that many of them have spent their riches wisely, modestly, and in a way still farther to increase the true riches; if this were not so, England would not be magnificent England, but cursed Ireland perhaps, or, if possible, some country more wretched than Ireland.

105. It is not easy to say what country loves bawbles most; but this may be safely affirmed, that savages and other ignorant people are most taken by them, and waste *proportionably* most of their money on them; and that, as nations pass upward through the different stages of civilization, they spend less and less upon these trifles *proportionably*, so that the best evidence of things going forward is to see gewgaws losing their hold upon the imaginations of the people, and the more solid pleasures taking their place.

106. These are some of the characteristics of property. 1st. There is property which is designed to last, and be permanent and useful, conferring happiness upon body and mind, or both, for a longer or shorter time, such as farms, cattle, tools, houses, pictures, gardens, books, &c. 2d. Property, in regard to which it is designed that it shall not last, but "that the fashion of it shall pass away" as soon as possible, so as to give room to some other extravagance of the like kind. This

kind of property is made with the express view of enriching some at the expense of others. It consists here very much of that immense mass of bawbles, finery, and pretty things imported yearly for the use of fashionable people, which, to be sure, nearly the whole people use according to their ability. In the year 1836 I saw at New-York such articles as the following: silk stockings at $12 the pair; ladies satin dresses with a silk embroidery at $80 the dress; a single dress of Mechlin lace for $500; a wooden box lined with silk and richly perfumed, to be the receptacle of ladies' pocket-handkerchiefs, for $40; ladies' cloaks at $80 apiece; a single box of laces, about 2 1-2 inches high, 8 inches wide, 15 inches long, said to be worth $2000; pocket-handkerchiefs at $50 a piece, and so on. The buyers and sellers of these pretty things are not people who enjoy lordly inheritances; on the contrary, their practice is to divide their property equally among their children, or nearly so. New-York is a city which, after being settled about two hundred years, is now making, for the first time, an effectual effort to introduce pure and wholesome water for the people, and which, as yet, is not as well paved or lighted as London, that owes its portion of a debt of eight hundred millions sterling. This is a city which has now (1837), as stated by the newspapers, three thousand paupers in her poorhouse. Here is an immense demand for that unproductive (unprofitable) labour which Mr. Paley, Mr. Malthus, and others think indispensable in England to stimulate labour, create enterprise and industry, and circulate money; and this will be quite true, too, in the United States, unless the people can get higher desires into their souls than for these gewgaws. Here is cause enough for our every now and then sending to auction laid-down coaches, eighty-dollar chairs, and the second or third set of fine furniture; cause enough for "panics," "pressures," broken merchants, broken banks, broken-down families, sighs, tears, and disgrace. If the rational people of the United States do not put their heads together and provide some better way of "paying labour, stimulating industry, and making money circulate among the poor," it will not be because they cannot. If they can, then Mr. Malthus's and Mr. Paley's political economy in this particular is not wanted in the United States. It is a pity that the people of the United States cannot be weaned from these foreign, aristocratic toys, considering what a grand material they have to work upon at home. Oh, what would become of trade, what should we work for, if not for fifty-dollar pocket-handkerchiefs and the little wooden boxes so exquisitely lined with silk and richly perfumed!

107. The pretty things I have above mentioned are, after all, poor trash, compared with the magnificent bawbles of England.

In going up Ludgate Hill in London, my friend stopped at the famous shop of Rundell and Bridge. Upon saying that he was from the United States (which we always found passport enough), and that he wished to see the establishment, a clerk gave himself up for that purpose. Among other things, my friend was shown a set of diamonds, bracelets, and earrings, valued at £70,000, about $350,000; the clerk informing him that there were instances, when noblemen married, of their paying £10,000 —$50,000—for a set of diamonds. He showed a number of brilliants of various prices, and the model of the Pigot diamond, about as large as two thumb nails, which Mohammed Ali bought for £30,000. He verified the old maxim, "that all is not gold that glistens," by saying that there was very little *gold* plate; that what is called gold plate is silver gilded.

The Pitt diamond was purchased for £130,000, and is now said to be valued at twice that sum. It was lately in the handle of the sword of Bonaparte. Many of the richest diamonds are obtained in Brazil, where they are procured at an immense expense of the labour of poor slaves; and then it is the labour of the poor men and women of England by which they are bought of Brazil. In the early history of Virginia, it is said that Captain John Smith obtained from the Indian chief Powhattan two or three hundred bushels of corn for a pound or two of beads. Mr. Burke says that the rich are the trustees of the poor; it will be more to the purpose when the poor become their own guardians. Rundell and Bridge will not then be able to exchange their diamonds for as many days of poor people's labour as at present. It would be better for us if all the jewellery in creation was melted into one shapeless mass of deformity, than to allow it to consume so much as it does of the labour of the world through an accursed vanity and pride, sustained only by unrighteous privileges.

How far the privileged system has stupified the moral and intellectual faculties of the higher classes by indulging them in indolence and pride, and by debasing the lower orders through servility and mean labours, can never be known till the world has got rid of it.

What, then, is the argument as to the people of the United States decking themselves in jewels? It is quite true that, in order to buy jewels, we must raise cotton, sugar, wheat, &c.; that this makes us industrious, and gives us trade, which is a good thing. The only sensible question is, whether the jewels be *the best things* that we can buy with our labour. Powhattan bought beads with his corn; we only buy a costlier toy. With such a glorious country before us, and so much real poverty, it would seem that the question is answered.

108. It is really worth our while, then, be we rich or poor, to know what labour brings about, how much it adds to what there was before, what it produces, whom it helps, and how much it helps; and particularly at a period when, in some way or other, we have so mismanaged matters, that not a few are turned out of house and home, and are obliged to begin the world over again.

109. Some people keep game cocks, and some game horses; what difference there may be in the dignity of the occupations they must decide between

them. As to what is said about improving the breed of horses in this way, every one knows that the main thing with these gentlemen is gaming; an exciting occupation for those who have nothing else to do. In the rearing and providing for these game horses, barns, stables, &c., are to be built, farmers, carpenters, masons, &c., to be employed. The colt is treated like a child, being trained at an immense expense of grooms, &c.; and all that some idle gentlemen, who have never been taught the true dignity of labour, may have something to do. What an occupation! I shall hereafter make some statements, though very inadequate they must be, of what it is in England, and how far this, with other kindred causes, have made about one eighth part of the people there paupers, and so pinched the greater part of the remainder, that life with them is nothing but an uneasy, troubled, anxious, feverish existence. It is a wonder that our people, considering what they have done and can do, should not reject these European follies.

110. The condition of labouring people has been so miserable, that it has led us into the most absurd ideas as to what they ought to do and can do. In England, it has appeared to be a great charity to support them; and it has been thought enough by people of property and political economists to give them wages, to employ them in any way. This we may see fully set forth by even as good and great men as Malthus and Paley.

The gentlemen who keep game horses, fly hawks,

pay fifty dollars for pocket-handkerchiefs for their wives and daughters, are, no doubt, more or less under this delusion. It is true they do some good with their money; they set people to work, they give them occupation, they keep them from idleness, they pay wages, they preserve them from the poorhouse. All this is good; but do they do all the good they can with their money? for this is the bounden duty of every man. Is it enough to set a man to work? There is another question: Is it not important what sort of work he does? And there is another very important inquiry, which the *labourer alone is to answer.* Is he an American labourer; has his independence secured him a choice of employment; and, if so, does he do all the good he can by his labour? Is it as well for him, and for other labourers like him, to be employed in keeping game cocks, game horses, flying hawks, making fifty-dollar pocket-handkerchiefs, distilling whiskey to be drank in tumblers as decent people drink water, as to work in a way to create some useful property? When wages are given, and no property is created by the labourer, or pleasure communicated that is becoming a man, and that he is entitled to, property only changes hands; the rich man gives and the poor man receives; it is merely the exchange of property for labour; but the poor man creates nothing that is *worthy of his labour.* When the poor man works only to get wages, as the grooms and riders of the game horses do, it is plain enough that there is nothing in the world more than there was before. Besides, this sort of extravagance, folly, and madness is catching; for as the rich man spends his money, so does the poor man. I have heard of many a strike on account of hours and wages, but not because of the contemptible, unworthy, wasteful employments in which labouring men are every day engaged, which would often be more to the purpose. Any man who has seen the unhappy, helpless-looking poor people of Manchester and various other parts of England, must acknowledge that they have many excuses for consenting to work in ignoble employments which the labourers of the United States, where independence is so easily obtained, have not. There is no valid excuse of poverty here, in most cases not the least; here a man ought to be ashamed to soil his fingers with any dirty work. It is this unprofitable labour, it is this dirty work, that will account for the miserable condition of the world. We can easily say why one eighth part of the people of England should be paupers. We were told there of an individual who had exhausted a property which gave him an income (no doubt every penny of it employed in setting people to work in some way or other) of forty thousand pounds sterling a year upon brood mares, the turf, and in the hells of London. What a disgrace that a man should be born into the world, and so beautiful a part of it as England too, leaving it just as he found it, even worse, so far as he is concerned, creating, producing nothing, not a plant, shrub, tree, or anything of value, either by the use of his hands or his mind, thus dying a pauper, and leaving nothing but his pernicious example.

111. Now let us reverse the case, and consider that kind of labour which not only brings wages to the labourer, but property or virtuous pleasure to the employer. Here two parties are benefited; the labourer has gained something and the employer something. The labourer has his wages, the employer the house which the labourer has built, the crop which he has produced, or the flower which has been caused to expand. But this is not all which the labourer gets when property is produced; he is inevitably a sharer also in the property, directly or indirectly, for it is impossible to create property without benefiting the whole society more or less; perhaps the house that has been built is for the accommodation of the labourer; if it be a crop got from the fruitful earth, he will certainly find an advantage; if there be many such crops, food will be abundant; if abundant, cheap; and in this every man is interested. If property is created, then every poor man knows there is a fund out of which roads are made, schoolhouses built, and poor children educated. Nothing is more certain than that wages are generally in proportion to the prosperity and riches of a country. *The number of the whole people, compared with the riches, is no doubt a very important point,* but that need not be discussed here. Where there is a great deal of property there is a great deal of work to be done; England and the United States are proof of that. When a country

is prosperous and great profits are made, then it is, of course, that property is increasing most rapidly, and then also wages are highest. The labourer, then, who lives by wages, has a certain interest, though sometimes an indirect one, in all the property that he creates. He earns something more than wages, he does something more than make property shift hands, something more for himself than obtain the dollar which his employer pays him at night after his work is done. The uses of all property should be such that the poorest man that lives should feel, as by a kind of instinct, that he is interested in the creation and preservation of it.

112. It is greatly to be lamented that the poor, the labouring people, the working men, and all people cannot fully realize that every increase of property by virtuous labour is for their advantage. It is true enough that this increase may not have been obtained in a way most favourable to their rights and interests. It may have been got at a most unrighteous expense of the health and happiness of the labourers; and still the accumulation is a good; it is a new fund to work with; it is a new mine opened, a new tool invented or created. It is very true that every such increase may not to-day or to-morrow be used wisely, or to the greatest advantage of those whose labour produced it; but the time will come when all property will be useful, it may be the next year, or the next generation, for the benefit of our children or our grandchildren. The labourer may be certain that it will become, some day

or other, an engine in his hands. The great thing is to improve the world as fast as we can. Much as every man may contend for his own ideas of economy, there can be no doubt that we know little yet as to what is the best form of laws or society for the accumulation of property or the right use of it. We may be pretty sure that, if we introduce good things into the world, good will come out of them. Let us, then, be candid; and, if we differ, get from the collision all the truth we can, which is often the golden mean between two extremes.

113. As all agree that some kinds of labour are more productive, more profitable than others, let us see, then, how the fabricating of fifty-dollar pocket-handkerchiefs or grooming game horses compares, for instance, with working for the public on a canal or railroad. As one of the people, the labourer is actually a part owner of the railroad; he is a partner in the concern. His labour not only gives him wages, but property wholly independent of his wages; and if a man who works for the public does not know this, it shows that he is a very ignorant citizen; and if he does not realize it, reflect upon it, and place a due importance upon it to himself and family, it shows how unthinking he is. A poor man, such as the greater part of those are who do the labour on our public works, and who is, of course, compelled to economize, can now travel on the Erie Canal for one cent and a half per mile; from Albany to Utica, about one hundred miles, for a dollar and a half. Before that canal was built there was no way in

which he could have travelled that distance for less, probably, than twice that money, unless he went on foot; and then, if the loss of time, extra meals on the road, and destruction of shoe-leather be considered, the cost would probably be double that on the canal. Here, then, is something to be got more than wages. Besides this, the transportation of provisions is cheapened in something like the same proportion, and certainly the poor man is interested in getting his food as cheap as he can. I have left out here the delights of travelling, of cheap intercourse with friends who are separated from us, and the glorious object of connecting this great country together with iron bands; all which are worth considering, be a man rich or poor. At any rate, they seem to be worth as much as fifty-dollar pocket-handkerchiefs,

114. We see, then, how much every man is interested in increasing property, which may be laid by for future use. Fifty years ago there was neither railroad nor canal in the United States; even had the people known how to make them, they were too poor to make them. Not only the rich, but the poor now enjoy better food, houses, clothes, &c., than then. This is owing, in a great degree, to the increase of property produced by the poor men who have in the mean time worked for wages. It is the increase of property which now enables the richer part of the people, or the capitalists, to build those railroads and canals which the public do not think it expedient for them to build. This property is

what has been saved yearly beyond what has been spent by the whole people.

It is, then, by labouring at a business which not only gives wages, but yields property to others, that a man becomes the member of a rich community like that of the United States, where, though he be a very poor man himself, and, perhaps, a destitute stranger in the land, still he sees such amazing industry and enterprise, so many public improvements going on, so much money stirring, such prodigious prosperity among the whole people, that, with prudence, he may hope, and with reason, that he shall be a sharer in these wonderful riches, though he may get a portion far less than his industry and virtues entitle him to.

115. Let the labourer, then, in the United States understand his position, look up like a man, and learn that he was created for something else than to earn wages from the rich man and make money fly; that there is something else to be done here besides working for those frivolous objects, that in Europe seem to be the great aim of life, that disgrace our name and standing with the world and the age in which we live.

How few trace out the consequences to themselves, their wives, and children, of virtuous, profitable labour on the part of the whole people! How few are able to say, when the sun has set upon their labours, "I have done a good deed; it is doubly blessed; I have not only earned a dollar for myself, but one for my employer, in property, or some virtuous pleasure that is an equivalent; I have not wasted my time and destroyed my health in fabricating, polishing, burnishing finery to deck out his person, to gratify his pride and vanity, in ministering to his gluttony and lust; I have not acted the part of a slave, exhausting my nature in waiting upon his midnight parties and revelries, nor in leading about game horses for idle gentlemen from one racecourse to another; among EO tables, gamblers, and drunkards, where labouring men are soonest corrupted and destroyed; I have performed no labour but that which is demanded by the various and virtuous wants, tastes, and conditions of mankind; I have replaced the dollar which my employer paid me with a profit; I am one of the producers of the riches of the world; I glory in that: I have been useful not only to myself, but to others; though a poor man myself, I have been working for the benefit of other poor men; by increasing property I have done all I could to equalize it; I have performed one of the first duties that God has assigned me here on earth; I am a happy man." There is no fancy in these ideas; they are but plain truth and common sense upon the subject of economy, and will sooner or later be realized in the United States. How soon would they change the face of the world, if the heads and hearts of labourers and their employers were thoroughly imbued with them! how mean and selfish would it then be thought to employ one's fellow-citizens or creatures as we often do at present!

116. What, then, is the conclusion? 1st. That

most of the disputes about productive and unproductive labour are idle, because so good is the Creator to man in his state of ignorance, that he has caused all, or nearly all labour to be attended with some advantage or other, either to the employer or the employed. The real question is, what is the *most productive labour?* It is better that the savage should be industrious, produce corn, and buy beads, and even whiskey with it, than not work at all; but then it would be better if with his corn he bought hoes and ploughs, grew more corn, and built a good house with the proceeds; so it is better for the people of the United States to work for good houses, gardens, clothes, and education for their children, than for finger-rings, earrings, bracelets, feathers, flounces, fifty-dollar pocket-handkerchiefs, fine capes to their coats, &c. And then, again, this is better than working for shiploads of brandy, rum, gin, whiskey to drink as they would water, or for rivers of beer, as the people of England do.

2d. That, as the American labourer has a choice of employments unknown in the Old World, the first object of his life should be to secure, through care, economy, and a good education, that independence which will save him from defiling his hands with any unworthy work, or with any that is not connected with his own advance in property and prosperity.

CHAPTER V.

117. In chapter eight, part first of this work, there is a statement as to what wealth is. It would be out of place to repeat those definitions here; most people know very well what it is without any such assistance. In chapter nine there is a very brief statement as to how wealth is obtained; and in this respect, also, people of common sense know that labour can only do it; that it is labour added to labour that makes either an individual or a nation rich. A nation gets rich as a farmer gets rich; and if the nation, taking the people altogether, spent their money as wisely as the farmers do, it would be better for them.

In chapter eleven the subject of consumption of wealth is treated of, or, in other words, the question is answered there as to what must be consumed, and what can or cannot be laid up. It is stated that there are two kinds of consumption, " productive and unproductive consumption." That it is productive consumption when a farmer consumes his food and wears out his clothes in ploughing, reaping, &c.; the food which he eats and the clothes which he wears out are consumed; the seed which he puts in the ground also perishes, but his food, his clothes, and his seed reappear in a new crop: that it is unproductive consumption " when an idler or drunkard consumes his food and wears out his clothes;" for they produce nothing. A horse in the stable will eat his head off, as the saying is; but a horse in the plough will pay his own way, and something more. In chapter twelve some account is given of the causes of poverty; among other things it is said "that one of the great causes of poverty is, that there are so many who do not produce the means of living." In section 202 there is the following statement: "There is a large class of vicious employments; these do not simply leave the world where it was, but make its condition worse." Some of these have already been alluded to. "Men who are employed in keeping and fighting game cocks, or in training horses to game with, or who spend their time in manufacturing and selling little pieces of red or blue paper, which they call lottery tickets, are engaged in occupations that are at once contemptible and vicious. These do not add to the general store by which the wealth of the world is increased, but they lessen it by corrupting themselves and their fellow-citizens, and thus taking away their working faculties. The working men who follow at the heels of these horses and their gaming owners do not understand what they are about; they have not studied their own interests."

118. In England no subject is either talked or written about more than its pauper laws. Much is said in English political economy about the duties of the poor; what shall be done with them, where they shall be sent, and something, although far less, what

the duties of the rich are towards the poor. They wonder, as well they may, in the richest country in the world, how one eighth part of the people come to be paupers. They cannot see how there should be such prodigious riches in the midst of such disgusting poverty. In this puzzle they attribute the poverty of their poor people to their bad poor-laws, not recollecting that there must have been many paupers before bad poor-laws were made for their provision. They lose sight, then, of some of those *first* great causes of poverty, against which so many shut their eyes. They forget that one of the greatest of these is the destruction by the rich of the riches which the poor create, and that the poor, in their turn, through bad example, are led on to the same destruction.

119. Mr. Hume says that idleness is the greatest of all causes of poverty. It is certain that the industrious must support the idle; nothing can be plainer. There is no cause of idleness like that of a man's knowing that he is working for others, and not for himself; and there is no cause for industry like the consciousness we have in the United States, that we are working for ourselves, our wives, and children. The puzzle of poverty would be in a great measure solved if the idle rich would remove from poor people their poverty-making example. We should then not want, certainly not for generations, any of that ingenious political economy by which the poor people of England are taught that it is best for them to abandon their neat comfortable cottages,

their green fields, their fertile lands, their beautiful hedges, for a frozen, inhospitable desert in Canada. This may be a very necessary economy to be taught in England as things are, but a stranger who has seen Old England, with all its beauties and glories, must think this a very hard lesson for the poor people to learn.

It is time, then, that we begin back at the beginning, and see if there are not other lessons first to be taught. This inquiry may be of some use in the United States, where *horse gaming* is just coming into high fashion. The labourers may put an end to it if they will, and to that *beautiful* array of EO tables under the Jamaica stand, by their own virtuous public opinion, without any legislative tinkering; and it is for them to determine whether they will or not.

120. On the — day of July, 1836, we left London for Holham, in the county of Norfolk, the residence of Mr. Coke, one of the firmest, most constant, and enlightened friends of American independence, whither we went to see its agriculture, for which it is more famous than any part of England. Newmarket was on our route, sixty miles from London. We left London at 7 o'clock A.M., and arrived at Newmarket at 2 P.M., the coach stopping twenty minutes for breakfast on the way. This I suppose to be about the average speed of coach travelling in England. In the economical use of time, the roads are but little inferior to railroads.

121. A man who does not, in travelling, open him-

self to an unrestricted intercourse, loses half its benefits, and more than half its pleasures. There is no one so uninstructed that he cannot give information to a stranger in a strange land. I adopted one practice invariably in England, and that was, under all circumstances, in omnibuses, cabs, hackney-coaches, in the streets, in London, on the highways, in the country, to enter into conversation for the purpose of information with people of all classes; and I can say very truly that, so far from having met with any rebuff, rudeness, or insolence, I found nothing but gentleness, kindness, and alacrity to answer my inquiries. To be sure, I generally prefaced them with saying, " that, being a stranger in those parts of the world," I begged the favour of asking about this or that. More generally I stated myself to be a stranger and an American, and this I am sure, in many cases, was a passport to pleasing attentions; for though the English see in us many things they do not like, they find many which they do; there is a certain respect which they do not wish to conceal. Our English descent (for how can a people fail in esteem for those who have come from their own loins?), our history, our deeds, our unexampled enterprise and increasing wealth, all claim the regard or admiration of an Englishman. Pursuing the plan I have mentioned, I received instruction from many cabmen, servants, and boatmen, and found on board a steamboat, *without introduction*, some of the kindest and most interesting friends that I met with in England. Indeed, if an American will shut his eyes, open his heart, and rid himself of the silly vanity and selfishness of being tormented about his own personal importance in England, where not one in a thousand of his countrymen has any, or can have any, he will hardly know half of the time that he is out of his own happy country.

122. On our coach were two jockeys on their way to Newmarket races, which were to take place in a few days. Newmarket is, or has been, the most notorious place in England for horse-racing. Races are held there seven times a year. Charles the Second built a seat there. One of these jockeys was the famous Chifney, a man of rank in his line in England, of *quiet aristocratic* manners, who is as well known in England in his line as Lord Lyndhurst is in his. By his side sat another, of very different calibre, who always addressed his superior as " Sir." The gradation of rank in England is a curious riddle. Chifney told us that racing was not declining in England; as to this, however, we heard different accounts, and so various that I am at a loss to know how the fact is. At Cambridge I went into a saddler's shop, and, upon examining some racing saddles, and inquiring about the state of racing at Newmarket, the man told me that racing had certainly declined there; that many formerly used to come over to Cambridge to lodge during the races for the want of lodgings at Newmarket, but that this was not the case at present. After we arrived at Newmarket we understood that Chifney had failed; that a commission of bankruptcy had

been taken out against him; that his plate was said to be worth three thousand pounds, about $15,000. I doubt whether there are five gentlemen in the United States who have as much.

123. There are, doubtless, some articles of plate for common purposes that are useful and economical; but that such immense masses should be set aside to be exhibited upon great occasions to show how rich we are, and, of course, how poor our neighbours are, is but a miserable use of the property in the world. How poorly are the greater part provided for ? how few of them possess houses, lands, gardens, flowers, books? how many that cannot afford a decent education for their children or pay their taxes ? how many delicate, well-educated, noble-feeling people are driven to such straights as not to know where to get a dollar, while these gorgeous, costly things, obtained by the degradation of the people, are resting unsoiled in solitary grandeur! If the rich were overruled in these vanities by a pure public opinion, what immense additional masses of property would be applied to useful purposes! This would not at all interfere with the rights of the rich, and would only turn their minds to the correct use of their property. It was said in the papers the other day that the plate exhibited by the Duke of Wellington at his Waterloo banquet on the eighteenth day of June last was valued at $1,500,000. If the account which I heard of the agricultural condition of his estate was true (if not, it does not affect the argument), it would be much more to the purpose

to turn a part of the plate, at least, into money, and the money into carts, horses, and ploughs, for the benefit of those melancholy-looking, eye-sunken people, his fellow-subjects, of whom I saw so many in England. Let no man be so simple as to suppose that the people of the United States are indifferent to the glory of these aristocratic bawbles. The glory is too expensive for most of us; but though the idols are few, the worshippers are many.

124. In England the magnificence of the riches of some can only be exceeded by the poverty of the many; and how is this to be accounted for? What sort of a *productive* labourer is Chifney in the political economy of England?

Being very desirous of getting information as to everything interesting in England, we went the next morning after our arrival at Newmarket to his house. We found a beautiful residence; a pretty garden appeared to be attached to it; a high brick or stone wall in front of the house, with a bell at the gate. This house, with the walls and outhouses, I think, would cost twice as much as any house, with the outhouses, &c., in our county of Berkshire. Chifney was not at home, but was out "*wasting.*" Most people are very desirous of keeping the flesh they have upon their bones, for generally it has cost them dear enough. But not so with the jockeys; they can let it come or go, as they choose. *Wasting* is a preparation for riding at a race by getting rid of more flesh than is wanted, the man bringing his weight down to the required standard. For this purpose he puts on three or four flannel shirts, as many pairs of drawers, stockings, &c., and in this dress he walks out five or six miles, and as many back, the perspiration all the while streaming from him as when in a vapour-bath. So we make money fly; these *wasters* are considered by many essential in England, in order to keep the rest of the people at work.

125. It is a wonder that these jockeys, riders, hostlers, and horse people of every description in England, do not see how they are for ever kept in the stables. That it is by their gaming, their dissipation, and following for ever at the heels of the profligate gentlemen of the country in all their wasteful extravagances. Nothing is more fatal to a common man than gaming; if he falls, there is no one to pick him up; the gentlemen can bear the fall; if they lose their property, they do not go to the workhouse; there are rich relations to uphold them, and then there has been a government in England to support all broken-down gentlemen by giving them offices in India, in the army, in the navy, in the colonies, or somewhere. But let the common people rescue themselves from this degradation; it is in vain to call upon the rich, upon Hercules; let them put their own shoulders to the wheel. The worst governments in the world are founded upon the vices and ignorance of the "lower orders," as they call them in England. Let the people in England, then, get knowledge and virtue by practising temperance and economy; forsaking beer, and dram-

drinking, and horse-gaming; let them get property; property will give them votes; votes will give them privileges, and then they will be able to make such a government as they choose; then they will deserve the best, and not before. Property is the great lever that moves the world; if the people are to be disenthralled, they must work off their own chains. This is the way in which the people of the United States have advanced, and this is the only way in which any people can. The times have changed; the people in England, here, and everywhere, must work out their own salvation. If a government fit for angels was now given to the people of England, or to any other people, they could not sustain it, they are not fit for it. Far enough shall we be from such a government, if the rich, idle gentlemen can lead the people about from one racecourse to another, as they do their dogs and horses. My object in making these statements about horse-racing in England is to show to the people of the United States distinctly what a wanton waste this practice is of their property, and how scandalously immoral and base it is to pamper a horse while a fellow-man is starving. A gentleman, who is now advanced to an honourable old age, told us this story: That, as soon as he got out of his minority, his father being one of the gentlemen of England, but not rich, told him that he might go to Newmarket, and for that purpose gave him a horse worth about a hundred pounds, and the same sum for his pocket. That the first night of the races he went to "hell" (so the gaming houses in London are called) and lost his hundred pounds; the second night he went to "hell" again, and lost his horse; that he then borrowed two or three guineas to pay his way home, and has never since been on the turf. From that period his life has been devoted to useful and honourable occupations. He told us that many of the nobility of England were running through their property at a great rate. It is thus that a sure process of regeneration is going on in favour of the working people. What a call upon them for increased efforts in favour of economy, temperance, and everything that gives value to a working man! How prodigiously it would push the working people forward in the United States if a thorough contempt could be got into their souls of the wasteful follies of the wasteful part of our rich people!

126. The extent of this horse-gaming, and the immense expense at which it is supported, can hardly be conceived of by those who have not been in England.

The morning after we arrived at Newmarket we went to see one of the training-grounds. It is said to belong to the Duke of Rutland, and that each horse that is trained upon it pays a guinea annually towards the rent. It appears to be a barren heath; but who can say what is *barren,* if these idle nobles, instead of spending their time in the stables with horses and hostlers, would try their ingenuity upon it, as we have upon *our* "barren" lands with plaster and clover? If plaster and clover will not bring out the natural fruitfulness of the earth, something else may. Barren as this land is at present, Heaven must have intended it for some sort of cultivation for the benefit of the poor people of England, and could never have designed it for so worthless a purpose as that to which it is applied. This heath, in one view of it, is not unlike, in the form of the ground, some of our high beautiful prairie, being skirted on the right, as you leave the town for Norfolk, with a growth of pine or some kind of furze.

As I came on the ground I saw at the distance of about a mile, and on what appeared to be the summit of a hill, a number of objects indistinctly in very slow motion. The view was so uncertain, the objects being in close line one after another, that in a desert they might have been taken for a train of camels bearing burdens. I soon made them out to be horses with riders upon a very slow walk. In other parts of the ground I saw afterward other squads of horses, some here and some there, scattered in all directions. I think there were not much fewer than fifty. We were told afterward that not less than 350 or 400 race-horses were kept at Newmarket through the season, and that, when we were there, there might be two hundred and fifty. The horses on the ground were ridden by boys. This is a part of their training, the horses having then been out from 4 o'clock in the morning; when we saw them they were all on a very slow walk. The books giving an account of the training of these horses state that it is common to take them out at this hour.

127. The riders being mere lads, there is often an older one put over them, who is then called the boys' lad. As we were retiring from the ground we saw one of these boys' lads, whom we asked to show us his stable and horses, which he declined, saying that it was not allowed, " as improper things were done." These "improper things" are called technically " poisoning horses for the race," a kind of fraud that has crept into very common practice, and is now so common that we were repeatedly told that these frauds and cruelties would finally put an end to racing, by rendering skill in training and the speed of the horse of no avail. Before we left England we heard of a case in which a noted horse called " Plenipotentiary" was " poisoned for the race" by giving him as much water as he would drink shortly previous to running, and which nearly destroyed him in consequence of his greediness, it being a common practice to stint horses in their water for some time before running.

One would not suppose it possible that the gentlemen of a country, the hereditary legislators, the owners of those beautiful fields, those green hedges, those superb palaces, costly parks, would consent to mix themselves up with sports necessarily attended by such low frauds and petty villanies as we know this horse-gaming and all gaming to be.

Before we left the ground a young lad showed us to Lord ———'s stables, he taking a shilling for going with us perhaps half a dozen rods. The lower orders in England, in consequence of their poverty, and being kept down by these gentlemanly vices, never scorn receiving any money for any service, however trifling it may be. These favours are received from the gentleman with cap in hand, and to us it was a source of perpetual grief to see men in such an abject state. I have seen three brawny fellows, who were in an open brick enclosure of high walls attached to a jail, who, upon being addressed by the gentleman who accompanied me, invariably threw up their hands, and, for the want of caps, caught hold of the elflocks that hung over their foreheads as a mark of respect. It may be said that these outward signs of respect are mere arbitrary conventionalisms, and prove nothing. This might be; but in England there are too many other proofs of the abject state of the lower orders, in their manners, voices, countenances, in their poor wages, and consequent poverty, to allow any doubt of the fact. Mutual self-respect lies at the foundation of all virtue and freedom, and is not to be found in Europe as it exists in the United States. The gentlemen of Europe may write about political economy, but they can never make their communities great, rich, and happy, like those of the *free* United States, until they have infused souls into all classes of their fellow-subjects, and until all men shall work with alacrity, as those do who know that what they work for will be their own, for their wives and children, instead of being thrown into the mangers for the horses or the kennels for the dogs.

128. The principal groom at this stable took from

us as a gratuity half a crown, his services being graduated by his superior rank. We found three ranks in these stables, and how many more there may be I know not. The lad, the boys' lad, and the groom; but they must all find employment, and what can the gentlemen do better than support the poor people by the money which the poor people earn? This groom showed us ten or twelve horses belonging to his stable, most of them being two year old colts. Each had a muzzle made of tin and leather to prevent him from biting the manger. They have a good practice of tying their horses in the stables. The halter is run through an iron ring fixed in the manger, at the end there being attached a small block of wood, so large that it will not pass the ring; this being done to save the horse from injury in getting his leg over the halter, as is sometimes the case in our mode of tying. The groom showed us two racing saddles, one weighing nine pounds, the other twelve; at Cambridge a saddler showed us a saddle which he said weighed but five pounds. These horses were fed then on hay and dry oats only. Three of the most famous trotting horses in the United States were sent to England, Tom Thumb, Rattler, and Rochester. Rattler and Tom Thumb were at Newmarket. The groom showed us a picture of Tom Thumb, Mr. Osbaldiston driving. This gentleman figured at Melton Mowbray, as may be seen in the account given in the Quarterly Review of fox-hunting there. Rattler deserved a kinder fate, for he died on the spot at Newmarket, having reached the goal in triumph, driven by Mr. Osbaldiston. The English acknowledge that no such trotting-horses as ours are known in England. Great trotting requires great strength and speed; so it seems that there are other modes of improving the breed of horses besides that of keeping them to game with! What a miserable excuse for gaming and taking the bread from the mouths of the poor!

It does not require any great knowledge in economy to know that these grooms, lads, boys' lads, and horses might be better employed; that they might be better occupied in ploughing and digging even the poor lands at Newmarket. Miserable as these are, they would produce a little, and that little is to be taken into account in a country where the poor every year tremble lest storms and rains should bring famine among them. Every account which we received of these horse people in England represented them to be, including masters and owners, among the worst in it.

The contrast between these disgusting sights and what is pure and noble in England, of which we saw so much, presents us an idea of different races of men.

We had the other day a specimen of the degradation to which the gaming part of the nobles of England (for it is happily only a part) are reduced, in a report in the London Times of the 12th February, 1837, in the case of Lord de Ros vs. Cumming. The plaintiff brought an action of slander against the defendant for accusing him of cheating in playing at cards in one of the hells of London. The attorney-general stated that his client, Lord de Ros, was at the head of the English baronage, and equally distinguished for his descent and virtues. It appeared that the parties played whist; that some of the cards were marked with the plaintiff's nail; that, with some French legerdemain, and the aid of paralytic hands, a fit of coughing, and holding the cards a little below the table when he dealt, he always had the extraordinary luck of turning an honour, which, as all whist-players know, is a great advantage in the game. The plaintiff was defeated: In the course of the trial one gentleman stated that he had won thirty-five thousand pounds in fifteen years.

We were told, by one who had a right to know, that the nobleman whose stable we saw at Newmarket came to an estate worth not less than forty thousand pounds sterling per annum, with two hundred thousand pounds ready money (a million of dollars), and that he had got through nearly the whole of it. A gentleman by the name of Craven, sixty years of age, after a race at Epsom a few years since, where there were said to be collected a hundred thousand people, and where he lost £36,000, blew out his brains. Upon the whole, everybody knows that horse-racing in England and here is nothing but a fashionable sport got up to enable the gentlemen to gamble and pass their idle time.

After all, political economy is a common-sense affair, for there is nothing like virtue, temperance, and industry to make property either for an individual or a nation, and nothing like vice, intemperance, and gaming to destroy it.

Sports are good; they are social; they make us stronger, happier, and wiser; we have too few of them. But, to be right, they must be simple, economical, and innocent pleasures. There is no country in which there are so many idle gentlemen as in England, whose regular business it is to kill time. The English have racing, hunting, shooting, fishing, archery, coursing, cricketing, rowing, yachting, and others. They had pugilism, but the increasing humanity of the people has nearly put it down, and so they will turf-gaming in its turn. There are but few who see how the world is going on; none but those who are in motion themselves can see it.

129. No person who has not been in England, or read its books giving an account of horse-racing, can conceive of the immense waste of time and property involved in pursuing this sport. There are twenty places mentioned as the principal racecourses,* some of them being graced by the presence of royalty, the kings of England having been great patrons of this "noble sport." In gaming very few escape contamination; the whole system being one of stratagem and deception, even among those who pretend, according to the laws of the turf or the gaming-table, to observe the laws of honour. Every one who has been familiar with a gaming-table knows it. George the Fourth, while Prince of Wales, was ac-

* Brown's Turf Expositor.

cused of the most dishonourable conduct on the turf. His friends denied the charge, and we hope truly. But think of the " first gentleman" in the kingdom, and the ruler over more than one hundred millions of people, falling under such a suspicion ! This was the man who, in the last periods of his life, when his heart should have been poured out in love and tenderness towards his people, used to ride in the lanes and by-paths of Windsor Forest in order to avoid the sight of them.

130. At Ascot, about twenty-five miles from London, we got down from the coach at a little country inn. Being unable to get a conveyance, I walked to Sunning Hill, an old man of about seventy years of age, a very melancholy-looking person, who was going on my way, undertaking to show me the road. We were soon in the neighbourhood of Ascot Heath, which is a racecourse. The old man pointed out the building used for the king's staghounds, the betting stand, and the king's stand. I asked him whether he had a wife and children. " No, thank God! I had a wife and two children, but they are all dead ; thank God for it. These are hard times for poor people ; I can only earn eight or nine shillings a week." This was an agricultural labourer, and this was about the average wages of agricultural labour at that time. But say ten shillings, and then you have about two dollars and fifty cents (the man finding himself) for the weekly support of a man, his wife, and children ; to pay for clothes, fuel, house-rent, lights, meat,

bread, drink, doctor's bills, &c. Mr. Bulwer states that one third, or nearly one third, of every man's earnings in England go to pay his taxes. I cannot vouch for the accuracy of this statement.

These gaming sports are, of course, at the expense of the labour of the country, for what else can sustain them but labour? An idle horse is for ever eating in a poor man's crib, and so are idle gentlemen too. Where, then, is the impropriety of a poor man's thanking God for taking his children out of a world, in which they must live to suffer by such a misapplication of the bounty of Providence as is constantly before our eyes in England?

It is high time that the people of the United States examine these vicious customs; for, after having had a certain growth, and people being long accustomed to them, even the best know not how bad they are.

131. There is a mania for horse-racing in England; wherever you go you hear of it. The king gives plate, and at Newmarket they have, or had, " the king's plate articles," by which the rules regulating running there are established. The seventh rule provides against foul play by the riders! What sort of a sport must that be where kings and gentlemen cannot prevent their servants from committing villanous frauds for the benefit of their masters?

132. While in England I saw an account of the Egham races, which the king was said to have attended. It was stated that the king made a *mag-*

nificent grant of " a free plate" (I believe a hundred pounds). The king was addressed, and returned an answer, stating that this was done to encourage " the rational and manly spirit of a free people." This is the puffy, grandiloquent language just fit for the occasion. So people and kings go on from generation to generation humbugging themselves, till a few, more rational than the rest, point out the ridiculous figure they are making. At *Tewksbury* (I think that was the name), on my way from Worcester to Manchester, great preparations were making for the races. We saw people on the road, men, women, and children, on foot and in carts, &c., hastening to the ground. At the inn in the neighbourhood where we stopped there were very respectable-looking and decently-dressed women, of an age at which one would desire to see them engaged in the nurture and education of their children, who had their hands full of cards for the race, which they offered us at sixpence apiece. All the persons inside the carriage agreed in the fact of the immense profligacy promoted by the races among the lower orders. I never heard a different account in England.

133. The author I have mentioned, though not over wise, is competent to point out the abuses of the turf. He regrets to be obliged to say that these have crept into the " thoroughbred system of racing," and that they are greatly in need of " a radical reform." Among these are *foul riding*,

PUBLIC AND PRIVATE ECONOMY. 161

gaming-tables under marquees gaudily fitted up, &c. At Ascot he says there are ten of these.

134. If you wish to see the most intelligent among the labouring people in England, you must go to the manufacturing districts. One of the most distinguished persons in office told us this, and we found it so. Such a fact ought to go far to diminish the fears of the people of the United States as to the evils of their manufacturing population. The growth of manufactures is inevitable here, and all that is left to us is to educate the manufacturing people as highly as we can.

At Manchester we were told by one of those working people, whom it is a happiness to know in any country, that the races in the neighbourhood of that place corrupt the people in a most shameful way; that a whole week nearly is given up to them by the operatives; that, during this time, many of the cotton-mills are stopped; that every device is resorted to by the moral part of the community to keep the children in the town; that, for this purpose, ten or twelve hundred are collected together in the Mechanics' Society Lecture-rooms, and amused with experiments in the airpump, electricity, &c.

135. By an act of parliament passed in the thirteenth year of George the Second,* it is declared, that any person who shall run a horse, &c., for

---

* As I cite from the book mentioned, I cannot vouch for the accuracy of the citation.

less than £50, shall forfeit £200. This shows the magnificent scale upon which this turf-gaming is got up. What a scandalous infringement of the liberty of the common people to make one law for the rich and one for the poor! Who will pretend that they do not use their money as wisely and virtuously as the gaming gentlemen?

136. I went to a country race about eleven miles from Reading, in Berkshire. Several races were run; one said to be for a ten-pound cup; one for a five-pound cup. Three horses started in the first race. It was a miserable affair altogether, as far as respected the race. The friend who was so good as to accompany me assured me that there was not a gentleman of his acquaintance on the ground. I had told him that I desired to see a fair unmixed specimen of the common people at a race, and it was plain enough that this was one. Still, if horse-gaming be an innocent amusement, why should not the gentlemen consort with the common people in their pleasures? why did God put the gentlemen and common people together in one world, rich and poor indiscriminately, but for the purpose of making them mutually useful to each other, and that they might teach each other lessons of civility, courtesy, and humanity? and how can this be done unless they sometimes come together and have common enjoyments? People seem to be blind to the progress of things, and afraid to open their eyes, lest the light should put them out for ever. But the

light is streaming in at every crevice, crack, and corner of that huge fabric of feudal barbarism erected by the Norman conqueror. From the moment it was finished, decay and destruction began, and now in England you may see plainly that it is tottering to its foundations.

There were probably a thousand people at this race. Many booths were erected, where fancy China-ware, toys, cakes, beer, &c., were sold. The people were neatly dressed with few exceptions; many labourers were in clean frocks, and, generally, there was much less finery than among our people. I left the ground at an early hour, and before the usual carousing upon such occasions begins. Though I was in the midst of the people in every direction, I did not see a drunken man.

137. What imbecility in the writings and opinions of a large class of men of learning, genius, and virtue, who set up as teachers of mankind! they know nothing of mankind, they have been acquainted only with ladies and gentlemen, and think that there is little worth having or enjoying out of that circle. In one of our passages, the ladies and gentlemen often played for money till a late hour in the night (a scandalous practice, and an outrage upon those whose sleep is interrupted), while the trusty sailors, at whose mercy we were, stood faithfully at the helm or the lookout. On one of those nights I read the following passage from Southey's Political Lectures " on the means of improving the peo-

ple:" "It is among the *lower classes* that those miseries, as well as those diseases are found, which become infectious to the community. The vices to which they are prone are *idleness*, drunkenness, *gambling*, and cruelty. Gambling is the least frequent, and might almost wholly be prevented, *were the magistrates to exert themselves and the parish officers to do their duty.*" Let us change the paragraph *a little*, and then see how near the truth it is; thus: " It is among the *higher* classes that those miseries, as well as those diseases are found, which become *infectious* among the *lower* orders by a pernicious example. The vices to which the higher classes are prone are *idleness* and *gaming*, which come from the misery of overgrown wealth, and having nothing to do; and *excessive eating* and *drinking*, which they call by any other names than gluttony and drunkenness. Which is the most frequent or most destructive of the happiness of the lower orders, it is impossible to say."

It is not the lower orders that *spread* moral infection in the community; that comes from a higher quarter; the lower orders are what the higher orders make them by example. When the upper orders become robbers of the privileges of the people, they teach the lower to be thieves upon a smaller scale; if the common people are playing thimble-rig, the gentlemen are on the same ground betting above the parliament standard of *innocent* gaming; and while the people are destroying themselves with adulterated beer and gin, the gentlemen are guzzling wine and hot whiskey punch. There is nothing more common in England than to see gentlemen in the hotels at dinner, and even sometimes a solitary individual, after drinking a half pint or pint of wine, crowning the repast with this vile compound. But the case is still more vulgar with us, for here this inebriating stuff is *sometimes* introduced even in ladies' parties, where Champagne and other delicate wines flow as freely as water.

But what is the remedy for gaming? Gaming might be prevented, says Mr. Southey, " were the magistrates to exert themselves and the parish officers to do their duty." This legislative quackery of whipping, cropping, branding, of appealing to magistrates and parish officers to make the common people virtuous, is pretty much scouted in the United States; and it seems, from the fact of the English and French sending commissioners to examine our prisons and prison-discipline, that, if we have made no other advance in the science of government, we have made some in the management of the "lower orders." We do not intend here to have one law for the rich and one for the poor; and this we think another advance in the science of government. It is, indeed, one of the grand onward movements we are making. The poor see the injustice of all but equal laws; they hate the makers of them, and then become ten times more hardened than before. If the history of the world has proved anything, it is, that the improvement of the " lower orders" will be soonest brought about through the virtuous example and instruction of the higher, and not by the treadmill and the parish officers. Those of the higher classes who corrupt the common people by offences, for which they would hand them over to the " parish officers and the magistrates," such as gaming, &c., are themselves the highest offenders. The treadmill has proved a poor schoolmaster. I saw it in England ; we have abandoned it. If purity is to prevail in the land, it must begin with those whose heads are not bowed down with ignorance, the temptations of poverty, bad education, and evil example.

138. I saw an instance in England at a court of sessions of the one-sided justice above described. A boy of seventeen or eighteen years of age was brought before the magistrates by his master, a farmer. The master being sworn, proved that the boy went out at ten o'clock at night against his master's orders, and stayed out all night. The boy did not deny the charge. It is proper to state that it was said he had once before been before the magistrates for some other offence. The magistrates sentenced him to one week's solitary cnofinement in the county jail. As I went out of the room afterward, I saw this boy in a little lock-up-place crying like a child, the tears streaming down his cheeks. Subsequently, in my presence, he was led with an iron chain about one wrist to the jail, in one apartment of which I saw common

felons on the treadmill. What ideas can such boys have of the morals of keeping *good hours,* when the ladies and gentlemen of London order their carriages for a route at ten or eleven o'clock at night, and roll home in them at daylight in the morning? When shall it be that we shall cease to have one kind of morals for the rich people and another for the poor? How soon shall we have one law for high and low? There was no reciprocal justice in this case. How many offences, equally heinous both in the sight of God and man, might not this master have been guilty of towards the servant without punishment by the magistrates?

The master told me that he paid this boy three shillings and sixpence per week, the boy furnishing his own food, and that this was common wages for such boys. This will show what portion of the good things in England is enjoyed by those who plough the fields, trim the hedges, and contribute so great a part of the labour which goes to bring forth that exquisite embellishment which there fills the soul with delight.

139. The world has been kept in slavery by its vices; the chains have been forged by the great, and the multitude have put them on at the word of command. As to those vices and vicious customs which have kept the people down and rendered them incapable of liberty, the people of the United States have made advances unknown in other parts of the world. They have done in a few years what Europe has not been able to bring about in

centuries. The people of the United States act with a full knowledge of these truths; and though they have made but poor progress compared with what might have been hoped, still the secret is discovered; moral reformation is the watchword, and constantly keeps alive that intense enthusiasm which drove them to these once desolate shores.

140. Gaming is one of these vices. It grows up naturally among the idle aristocratic part, and then descends to the labouring portion, who, being ruined by it in their independence and property, become mere tools, of course. A common man, a labouring man, who has neither property nor the desire of it, is fitted at once to be the slave of power and despotism. The people of the United States, with their clear sight, in a new world and pure atmosphere, saw at once the truth. They knew the theory, and had seen the practice in the Old World; that is, that vices among the people were not destructive of *despotic* government, but essential to it. Virtue and republicanism, therefore, with us are synonymous; we have no hope of the latter without the former. We all know that the creatures and minions of despotism look for their strongest support among the worst of the people. Their dregs form the armies. The people of the United States, therefore, have set themselves to work in earnest to put down those national vices that can be reached by public opinion, and which, through custom and fashion, become common.

Gaming is a remarkable case; intemperance is another; licentiousness between the sexes is another. I shall speak of these in their turn. He who in the United States, trusting to his riches, influence, and power, dares to spread these vices among the poor, ought to be marked and branded by public opinion as their destroyer. He is the enemy of free government and poor people, let his party name be what it may. The people can put him where he belongs; this is their real power, and far greater than any they have given to their rulers.

141. I remember when there was turf-gaming, and not a little of it, in some parts of New England, and particularly in our own village, upon a large scale, but I doubt whether ten dollars have been lost or won among two millions of people in New-England upon a horse-race within the last ten years. I do not assert this absolutely, but can, that the *practice* of horse-racing no longer exists among us. If the gentlmen of the cities here should attempt to revive it under the idea of improving the breed of horses, they would be laughed at. This is the charm that works in the United States! The people would laugh, because they know that the breed of horses can be improved, if that is what the turf gentlemen have determined upon, without the aid of EO tables; without an enormous waste of time on the part of the gentlemen; of property on the part of the people; and without that brutality to the poor animal which goads him to death. There was, probably, never

a more contemptible idea got up by gentlemen at the expense of the public morals than this of the necessity of horse-racing to improve the breed of horses. It is not horse-racing nor the breed of horses that most of them desire (though there are, doubtless, public-spirited men among them that have these opinions), but the delights of gaming, of getting rid of idle time agreeably.

But it is not horse-race-gaming alone which is to be spoken of here. Every kind of gaming has greatly disappeared from among us in the country parts in New-England, and in the Northern states generally. I speak of these with certainty, because to these, upon this subject, my personal knowledge is confined. It is absolutely disgraceful for any class of people here in the country to be seen engaged in it. But the time was, thirty or forty years ago, when the passion for it was excessive; there was gaming in the smallest villages, in private houses, at the taverns, at the courts, at balls, dances, militia musters, and wherever there were collections of people. There is yet a good deal in the cities; but even in them there is an improvement, which, I do not doubt, is going on in every part of the United States, though in some, perhaps, very slowly. What a people are to do or to be is best known by comparing what they are doing with what they have done and been.

142. I have been more particular upon the subject of horse-racing in England, because it is one of the most wasteful of all the fashionable aristocratic modes of destroying the property of the

country; because gaming is one of the most demoralizing of all vicious practices; and because this vicious sport in some, though a few, parts of the free States is getting great popularity. The vicious, aristocratic sports are among the best devices that ever were contrived to keep the common people down; and it is a wonder that they have not always looked at them in this light. They rob them of their property, increase the number of poor dependants and the lower orders, and then make slaves of them, of course.

143. Nothing is more common than the mistaken opinion that it is a matter of no moment how rich people spend their money, so far as the poor are concerned, only that they spend it. The difficulty lies here; as the rich spend their money, so do the poor. "Like master, like man," is the old proverb. It is a mistake to suppose that, if the rich waste their property, the poor will get the benefit of it, of course. They may get the property, but they do not keep it; the great man's vices have spoiled them for that, and this is the grand difficulty in the way of the lower orders in England shaking off their chains. They are so extravagant, intemperate, wasteful, sensual; and still, no doubt, a great reformation is going on in these respects. A single age of determined virtuous economy in England among the people would wholly change the face of things there.

144. The true way to spend money is that by which the poor people, and all people, may not only

get, but spend virtuously more than they had before. If the idle horses at Newmarket were put into the plough at Ascot Heath, on the Hampshire Downs, and the other poor lands of England, so much the better for rich and poor. There would certainly then be more food than there is at present; and if the people did not increase in as great a proportion as the increased food, according to Mr. Malthus (of which I shall speak hereafter), the poor people would be better off than at present. It would not be so necessary as at present to send them penniless from the parishes to the United States, as is now most cruelly the case. If a man ploughs land that never was ploughed before, he hires labourers and pays them wages, and has one crop more than there was before; if he keeps a stable of horses, he hires the groom, the lad, and the boys' lad; he pays wages, of course, and what has he? Fine horses, their skins as sleek as polished marble, grooms and servants in abundance, to come and go as he orders. But there is the end of it. He spends his money and produces nothing; the world is none the richer for him; he is a cumberer of the ground; he will leave the world just as poor as he found it; he earns nothing; he does nothing to improve the condition of the poor; he does not make roads for them to travel on, nor open the bowels of the earth in search for coal to warm their houses; nor does he build ships or plough the land, by which poor people who want work get wages; by which work they pave the way for more work; and thus there is an infinite succession of labour and wages. Hence flows an infinite succession of riches; and upon this plan they are always increasing. Upon the whole, there is proof enough that the world is in a disgraceful state of poverty, and that the people of the United States are beginning to understand the subject, and that they will take care that property is not wasted here as it is and has been in other parts of the world. They will soon find out that, even allowing that horse-racing, not horse-racing, but horse-gaming, does improve the breeds of some sorts of horses, it does not improve the breed of any sort of men; that horse-gaming is not a sport for hard-working people; that on the turf they are mere hangers-on, for they cannot afford to keep horses nor grooms, nor partake with the gentlemen in their lordly bets; that this is one of those high aristocratic recreations where the great body of the people who go to partake of it are looked upon as underlings, understrappers, a mere mob. How, then, is it to be put out of countenance? I answer, that the hard-working people of the United States have all power; there is nothing above or beyond the public opinion which they can create. Let them, then, combine, join hands, turn their faces the other way, and permit the gentlemen who own the horses to go to the racecourses with their grooms alone. This is an easy process, a remedy quickly administered, sure, and far better than all the legislative quackery in the world.

CHAPTER VI.

145. A voice has gone forth commanding the whole world to be temperate! to use the things of this world as not abusing them. It denounces drunkenness as one of the greatest curses; it orders the rich to set an example of godliness to the poor, over whom they have so great a control; and the poor to forsake all evil examples of the rich; to stand erect in the likeness in which God made them, and to forsake all those vicious ways by which they are deprived of their natural portion of the earth, its blessings and comforts. It teaches that the chain that is about the soul binds harder and cuts deeper than that which confines the body.

146. Let us make what parade we will in our fourth of July orations and election speeches about our excellent republican constitution, our free institutions, and universal right of suffrage, all will come to nothing without *temperance* in the people. From temperance comes property, and from property virtuous pleasures and independence. These are not gained without industry and economy, without spending a little less than we earn. There are hundreds and thousands of people now in the United States who, at twenty-one years of age, become citizens and voters, and still have nothing, or next to nothing; perhaps the clothes on their backs and some trifles.

PUBLIC AND PRIVATE ECONOMY. 175

For this, in most cases, there is no inevitable necessity. The necessity lies in the want of a noble determination. Suppose all the poor people go on spending all they earn from year to year, they must, of course, *remain* poor as long as they live. Doctor Franklin was once a poor man, and always a working man, that is, a man of honest, useful industry, which is the true idea of a working man. In London, where he went to make his fortune, he lived upon bread and cheese, instead of beer, to make him "*strong.*" A story is told to this effect: A person applied to him to insert some vulgar, libellous matter in his paper. He said he would take it into consideration, and give an answer the next day. The next day came, and he gave *this* answer: "I went home, sir," said he, "and supped on bread and water; I slept in my cloak on the floor, and I breakfasted as I supped, and I think, upon the whole, that I can live without doing your dirty work." A man who is destitute should have the heart to live upon a crust of bread and cold water, rather than waste his strength in whining about poor wages and the monopolies and privileges of the rich, which the people here can always overthrow, if they have the true soul. No wages can save a drinking man from destruction; and as to the rich, they will keep their privileges as long as this destruction lasts. This general truth in the United States no man can gainsay; and that is, that neither a virtuous *man*, nor a *class* of such men, can be kept down; the stronger the pressure, the more sure they are to rise.

147. In part first, chapter third of this work, there is a brief history of property, in which it is shown that the common people have advanced just in proportion as they have gained property as a body. In the United Kingdom there are now about eight hundred thousand voters. This is a noble effort on the part of the poorer and middling classes, when you consider how they have been taxed, and how their earnings are wasted. When William the Conqueror became master of England, the whole landed property was divided among a few thousands. Since that time, the nation has advanced in those useful arts which distribute property wisely; for these arts themselves are great dividers of property; and here we see that there can be no assignable limit to the increase of property; for no man can point it out. It is easy to believe that a nation can be a hundred or a thousand times richer than it is, because we know that a civilized nation may be a hundred or a thousand times richer than a savage people. England may now be a thousand times richer than she was under the Conqueror; there is no way of ascertaining that exactly. One thing is certain, that all the common people were then little better than slaves; many were slaves, in fact. After all, riches are not worth a thought, but for the purpose of obtaining those material things which enrich the mind and purify the souls of the people.

148. It is high time for the people of the United States to think seriously of what they *can* do; to boast less and do more. The day has gone by for

teaching political economy aside from the character of the people. No man can get food and clothes for his family, and keep them well supplied, without virtue, sense, and temperance. The nation stands on the same ground: the common people, therefore, must turn their backs upon all the vicious and fashionable follies by which so much property is destroyed by the *wasteful* part of the rich, always taking care to distinguish between the rich who are faithful and make property and those who *destroy* it. If one man drinks more Champagne than he can afford, that is no reason why a labouring man should empty his pocket into the till of the grocer and tavernkeeper. It was never intended that all men should wear the same clothes, live in the same houses, drink the same drink, or eat the same food. It is a childish imitation of the upper classes that enfeebles the lower in the United States, and deprives them of a great portion of their power. It is this that hitherto has so much tended to take from them the means of carrying out, to their true ends, the principles of a free government. The labouring people, therefore, should learn the just harmony of their relations, as they would be taught fine music; it is in this way that they will find out what they can do for themselves. People complain of poverty; intemperance has been the greatest single cause of it in the United States; the next is covering up rags with finery, in order to appear like the rich and fashionable. If the people are childlike in their understandings, there will be bad government, of course; for the cunning will do with them what they choose; if they are virtuous, there will be good government, of course. Many complain of monopolies and of government doing everything they can for particular classes. There is a power of preventing all this, of avoiding the accumulation of the great heaps to the destruction of the small; monopolies will then tumble down, of course, and the few very rich that remain (rich by comparison, for this is the only way in which we can speak intelligibly of riches) will prove a good example of what men can do by extraordinary industry, skill, and perseverance. To pull down the rich who become so in this way is to destroy the hen that laid the golden egg.

149. If a single individual is prudent, economical, and industrious here, in most cases he can obtain property; this gives him influence at the ballot-boxes and everywhere else; the same is true of a thousand and of the whole nation. Let the people, then, Heaven directed, work out their own salvation! let them keep their minds constantly turned to their pole star, the great principle of *a more equal division* of property, to be brought about by their own improvement in virtue. A more equal division, for two reasons: *First*, a more equal division is best in itself for the virtues it would bring forth, and the pride, vanity, and sensuality it would keep down. 2d. These virtues would increase without any limit that can be assigned the property there now is. The despairing, the hopeless, the miserable, of whom there are such multitudes in England, do lit-

tle or nothing to increase property. It is the unbounded hope here that gives such animation to the scene. There are many good and honest people in the United States who, guided by the experience of other countries, do not think that the multitude are fit for so ample a liberty as we have. Let the multitude entitle themselves to it by a respect for property, by moderation, by *temperance*, by self-government. If they can govern themselves they can "rule a city," and the work is done. Let the people, then, wherever gathered together, proclaim temperance *and shut up their dramshops.*

150. What, then, can we do here to push forward these principles? Much. I have stated in part first that a large portion of those who subsist upon wages in the United States could live comfortably, decently, and, in all material things, as well as they do now, and still not expend more than one half of their wages. Let it be a *third*. Reader, if you doubt it, take the average; examine the working people themselves. To this let there be added, the power which the *common people have over prices* in things that have respect to their common ways of living, which I shall endeavour to explain fully. If a man determines, in his own soul, that he will be independent, no power can oppose him; his will is his own, that he is sure of. If he lays up ten dollars this year, the next will see him in possession of twenty. If property is worth getting, it is worth keeping. Let the mobs of brutes, then, that go about trampling

upon the treasures of the earth, burning convents, throwing their neighbours' flour into the gutters, &c., be put down at once. In England, it was thrown in our teeth that mob-law had become the established code here, whereas we know that the people of the United States have been distinguished for their love of order, and that mobs have been tolerated for the moment only through our superior humanity and aversion to blood and punishment; that much of this disturbance has often been made by mere boys and ragamuffins under the influence of liquor, whom the breath of the rational people may destroy, as the dry leaves are scattered before the whirlwind.

151. The people of the United States have taught Europe the greatest practical lesson in economy that has ever been learned at all, and this is in showing how property can be increased, wages raised, the upper classes purified, and the poorer elevated by *temperance*. The people of England know nothing, scarcely, of what is going on in the United States in this respect, or of the results of it. If you tell them, they stare for a moment; but it is evident that what you say goes in at one ear and out of the other. There are interesting exceptions. It is equally true that the few people in Europe who have any adequate idea of us are astonished at the progress we are making in wealth, for there is no parallel among them. They account for it in their way of reasoning upon such a

subject by ascribing it to our working a new virgin soil, and so on. That is not the only or the greatest cause; for there are other new and virgin soils in countries where no such wealth is seen. The greatest cause is the improved moral tone of the people, at the bottom of which lies *temperance.*

A great moral and economical truth is very feebly illustrated by figures, but they may do something. If we suppose there are fifteen millions of people in the United States, and that each consumes, upon an average, *two cents* a day less than heretofore in spirituous liquors, including wine, ale, beer, cider, whiskey, &c., we shall have an annual saving in this item alone of 109,500,000 dollars. I think no one will deem this an extravagant calculation; but to this we may fairly add the time wasted; the health destroyed; the useful labours abridged; the money spent in repairing wornout constitutions; the property destroyed or diminished in value by imperfect work; by fires in ships, houses, stores, manufactories; by the neglect, carelessness, and recklessness of drunken people, and we shall have an amount truly incalculable! The world will know nothing of the magnificent provision made for the wants of all mankind till the privileged have ceased to oppress the poor, and the poor shall cease to oppress themselves by that stupid intemperate way of living and spending by which all have squandered their property and wasted their power. The poor complain of the ways of Providence and of the unequal distribution of the goods of this life. They will never know how generally comfort may be diffused till they have turned their backs upon the dramshops; till universal temperance shall strengthen their arms, and they have put their own shoulders to the wheel. No man knows what he can do in obtaining property till he has tried; and few will try in earnest till they see the true end of it, the godlike uses to which it may be applied. Still less do the hard-working people know how large a portion they might take, not by robbery or agrarianism, but by *temperance,* frugality, and industry (for here is the true agrarian code), from the great heaps of those who now, through folly and passion, consume so much; least of all do any of us know what enormous additions will be made to the *total* amount of property. Hitherto the world has gone on consuming nearly as fast as it has been producing, and all the while we have been complaining of Providence! The powers of nature are conspiring with the moral power, and God is evidently making new revelations to man of what he can do for himself. It is in very modern times only that the amazing forces of production have clearly made themselves known. Machinery is displaying its wonders; a steam-engine will perform what a thousand men could not. Is it not certain, then, that the mass of men may obtain for themselves the necessary supplies for a pure, simple, tasteful, healthful existence? is it not certain that the poor man is rising, and will rise, if he enlists under the banner of virtue and *temperance?*

152. Some people in the United States suppose that the temperance reform is not growing; but it is as certainly growing as that the trees are growing; all know this who are in the habit of inquiring into the facts. The extent of it in great portions of the United States (I shall here confine my observations principally to the northern and northwestern states, to which my information principally extends) may be known from a few facts and considerations which can be accurately stated.

First. The farmers of the free States are the most powerful and influential body of men in the country. In part first, chapter third, in giving a history of property, I have shown what the tenures are by which farmers hold land in England, and that they are universally, or nearly, tenants holding from year to year, or for seven years, fourteen, twenty-one, or for life, &c.; that a holding for seven is probably as common as any other.

In the United States, on the contrary, nearly all the farmers are tenants in fee, and hold their lands to them and their heirs for ever. Of the cultivated land, the farmers hold nearly the whole by this tenure. Tenancies here are very rare. So that it may be said that the farmers *own* the country; and to what extent it may be asserted that they *rule* the country can only be well known to those who live among us.

153. Second. Previous to the temperance re-

form, which may be considered as not having advanced extensively till within about ten years (1836), it was a practice so general as to be called universal, for farmers not only to use distilled liquors themselves as a general beverage, but to give them to their hired men. These were most commonly cider, brandy, whiskey, and West India rum. These liquors were supplied very freely to the men at all seasons of the year, but in the harvest nearly without limit. A pint to each man was not uncommon, and many instances were known of labouring men drinking a quart or more in a day. As might be supposed, under the influence of such a practice, a large proportion of the agricultural day-labourers were strictly drunkards. This was far from being the case with the farmers, whose pure employment and general respectability secured them from such frightful consequences, and they were as temperate, at least, if not more so, than any other class.

154. Third. At present, a large proportion of these farmers are members of those temperance societies which adopted the pledge of abstinence from all *distilled* liquors, and some, of those which refrain from all *inebriating* liquors, having signed the total-abstinence pledge, and called in England " *Tee-totallers.*"

Besides, as to a great proportion of the farmers in the free States, it may safely be affirmed, that at present they do not give any spirituous liquors to their labourers; but, on the contrary, the bargain is either directly made or understood that the labourer shall have none; and a very large number deny to their labourers any kind of alcoholic liquor, such as cider, ale, strong beer, &c. So that the common beverage of the labourer while at work is milk and water, vinegar and water, with an infusion of ginger, home-made beer without malt, molasses and water, &c.

155. Fourth. It has never been the practice in the United States for the master manufacturers and mechanics to give liquor to their labourers as it has for the farmers. Till the temperance reform, it was a common practice, however, to permit their labourers to drink what they chose; and as all others drank freely, they fell into the general habit of indulgence. Now, a tacit or an express agreement is very general that the labourer shall abstain altogether while at work; that he shall drink nothing on the premises; and some go so far as to reject any labourers of whom they have proof that they drink ardent spirits at all.

156. Fifth. On most of the public works, such as railroads, canals, &c., there is a very general practice on the part of contractors, prohibiting by express contract the use of liquor on the premises. No doubt this stipulation is very often departed from.

157. Sixth. All statistical accounts upon such a subject, and particularly those that proceed from the ardent and enthusiastic friends of the societies, are to be dmitted with due caution. At the same

time, I believe that there are now more than 1200 strict temperance ships sailing under American colours. The London Times newspaper of the 15th November, 1836, contains a report of a committee of the House of Commons, showing the causes of the numerous shipwrecks of British ships, and, among other things, states that drunkenness is one of them, and that there are now more than 1000 temperance ships in the United States.

Seventh. There was a universal practice of drinking cider in the northern States as a common beverage in the same way, and probably to the same extent, at least, as beer is now drank in England. Among great numbers, this practice is wholly abandoned, and a very inconsiderable portion, if any, drink the same portion of cider as formerly. On the contrary, apples are now extensively used as food for animals.

158. Eighth. Previous to the temperance reform, the country shopkeepers were the wholesale sellers of nearly all the liquors that were carried into the country. They were also sold by them at retail generally. At present, a very large proportion of these shopkeepers, whose profits upon the sale of liquors were very large, have discontinued the sale altogether; some few keep a small portion of liquor on hand for sale in case of illness and other emergencies. Besides, there are a considerable number of temperance inns; and many of those who do not strictly keep temperance inns very honourably and conscientiously refuse to sell liquors to those

whom they know to be given to habits of intoxication, so that it is really no uncommon sight in Massachusetts to see drinking people go to a neighbouring town where they are not known to get their accustomed drams.

159. Ninth. Previous to the temperance reform, it was a common practice to put bottles of spirits upon all, or nearly all, the public tables in the inns, boarding-houses, steamboats, canalboats, &c., for which no separate charge was made. It is almost wholly discontinued.

160. Tenth. The force of public opinion upon this subject in the United States proves more than everything else. The devices and shifts which the most degraded people resort to, show it. It is the public opinion which drives them to these shifts that it puzzles M. Tocqueville so much to understand. The whole people here are hammered into one great chain, in a manner unlike anything which exists in Europe; if you touch one link you touch the whole.

In a neighbouring store, a man applied with a bottle half filled with the flour of sulphur for spirits, which he said he wanted as a medicine. As soon as he left the store he drank off the spirits, leaving the flour of sulphur as another heel-tap. I have seen a man go through the village with a pair of old boots in his hand, as though he was pushing for the shoemaker; when, in fact, he had an empty bottle in each boot, about to be replenished. In the country we constantly see the sly, sneaking tricks to shun the eyes of their neighbours, resorted to both by those who keep up their old habits of drinking and those who sell the liquor. In those stores in the country in which the contraband article can be had, it is often asked for under some feigned name, as the House of Refuge lads call trousers, " kickers ;" watches, " thimbles," &c.

I know that this is a very feeble statement as to the improved state of temperance among us. I have intentionally avoided, as before stated, a large mass of statistical facts that might be added, such, for instance, as that, through the same force of public opinion, there are whole counties in the state of Massachusetts in which not a single license to retail ardent spirits is granted, and so on. If we add to all these considerations the improved health (a fact known to us all), the improved countenances, apparel, food, household comforts, manners, of even the poorest classes of labourers, no man can doubt the beautiful and sublime process of moral reformation which we are undergoing in the United States.

Upon the whole, no attentive observer needs any other proof than he has that a great moral reformation has commenced and is progressing. Still some doubt; and it is certain that in the cities and large villages the progress has been slowest. For this there are many reasons; such as the state of the foreign population, and others too obvious to be mentioned. We have in the large cities the extremes of the very rich and fashionable on the one side, and the poor and degraded on the other, which are the last (there are beautiful exceptions) to be touched by any new moral sentiment. This temperance reformation is giving to true democracy, to the people, a grander moral triumph than they have ever beheld; and, if carried out by them like men, will be followed by a corresponding political consequence. Moral reformation is the only sure basis for political power in the mass of the people; without it they do not deserve power; without it they will certainly not retain in the United States what they have; nor will any rational man wish that they should; for an ignorant, drinking, depraved people with power is a many-headed monster let loose.

161. No one can have any adequate idea of the importance which the people of England attach to strong beer and ale. Beer is another of the gods worshipped there, and John Barley Corn is certainly one of the greatest men in the United Kingdom. Beer is a very ancient liquor; as early as the fifth century there is this account of it.* " The grain is steeped in water, and made to germinate; it is then dried and ground; after which it is infused in a certain quantity of water, which, being fermented, becomes a pleasant, warming, strengthening, intoxicating liquor."

Hops were not introduced into the manufacture of beer till about the year 1524, when it was said,

"Hops, reformation, bays, and beer,
Came into England all in one year."

* Domestic Life in England, p. 197. London, 1835.

The Anglo Saxons did honour to beer by drinking it out of cups of wood ornamented with gold and bone. They had a peg tankard, introduced by King Edgar, to check *excessive drinking;* of which, from what we saw, there must be very few specimens left in the beer line. This is the story of the tankard: "It had in the inside a row of eight pins, one above another, from top to bottom; the tankard usually held two quarts; so that there was a gill of ale, i. e., half a pint Winchester measure, between each pin. The first person that drank was to empty the tankard to the first peg or pin; the second to the next, &c.; so that the pins were as many measures to the drinkers, making them all drink the same quantity; and as the distance of the pins contained a large draught of liquor, the company would be very liable, by this method, to get intoxicated, especially when, if they drank *short* of the pin or *beyond* it, they were obliged to drink again."

162. From ordinary appearances, you would suppose that all the water in England had been turned into beer. You see it constantly travelling about the streets in London in pint and quart mugs. In the west end, I saw coachmen and footmen, after having got rid of their masters and mistresses, stop at the beer-shops and partake of this enlivening potation, the coachman not leaving his box. The people of England, in regard to beer (1836), seem to be nearly where we were in respect to ardent spirits ten years ago. If you were to tell

them that men here in the ironworks, the forges, the glassworks, and firemen at the steam-engines, are often mere water-drinkers, they would think the story a fable. They verily believe that beer is indispensable; that they cannot work without it; that it is essential to make them *strong*.

163. The English common people drink beer of various degrees of strength. At Highgate, near London, at a village inn, I fell into conversation with a man who was going into London with his cart drawn by three excellent horses; the harness strong, clean, and in perfect order, and the cart newly painted. The common farming utensils in England are kept in such beautiful repair, that it would seem that it was designed that they should never wear out. There is very little poverty on the outside of things in England, and it argues much in favour of the manly pride of the poor people that they are able to keep up a good appearance in the midst of so many trials and difficulties. This man had been drawing hay, and told me that the wages of pitchers and stackers at that time were three and sixpence per day, but no beer. That he drank three pints of porter a day, and generally paid a penny halfpenny a pint. That he did not know any one who did not drink porter, meaning, no doubt, some kind of ale or strong beer.

164. In going from London to the neighbourhood of Windsor, my seat on the coach was next to a woman who told me that she had been a servant in a gentleman's family. I never failed to

avail myself of such an opportunity of conversation, whatever might be thought of the gentility of the thing. She said that she knew Lord ——'s family in town, mentioning a great legal character whose name has long been well known in the United States; that in his town-house he had eleven domestics, one of whom was the butler; that a butler's place in such a house was worth forty-five or fifty guineas a year; that he is at the head of the servants; keeps the plate; cleans it; draws the beer for the servants at dinner and supper; that each, as a general rule, is entitled to a pint twice a day; that she drank a pint at dinner, and another at supper, as regularly as she drank her two cups of tea; that beer " was good for her; that she could not live without it." I beg that the reader will observe that I do not rely upon the exact accuracy of all these statements, nor are they important. In such cases, the story is told to illustrate some main truth, which, in this case, is the beer-drinking habit of the people. By this faith, that beer is a life preserver, the English live, and by this they die.

165. Being desirous of knowing how far she had studied political economy, without, perhaps, knowing the name, I entered into some conversation about the wages of servants, &c. She told me that servants, in respect to their wages, were not as well off as they had been; that there might be a difference of a quarter. It must be remembered that, since the war and the reign of paper money, prices in England *generally* have fallen. Being

desirous of knowing how far she understood Mr. Malthus, I asked her the cause of this fall in wages; upon which she said it was owing to the " popularity" of the people, meaning, doubtless, populousness, or that the people had overbred, and that there were more " guests than plates," according to Mr. Malthus's favourite economy ; never for a moment dreaming that the more property servants waste, the less there is to pay them in wages; that servants must, of course, have less wages there in consequence of the seas of beer they drink ; nor imagining that the millions they pay in taxation on malt have anything to do with their comforts. If common labourers do not get some common-sense ideas into their heads upon these subjects, they will go on here just as helpless, dependant, and destitute as they have elsewhere.

166. At Bristol I went out upon the great Western Railroad then making in that neighbourhood, and had several conversations with the men. They told me that their average wages were from two shillings and ninepence to three shillings per day; that the price of beer was twopence a pint, and that two quarts a day was a common allowance for a man there; that is, about fifteen cents of our money, or about a quarter of their wages. And what would become of the rich people if they swallowed in sherry, port, Chateau Margaux, Johannesbergh, one quarter of their daily incomes, and lived in other respects in the same proportion !

167. In passing through Staffordshire, a man on

the coach engaged in the coal-trade told me that very few of the coal-men laid up any money; that the contrary was nearly universal ; that they drank beer at the price of five or six pence a quart; and that it is thought by many that there is an infusion of tobacco-juice in some of it, to give it an *intoxicating* quality and make it *strong*. Accum states* that beer is adulterated in England by "black extract," &c. The brewer is prohibited by act of parliament from using any other materials besides malt and hops; and still we know that adulteration constantly takes place. Certainly I do not mean to assert that tobacco-juice is put into beer in England.

168. When in Wales I went to see the iron-works at Merthyr Tydvil, which are some of the first in the world. The men here drink excessively, and, from the nature of their occupation, more than most other labourers. Very few, consequently, lay up any part of their wages; they pay fourpence and fivepence a quart for beer, buying at retail, which is the case in everything with wasteful, childish people. One of the overseers told us that some of the men drank little less than a pound worth of beer in a week; the rollers, or a part of them at least, then earning two pounds a week. At what speed might not a poor man go ahead in England, earning ten dollars a week, and practising the prudent, temperate ways of the economical part of the people!

* Accum on Adulteration, p. 140.

It was said at Merthyr when we were there (1836) that the price of iron had advanced from about five pounds in the years 1830 and 1831 to eleven and twelve pounds then; that the Emperor of Russia was getting railroad iron there for a railroad leading from Petersburgh to Moscow; that the Pacha of Egypt had already obtained there the necessary rails for at least one half of a road across the Isthmus of Suez. At Cardiff we saw several American vessels which had come to that port to get Merthyr railroad iron for the United States. Such is the progress of the industrious temperance people; fifteen years ago there was not a foot of railroad in the United States, except about three miles at Quincy, in the State of Massachusetts!

169. *The most remarkable feature in the present times is the elevation of the labouring classes.* Walter Scott, in his " Ivanhoe," presents this picture of a man towards the end of the reign of Richard I., in the West Riding of Yorkshire: " His garment was a close jacket, with sleeves composed of the tanned skin of some animal, on which the hair had been originally left, but which had been worn off in so many places that it was difficult to say to what creature the fur had belonged. Sandals bound with thongs made of boar's hide protected the feet. He had no covering on his head, which was only defended by his own thick hair matted and twisted together. There was a brass ring resembling a dog's collar soldered fast round his neck, so loose

as to form no impediment to his breathing, yet so tight as to be incapable of being removed, except by the use of the file. On this singular gorget was engraved in Saxon characters an inscription of the following purport: 'Gurth, the son of Beowulph, is the born thrall of Cedric of Rotherwood.'"

Here are the materials for a contrast between the past and the present; this shows what a change has taken place, and no one can believe that the progress of things is to be arrested here. And what constitutes the true elevation of the working classes but their virtues? What surer foundation to build on than *temperance?* It is the moral energy that raises men in the scale of being. The working people form trades' unions and combinations to lessen their hours of toil. All this is well, if well done; but what signify increased wages, if the money which a man earns is spent in those sinks of corruption, dramshops, in riot and debauchery? With many it is a strong argument against high wages that the money is so often squandered; and were this universal, the objection would stand good. Let the working people, then, whenever they combine, as they have a right and ought to do for all worthy purposes, proclaim temperance as their watchword, and mutual respect for each other's virtues as the law of their order. They have a very feeble conception of the extent to which poverty and the unequal distribution of property proceeds from their vices; from excessive beer-drinking, dram-drinking, gaming, and the belittling of themselves by following the fashions of those who are ten or a hundred times richer than themselves. Kings, lords, commons, tithes, and taxes might soon be brought within the control of a moral people. If they will, however, drink, eat, and wear twice or ten times as much of the proceeds of their labour as they need, why, then, there is an end of so much power for ever; it is letting the lever slip through their hands; a man cannot have his cake and eat it. If one Englishman can economize and lay up, and thus save himself from being turned into the snow-drifts of Canada, so can thousands, and thousands make up millions. It is true that there are a prodigious number of people in England who, with all their efforts, have no surplus; so it is as true that a great number have, or might have. All this surplus may be made a *capital* for those poor people to work with and give them wages who have no capital of their own. A poor man, even with a little property, may help another poor man without giving him alms, and thus making a pauper of him; let those, then, who can lay up, save for the benefit of themselves and the rest.

The property of industrious people does not remain idle like that of many of the rich; there are no splendid palaces, parks, coaches; no game horses, kennels of hounds, services of gorgeous plate to take care of. There might be an increasing ratio in the property of the labouring classes if they would make it so, which would push them forward at an amazing rate if they could see their own interests.

The greatest reform, then, that can take place, is a *reform* of the people. Monopolies, abuses, privileges, cannot stand before a *reformed* people.

170. Let us look at a few facts and considerations which will show the amount of destruction of property there is in England in the single article of beer, first deducting from the whole amount such portion of the cost as any one shall allow for a prudent, moderate, and healthful use of this beverage. Such a calculation will give the people of the United States some adequate *ideas of their own wasteful destruction.*

171. One of the most beautiful sights in England is the barley standing on the ground just before the harvest. I saw it in various parts in immense quantities, some of the best land being occupied in producing it. A great number of ploughs, drills, horses, and men are employed in bringing to perfection a harvest, not for the purpose of feeding the people who stand so often on the brink of famine, but to afford an intoxicating liquor to stultify their understandings. Let it be understood here that I do not speak as a temperance man, but of excess, of the enormous quantity of beer drank beyond what any man can pretend is salutary to the people.

172. The quantity of malt made into beer in the United Kingdom in the year ending October 10,

1833, was 5,020,599 quarters, which, at 8 bushels to the quarter, is 40,164,792 bushels, yielding a duty in taxation of £5,153,574, equal to about 25 millions of dollars.*

Such statements confirm the almost incredible accounts of the beer drank in England in former times. Hume relates that, at the entertainment given by Leicester to Queen Elizabeth at Kenilworth Castle, there were drank 365 hogsheads of beer, or 23,000 gallons. It is stated by M'Nish "that seven English pints are quite a common allowance, and not unfrequently twice that quantity is taken without any perceptible effect; that many of the coal-heavers on the Thames think nothing of drinking two gallons of porter per day, especially in the summer season."

173. Beer is not the only destroyer of morals and property in England; gin comes in for its share. For this they have the high authority of Mr. Burke, who says, "Whether the thunder of the laws or the thunder of eloquence be hurled on gin, always I am thunder proof."

Everybody has heard of the gin-palaces in England; few, however, can have any adequate conception of them. These are fitted up in a style to be as seductive as can be to the unhappy victims that enter them, and in a way to appear as little like common dramshops as possible. They often occupy the best positions at the corners of the streets, and may be known by the splendour, the

* Companion to the Almanac, 1834, 1835.

profusion, and fanciful variety of their gaslights. In the Manchester and Salford Temperance Journal there is this description of some of them : " In the section between Old Gravel Lane and Shadwell New Church, within the space of one hundred and thirty paces, there are seven splendid ginshops recently fitted up in the modern gin-palace style, highly decorated with paint and gilding, and exhibiting in front gigantic lamps with magnificent gaslights. At one, a revolving light, with many burners, playing most beautifully over the door; at another, about fifty or sixty jets in one lantern, throwing out their capricious and fitful, but brilliant gleams, as if from the branches of a shrub."

174. We went into three ginshops on Holborn Hill and in that neighbourhood, which were said to be some of the most showy in London. They were filled with men, women, and children, who generally went in at one door and out at another. None stayed long, as far as we could see; they came in, drank, and went off. We saw none who were not quiet and orderly. A man entered with a woman and little girl, whom we supposed to be his wife and child ; the child appeared to be about eight years of age. The man drank, and then the woman, who gave what remained in the glass to the little child. We bought a glass, for which we paid a halfpenny. This was undoubtedly adulterated ; it seemed to be sweetened, and certainly had not the flavour of pure gin.

Mr. Bulwer says that, in taking off the duty on

gin, "there commenced a most terrible epoch of natural demoralization," and he quotes the Bishop of London as saying, " When I first came to London, I never saw a female coming out of a gin-shop; I have since repeatedly seen females with infants in their arms, to whom they appear to be giving some part of their liquor." And why should not a bishop (if the bishop meant here was Bishop Porteus, he was one of the best of men) enter the ginshops, and know what these poor women do give to their children ? Such are the false ideas of duty which grow up under a false system.

175. Notwithstanding all that is said about the infatuation that reigns in the gin-palaces and the horrible amount of dram-drinking in England, there are certain proofs of an amendment. The superficial opinions picked up in England in every day's conversation, and particularly in London in that class who only know the poor by representation, and who do not go among them, is not to be relied on. In London you may converse with half a dozen people in succession who hardly know that a temperance society exists in England, or, if they do, it is only the name that they are acquainted with. There is now no so great mistake made by those who govern, and by the higher classes, as in underrating the improvement that is going on among the common people.

176. A stranger in England will be cautious in forming his judgments, but it seemed to me that the gin-palaces, frightful as they are in the contrast be-

tween so much splendour and so much misery, must be a decided improvement upon the dramshops, those holes and dens where these unhappy people have been accustomed to congregate, and such as our own cities are filled with. In these palaces everything seems to be exposed to light; what a man does is seen; and besides, it is, I believe, the fashion not to spend time there. But in the cellars and holes, where a few only assemble, they get together for the pleasure of long protracted drunkenness, which ends in producing in some a brutal stupefaction, and in others in setting on foot all manner of deep-laid plans of wickedness.

England is free of the disgrace, so far as we ever saw or heard, of the common *American bar-room*. In Norfolk we saw a tap-room resembling our vulgar dramshops attached to an inn, in other respects very decent. At one of the best inns in Manchester we saw, after having been some days inmates in the house, without knowing of the existence of such a place, a sort of smoking-room, where gentlemen tiplers, or, at any rate, those who appeared to be gentlemen, were drinking just as our gentlemen tiplers do; it was in the back part of the house, and seemed, from decency, to be as far removed from observation as it could be. But as to our vulgar *American bar-rooms*, usually the most common entrance to our inns, with a bar duly shelved to hold up to view, in the most seductive way possible, bottles of brandy, gin, rum, lemon-peel bitters, whiskey, wine, with all the apparatus of hot water, sugar, sugar-sticks, lemons, mint, bitters, to make the compounds pungent and agreeable, with the accompaniment of gentlemen, who come to get an appetite for their breakfasts or dinners, perhaps to drown their sorrows, but certainly to send, by their base example, their poorer, less educated, and unfortunate fellow-citizens to the dramshop; thus destroying their morals, and, of course, the true democratic, republican power; I say, we never saw anything in England resembling this barroom; whether the tap-room, the smoking-room, or the gin-palace be more vulgar, destructive things, I cannot say.

177. There are conclusive evidences of improvement in England. Stupid as the fashion is, for, with many, it is little better than the fashion, of swallowing ten or twenty times more wine than they believe to be useful, still, with the gentlemen of England as with us, the midnight orgies, the carousals, the full bumpers, with keys turned to prevent any man from going home sober, have greatly disappeared. We were told, also, that there was a great improvement among the farmers; that they tippled far less in going to market, and upon all occasions, than formerly. There never was, and never will be, a moral improvement among the favoured classes that does not descend, sooner or later, to the lower; hence the responsibility of the rich.

178. To form any just idea of the labouring people in England, you must go among them, among their friends, counsellors, and teachers, and espe-

cially in the manufacturing districts. From the latter we never received but one opinion, and that was always in favour of the increasing temperance of the poor people.

Manchester is the greatest manufacturing town in England. In its manufacturing establishments we found some of those very intelligent men of the working class who are capable of giving the best information in regard to the subject. Some of these are overseers, or "overlookers," as they are called there, and those we saw so like in intelligence the same class in our own country, that you would not know them apart. At Roberts and Sharpe's Machine-shop, which employs five hundred men, one of them told us that he was an "overlooker;" that he had been a common labouring man; that the character of the workmen had improved very much; that they did not drink ardent spirits as formerly; that the temperance societies had done a great deal of good, but that these did not generally exclude *beer*, which was a "great loophole" for the escape of temperance. That he himself, however, was not a tee-totaller.

179. At Messrs. Houldsworth's great cotton establishment we saw another of these valuable men. It was said that at this mill finer cotton was spun than in any in Manchester; that a thread was drawn out from a pound of cotton that would reach one hundred and fifty miles. What a minute fibre may serve as the connecting chain of good-will and peace between two great nations! This man told

us that the people drank a great deal, but not so much as formerly; that the Mechanics' Institute in Manchester was a great means of improvement! We knew some of the excellent persons connected with this admirable institution. I have avoided all discussion of the principle of the temperance societies. That they have done great good in the United States is certain; that they will do a great deal in England is equally so. I have a very imperfect knowledge of their condition there.

180. There is a British association for the promotion of temperance upon the total abstinence plan, which was established on the fifteenth day of September, 1835. An account of this association states that there are 47,178 tee-total members. In a temperance paper of the Isle of Man of the fifteenth of April, 1836, it is stated that there were then in England and Wales 139,058 members of temperance societies. This is a small beginning, but small beginnings sometimes make great endings: there are those alive who remember the period when not one twentieth part of this proportion of the people then inhabiting the American colonies were in favour of American independence! At Manchester we found great activity in favour of the temperance cause.

It is a good omen that the most intelligent of the common people of England should so soon have followed the lead of the United States. It was said at Manchester that there were not less than ten or twelve hundred members in that town. The town of Preston has been a leader in this cause; and in the temperance paper published there have appeared, from time to time, speeches delivered by operatives so full of true common sense, pathos, and eloquence, as to do honour to any public assembly, and such as have never been witnessed in the same class in the United States, so far as I have seen.

This is a good forerunner of what is to be. The work of regeneration among these operatives must be their own work; for who can do so much for another man as he can do for himself? Of one thing we are certain, and that is, the good work does go on; and the people will see, sooner or later, that it is harder for a man to knock off chains of his own forging than those which others have put upon him; that intemperate people are but mean supporters of the true democratic cause. I do not speak here of any *party* cause.

181. Let every man among us, then, take heed to his own ways, and how far he himself is the cause of poverty, of aristocracy, of overgrown riches, of heaping them up in the laps of those who already have too much. If any now have unjust privileges, let him take care how he increases them by his own folly. In part first I have stated that one of the most fruitful causes of the unnatural distribution of property is, that the poor people are for ever emptying their pockets into those of people who are already richer than they should be. No man is bound to spend his money at a dramshop or any other shop where his pocket is picked. Look at

the enormous establishments in every country, such as breweries, gin-palaces, distilleries, and the fashionable money-catching shops that are built up mainly (for I speak of excess) by the vanity, pride, and sensuality of those who complain most of the unequal distribution of property. The common people are the great props of these establishments; the labouring people, from the fact of their superior numbers, are their greatest customers. All this shows that the common people of the United States may do what they will, *if the will be a right one.*

It is not unbecoming to bow down and kiss the very earth that bore such men as Milton, Locke, and Sir Harry Vane; they saw clearly through the ennobling Christian principle of the republican system near two centuries ago, but the people were not intelligent and virtuous enough to follow their leaders; and the consequence is, that they have been grovelling in the dirt ever since. Privileges, monopolies, abuses, have hung about their necks like a millstone, which they have not had character and sense enough to get rid of.

182. The breweries of London are among the great sights of it. We went to Barclay's, said to be one of the greatest. I wish it were in my power to give an account of the enormous masses of hops and malt, the immense extent of the buildings and stables, of the vast processes and ingenious contrivances which are here in motion to keep down the common people, to destroy their property, and stupify their minds. Let it be remembered that I

do not enter into the question of total abstinence, and only speak of superfluous destruction, of suicide. In this brewery we were told that there were a hundred and twenty-eight vats, of which six contain three thousand three hundred barrels; four, two thousand seven hundred barrels; that the residue were of different sizes. That from two to three hundred men are employed, and one hundred and thirty-six horses. In one vat, that was reeking with steam, we saw three men throwing out the mash naked to their waists, the perspiration running in streams from them. In the stables we saw thirty or forty horses.

This is the Lincolnshire horse; and he is, to be sure, a curious animal, as fat as a hog can be made; his flesh stands in folds, and rolls upon his ribs; and they say in London that, when he falls, he can never rise again. This is not quite true, for I saw one instance of a resurrection myself; but the fall was horrible; it seemed as though an elephant had come down, not by degrees, but by one awful sprawl. This fancy hog-horse is, of course, kept mainly at the expense of the common people, for they, numbers being on their side, drink twenty glasses of Barclay's beer to one drank by the gentry.

When Thrale's great brewery was put up at auction, Doctor Johnson, who was an executor, amused himself by appearing for a moment in the character of an auctioneer, and cried out, "We are not here to sell a parcel of vats and boilers, but the potentiality of getting rich beyond the dreams of avarice." The opposite thing it was the duty of an auctioneer to leave out, that is, the "potentiality" *of making poor.* It is one thing to make a rich man richer than he should be, and another to make a great many in middling circumstances or in poverty poorer than they need be. A science very well understood in England, long practised upon, and which we have largely introduced into our own country; that will certainly produce its natural aristocratic fruits, unless the labouring people take warning in time, resist it in the onset, and forsake their dram-drinking, their gaming, and all those fashionable gluttonies and luxurious ways of the idle and sensual by which they are enfeebled in body, mind, and estate. There is but one certain, proper, absolute divider of property into natural parts, and that is the virtue, the economy, the unconquerable resolution of a free people sustained by a universal system of proper education. This division supposes perfect freedom and equal laws in the acquisition of property. Can any man object to them in the United States? if so, upon what ground? This is an honest, healthful division that will last; it is not brought about by commotion, riots, throwing flour into the streets, burning up convents, by agrarian laws, which other laws will soon repeal, by monopolies hateful in the sight of all righteous people, but by the power of God in the heart of an industrious, temperate, painstaking, self-denying man; a greater power than which on earth there cannot be. This is the true reform; there is no other to be relied on; it must and will precede all others; a people who can reform themselves can reform the laws; the very act of reform gives them the property, and, with the property, the education, the enlightened mind, the mental qualities fitted for the work. Let those, then, who set up for reformers, for enlighteners of the world, for *democratic leaders*, for just laws, and a healthful division of property, take heed to their own example. There is a revolution going on which is little thought of on the surface. The people are getting sick of pretenders in every party, and they know that the great work which they have marked out to be accomplished in this New World will be brought about only by the disinterested.

THE END.

PUBLIC AND PRIVATE ECONOMY

ILLUSTRATED BY OBSERVATIONS MADE
IN ENGLAND IN THE YEAR
1836

BY

THEODORE SEDGWICK

PART THIRD

[1839]

AUGUSTUS M. KELLEY • PUBLISHERS
CLIFTON 1974

First Edition 1839

(*New York:* Harper & Brother, *No. 82, Cliff Street*, 1839)

PUBLIC

AND

PRIVATE ECONOMY.

ILLUSTRATED BY OBSERVATIONS MADE IN ENGLAND
IN THE YEAR 1836.

BY THEODORE SEDGWICK.

PART THIRD.

NEW-YORK:

PUBLISHED BY HARPER & BROTHERS.
No. 82 Cliff-street.

1839.

Entered, according to Act of Congress, in the year 1839,
By HARPER & BROTHERS,
In the Clerk's Office of the Southern District of New-York.

CONTENTS.

CHAPTER I.

War, its true Character—England a great and powerful Country—Number of Voters in it—Committee of the House of Lords—Principle of the Constitution of the United States, as to taking private Property for public Use—Importance of Cotton Trade—Committee of the House of Lords—Marquis Bute, his Income—Lord Wharncliffe—Education—Importance of it—Manner of Speaking in the Lords and Commons—Good Speaking—Importance of it—Changes that are going on in Civilization—Fees paid for Seats in the Gallery of the House of Commons - Page 13

CHAPTER II.

Boatman, his Wages and Ideas of Political Economy—Desire in England among common People for Information about United States—Nature of Property to multiply itself—Cleanliness of London Hotels—Value of Cleanliness—Porters' Wages—Overwork of People of England—Miserable Appearance of Menservants in our Hotel — King's Opera — Late Hours—Covent Garden—Brown Bread in London—Strawberries, their Price—Devonshire Cream—Butter sent to London by Coaches from Norfolk — Devonshire Cider — Zoological Gardens—Riches of West End of London—London Pavements—Picture-shops in Pall Mall—Character of London Populace—Pugilistic Exhibitions—Westminster Abbey—Fees paid there—Waterloo Banquet—Poor sent from the Parishes in England to the United States—An Imposition—Agriculture in England - - 28

CHAPTER III.

Pageants in England—Battle of Waterloo—Military Show in Hyde Park—Expense of Military Foppery—Embroidered Coat of Midshipman—Savings of Massachusetts Farmers—Tower of Lon-

CONTENTS.

don; Fees paid—Mr. Malthus, his Economy as to Non-producers—Crusaders, their Employment—Jewel Office—Mr. Burke's Efforts to Reform it—State Trinkets—India House—Royal Exchange—Pay-rule in House of Commons abolished—Tendency to Aristocracy in England—Division of Property in United States —Importance of useful Employments—Greenwich Hospital— Mourning Procession, its Expense—Pensioners in Hospital— Their Fare—Sir Thomas Hardy—Picture Gallery—Nelson's Coat—Lady Hardy—Park attached to Greenwich Hospital— Character of the Pensioners - - - - - Page 53

CHAPTER IV.

Excessive Labour of the Poor—Unseasonable Labour—Midnight Slavery—Effect of, on Temperance—Habits of London People as to rising in the Morning—Time for Breakfast and Dinner— Great Routs—Hume's Account of an old Earl of Northumberland—Habits of his Family, Hours, Diet, &c.—Five o'clock in the Afternoon Breakfast of the Duke of ——— —His Style of Speaking in the House of Lords—Style of Routs in the United States - - - - - - - - - - 82

CHAPTER V.

London, Doctor Johnson's Account of—London Jews, their Cries —Mr. Rush, his Account of the Prince Regent's Levee—Of her Majesty's "Drawing-room"—Of an Entertainment at the Duchess of Cumberland's—Expense of a Lord-mayor's Feast—Of the King's Harness—Contrast here—Ministers, their Salaries— What additional Duties they ought to perform—Sight in St. James's-street—Degraded State of Servants in England—Sumptuousness in Ancient Houses—Livery, its Origin—Variety of Livery—What Objection to it - - - - - 94

CHAPTER VI.

London, Tacitus's Account of—Number of Soldiers in London— Hyde Park—Stages and Hackney-coaches not allowed to enter it —Cost of Royalty in England, as stated by Mr. Bulwer—Gaming-houses of London, where situated; Crockford's—Play in them —Expense of them—Westminster Abbey and St. Paul's Church,

Labour expended in building of—St. Giles, its Appearance—Mobs in London; in the United States—Population of London—Causes of the great Population of London—Mat de Cocagne—Freedom in Trade great Cause of the Population of London—Large Cities not Evils, of course—Advantage of a dense Population; of a great Division of Labour—Unnecessary Evils in Cities—Physical Evil great Cause of Vice—Manufacturing Population in Manchester—Little Ireland—Musical Festival in Manchester—Gaming there—Village and Rural Population of United States ; of England—Contrast of—Character of Country People here - - - - - - - - - Page 112

PUBLIC AND PRIVATE ECONOMY.

PART III.

CHAPTER I.

SEC. 1. In this third part of my work I shall continue to avail myself of observations made in England in the year eighteen hundred and thirty-six.

I trust that it has appeared to the reader already that I do not write about England with spleen or ill-will. Those odious libels and caricatures that are to be found in so many books of travel calculated to excite hatred and division between the two countries, and finally to produce war, deserve the execration of both.

2. There are cardinal points of all true democratic policy. Causeless war is one of the greatest enemies of democratic liberty, and often a mere aristocratic device to keep the people down. When causeless, it is the greatest of all political curses to poor working men and those who live upon scanty means through regular industry. It is the great destroyer of the property of both rich and poor; but there is this difference between them generally, the poor man too often loses his all, the rich man but a part. At best, war creates the necessity for great

power, numerous offices, and a large expenditure. While it is going on, few flourish except spendthrifts, usurers, contractors, job-seekers, office-holders, and all that race who in times of disturbance fatten upon the miseries of the people. We have some experience of the evils even of *unavoidable* war. It begins with great loans from great capitalists at a high rate of interest, of seven or eight per cent., who in time of peace usually can get only four or five; by-and-by, banks stop payment, and then we have paper money alone, and paper-money prices for all the poor, *whose wages do not rise, in such cases, in proportion as the prices of their bread, meat, and other necessaries rise.* And now the work, and, of course, the wages of poor people stop too. Labourers leave the land for the camp; production, of course, diminishes; dearness, scarcity, and a monopoly of necessaries follow; schemers and idlers begin to think that labour was not made for them; speculation rages, and the rich man, by his control over indispensable articles, has an immense advantage of the poor man. At length the bubble bursts, the dream ends, and people awake in horror at the sight of the destruction which has been going on. Now the rich contractor, who paid a shilling for a loaf of bread and sold it for two, rides in his coach, and many a poor man's horse, cow, and other little property go into the sheriff's hands.

The country, too, is overwhelmed with debt, and all the people, rich and poor, must be taxed to pay the rich capitalist his principal, with his seven or eight per cent. interest, though money, which is now *gold and silver*, be worth the double of what it was during the war. All debts, also, must now be paid at a much higher price than that at which they were contracted. During all this while, public works have been put a stop to ; the education of the people has been neglected, and all that rational reform that produces a natural and beneficent equality has been arrested. This is but a feeble and partial statement of the evils even of necessary, unavoidable war.

3. England is a great, powerful, beautiful, civilized country, and instead of being governed by rotten boroughs, it was ascertained, after the passage of the Reform Bill, that there were eight hundred thousand voters in the United Kingdom. Though far behind what we believe to be the true standard of good government, reform is going on in that country, perhaps, as fast as the people are prepared for it. The history of the world proves that government will be adapted to the existing intelligence and virtue of the people. War between us and England would, for the present, be destruction to the cause of reform, and a great hinderance to all poor oppressed people throughout the world who are struggling for their rights. It would be a disgrace to the cause of democracy : I do not speak of democracy in a party sense, but to all those here who delight to see the extension of just democratic empire. It will be a most favourable omen

for the continuance of it if the people can be made to *reason* about unnecessary war, and comprehend how the poverty of the poor man is increased and the riches of the rich man diminished by the barbarous strife which it generates.

4. The Christian religion holds out a clear promise to us of a better lot even in this world. This supposes, of course, that we will lay hold of the promise, and do all we can to make it effectual. When the poor oppressed man is put upon an equal footing, in respect to rights, with the rich man, this promise will be fulfilled, and not till then. To place himself in this New World, the poor man, the working man, has a great work to do himself: this is to enlighten his mind, to keep down those evil passions which destroy other poor men, and make him the tool, the understrapper of the ambitious, who stir up war for their own good. These sentiments are not out of place at a period when there have been so recently on our borders, among our own happy people, so many reckless agitators.

June. I went to see a committee of the House of Lords which was sitting upon a Railroad Bill. These bills have been carried, in some instances, after great opposition, founded on their encroachment upon private property. All property ought to be at the disposal of the public for public good; if the public take it, however, they should do so upon the principle of making compensation to the owner, which principle is ingrafted into the Constitution of the United States in these words. "Nor shall private property be taken for public use without just compensation."*

5. There were eight gentlemen, I think, sitting at the table, not distinguished by the insignia of their orders, stars, garters, &c.; nor are they when in attendance upon the House of Lords upon ordinary occasions. Witnesses were present, to whom interrogatories were put by barristers from briefs which had been prepared by attorneys or other agents. This is one of those nice divisions of labour which spring up, of course, where business is done upon a great scale. These barristers managed their cases very much as we do, except with much greater economy of time.

The room was large, and there were scattered here and there many empty chairs: very inviting objects in London to those who go about seeing sights! But, alas, the empty chairs were like a great many other good things in England, to be looked at, not enjoyed. The friend who conducted me, seeing this forbidden fruit, and knowing that I must long for it, suggested, very courteously, that I could not sit, but that I might *lean* against the wall. Fortunately, I did not need this information. A sitting and a *leaning* "privilege," to a man exhausted in traversing the streets of London, are very different things. Actuated by a little malicious curiosity, I was determined to know from headquarters whe-

* Amendments to the Constitution, Art. 5th.

ther I could or could not, among these dignitaries of the empire, take an empty chair, and appealed to a messenger, distinguished by a large gold or gilt ornament worn upon his breast, who very civilly said, "No, sir." These barriers may seem to be very important in England, but we in the United States look upon them as the people in the north do upon the high rail-fences in Virginia, which seem to be three or four feet higher than any animals there can jump over. The tailors and shopkeepers might, for aught I know, drop into the empty chairs if allowed to do so; but what then? they could not carry the chairs off with them. It is to us a painful idea, that a great people should at this late day insist upon distinctions which are removed from our minds, and gone for ever. It is astonishing that the privileged people of the world should not be able to comprehend that they are placed in a new position; that their whole system has been moved backward a little, while that of others has been pushed forward. The question is now agitated in England, not whether others shall sit in the presence of the lords, but whether the lords shall sit at all where they do. Besides, why forget the laws of hospitality? why pass by the stranger? why not offer an empty chair to him who comes from a long distance to see his fatherland? why should not these lords overlook a little blunt republican rudeness, simplicity, and want of polish, if you please, taking the man according to the goodness of his heart and the light of his mind (some do so), and thus throw open their arms and hearts to the people of a great nation, that is speaking and spreading their language, reading their books, buying their goods, furnishing their looms; that is descended from their loins, whose love and respect for all true British greatness and goodness yet predominate? See with what a fine fibre we are bound together! What would become of multitudes of these lords if cotton should cease to-morrow to grow in the United States? The world is changing; sometimes the proud and lofty are abased, and the poorest and most miserable raised from the dust. Everywhere we may read lessons of wisdom, if we will but open the book. There is a gentleman in Boston, whose memory will be fresh after that of multitudes is obliterated for ever, who wears a pair of spectacles divided into two parts, the one for far, the other for near sight, said to have been contrived by Franklin, who wore such at the court of Versailles. The story is, that the queen, observing them, said to one of the ladies of the court, " I hear that the Americans are a very clever people ; but is it true, as I am told, that they are so poor that he cannot afford to buy a pair of whole spectacles?" Whether the story be true or false, the moral is, that we live in a changing world, in which the rich become poor and the poor rich; and what is better still, in some parts of which many poor may and do attain to that happy middle state which the wise man pronounces to be better than riches or poverty. When these lords sojourn among us, they are ever ready to receive our kindness, the existence of which is known, felt, and acknowledged by strangers. One of these gentlemen, who was lately in our country, never refused the hospitality of any class here; saying that this opened to him many sources of information, a privilege which his rank denied him at home. It is true, that at home he could not dine with small traders, common farmers, shopkeepers, and such sort of people. There is a higher rank approaching than heraldry ever knew, and to that they and all of us shall be obliged to acknowledge superiority. No mean pride should keep these great nations asunder, but every device be resorted to to bring them closer and closer. It is true, that in our "poor estate" we were grievously sinned against, but the magnanimity of forgiveness is one of the privileges of the prosperous.

6. From this committee-room we passed to another, through a private passage made by the late King George the Fourth for his own exclusive use. It was very magnificent, and is said to have cost a large sum of money. These are some of the solitary selfish enjoyments which our more benevolent system forbids, and which all great and generous rulers have ever despised. To take the property of the poor people who live on ten shillings a week, pay a rent of four, and are obliged to begrudge themselves a glass of beer, for such a paltry distinction, seems to be the perfection of meanness. The day must come when the rich will better understand their duties, and the poor their interests.

7. About fifteen lords sitting about the table

were well and simply dressed, as gentlemen should be. It is said that the gentlemen of the Lords and Commons are the best dressed men in the kingdom.

The Marquis of Bute was pointed out, who is said to have an income of sixty thousand pounds, about $300,000, which is in the second or third class of incomes in England. Lord Wharncliffe was present, who spoke intelligibly, an attribute not common within these walls, as I shall have occasion to mention again. Lord Wharncliffe mispronounced the most important word to the lords in the English language, saying "my luds" for "my lords." This, however, is according to ancient usage in that country; and as the oracles of fashion are to most people the oracles of wisdom, there is no use in disputing them. In another case, it would have been "lords." If Lord Wharncliffe should have occasion to say, "that there was an ancient and venerable custom by which the commons were obliged to appear before the members of the Upper House with their hats off, while their superiors remained covered," he would have said "before the lords." This, however, is but a fashion; and as there are so many all over the world much worse, it is not worth while to be vexed with it.

8. If anything in political economy be important, it is education: if anything be important in education, it is good speaking. Mr. Bulwer, in giving an account of the tone of conversation among the

aristocracy in England, says:* " And our rational conversation is for the most part carried on in a series of the most extraordinary and rugged abbreviations, a species of talking short-hand. Hesitating, humming, and drawling are the three graces of conversation." He goes on by a striking caricature to represent this style of speaking to be even worse than I can from my little information acknowledge to be true.

As to the speaking in the House of Lords and Commons, having heard it upon various occasions, I can say (so far as my small experience goes) that I know not even any State Legislature in the United States in which the average merit of the speakers is not greater than that of the Lords and Commons. I speak of *manner*, and mean to except a small number of the more eminent speakers, as to whose merit all think alike. It is equally shocking and indescribable; it may be called a hesitation, a drawl; producing the same effect upon the nerves as the twitchings of a balking horse, who seems to want to go, and can go, but won't go. In the House of Lords, I heard one of these gentlemen (whose name is well known), of whom I learned that he was a man of sense, who possessed this "curious felicity," as Mr. Bulwer calls it, in an eminent degree; and I can assure the reader, that in tone, manner, voice, gesture, I never saw in state, county, or town, a grown up man make a

* England and the English, book ii., ch. ii., Conversation and Literary Men.

worse appearance. He seemed to have swallowed his pocket-handkerchief; and, still, great as his own and the sufferings of his audience, under such a misfortune, must have been, on he went, twitching, drawling, floundering, for half an hour.

Among all the rational powers of man, there is none that distinguishes him more than that of speech; none gives more pleasure or confers more power. It is surely, then, most unaccountable that the hereditary legislators of so great a country should seem to hold it in contempt. It is a gross affectation; it marks an indifference to the attributes of a common nature. Good speaking is an accomplishment which can only be enjoyed in common with many; there is no royal road to oratory; but there is to titles, to lordly estates, and magnificent castles. We saw mechanics and manufacturers at Manchester who are certainly learning the science of oratory; their condition will loosen their tongues, and the world will see their hearts poured out, one day or another. We here cannot conceive that a public man should be indifferent to the graces of speech, more especially that he should despise them. The English say that we are fluent, but they may not see the cause. We attribute it to the blessings of free institutions, which not only call forth all the powers of men, but of all men. It is, then, a just and rational government, giving a stimulus to every faculty of man, that lies at the foundation of his highest exaltation.

9. From these strictures as to public speaking

in England, everybody knows that there are great and numerous exceptions. Besides, in the melody of the voice, the English claim a superiority, and I suspect justly. They say that we speak with a nasal tone; it may be so. To my ears, the English voice appeared, generally, like our own, with this exception, that I heard some which seemed to give forth sweeter notes than I ever heard at home. This may be owing in part to climate, the general cultivation of music, and to a long course of refinement in the arts of civilization, or to other causes. Be this as it may, let lords, commons, and people everywhere cultivate the powers that God has given them; all must rest, finally, upon this basis. The times are changing, and will change. The days have gone by when it was said, " It is enough for the sons of noblemen to wind their horns and carry their hawk fair; and leave study and learning to the meaner people." If the lords will go to Manchester, and hear the people talk to whom Lord Brougham sometimes lectures, they will find that the wheel of time has whirled very fast since the price of a slave in England (white slave), in the reign of Ethelred, about the year 997, was said to be £2 16s. 3d.; of a horse, £1 15s. 2d.; that of a hawk or a greyhound the same as that of a man; and when the robbing of a hawk's nest was as great a crime, in the eye of the law, as the murder of a human being.* So the world changes; the hour-hand moves, though no man perceives it to

* Jacob on the Precious Metals, vol. i., ch. xii.

move; the sands are washed away, and the wall falls, though no one can see the process of destruction.

But few people observe the change that is going on, probably few of the lords see it; though the loss to them will be great, the consolation will be great. To be compelled to do justice to all men, and extend equal privileges to all, will take nothing from the greatness of the great man, but that to which he is not entitled; and then, to be sure, his pride will have a fall. This solace will be left for all: the great will be greater than they ever were before, for they will have more competitors; and there will be many who dare undeceive them in their pride and folly.

10. June. This day we went to the House of Commons, it being expected that the great debate upon the Irish Tithe Question would come on. Two and sixpence English was the usual fee paid for a seat in the gallery of the House of Commons, it being paid at the door. Owing to the importance of the occasion, we paid twenty-one shillings for three seats (about five dollars), with the understanding that our seats were to be kept from six o'clock P.M. till eight in the evening, when it was said that the debate would commence. It was postponed, nothing but ordinary business being transacted. The house, for the want of something important to do, I suppose, was in the greatest disorder in which we had ever seen a legislative assembly in our lives. Some were walking to and

fro, some greeting their acquaintances, some laughing, some talking audibly; so that it seemed to us that Bedlam itself had broken loose. We saw one member a little in the rear of, and on one side of, the speaker's chair, lying prostrate, and apparently asleep, for half an hour. Some half inclined, with both feet hoisted upon the table in front of the chairman's seat; the speaker having left the chair while we were in the house. He was in full wig. Twenty-one shillings for such a sight appeared to me an odd contrast, and we thought that this money, like a great deal more, might have been better spent. We saw bills brought down from the House of Lords by masters in chancery in flowing black robes, they being in full wig also.

How far the wigs of England upon gentlemen, coachmen, &c., for two centuries, would go to pay the national debt, I cannot say; but there is no doubt that the bill would present a grand array of figures. These masters had under their arms immense rolls of parchment, and were followed by several persons carrying others. The sight of these massy documents, which looked like bales of cloth, raised a great laugh in the house. The masters made three most reverential bows as they approached the speaker's chair, and in returning, with face to the chair, three more in the same form. It will take a good while for the people of Europe to find out in what way the people of the United States are shooting ahead so prodigiously, of the rest of the world. There is not a great deal of time spent here in making wigs and bows; perhaps that is one of the reasons. Besides, the ideas of greatness here and there are not the same. Lord Anglesea was, by special grace, permitted, at the coronation of George the Fourth, to turn his back upon royalty, and go face foremost down a flight of steps, in consequence of having lost a leg at Waterloo. Perhaps the time will come when greatness will be measured by what it accomplishes.

11. It is to be hoped that the people of the United States will, in all their economical regulations, avoid the mercenary usages of England, so mean and selfish in regard to the poorer people. Nothing hardly there can be seen without pay. Customs founded upon the godlike principle of conferring equal advantages, so far as power can dispense good, are strangers in England. There are two opposite systems in the world, the *selfish* and the *benevolent.* It is the selfishness of the exclusive system that is its curse, and will be its destruction The theory of republicanism is the theory of benevolence; and if it cannot be carried into practice, it must be owing to the utter depravity of mankind. We shall try.

12. Certainly the whole population of London cannot be admitted into so small a gallery as that of the House of Commons; but that does not at all justify this two-and-sixpenny fee at the door. The distinction is odious. There are thousands in England, gentlemen, scholars, men of science, good subjects, who cannot afford to pay the fee; there

are too many claims upon their half crowns in that dreadfully dear country. The house has at length seen this fee to be as odious as it appears in our eyes; and while we were in London (1836) the venerable usage was given up, and, in the place of it, strangers are now admitted upon the order of a member.

CHAPTER II.

13. June. I went with a friend in a boat from Westminster to Blackfriars' Bridge. The boatman told us that he earned two and sixpence a day! that his work, when on the water, was sometimes very hard, as he must often pull against wind and tide; that in bad weather he worked at shoemaking; that when he learned the trade he was obliged, as an apprentice, to pay a premium for learning, which was not the case at present; that he paid a rent of four shillings a week for himself and two children; that he should like to go to the United States if he could get away; that there were too many of the labouring class in England; that as soon as the railways were all finished it would be worse than ever for poor people. I asked him why; to which he replied, " that there would not be so many horses to be reared, and that it could not be that the poor people

would then do as well as they were now doing." Certainly, two and sixpence a day, the man finding himself, and being obliged to provide a boat, and work at a very hard business, is a miserable pittance; and still this is higher wages than many earn in England. Nothing marks the wretched feudal barbarity of Europe more than the miserable wages that the poor are working for. The pride and power of the labourers in the United States will sav' them from this degradation. Pride has much to do with it; the pride of having a good house and home, and a little laid up that saves a man from bows, scrapes, and, cap in hand, begging a job.

Prudence, prudence, is the deity that presides over the prosperous! Economy is the mother of good wages. A man of sense will earn more than a fool; and the people here, inspired by hope that drives them to incessant industry, are producing more, aside from the bounty of nature, than men ever have produced elsewhere. Every step in education will give better wages to the people of the United States, and bring about a wiser distribution of property, that best of all fruits, both moral and physical, of the democratic system. The proportions in the Old World are shocking; and this giving the lion's share to the king of the beasts makes a glutton of him and starves the rest. It is the greatest cause of the wretched poverty of Europe.

14. I often found in England, among the lower classes, though many are too ignorant to inquire about anything, an earnest desire to know what they

could about the United States; many seeming to consider this country as a sort of heaven, to which their hopes, in the deepest gloom and despair, aspired. Such we ought to make it to these poor outcasts, as far as we can, of whom it may be said,

"Homeless, near a thousand homes they stood,
And near a thousand tables pined and wanted food."

The great political economists of England had taught the poor man that God had set no plate for thousands and tens of thousands like him; when it is as certain as the existence of that good Being, that he has not only done that, but ordered their plates to be filled. What sort of political economy is that which teaches those who first open their eyes upon the beautiful hedges and green fields of old England, that *home* is *abroad;* that they must emigrate, go to Van Diemen's Land, or to the wilds of Canada for bread. It is true enough that there are too many in England at present for the bread there is there. But let it be repeated, the first question is, how comes there to be so little bread? Let those answer who, in insisting upon the corn-laws, forbid the people from buying cheap bread; who use the land that God gave to the people for a "people's farm," in feeding idle horses and grooms, pampered and powdered servants, with wigs and white gloves, and many more servants of every description than are required by a proper division of labour or the desirable refinements of mankind. Let the land, then, be exempted from paying a rent to vanity, gluttony, and all sorts of sensuality; for a man is a better animal and a nobler being upon a one, two, or four shilling, than a five pound dinner. Let the first lesson, then, in political economy be taught to the rich, who possess the land and the food, and not to the poor, who have not ten pounds to enable them to reach Canada, and who sometimes are obliged to live for weeks on frozen potatoes after they have arrived there. This I know. If there is to be a true political economy, we must begin at the beginning, and teach those who have the sway, that if they desire to provide the people with bread, they must employ them about something that produces bread. A new code of morals must precede the new book on political economy.

15. But let us go back to our boatman. He says, "That after all the railroads are made, there will be no more horses to be reared, and, of course, there will be less work for poor people." If this one delusion could be got out of the heads of rich and poor, and utterly exploded, that is, that there cannot always be found profitable labour enough to support the labourers, it would be a great move in political economy. "All the railroads" will never be made if England suffers her people to get bread and other kinds of property, according to their wants and tastes, where they will and how they will, and does not force them to labour for "gold sticks," "silver sticks," gold-headed canes, coachmen's wigs, coronation robes, and all that sort of tinselled trumpery, which is certainly doomed to be buried

in the dust of ages, like the old Scotch regalia, for which there was a great hunt a few years since, nobody knowing exactly where they were, or whether they existed at all.*

16. Again, our boatman made another mistake. Neither he nor any other man can yet foresee a hundredth part of the benefit of railroads. The railroads will create a demand for many horses, where there is one now, for transporting persons and property to and from the railroads, and in doing the increased business created by them. So true it is, that property, when rightly used, produces more property, and, of course, more employment for labourers, and as certainly more wages. Nothing is plainer than that the more property there is, the more hands there must be to keep it in use, to take care of it, and preserve it from wasting. It is in the very nature of property to multiply itself, just as animals will multiply themselves, if they have food enough. If the minds of the people could be imbued with this one simple idea, that is, that all property, public and private, may be made to redound to the advantage of the people at large, they would consider it as a sacred gift from God for the support and comfort of all his creatures. Whether belonging to rich or poor, therefore, let it be preserved.

We made in the United States the same mistake that the boatman made; for I well recollect, that when the Erie Canal was about to be construct-

---

* See Life of Sir Walter Scott.

ed, it was said that it would greatly lessen the demand for horses, whereas there are now, probably, two horses for one before, even in that part of the country.

17. An American lady told me that the beds in the hotel in which she stayed, which I knew to be a fashionable establishment in the west end of London, were filled with vermin! I suffered only once in England in this way, and that was in the city part of London. There is but one mode in which the evil can be corrected in public houses, and that is, not to submit to it, but make your complaints on the spot. The English boast of cleanliness in their inns, and, according to my experience, they have a right, certainly, compared with us; for though we are not, by comparison with many others, a dirty people, we have not arrived at their refinement in this respect. As to the *niceties*, a lady's eye is the best detecter of blemishes in this particular, and I was told by a female friend that she did not find the coverlids, blankets, bed, and window curtains as clean as she expected. As to these enemies of the human race, however, there is no excuse for suffering them to exist in the settled parts of the country, either in inns, packet ships, or steamboats. In the latter they are shamefully common. It is said that beds cannot be kept clean where so many persons, with bags, trunks, &c., are constantly travelling. It is a mistake; care will do it. Travelling in the United States, not only among ourselves, but on the part of for-

eigners, has become so great, that it is an important interest to study the arts essential to the traveller. A clean house, therefore, ought to be talked about and pointed out, as we would point out a safe steamboat or a well-regulated packet ship. Upon the whole, the neatness, order, quiet, and cleanliness of the inns in England, and especially those of the country, are, according to my experience, among the most interesting things to be witnessed in England; and if an ambassador should be sent to that country to learn all their cleanly ways, I think he would as well earn his money as some that have had that honour. They say in our western country that they are too poor yet to be clean; and the truth is, that this is the best apology that we can offer, in any part of it, for violating that precept which declares that cleanliness is a virtue. A pious man has declared, that, in his opinion, a man could not get to heaven with dirty hands; certain it is, that clean hands are an emblem of it.

18. Upon returning to my lodgings to-day at the colonnade, the porter told me that his wages amounted to from twenty to twenty-five shillings per week, and that he slept, upon an average, about five hours. This is one of the plague spots of England, an overwork of her poor people. There is nothing that sooner breaks down the resolution of a man than overwork, too little sleep. Every man knows what the loss of a single night's sleep is. What, then, must be the condition of one who loses a part of every night? If the nerves are

shattered, the mind will be weakened, and the man unavoidably resorts to drink to restore him; he loses his resolution; his courage is gone; his sight of virtue becomes more and more dim; he does not see far enough to recognise vice in its distant approach; he becomes selfish, submits to temptation, and is ruined. The condition, in this particular, of many of our servants in our fashionable hotels and boarding-houses, is a shame to a Christian country; it is a disgrace and an outrage to these poor servants. They ought to combine and resist; it is a good cause for combination; they can combine; they are not such slaves as to be helpless; the good and generous part will combine with them. They are entitled to the greatest natural blessings of their condition, health and sleep; but the fashion of late parties and midnight dissipation is at war with them. We complain of bad servants! Who make them bad? What a gross injustice!

19. There could hardly be a more melancholy sight than the haggard looks and sunken eyes of the men-servants in our coffee-room, who were so exhausted in the morning as to be stupid, and scarcely able to answer a common question; and the women, who were dragging pails of water up and down the stairs, seemed equally wretched. And who is in fault if the poor people are demoralized? who but those who turn day into night? who but those who compel these menials to serve at their midnight banquets and carousals?

The King's Opera was in the immediate rear of our lodgings; the streets and passages were crowded with carriages and people, and at one or two o'clock in the morning I have heard the loud and deep curses and execrations of wretched people, who seemed mad with the idea that their midnight debauch must soon end, and be followed with a day of ceaseless toil. And when will people begin with righteousness in their own households? when will the rich set up the law of love and charity? when will they see, to the full extent, the evil of their bad example in midnight dissipation, upon the poor and uninstructed? when shall we find out that true political economy can no more be separated from the love of one man to another, than soul and body be divided? When will they abandon in England the delusion of sending people to the wilderness in order to get rid of poverty and make the nation rich? There is nothing that will either create the riches of the soul, or the material riches, which the eye sees and the hand feels, so fast as that divine spirit which now begins to stir in the world! Let it not here be supposed that I oppose emigration to a starving people, but, rather, that I propose what will save them from being brought to this pass.

20. June. Went to Covent Garden, " so called (as the guide-book says) from having been the garden of St. Peter's convent." This is the great vegetable and fruit market of London. On my

way I stepped into a baker's shop, who sold his two-pound loaves for fourpence. Some of the bread was mixed with dried sweet currants, which he said were used by some people in that way instead of butter. In the United States the people live as though they thought they could eat their bread spread with butter on both sides, instead of leaving out the butter altogether. He had in his shop brown bread, which is often seen in London; by which I mean bread made of wheat flour not bolted. Upon another occasion, I inquired for brown bread, when the shopman told me that he did not sell it; "that it was principally used by the fashionables, and only because the doctors told them it was healthy." I could wish, that all the prescriptions of the faculty were as useful.

21: At Covent Garden I saw strawberries at fifteen pence the pottle. The pottle is a basket, which I think will hold a little more than a pint; it is much larger at the top than at the bottom; it runs off so much to a point, that it looks as if two strawberries could not lie alongside of each other. The basket is so filled to overflowing, that the fruit is sometimes bound on by strings of matting. This the London gardeners call "turning the best side to London," just as our sweet-potato boys in New-York crown their loads with the finest specimens. It is a pity that the labouring people in Europe or anywhere should ever resort to these petty frauds, which seldom turn to much account, for they are soon found out; and then they are returned by the great and rich to the poor in the "poisoned chalice," overflowing. One fraud naturally begets another, for the man says, "if you cheat me I must cheat you." This "turning the best side to London" is a peculiar disgrace in the United States, where it is mostly one working man robbing another. These strawberries are very large, though I think, for the want of sun enough, not generally so good as ours. I saw them afterward in London at ninepence and at sixpence a pottle. At best, according to my observation, they are a dear fruit in England, and I believe a rare luxury to the poor. And why should the good *natural* fruits of a country be a rare luxury to the poor anywhere? One day or another, if the world prospers and gets to understand the true political economy, it will not be so; but that day may be a good way off: and what then? To the virtuous labourer, who goes on with an unconquerable perseverance to get knowledge and education, which are at once the creators and dividers of property, many days are as one day; what we do not obtain for ourselves we shall get for those who come after us.

22. On returning to my lodgings this morning, I found my old acquaintance at the door, as usual. I seldom failed to get some conversation out of him, which was a real pleasure in that, to a stranger, *solitary* place, London. He told me this morning that

it was common in his county (Devonshire) to heat milk (as many of our people do) to produce cream; that this was done in twenty minutes; that Devonshire cream has a great reputation in London, and is constantly sent up in the stagecoaches. When we went to Norfolk, our coachman stopped at the house of one of Mr. Coke's tenants, about a hundred miles from London, and threw off baskets, in which butter had been sent there. Butter in this way was then sent daily, the coachman receiving one penny per pound for freight. On our return from Norfolk, the full baskets were taken on the coach. These are the advantages of perfect roads!

The old man farther told me, that little beer was drank in Devon compared with other counties; that most people there prefer cider; that Devon is a cider county; that he had, in former times, known cider as cheap as five shillings for 63 gallons; that the common price was from 20 to 25 shillings the hogshead; that agricultural wages then in Devonshire (not in the harvest) were only eight or nine shillings the week, with a quart of cider a day, the man finding himself. That there were many Methodists in his part of the country; that though he was not one of them, he knew there were good men in all persuasions; that religion was in the heart, and that any man was good who was good to his fellow-creatures. If all the people of England had as good a religion as this man professed to have, there would be a much better political economy, and far less cause for emigration to Van Diemen's Land.

23. June. We went this day to the Zoological Gardens, an institution that belongs to private persons. The gardens were opened in 1828. You are admitted, by an order from a member, upon paying one shilling at the gate. This garden lies beyond Regent's Park, which was crown property, but has been given up for the benefit of the people. At the gate is a register, which, by the means of a covered dial, tells the number of people that pass in a day. We saw the giraffes, a very curious animal, eating hay from a manger not less than nine feet from the floor. As they lie down, the foot to the fetlock doubles under, as though there was a perfect joint in it. They were attended by an Arab, who, it is said, came over with them. In this garden we saw the gazelle. The animals and birds are exhibited in paddocks, dens, and aviaries suited to them. The garden is filled with flowers and ornamental trees. There was a large crowd, but I saw no rudeness or vulgarity. It is a noble establishment; my view of it was, to be sure, very superficial, but it seemed to be worthy the taste and industry of a great people, furnishing not only an amusing and innocent recreation, but the means of obtaining useful information in natural philosophy. Here was a great and an innocent enjoyment for many people at a moderate expense. How much better, though, if it were a national enjoyment for rich as well as poor without expense! How

many of the like enjoyments might not even the poor possess if the rich would renounce the enormous charges of their frivolous distinctions, and the poor their dram-drinking and other sensualities, and all live like rational beings, Then the poor would have something to fill their souls as well as bodies, and cause them to raise their heads to Heaven in gratitude, instead of slinking away from sight to hide their miserable rags!

The Zoological Gardens lying beyond Regent-street, we passed through that street and Portland Place in going to them; and here you have as full a view as can be had of the palaces of London and the immense number of rich equipages and liveries, that are as various and gorgeous as the clouds. There is nothing in the United States that gives us any adequate idea of the riches of the west end of London; it seems, for the moment, as if all the ladies and gentlemen of the world had come there to ride in coaches and chariots, to build palaces and live like kings. But there are sad contrasts here!

24. At the door of our hotel to-day I had a conversation with an Irishman, who was laying down gas-pipes. He told me that he paid a rent of five shillings a week. The paving-stones he was then taking up were blocks about twelve inches square. They appeared to me to be of the size of the paving-stones in London generally; he stated that in some parts they were smaller. London is

much better paved than New-York; the holes and inequalities in the sidewalks, which are so dangerous and disagreeable in New-York, do not exist to the same degree in the London pavements. Roads, streets, lights in cities, &c., are for public convenience, and it is therefore for the public to provide them, which must be done out of the property of the whole people. In England it is not in the power of the mass of the people to dispose of the property of the whole for these objects, as it is in the United States. It is a wonder, then, that here, where the people have the power, they should not insist upon these great objects, in which they have so large an interest, being first accomplished. After that, if there be a surplus, and if the rich have money to throw away, why, let them do it. The people of the United States will never have any adequate idea of their destiny, till they are weaned from petty sensualities, and insignificant ways of spending their money.

25. I saw in the neighbourhood of my lodgings on the signs, "Tea Man, Poulterer, Grocer," &c., "to his Majesty," and I at first imagined that these were the distinguished shopmen who had the exclusive honour of his majesty's custom. But, upon observing the same thing in many other parts, I concluded that his majesty could not be so large a customer, and that this was but a cunning device; which was the fact, as I was told.

The English are adorers of riches, and of the

king as their great emblem. This flows from the nature of a government dispensing so much patronage, power, and greatness. Man-worship in the form of a king is as belittling to the soul, as is the god-worship of an idol. The tendency downward of the mind is the same. To be obliged to bow low to a miserable creature like George the Fourth, in the shape of a king, confounds the just ideas of greatness and goodness in the human mind. The very prayers taught to the children and people are hypocrisy and falsehood. At Cardiff Church I heard an excellent sermon from the rector, plain, bold, direct, with every appearance of manly sincerity and pure religion. He read from the Litany these words: " We beseech thee to hear us, good Lord, that it may please thee to bless and *preserve all* the royal family." To pray for the *preservation* of such creatures as Charles the Second, George the Fourth and his queen Caroline, &c., is a mockery. After all, there are so many good people and good things in England, as to show that there are great compensations for these blots. Let us, then, who have begun a new career, and who have our own follies and vices to atone for, steer clear of man-worship, which we certainly shall not if we suffer a few thousand to possess all the comforts. There is no more reason, in the nature of things, why a few thousand in a country should enjoy all these, than why they should breathe all the pure air. The *comforts* are much more widely diffused in England than is generally supposed, but not as they are in the United States.

26. There are in London many beautiful picture-shops; some were in Pall Mall, in the immediate neighbourhood of our lodgings. I saw day after day crowds of common people stop and gaze, showing clearly that the germes of taste and love of beauty were in their souls. This love ought to be cultivated, and all the people admitted as much as possible to such enjoyments. This is one of the designs of property. Many of the English say that the London populace is the most depraved in Europe; their writers confirm it. And what can make the poorer sort so depraved, but neglect on the part of the more fortunate? In other parts of London, I have seen at the windows of the picture shopdealers the most wanton exhibitions. But this is nothing worse than I have witnessed in a Broadway shop, where a *woman* was left to do the loathsome work of showing to *men* for sale, one lewd picture after another. These panders to the aristocratic vices of lewdness and debauchery (I shall state hereafter the reasons for calling them the *aristocratic* vices) are the destroyers of the people, enemies of democratic government, and the human race; they bring upon the heads of the common labouring people the curse of poverty, base subservience to the rich, disease, and death. A damning virtuous public opinion, among the labourers, as their own public opinion, issuing forth in groans and maledictions, ought to ring incessantly in their

ears; the hatred of the people in public, in private, through the press, and in every appalling form, ought ever to be present to them. Any labouring man in the United States who employs in his art or trade any power which God has given him to debauch the mind of another; to seduce him from the industry which supports his wife and children, ought to be put out of the pale of honourable labour, and cut off from all generous associations and sympathies with his class.

27. I saw to-day, in one of the papers, a notice stating that there was a fancy pugilistic exhibition by some first-rate performers, for the amusement of the sons of the Prince of Orange, who were then visiting England. Pugilism has been the gladiatorial show of England; but, thanks to the progress of a virtuous public opinion, is nearly extinct. I was not aware of this to such an extent till I arrived in England. The gradual disappearance of any vicious cruel practice among the people ought for ever to be distinctly marked, that all may see, for their encouragement, what the Christian spirit is producing and what the world is gaining. The papers mentioned the lords who were present. It is a pity that these governors of so great a portion of the world should not be able to find some more worthy occupation of their time.

28. I went yesterday to Westminster Abbey! A gentleman who visited England some years since told me, as an evidence of the admirable preserva-

tion of things in England, that a broken pane of glass was not to be seen in the whole country. I did not find the fact just so, for I counted four in the Abbey, or in Henry the Seventh's Chapel, which is usually considered a part of it. This was probably accidental, for the preservation of things in England is admirable! The care with which they are mended and kept in order may well put us to the blush. It shows a love of home, of kindred, of country, which can be kept in full vigour only by retaining the memorials of them. If there be broken panes of glass in England, there are few, and these are not replaced with old coats and hats. The marks of decay in England are most visible in ancient lordly palaces and castles, many of which are going to destruction, because there is no good reason why they should be preserved. Long may their ruins remain as beacons to warn mankind that labour should have for its object the happiness of the people!

Westminster Abbey! Everybody goes to see Westminster Abbey. This is a grand object; and still there is a strange mixture of the noble, the beautiful, the grotesque, and the ridiculous in it; there are magnificent points in the architecture; there are statues of surpassing beauty, and so there are miserable wax daubs. There are to be seen here statues of the meanest and basest of mankind, whose memories, if possible, ought to have been permitted to perish for ever, so that men might escape from the corruption of knowing that such beings ever existed.

Many of these statues are shamefully mutilated, without reference to the demerits of the dead; heads, toes, fingers, noses, &c., being broken off. There is a monument to Andre, containing several figures; two in that, I think, are decapitated. Nelson, Queen Elizabeth, and Charles the Second are in wax! One can hardly realize that the respectable English people whom I saw over their own happy firesides, with their innocent wives and daughters, should come to gaze upon so low a debauchee, a bribed king, and the murderer of Sir Harry Vane! What a confusion in our ideas of virtue! Some of the wax figures were such things as we see at our country shows. There is a noble statue of Watt. No Watt could have found a place there in the reign of Charles the Second. No Charles the Second can now live in the country of Watt.

Here we see the chair in which the kings of England have been crowned, even down to William the Fourth. The seat of the chair is cracked or broken; is this ominous? Several plain country people were with us; some of the women sat down on these kingly ornaments, perhaps because they were as tired as I was; perhaps, but probably not, to show their contempt of dead or living royalty. All who go to England should see Westminster Abbey; it is a history of mankind; it shows their rank and employments; what they have done and what they have been; it is a mixed monument of human creatures and things, in a less enlightened and a less benevolent age ; of great conceptions, beautiful designs ; of pride and vainglory ; of great deeds, misdeeds, and waste of labour. I have been delighted with England, but I cannot but love a country more where there are fewer memorials to testify to the splendour of a few, and to the meanness and poverty of the multitude.

At the Abbey we pay an entrance fee of fifteen pence ; *threepence* for the Poets' Corner, which you may see separately ! There is no limit to this kind of meanness in England. The day was warm ; after a long walk, being in a state of profuse perspiration, we kept on our hats, but were soon admonished by the doorkeeper to take them off. We remonstrated, and stated the reason. The doorkeeper pointed to a gentleman in black who was just going out of the door, and said that his lordship would blame him if he allowed us to remain uncovered. We were, of course, obliged for an hour and a half to stand upon the stone pavements with our hats off. All this might be expected, of course, for aught I know, among a parcel of ignorant monks in Italy or Spain, but not in England. It is true that the Abbey is a place of worship ; that is, a small part of it, there being divine service in the chapel every day. It is a pity that the countrymen of Washington, the citizens of a country without whose industry England would be, in this cotton-growing and cotton-wearing age, comparatively a beggarly land, should be compelled to be disgusted with these trifling annoyances; that these petty observances should not give way to the laws of hospitality; that the clergy, and all men, should not see that the time has gone by for observing a religious punctilio, at the sacrifice of health and comfort, and that brick, stone, and mortar are no longer holy things.

29. Waterloo Banquet, Apsley House. The Waterloo Banquet is in honour of the battle of Waterloo, on the 18th of June, and is given at Apsley House, Lord Wellington's residence in Piccadilly, Hyde Park Corner. The iron window-shutters still up (1836) are among the memorials of a London mob, which a few years since rudely broke in upon his lordship. The Spanish proverb says, "Never mention a rope in the family of a man who has been hanged." Mobs have been a pretty delicate subject in the United States for two or three years past.

It was stated in some of the newspapers, that the tables were shown to a great number of the nobility, &c.; that the centre exhibited an extraordinary display of gold and silver in triumphal columns, presented by the allied sovereigns after the battle of Waterloo; that the magnificent service presented by the King of Prussia was used. This is another idol set up at their own expense that the people of England worship; that is, the magnificence *of the gold and silver* of their great men. They seem to delight in it as a part of their own glory. If a man can obtain the means of erecting triumphal arches of *gold and silver* by his own skill and genius, and if he has that sort of taste, why, let him do it. It is seldom done but at the sacrifice of the poor people, who earn a shilling a day, or perhaps eight or ten shillings a week. The wages earned by many of the subjects of these magnificent sovereigns are far less. Nothing argues more strongly against the barbarism of the age in which we live, than that a gentleman should be willing to accept such a present upon such terms! These are the natural fruits of war, of contracts, and jobs, abundant, of course, to a few, but very meager to the people. War may sometimes be necessary, but it seldom sets them down to rich banquets. The expense of these triumphal arches of *gold and silver* is said to be justified as the reward of great actions; and so it will be till great actions are followed by greater rewards. How can men's hearts be reconciled to the splendours of a show, a mere pageant, wrung from the miseries of the poor people?

30. June. It was stated in the Observer of the 20th instant, that one hundred and sixty steerage passengers were going out in the American packet Westminster; "that a majority of the farming labourers are from the counties of Norfolk and Suffolk, and that their passages are paid by the parishes to which they have become chargeable." These are the poor people that Mr. Malthus and his disciples can find no employment for in England. They think that the best that can be done

for many of them is to use them in fashioning the "triumphal arches," preparing the Waterloo banquets, and waiting at the tables. Candour must admit that we have followed these old baronial fashions as closely as our riches would allow; but it is equally certain that causes are slowly but surely at work here that will hereafter save the earth from sterility, and the poor from their accustomed wretchedness. The "triumphal arches" of gold and silver neither reap nor sow, nor yield increase in any way. The arches being once erected and the banquet enjoyed, there is an end to what they yield to the labourer. He gets his wages, to be sure, but the fund for more wages is consumed. Let the great men in England, then, instead of suffering this imposition of forcing their paupers upon the people of the United States, give up their rich banquets; a simple repast is better, healthier, and more worthy; then let them apply the money which the people permit them to enjoy, or some part of it, in improving the earth; among other things, in rooting out those vile poppies from the oats, barley, and wheat, of which we saw such immense quantities on the road from London to Norfolk. In this way they will produce two sheaves of wheat and blades of grass where there was one before. This would be better than to send the poor people by a heartless political economy to wander houseless and homeless among strangers here. It is affecting to see these poor foreigners driven away from a rich home, and crawling about for crumbs, like cats and dogs that have overbred. But if they must quit their own beautiful country, may God give us Christian hearts to receive them.

31. Of all the miserable fallacies that ever got into the heads of men, and then into their books of political economy, this is one of the worst; that is, the impossibility of furnishing profitable labour for all. The proof of the contrary is, that God has furnished man with an exhaustless power of creating property out of the materials of the earth. A few years of peace in the civilized world have proved it. Let the people, then, reflect upon this cardinal rule, upon this undeniable truth; wherever property is created, preserved, put in use, and thereby increased by agriculture, manufactures, or commerce, there will be improved wages, there will ever be a growing prosperity, there all will flourish together.

32. To go back to the poor people who are shipped from Norfolk and Suffolk. It is a breach of the laws of hospitality to cast them naked and forlorn on our shores. It is more unprincipled than to turn a poor beggar from your own door upon your neighbour; it is a fraudulent imposition upon the charitable; and our government has a right to consider the continuance of the practice as a violation of the laws of good neighbourhood. But between us and these poor children of want let there be no controversy.

33. I have alluded above to the agriculture of England. I paid every possible attention to it, considering my short stay there. In this and in every statement I wish to be perfectly accurate. In re-

gard to several points I cannot be mistaken, and I shall speak of it more particularly upon another occasion. Superior as it is to that of the United States generally, it fell far short of my expectations, and of public opinion here. We often talk of England as a garden: it is not so, as all intelligent English farmers well know and acknowledge.

CHAPTER III.

34. PAGEANTS in England consume an immense amount of the people's money; no one can tell how much. On the 18th day of June we went to see the military show in Hyde Park, in commemoration of the battle of Waterloo. It was stated that five thousand soldiers were on the ground. The king, many royal personages, and the Dutch princes were present. Some were in splendid coaches, others on horseback, while the gentlemen who made up the party of which I was one, were elevated about two feet from the ground on an oak plank, for which privilege we paid sixpence each. This is a considerable elevation in England, when you reflect how many are prostrate in the dust. There is nothing so difficult to reconcile in England to our ideas as the superiority of rank. We hardly know what

it means, whence it comes, what it is good for, or how to treat it.

35. We saw the king and the court carriages as they came within the circle. The whole line of the military extended, I think, about two thirds of a mile, but I cannot pretend to be accurate. The flying artillery moved upon a full gallop, the horses being nearly upon a run; there being four, and, I think, sometimes six horses attached to a gun. As soon as the horses stop, the men who are on the horses and carriages fly from their seats; the hind wheels of the carriage, to which the gun is attached, are immediately disengaged, and the firing begins. It was the opinion of our party that each gun was fired four times in a minute. This is murder, to be sure, on a great scale, when people are in earnest. The populace, of which we were a part, was kept out of the military lines by a chord extended around the enclosure. Within the lines, besides the military, court carriages, &c., there were a considerable number of well-dressed people, said to be officers' friends, &c., admitted by order. Our stand was about twenty-five feet from the enclosing lines, between which and us was a constant stream of people passing to the head of the line, where stood the court carriages, we being perhaps eighty rods from them. As the cavalry were rushing at full gallop from one side to another of the field, one of the Horse Guards' men fell. It was an interesting moment! Some one or more of the young Princes of Orange left the ranks and sprang forth to the man's assistance, as was said in

the papers the next day. I saw a dozen infantry men rush out for the same purpose. The man afterward led his horse off from the ground, and did not appear to be injured. I saw the king, queen, &c., at the distance of about twenty five feet, as they left the place, and afterward Lord Wellington. I doubt whether any of these great personages, surrounded as they were with military and courtly splendour, were more happy than I, a humble citizen of the United States, was on that day on my sixpenny stand. At least, our pleasures were probably very different. Of the military show I was no judge; besides, being at a great distance from some of the evolutions, they were seen indistinctly. For three hours my attention was closely riveted by a near observation of the dress, manners, looks, &c., of the groups of people in my neighbourhood, and of the immense number that were passing directly before me, who were going to or returning from the head of the line, where the royal carriages stood. I must have seen many thousands distinctly, men, women, and children; and I can say that I never before saw so many thousands of better-looking or better-behaving people together. I did not see a drunkard or hear an oath. Having a good opportunity of observing so large an assembly of the populace, I did not fail to scrutinize it closely. There were exceptions; some few, and only a few, miserable-looking people, who were evidently of that depraved class of whom you see so many in various parts of London. Even these seemed to be overawed by the general decency and propriety. Although I had already seen many of the sights of London, still this view of so vast an assemblage of well-dressed, well-looking, and well-behaving people, was the most refreshing and delightful one I had yet witnessed; and I must say that it gave me a higher opinion of the general character and condition of the people in that part of the world than I had expected, which opinion was confirmed by all my subsequent experience, an experience, to be sure, very limited and imperfect. It is impossible to witness such a scene without realizing the fact of the immeasurable distance of the people from their former degradation, or to suppress the conviction of the great improvement which they are now undergoing. It is a sure omen for the future, and affords the most consoling reflections to all those who see in the growth of the people in virtue, a certain evidence that civilization is advancing, will advance, and end in preparing Europe for the enjoyment of liberty. This is too great a blessing to be expected, however, without self-government, self-sacrifice, humanity, moderation, and temperance on the part of the people.

The people of England cannot, however, hope to keep pace with those of the United States in the race of prosperity, so long as so many of these pageants are preserved at such an enormous expense. Armies may be necessary, but military foppery is not; of the pageants we have fewer, but of the foppery of them perhaps little less. In part first, section 206, I stated that in the year 1830 the then Secretary of the Navy issued an order regulating the costume of several of the officers; and that accompanying these orders were patterns of the dresses required: that by that order an *embroidered* coat is directed for a midshipman—an unfledged boy. This coat then cost *fifty* dollars at the shop of a fashionable tailor in New-York! The people who have, by their hard work, economy, and contempt in their own persons and families of expensive folly and foppery, brought the United States to that degree of glory and happiness which they are now enjoying, ought to set about in earnest to calculate the whole amount of it in their public expenditure, and then send men into their councils who will make thorough work in lopping off perhaps a third, perhaps a half from the total amount of the expenses of their government. This, or something approaching to it, is undoubtedly possible without encroaching upon the dignity of the United States or diminishing the rewards of any man for real service. Do the people expect to make naval heroes of their youth by setting the tailors to work silk braid upon their coats?

Even the *prosperous* part of the farmers of the State of Massachusetts, who are able to accumulate at all, do not lay up, *upon an average*, more than two hundred dollars annually. I state this fact after a good deal of inquiry. They have no money for *embroidered* coats; what, then, becomes of that part who have no surplus for coats of any description?

36. Extravagance, after all, is a vulgar thing, for

it requires neither genius nor skill to waste the people's property. Even the most ignorant would sooner acquire truer ideas of real glory, if any proper pains were taken to infuse them. In Europe, at present, all ideas of greatness seem to suppose, as an indispensable accompaniment, palaces, coaches, jewels, diamonds, laces, epaulets, liveries, &c., &c., and thus tens of thousands work to produce little or nothing, and then come the poorhouses; the eight hundred millions of debt; and the eighth part of pauper people! Nothing can keep the people of England in their position but the infusing into their minds that which Mr. Bulwer says that the people of England want, common sense upon this subject. However closely we have imitated many of the stupid fashions of the Old World in our ways of living, they are not ingrafted into the frame of our government, and sustained by the same train of monopoly privileges.

37. June. We went to the Tower. Here again we pay; all pay, rich and poor, strangers and subjects. It strikes us as rather curious to see a man paying for the sight of his own curiosities! They have a way in England of considering Towers and such sort of things as belonging to the king, which we very foolishly take to be the property of the people, and to be enjoyed by them accordingly. I suppose the Tower is one of these, for it is said to have been built by William the Norman, who established the principle that all lands were held

under the king; and if the king had all the lands, he should have the fortresses by which they were protected. Here, too, is a governor, by the name of Constable of the Tower, with a good salary, I suppose, according to the English standard of salaries, which are essential to keep up the dignity of the palaces, parks, coaches, diamonds, laces, liveries, &c.; and as long as true dignity in the minds of the people consists in these, so long will such salaries be so too. The governors and constables are a part of the "*nonproducers,*" who are indispensable in keeping the producers at work, according to Mr. Malthus; for in the summing up of section tenth, eighth chapter, of his " Principles of Political Economy," he says, "*It has been repeatedly conceded that the productive classes have the power of consuming all that they produce; and if this power were adequately exercised, there might be no occasion, with a view to wealth, of unproductive consumers. But it is found by* experience, *that though there may be the power, there is not the will; and it is to supply this will that a body of unproductive consumers is necessary.*" It is a pity that so many of even the wisest and best men of these countries should consider their "experience" as what must be the experience of all time and of all countries. This is not the experience of the people of the United States; their common sense has rejected much, but not all of the teachings of this experience. They believe that the productive classes have the "*power,*" and the "*will,*" too, to consume all that they produce. Let a man have the opportunity of building a good house, and he will not be apt to make his bed under the arches of London Bridge. The plan of putting a cocked hat upon one man's head, an embroidered coat upon his back, epaulets upon his shoulders, gold rings upon his fingers; of giving him a fine house to live in, and coach to ride in, so that he may be idle and a nonproducer, in order that another, after having worked like a slave to fit out this baby-house man, may clothe himself respectably, seems to us very strange political economy! The plan of sustaining a body of idle people in order to make the rest industrious, appears to us very preposterous. Still it is natural in Europe; for the labourers there have so long been degraded, they have had so little, they have enjoyed so little, that they have hardly been taken into account. Things, however, will go on in this train for a while, and but for a short while, before the United States shall have waked up the Old World from a long dream, to some very striking realities!

38. We paid seven shillings for the sight of various curiosities at the Tower. The fee for the exhibition of the whole was said to be eleven shillings, but we had not time for all. We saw the horse armory, exhibited in an apartment said to be one hundred and fifty feet in length. Here are men bristling in complete armour from the crown of the head to the soles of the feet, sitting bolt upright on horseback, the whole face

being enclosed in iron. These iron men show the iron age in which they lived. One of the figures is a woman crusader on horseback in complete chain dress, the whole stated to be a perfect thing, and now in the same condition in which it was found. These crusades, set on foot to take the Holy Land from infidels, lasted more than a hundred years. This change of employments from the running over Europe to seize other people's lands, to the cultivation of our own, is a change indeed! If so, the crusaders' "experience" was very different from that of Mr. Malthus. I wonder how many of those neat beautiful cottages that I saw in England were in existence in the age of these iron men! So it seems that people in different ages want different things, enjoy different things, and, of course, work to obtain different things. Perhaps the world may yet advance in this way; for there is no great evidence of a stand still just now either in England or here, or in many other parts of the world. If this be so, much may yet be brought to light; and if the labourers get to have "the will," that is, certain wants of decent houses, homes, and other rational comforts, that hitherto they have little thought of, but which now are not a little talked of among us, then there will be not only a prodigious increase of property, as well as a better division, but a far more just distribution of it than was ever dreamed of in our philosophy.

39. *Jewel-office!* Rather a petty establishment

for a great nation to keep! Mr. Burke tried to reform it, but the old woman at the door who received our shillings, and the old women in the government, were too powerful for him. This is a little dark room, perhaps twelve feet square. There are a few seats for spectators arranged immediately before the objects to be seen, and I think in a semicircular form. The entrance is small, and the apartment looks like a cave or den, where a wild beast might choose to lodge. We were conducted over the place to the Jewel-office by a stout, brawny man, one of the "nonproducers," fit in strength for a forgeman or miner, whose insignificant employment and beer-drinking habits were stamped upon his vacant face. These are some of the miserable employments to which so many able-bodied men are put in England: because they want "*nonproducers;*" there must be a place for them to save them from begging in the streets or robbing on the highways. In most of these places, errand boys and girls would answer the purpose just as well as men and women, and at half the expense, and then these might be put to more necessary occupations. Oh! but where are the necessary occupations? Where is the capital that would go to create them? There is capital enough, and would be a hundred or a thousand times as much, but see how the nation destroys it; see how the people waste it! Besides, who would trust the jewels of the nation, these pretty things, these invaluables, to the care of boys and girls?

We were conducted by our forgeman, in the livery of a red coat, to the entrance of the cave, where we were received by an old woman with a candle in her hand, who ushered us into it with as much caution as if she knew us to be robbers. A vain attempt was formerly made by one Blood to carry off these pretty jewels. They are secured by an iron grating, made, I think, of about half inch or inch iron; a lamp burning within. These "*splendid*" objects are said by the Guide-book to consist of the golden orb, the golden sceptre and its cross, the sceptre with the dove, St. Edward's staff, state salt-cellar, curtana or sword of mercy, golden spurs, armilla or bracelets, ampulla or golden eagle, and the golden spoon. These are the regalia! The reader, by referring to the coronation of George the Fourth, will find that they were used upon that memorable occasion, when one of the meanest and most selfish men in the nation was crowned as the sovereign of a great people. The memory of this sovereign is very distinct in their recollection. The showmen in England are very communicative; great men in their lives never seem to imagine what tales of them will be told after death. The showman at Windsor, having left a group of people in one corner of the room, attended me in another. I asked him if he knew George the Fourth, and what sort of a man he was. "Oh," said he, "at the last of it he got very bad;" and pointing to his head, said, "he would take anything." The truth is, that he died a confirmed sot.

40. My recollections of the state trinkets is very indistinct, for the old woman in her account of them jabbered so fast, as all these show-people do in England, that we could not understand her; and after she had reeled off one third or more of her lesson, we several times compelled her to go back, till she got quite out of temper and we into a frolic, and then left the place, knowing less of the jewels than most people who see them. The names I derive from the Guide-book. There they are, a single ruby in the crown of George the Fourth, being said to be of "inestimable" value, and all the regalia to be valued at millions! Whether the real value be one, half of one, two, or ten millions, perhaps no person will ever know. Mr. Cooper suspects that most of the stones are false.* What matter is it whether true or false, when it requires the skill of a jeweller to make it certain, and when, at the distance of half a dozen feet, not even he can discern the difference? What homage to a bauble! In a just state of society, it would be impossible that the people's money should be thus squandered.

I have thus given a brief account of the regalia that are shown for a few shillings as some of the great things of England to the countrymen of Washington and Franklin, by the descendants of Shakspeare, Milton, Locke, Chatham, and Burke! But they are not shown even to the poor English without pay. Why not make common property

* Gleanings in Europe. England, Letter xxi.

contribute to common enjoyment, if there be enjoyment in the sight of these pretty things? But, what would be more to the purpose, why not sell this trumpery, if there be no moral objection to putting off such trash at any price, to the Grand Turk, or the King of Siam, or any other barbarous prince, and invest the proceeds for the education of the poor people, or in some other useful way? Only think of the good that may be brought about by even one million sterling; of the industry it may put in motion; of the poor children it may educate; of the comfort and abundance which, rightly used, it may create!

41. The people of the United States are quite too much addicted to these aristocratic distinctions; their institutions point to another course. As to the principle, however, of true Christian civilization, it matters little whether so many precious stones glitter on the head of royalty, or around the fingers, arms, and necks of a republican people. Property well used produces more; one dollar yields another. Where would be the end of this progression, if men did not trample upon the fruits of their labour, as brutes do upon those of the earth! After all, it is plain that the more rational people, both here and in England, are beginning to despise this expensive pomp and vanity; that their hearts are yearning for something more noble and Christianlike; that they are grieved and disgusted at the sight of so much unnecessary poverty, and that, instead of a sentiment of admiration for this

parade, there is a growing scorn pervading their souls towards those who will not use the superfluous bounty of Providence for the common good.

42. June. To-day we saw many of the sights of London; among others, the India House. At the door we found a porter, another stout, able-bodied man, clothed in a flowing robe of livery, with a cocked hat. There are few things so disgusting in England as the never-ending finery of this livery, used mainly to distinguish the glory of the master and the degradation of the man; the national expense of which no mortal can compute. Our major-general conducted us to a room where merchants appeared to be selling silks at auction; and when we had arrived at the entrance of the room where the business was done, he doffed his flowing robe, and exposed his dirty, greasy under-clothes; a sight not so common in England as in the United States. Setting aside livery and some other trumpery things of the like kind, the English have a better taste for what is good, durable, and truly becoming in apparel, than we have.

To-day, also, we saw the Royal Exchange. Here it is that, they say, every great merchant has a particular stand in business hours where he may be found, which otherwise would not be possible in so great a concourse. Here was the pillar against which the great Rothschild leaned, who was then alive, but not present, his son occupying his place. The father, by being able to loan money to kings, and the greatest of them, has taught them a new lesson; that if they are to be upheld at all, nothing but the industry of their people can do it; so that true economy is forcing its way by inevitable circumstances whether the great people will it or not.

43. Last night we went again to the House of Commons, upon the order of a member, the pay rule having (I know not after how many generations or centuries) come to an end, as I have observed before. Oh times, oh manners, how changed! "The turnspit in the king's kitchen is no longer a member of Parliament." What disaster may not fall upon the kingdom from this headlong passion for change! Who can say that it will not blow up the House of Commons, and if the lords should be in the neighbourhood, blow them up too!

There being nothing important to call out the great men of the house, there was the same stammering and hesitating that I had heard before, with few exceptions. Our popular institutions, where every great question is debated by the people at large, and where there are no hereditary legislators or orators, give the rein to the mind and tongue, thereby producing a common, manly, bold, natural eloquence, unknown to the same extent in England; whatever the half-minded people may say to the contrary, who see excellence only on one side, and who cannot shove up the little windows of their little minds high enough to look abroad, and acknowledge that these great nations have their respective excellences to be admired and followed.

44. June. To-day we dined with excellent friends. Some gentleman at table said that everything in England tended to aristocracy; that if a man died worth £20,000, he would probably divide his property among his children; if worth £200,000, he would certainly give the bulk to his eldest son.

It must be remembered here that the proportion of those who die worth only £20,000 is constantly increasing in England. Few people realize the progress of things; the right of primogeniture cannot prevent a still greater diffusion of property. When we hear of the enormous property of a few in England, we are apt to think that there is no middle class. This is far from the fact. The Reform Bill gave eight hundred thousand voters to the United Kingdom; and what ever gives to the middling orders the power of voting but their capacity for obtaining property? The time was when comparatively a few great feudal landlords possessed nearly all the property, but that day has gone by. There was in those times little other property but land; but now commerce, manufactures, and mechanic trades have produced new orders in the state. Nothing is required to change the condition of things on the part of the working-people everywhere, but industry, skill, temperance, economy, and the manly virtue of putting their heads and hands together to help each other. From hence comes property, of course. Property gained by the virtues of those who labour for their daily bread can do what it will. But all this cannot be brought about in a moment; and what then? He who plants a tree not expecting to eat the fruit himself, but hoping that another may, has his reward. Far as England is removed from a just and Christianlike division of property, you are astonished at the immense number of people there who have arrived at a comfortable independence. What a lesson for frugality and virtue on the part of the American people, when they see how many comforts can be gathered together by those who are bowed down by such a load of taxation!

45. As a test of our republicanism in the United States, we were asked if people looked forward to it in future, and made their wills accordingly, or whether they gave the bulk of their property according to primogeniture. To this question there could be but one answer. It is not probable that ten men in the United States have in ten years given the bulk of their property to the eldest son, with the view of building up an aristocratic family. An equal division of property among children may be said to be the universal rule, as opposed to the practice of giving the mass of the estate to one. It is true that in many cases more is given to sons than daughters. In New-England it is, I think, a general rule to give about half as much to daughters as to sons. At the same time, a man may bequeath his property in such proportions as he will. This shows that a public opinion here in favour of a reasonable division is paramount to all law, and clearly indicates what must take place in the United States, which is a greater division of property than has ever been

known in a great and rich nation. To bring this about, there must be added new stories to the souls of the people, instead of their houses; in public expenditures there must be a noble provision by which rich and poor may participate in equal pleasures, and the mean passion for pomp, parade, and sensual enjoyment must be renounced as belonging to little minds and a barbarous age. Then, through the influence of a pure, holy, equalizing religion, all will scorn to live upon the robbery of the poor, and without labour either for themselves or for others. All political economy that is not based in the love of man wants an essential foundation; it is selfish and soulless, and will come to nothing. The world is beginning to wake up from a long, painful, feverish dream. Though emigration from England to the United States and elsewhere be proper to recommend to many, it will not always be the case that the people of England will suffer their poor countrymen, who have souls to enjoy that glorious country, to be driven, by a barbarous political economy, into the deserts of New-Holland or the frozen regions of Canada, because there is not work enough for them at home! Some think, that in order to have the elegances and refinements of life there must be one class to produce and another to spend; this, they say, creates the greatest division of labour and multiplicity of employments. What can create such a multiplicity of employment and amount of labour as large enjoyments on the part of all classes? This is one of the great problems that we are beginning to work out. Compare the rich man in the great house, his wide-spread table, his stable full of horses, his kennels of hounds, his long train of servants, and poor tenants, with an equal number of independent farmers, mechanics, and manufacturers, and you will soon find out which are richest; which create the greatest division of labour and multiplicity of employments; which are the greatest customers to all sorts of trade. Compare the old pauper world under the despotic governments with these youthful States just beginning their career.

The true thing is to have as many useful employments as possible, and to make it honourable for every man to work in some way or other; if he be not yet comfortable and independent, then on his own account; if that be his happy lot, then for his friends, neighbours, and the public. This is true charity and true political economy.

46. June. This day we went to Greenwich Hospital, a sight which, if life were not so short, and our means so narrow in consequence of the accursed dearness which ostentation and fashion, by an endless chain of expense, have introduced into every department of life, it would be worth crossing the Atlantic to see. If people would make their dinners as though life were valuable to them, instead of gormandizing as they now do, ten might see Greenwich Hospital where there is one. So there would be ten Greenwich Hospitals where now there are none. They must choose between these pleasures.

47. On our course through the city, as we were winding our way up Ludgate Hill, being jammed in like driftwood in a narrow stream, in consequence of the immense crowd that dammed up the street, we passed a *mourning procession.* I saw several afterward not very different in appearance. The hearse was drawn by four black horses in mourning, which was followed by five or six mourning coaches. Besides the driver, there was a man on foot at the side of each coach; but whether a servant, I know not. The hearse was decorated with a profusion of large flowing black feathers, with one of the same on the head of each horse. So it is; in the cradle, in the world, in the coffin, ostentation often costs us ten times more than all the rest. Oh, but, then, the making of the feathers and the flowers employs poor people! Yes, it does; and what then? Then we have but one Greenwich Hospital in the world; and would not the erection of another, and another, and another, employ poor people too?

This hospital was built for a palace by Charles the Second. This was the bribed king, the companion of buffoons and courtesans, the son of a man who lost his head on a block. But this mended neither his manners nor morals. How irreclaimably vicious are most of those people who are not driven either by necessity or public opinion to virtuous labours. It is labour, care, moderation, and anxiety in the business of life that bring people, for the most part, into a decent way of living and behavior. The more that are forced into it, the better for government and people.

Greenwich Hospital is on the Thames, about five miles from London Bridge, and is a retreat for seamen disabled by age and infirmities. We were told that there were 2710 pensioners, besides whom there were said to be, in the Guide-book, 32,000 out-pensioners, who receive an allowance from the hospital. The hospital is said to be supported by a revenue derived from various sources, partly from the payment of sixpence a month from every seaman. It is a pity that a people indulging themselves in such enormous luxury as the people of England do, should not be willing to relieve these brave fellows from paying this poor sixpence.

48. It is said that there are two things that man can never get rid of, death and taxation; in England there is a third, and that is, paying for sights. It would seem that, in order to render the practice as mean as possible by exacting as much as possible, they make you pay by dribblets, that is, at the different entrances of the establishments. For instance, here we pay at the picture gallery three-pence, and so on. It is a pity, likewise, that a people who are so rich as to be able to clothe their coachmen in white gloves, silk stockings, and wigs, should not be able also to let their poor neighbours see their fine sights "for nothing." We saw the men just after they had dined, and the following bill of fare: Three pints of beer; bread, one pound; meat, three fourths of a pound; potatoes,

half a pound. In the morning, one pint of cocoa, with milk and sugar; bread, but no butter. At evening, one pint of tea, with milk and sugar; bread, and half an ounce of butter. I tasted the bread, which was excellent wheat bread. We conversed with several men who had been employed in the stupid work of fighting us during the last war for the maintenance of principles which will never be reasserted by England. In the chapel we saw a magnificent picture by West, of St. Paul's shipwreck. The man who showed us into the chapel squirted mouthfuls of tobacco-juice upon the very nice mat that covered the floor. This, though, is a rare sight in England. We witnessed one other only of the same kind, and that was a showman, who, sitting at the entrance of the chapel at St. Paul's, defiled the floor in the same uncleanly way. The common people of England do not seem to consider themselves under a vow to chew tobacco, as one might suppose to be the fact with the people of the United States. It is true that many of the common people there chew, but I think that more of them smoke. I wonder that the clean people of England do not turn their showmen out of office who chew tobacco, for surely it would be a much better cause of removal than that often assigned here for removals from office. As to any person chewing tobacco in England who is said there to be a gentleman, I never saw one; no, not one. Nor do they spit, except in their handkerchiefs; which when done, the handkerchief is neatly rolled up and put into the pocket as usual! The one-sided people see nothing unseemly in this, because they do it. But why should men spit into the fire, or on the floor, or into their pockets? *ladies never do;* and they say the Persians abhor a man who spits at all. Your prejudiced people never see but one side of anything.

49. There are in the hospital many labouring pensioners, such as cooks, &c.; some of these told us that they received nine shillings per week. The men generally appeared contented and happy, and said that they were so. Several spoke in the highest terms of their governor, Sir Thomas Hardy. Many that we saw not engaged in work in doors were clothed in blue, wearing cocked hats and long coats. The men were very grave, serious-looking persons, cleanly, orderly, and as unlike the common sailor as can be imagined; showing the extent of the humanizing influence of such a place, and of such treatment upon the mind and heart of man. They seemed to be beings whose souls had passed from one body to another, and you could not realize that they had ever been those unreflecting, reckless creatures, those " six weeks lords" that we see about the docks and in the sailors' boarding-houses. Notwithstanding the instance of tobacco-chewing that I have mentioned, nothing can exceed the cleanliness of the place, the walls, floors, walks, &c.; it seemed as though the whole had been rubbed and polished like a mahogany table. No one can wonder that the dirty defile-

ment of tobacco in our public places is so abhorrent to the English.

50. The picture gallery contains pictures of naval heroes and of naval actions from the earliest English history. There is preserved here in a box the coat that Nelson wore at the battle of the Nile. As we stood in one of the doorways, one of the men said to us, " That is the governor, that is Sir Thomas Hardy." We immediately crossed him in a walk at a distance ; and upon announcing ourselves as strangers and Americans (not, perhaps, according to strict English etiquette in such cases, but after our own manner), he in the kindest way, and without request on our part, showed us what he could of the place, &c. Sir Thomas Hardy is the man to whom Nelson, in his dying moments at Trafalgar, said, " Kiss me, Hardy." Among other things, he showed us the infirm wards, where the oldest and most decrepit men were. Being himself advanced " into the sear and yellow leaf," these men seemed to regard him rather as an old friend than a master. There were some sad spectacles here, men in the last stages of existence; one of eighty years of age, who had sailed with Captain Cook ; one perfectly blind, who had been in the hospital fifty years, who was at Boston at the time of the battle of Bunker Hill, and mentioned the period accurately. He was afterward taken in a transport by a Captain Tucker of Marblehead, and declared that he was never better treated than by the Americans. Sir Thomas

showed us the burying-ground, where we saw two coffins, one upon another. These graves, when full, hold nine coffins placed in the same way. After about twenty years there is nothing to be found in the graves but a few bones, the soil being such as to decompose everything else. Out of the whole number in the hospital, one a day, upon an average, goes to his long home, and reposes in this place. The yard was full of flowers, a *cheap* beauty; we saw it almost everywhere; in the buttonholes of the men's coats, and on the headpieces of the horses' harness, in gigs, cabs, &c.

In the garden at a distance we saw a lady cutting roses, which, when severed from the stalk, dropped into a basket. Sir Thomas told us, that if we would walk in that direction, he would introduce us to Lady Hardy, which he did as Americans. She gave each of us a rose very gracefully, upon which we made our bows and departed. The reader will not suppose that these personal details are deemed of any importance, any farther than to show the delicate attentions which we so often met with in England from entire strangers, and to prove to him that there are other feelings there towards us than hatred and long-treasured resentments, even on the part of these men of war. May all those who go to see that glorious country find in it as many good people as there seemed to us to be. In truth, in going to England we desired to see a great people, our ancestors, and we found them; to enjoy hospitality and kind attentions, and we received them; not to show our own importance, but to be happy, and we were so. Indeed, we did not see things in the same light that some of our travellers have; probably we showed our ignorance, and were grossly mistaken in suffering ourselves to be so happy.

51. We then went into the Park, where we saw some of the noblest trees that can be found anywhere, chestnuts, elms, fir, &c.: elms as large as any I have seen, if I except some on Connecticut River. But the trees were more clumped than our branching eln s, the leaves greener, and appeared thicker. The Park was filled with deer; I saw perhaps fifty, and could hardly rouse them by waving my pocket-handkerchief. We went the full length of the Park to a wall, where we found Black heath. Here is a large open space of barren country, which God gave to man when he told him "to increase and multiply," that the poor people would cultivate, of course, if they had their portion of the property; but the rich and titled, by the aid of their privileges, waste it upon port, horses, dogs, livery, &c., and the poor, through a bad example, upon gin and beer. Of course, they cannot have their cake and eat it. Who can believe that Heaven ever intended that there should be a barren heath within five miles of two millions of people, or that God ever created such portions of the earth to remain steril, while his creatures are wandering over oceans, sands, forests, and deserts, houseless and homeless?

52. Here we saw a dozen or more melancholy, forsaken-looking donkeys, with side-saddles, which are let to those who choose to ride over the heath. These donkeys are very common in England; they often draw in and about the towns small vegetable carts. The ass lives upon poor fare, and he may perhaps be an economical animal for certain purposes, though I have seldom known him here to be used by those who could afford good horses and oxen. Donkeys and postboys are the animals of which the Pickwick papers, a high authority, assert that no man ever saw a dead one, and that without being able to say, as some very sensible people have, that postboys and donkeys are immortal; suppose, that whenever they get stiff, and past their work, they ride off together, one postboy to a pair, in the usual way; that as to what becomes of them afterward, nobody knows; but that it is very probable that they start away to take their pleasure in some other world, for there is not a man alive who ever saw a donkey or a postboy take any pleasure in this. I thought I saw in England many melancholy, downcast-looking people, such as agricultural labourers, earning nine or ten shillings a week, and manufacturing labourers at Manchester, who also had very scanty pleasures in this world.

53. Here, also, we saw a few miserable cabs, the horses in them being wretched creatures, their knees often horribly swollen or lacerated from falling. These cab and hackney-coach horses are

among the most disgusting sights in London; the whole people ought to be ashamed of them, and at seeing them whipped so unmercifully. People might get rid of these miserable sights, if they would only think so. We also have quite too much of the same sort of abuse of the faithful animal in our stagecoaches and omnibuses, but I think not so scandalously cruel. Any man who abuses his horse deserves to be put in his collar; his heart becomes hardened, and he passes, by a quick transition, from maltreatment of the brute to cruelty towards his fellow.

54. This park may contain hundreds of acres; but I cannot speak with any accuracy, as I do not know its bounds. In one direction at least, as you pass the common avenue, they are not to be seen on account of the trees.

As we returned from our walk in the Park, we saw the pensioners as they went to their tea. In one room there were said to be eight hundred; in another, six. The fare corresponded with the bill we had seen. Here were the real half ounces of butter, that looked as sweet as though they had come from the churn of a Philadelphia marketwoman. They have much excellent butter in England, but it falls considerably short of the Philadelphia standard, so far as my experience goes.

The men were orderly, and appeared very well at the table; none were noisy or boisterous. The blessing was asked by a one-armed man. Such is a very imperfect description of Greenwich Hospital; we left the place with the deepest impression of its beauty, grandeur, and moral sublimity. It was the most refreshing whole day we had enjoyed across the water. In such a place, you seem to be sanctified, redeemed, and set apart from all that is unholy and unclean in the world: you are in the midst of the most abused, neglected, and wretched part of mankind, but you forget it; you cannot realize it; death seems to have passed over you, and all is changed: you see the same individuals, but with different garments, manners, countenances; all is bright, cleanly, and beautiful; there is enough, there is simplicity, no gluttony, no intoxication. You see here men that must have passed through scenes that are disgusting and horrible, and this assures you that there is no part of mankind so abandoned but that they may be brought into a state of improvement; and if to one degree, then why not to another? there is no end that can be seen or pointed out; if so, let us hasten on our course with the cheerful step of Christians and rational beings, made for the enjoyment of each other. If this pure kind of existence, this simplicity, this temperance, this economy, reigned in the world, what fulness, what grandeur, what beauty should we not find!

CHAPTER IV.

55. In Part I., Chapter V., Section 64, there is this statement. "First, This, then, is the first mark of the poor that will be mentioned, *excessive labour ;* that degree of it which, exhausting the body and mind, wears out both prematurely; so that a man may be said not to live out his appointed days. The manufacturing population of New-England, taking summer and winter, and exclusive of the time occupied in meals, work upon an average not less than twelve hours out of the twenty-four. In many establishments they work a longer time. Many mechanics and day labourers, even in the United States, labour not less than fourteen hours out of the twenty-four. It must be remembered, that the labour here taken into consideration is that only which the manufacturer or mechanic performs in the service of his employer. There is more labour still for a large class. These are compelled before their working hours begin in the morning, or after they are over at night, to provide conveniences for their wives and children ; to do the chores of the family ; and they find that this additional work bears upon them with great severity. Some are obliged to walk miles to their tasks in the morning and to their homes in the evening, and this is the hardest of all their labours."

I shall now speak more particularly of *unseasonable* labour, of midnight slavery. Of the working-hours in manufactories, &c., I mean to give an account hereafter. Work late at night is sometimes indispensable, but where it is not, the labouring people, and servants especially, have a right to consider it, when forced upon them, as a causeless and cruel abridgement of their comforts, property, and wages. How is man or woman to get good wages but through good health, and how is good health to be kept but by means of sufficient sleep? I have spoken of temperance; if the people of the United States desire to be temperate, to make anything respectable of themselves, or of their government, they must begin betimes, and resist that aristocratic pride and folly by which, in the great cities especially, fashion has turned day into night, and so many of the labouring people are compelled to work like animals.

56. The subject of excessive and unseasonable labour is necessarily connected with the cause of temperance. The people of England are not only overworked, but worked at unseasonable hours; and this we heard often spoken of as one of the great causes of intemperance. The overworking and unseasonable working of her poor people is a disgrace to England. A man who is exhausted by labour, and who has no proper moral education to sustain him, drinks of course. The most temperate people in the world know how prone they are, in case of great bodily fatigue, of watching, of corporeal, of mental suffer-

ing, to resort to stimulants; it may be a slow poison, but they are willing to take the poison for the immediate relief. This is the reason why large classes, whose labours are particularly exhausting, as sailors, drivers of stagecoaches, forgemen, enginemen, glassblowers; tailors and shoemakers, who are enfeebled by sedentary work, and paper-manufacturers, who are exhausted over heated vats, are given to intemperance.

57. One of the first things that strikes the observer in London, is the extent to which the people have contrived to turn day into night; to change the order of nature, to sleep when other creatures are awake, and to be awake when they are at rest. Next door to my private lodgings in London there lived an old man who was a shopkeeper, with whom I had frequent conversations, and who told me that the average time of opening the shops in London was about half past seven in summer. It must be remembered, that at that hour in London there have been about four hours of daylight; that is, with light enough to enable a man to see to do ordinary work. I do not speak with certainty, though I think it must be so, as there is twilight in London during a part of the summer season the whole night. I found, by actual observation, this man's statement to be correct. A large number of shops in London are not open till eight o'clock. On the fourth day of July I went to Smithfield Cattle Market. In going up the Strand, one of the great arteries of London, and filled with shops, at

a quarter before six by the watch, there were no shops open, except perhaps half a dozen; in returning through the same street at a quarter past seven, not one shop in ten was open, these being generally bakers' shops, or belonging to that class that sell refreshments.

58. One of the proudest distinctions that exists in England for the great people, is that between the workers, and the fashionable and idle. The power of fashion there is an absolute despotism, as it is here in many things, and will be in more unless the rational people who are compelled to work, and who can here do what they please, shall choose to set up their purer standard of morals, and thus bring the fashionable under the yoke of it, as they have the power to do. There is nothing more disgusting in the United States than to witness the power (every day diminishing, however) which some of the most insignificant people have acquired over the best from long habit and the aristocratic fashion of other countries. But the bubble will burst, the charm cannot last long. By fashion here I do not certainly mean that capricious thing which consists in the length of the skirts or the cut of the capes, but something far more important. One of the first objects of these merely fashionable people in the Old World, and just as much in the New too, is to change the natural order of things; to turn things inside out; to be as unlike the common people as possible; for the nearer they are to them

the greater is the danger of vulgar contamination. Nothing is so shocking and horrible as to be like those common labouring people whose hands are in the dirt, it being forgotten that these are the hands which produce and fashion nearly all that contributes to the sustenance and comfort of man.

59. In England these people breakfast from ten to twelve in the morning; they dine from seven to eight in the afternoon. Great routs and parties at great men's houses are said to begin at eleven and half past eleven, many persons going the rounds to several in one night. These parties often last till daylight. It is quite common in the London hotels to see people breakfasting at twelve and one o'clock. Mr. Rush, who was about seven years our minister in England, says that he went to Lady Castlereagh's parties after the *opera* (her cards of invitation specifying that time); that the opera breaks up at twelve o'clock at night. An opera-going lady lately told me that at present it breaks up at one. Mr. Rush also tells us that parties beginning so late last till two or three o'clock; that most of those who have been at them do not rise till towards noon; that at about two o'clock in the afternoon commences the roll of carriages for Hyde Park; that at six in the afternoon the morning ends; that then, but scarcely sooner, the throngs of carriages, with gentlemen and ladies on horseback, disappear from the streets and parks, the hour of preparation being then at hand for dinner and for evening parties. He adds, "this is

no overdrawn account, but the daily routine ; it seems strange that health should be preserved with such habits ; yet the men look well and the women blooming." What men look well and what women look blooming? Some persons seem to think that there is but one description of people in the world, and these are the born ladies and gentlemen. If these look fair and blooming, all is well enough. The ladies and gentlemen in England are in a very different category from that of those who wait upon their pleasures. If the ladies and gentlemen spend the night at Almack's, at the opera, or the theatre, many of them at least can pass the day upon their pillows ; while the waiters, the chambermaids, the cabmen, the coachmen, &c., are compelled to begin the day as they ended it. The horses are hardly cooled and well rubbed down, before they must move into the harness again, while the ladies and gentlemen, having closed their window-shutters against the sun, order the servants to call them at twelve or one, as suits their convenience.

But, says Mr. Rush, "the men looked well and the women blooming." He cannot mean the waiters whom I saw in our hotel ; for there could hardly be a more melancholy sight than the haggard looks and sunken eyes of the men-servants in our coffee-room, who were so exhausted in the morning as to be stupid, and scarcely able to answer a common question ; nor could he mean the servant-girls whom you see cleaning the floors and dragging pails of water up and down the stairs, and who seem as wretched as the men; nor the exhausted cabmen and hackney-coachmen, who, among the most miserable of the unhappy people of London, are often seen sleeping on their stands amid the eternal din of a throng where no man could sleep whose nature was not worn out. These our fellow-men of the same flesh and blood are too often the victims of intemperance; they then abandon their wives and children; they drink to kill misery; being unable to govern themselves, they must be governed; and here we have creatures who should have been trained to virtue and honesty by the well-born, the favoured, the ladies and gentlemen, now transformed into the mob, the low people, the canaille, the servile, the menials; the desperadoes whom every good man justly fears, and whom none dare trust with free government; and then we must have a strong government, soldiers, gendarmes, to give a man safety in his own parlour. And who is most in fault if these unhappy people are demoralized, are sent to the poorhouses, to the jails, to the penitentiaries, and to the gallows? who but those who turn day into night, who compel these menials to serve at their gaming-houses, midnight banquets, and carousals? Well has it been said, "that the slavery of fashion is the dark side of civilized life." There are strong reasons why it should exist in the Old World, but not in the New; for the *slaves here must be the free-voting working people.* Whether they will yield to this empire of vanity and pride set up by a few thousand,

and a large number of these the most insignificant people in the nation, they must decide. In England they allow three or four years for working a stage-coach horse to death; what time is allotted to cabmen and hackney-coachmen, and to the waiters and chambermaids in the London hotels, I cannot say. These overworked people did not seem to me to belong to the same country with the healthy-looking part of the British nation. Lord Chesterfield predicted, in his time, that in a hundred years the trade of a monk and a gentleman would be greatly changed. By gentlemen in England they often mean a man who can live without what most of us are doomed to here, labour. The change since Lord Chesterfield's time is great, but we must not be astonished to see a greater.

60. The caprices and fashions everywhere would be merely ludicrous, if they were always as harmless as they are absurd. They have an odd hour among the great people in England for great breakfasts, or, rather, what we call a dinner, or *tea*, they call a breakfast! So they have an odd manner of speaking of their dinners; for I saw in one of the London papers a great lord's dinner announced in this way: " Lord A. entertained a select party at dinner last evening." I am not here about to discuss the question of late dinner hours, for which, in great cities, for some classes there are strong and good reasons. It must be admitted, however, that the fashions have changed greatly. Hume gives an account of an old Earl of Northumberland who lived

in the reign of Henry VII. His family rose at six in the morning, dined at ten, and supped at four in the afternoon; it consisted of a hundred and sixty-six persons; fifty-seven strangers are reckoned upon as guests every day, making in all two hundred and twenty-three persons. No sheets were used! "The drinking was tolerable, namely, ten tuns and two hogsheads of Gascony wine," I suppose per year. The lord and lady had on their table for breakfast a quart of beer, as much wine, two pieces of salt-fish, six *red* herrings, four *white* ones, or a dish of sprats. The lord kept *only* twenty-seven horses in his stable at his own charge. He passed the year in three country-seats, but had furniture only for one. One cart sufficed for all his kitchen utensils, beds, &c. He had eleven priests in his house, and only two cooks for two hundred and twenty-three persons! There is not so great a man in England now!

61. Parliament-street is the great avenue from the two houses of Parliament to Charing Cross, where you pass to the right up the Strand into the city, as the business part of London is called, or to the left up Pall Mall, which leads to the west end, the region of idleness, splendour, and fashion. As I was passing up Parliament-street I saw a number of showy carriages going out on my right, and a large collection of people standing on the pavement at the turn, some appearing to be merely gazing at the spectacle as I was, and others waiting a moment till they could avoid the rush and pass in safety. As I arrived at the spot, I found there were

some police-men stationed at the turn in the street where the carriages defiled, and, as I supposed, to keep order. Such are the excellent manners and character of these police-men, that you need never fear to ask them any proper question. I was curious to know the occasion of such a concourse of equipages, and asked the question. The man told me that it was the Duke of ——'s breakfast! It was then five o'clock in the afternoon! This was a great lord, of whom I had heard that, in travelling over the kingdom a distance of four hundred miles, he could, at moderate stages, sleep each night at some one of his numerous castles or palaces. I suppose, however, that in these days many of the stories they tell of great lords are about as true as those formerly told of great witches. Be this as it may, this gentleman is so well known in England, and so much is said about him, that there is nothing equivocal in respect to his fortune or celebrity. I afterward saw an account of this breakfast in a London paper, for there is very little that lords do that can be brought to light, and very little that they never do and that cannot be brought to light, that is not reported of them in the newspapers. I also afterward heard this gentleman in the House of Lords; and though he was not one of the stammerers whom I have heretofore mentioned, I really could not discover anything about him that entitled him to the distinction of taking his coffee so late in the morning, when the London coalmen had emptied their carts, and were getting homeward to their supper, and when we simple souls in the United States (at least some of us) take our tea! Nothing is more repulsive in the eye of reason and religion than the immense power of the idle, dissipated, fashionable people in the Old World over all its institutions, manners, and fashions. Let it ever be remembered, that it is *property* that wields this power.

This breakfast was a *rout*. We have our routs too, but seldom, if ever, at so early an hour in the day. Ours are evening routs, and the most fashionable begin at about ten o'clock. I certainly am not familiar with London routs, but I believe they are very different affairs from ours in the United States. The ladies and gentlemen who give them here possess neither castles nor palaces, nor are they able to employ upon their estates nine hundred and fifty labouring men, as Sir Walter Scott relates that the Duke of Buccleugh did at one time; on the contrary, the ladies and gentlemen here are often people of very moderate property, when estimated by the standard of these ostentatious pleasures; and all the sure estate, the terra firma, they have, is covered with a house having a front of not more than twenty-five or thirty feet, into which they occasionally squeeze two or three hundred people, sometimes taking down the children's bedsteads and sending the little ones to their uncle's and aunt's to sleep, which, I believe, is not the fashion at the Duke of ——'s.

To be serious, these routs do not conform to our fortunes; it is neither society nor hospitality, as it should be; it is the old story of the frog straining himself into the size of the ox; it is high life below stairs; it is a mean imitation, a foreign thing, a poisonous thing; and, above all, late hours are subversive of the comfort and morals of the labouring classes. This is the true and solid objection with the rational, humane, temperate people, who may in all important respects that involve the health, independence, property, and virtue of the labouring part, give the law if they will. That is, if they will assume and exert the power which naturally belongs to them. By every law of love and charity, they ought to become the protectors of the unprotected, the friends of the friendless. The vicious part of the influence of cities may be resisted here; it is far more difficult in Europe. It will be our own fault if we suffer these immoral practices, this midnight slavery, this degradation of the poorer classes, to stalk over the country and get a footing among our uncontaminated people. It is surprising that any among us should be willing to degrade their fellow-citizens in the shape of servants. It is not the degradation of serving, of helping another in his lawful business or pleasures, of which any man has a right to complain. In civilized countries all kinds of necessary useful work must be done; and the more civilized, the more various these employments. There is as little sense in objecting to be a servant, if that be a man's lot, as there would be in refusing to dig a ditch or clean the streets; the streets must be cleaned, and so must the houses. The true degradation consists in being put to work which unnecessarily impairs the strength of body and mind. To corrupt the soul of a human being; to expose him causelessly to temptation; to break down his love of virtue, in administering to our unlawful pleasures, has ever been ranked among the worst crimes. The fashion of other countries has depraved our moral sense; and it remains for the people of the United States to take the subject into their serious consideration. The highest perfection of physical existence consists in the due appropriation and division of labour; of moral, in the enjoyment of such pleasures as neither debase us nor those who serve us.

CHAPTER V.

62. A GOOD account of London would, to the people of the United States, be one of the most amusing and instructive books that could be written. I wish it were in my power to perform such a service.

Dr. Johnson wrote a poem called "London," which has merit; but not that of letting us know what London was; for it is little more a description of London than of any other great city. He says,

"London, the needy villain's general home,
The common sewer of Paris and of Rome."

One of the first sights that you see in London at seven or eight o'clock in the morning, for earlier than that a great many do not open their eyes, is a man passing rapidly with a bag under his arm, casting his quick, keen glances from one side of the street to the other, and crying, " clo, clo, clo," and sometimes "old clo, old clo, old clo." This man is said to be a Jew, who buys old clothes in the west end of London, and in other parts, for aught I know, of servants and others. From the numbers of these people, and the frequency of the cry at that hour of the day, strangers might suppose that all the inhabitants of the city wore cast-off clothes purchased from the inhabitants of some other city much better clad than those of London. I assure the reader that this is not the case, for nothing can exceed the pomp, splendour, and expense of outward appearance in some parts of London, unless it be the meanness, poverty, and misery of other parts. Ostentation and nakedness are generally very near neighbours to each other; it is but a very short distance from St. James's-street, or Hyde Park, to St. Giles's.

63. I shall here again cite Mr. Rush, whose opportunities were so much greater than my own. Speaking of the prince regent's levee on the 12th day of February, in the year 1818, he says: "The yeomen of the guards had halberts in their hands, *velvet* hats with wreaths around them, and rosettes in their shoes. There was the lord chamberlain with his gold stick and silver stick;

the cabinet ministers with bag and sword; the lord chancellor and other legal functionaries with black silk gowns and full wigs; bishops with aprons of black silk." He describes "a drawing-room" held by her majesty (upon which occasion it is customary for young ladies of fashion to be presented at court, when the queen kisses the cheeks of those who have the proper rank to be entitled to that honour), and says, " that the glitter of the carriages was heightened by the appearance of the numerous servants in glowing livery, there being generally two, and often three footmen behind the carriage." That " the horses were all in the highest condition, and, under *heavy emblazoned* harness, seemed, like war-horses, to move proudly." He describes "the hoop dresses of the ladies sparkling with lama," their plumes, lappets, &c. This was, according to Mr. Rush, very near " to the last of the hoops;" the glory of which may now be traced to rag-bags, garrets, and other lumber-rooms. He mentions an entertainment at the Duchess of Cumberland's, where there was a table set out with " golden urns for tea." And another upon the marriage of the Princess Elizabeth, when there were " on the table urns and teakettles of fretted gold." There is an old proverb, " that it is not all gold that glistens," of which we saw many proofs in England, besides those stated to us at Rundell and Bridge's, as heretofore related. He further states, that upon the dissolution of Parliament, the prince regent appeared in person, drawn by eight horses, " with golden bits adorned and purple reins." "The royal carriage drew up before the entrance of the House of Lords, a groom held each bridle, the horses champing the *foaming gold*." Upon which he makes this reflection: "Even in the insignia and decorations of a state carriage, England has not forgot the *field of her power*." He thinks "that what cripples the resources of other nations serves but to invigorate and multiply hers; and that a lord mayor's dinner will make any man hesitate whether England is to be destroyed by her present financial difficulties." It is not every one that counts the cost of these dinners, or considers who has to pay for them. A lord mayor's feast usually costs about £3000, fifteen thousand dollars. That given to George the Third cost £6898, or about thirty-four thousand dollars.* A useless charge, of course, upon labour, for who can indulge in this sort of parade and gluttony without it? This, then, is the glory that is to be held up for the admiration of the people of the United States! This is to invigorate and multiply their resources, so as to give them fair wages and a good living!

64. When the lord mayor's dinner is eaten, there is an end of it for ever. A dinner a man must have, but he need not have a dinner at the expense of poor people that costs a hundred times as much as will satisfy his appetite. If all the people of England had good dinners and other reasonable

* Percy Histories, part ii., London, 1823.

comforts, and were not obliged to buy old clothes from the Jews, there would be some sense in the argument, that it is necessary to set them to work, in order to get wages, in making velvet hats and rosettes for the king's yeomen of the guards; gold sticks and silver sticks; bags, swords, wigs, and black silk aprons; glowing livery, heavy-emblazoned harness, hoop dresses sparkling with lama; plumes, lappets, golden urns for tea, and teakettles of fretted gold; golden bits, purple reins, lord mayors' dinners, &c. That the privileged people are able to turn labour to such an account is the millstone that hangs about the neck of England. The people begin to feel the weight, and any man who goes to England may learn that fact. Men must be addressed according to the light they have; considering, therefore, what we know now in the present state of civilization, and what we want in the present state of destitution, the argument, that it is essential for the rich to indulge in this kind of expense in order to " compel the lower classes to work *even for necessaries*," is unworthy of being addressed to a Christian people, or to those who have common sense.

65. Besides, it is not the opinion at present of the real statesmen of England, that the lord mayor's dinners or the wigs of his coachmen increase its finances; for the most prudent of them have been very desirous since the war to save by cutting off pensions, and by all sorts of economy; which, to be sure, are forced upon them by the stupid waste

and destruction of property to which they have so long been accustomed: the common fate of all spendthrifts.

66. While we were in England Parliament was prorogued; and it was stated in one of the papers that the king's harness used upon that occasion cost three thousand five hundred guineas: a pretty robe for eight horses! The interest of this sum at three per cent. is 105 guineas, and more than sufficient to support four men with their families, according to the rate of agricultural wages when we were in England. Kings do not understand the common people as well as we who live with them, hear their conversation, and know what thoughts are in their minds; but they may rest assured that their race will not live the longer for jingling in the people's ears these gilded bells bought with their labour. They understand that property first comes from the earth, and they know pretty well by whose hands.

About thirty years ago, a governor of Massachusetts, and a very respectable man, travelled through our state in a coach and four, which might sometimes be seen on a Sunday at the doorsteps of our plain country meeting-houses. Such parade would now be laughed at; the present governor, in purer taste, makes his circuits in a stagecoach. When young children have outgrown their playthings, it is not worth the while to buy them any longer. State pomp is for grown-up children, and the people of the United States have made at least one good move forward by a hearty contempt of it. It is to be regretted that Mr. Rush, with the opportunities he had in a seven years' residence as minister, should not have presented to his countrymen more ample means of instruction. But the fault is not so much his as in the system. Our ministers generally, in the present state of things in the world, cannot be overburdened with business. If any man eat the bread of the people let him work for it. Let the government, then. make it the duty of the ministers to present full reports with regard to the state of agriculture, as well as the condition of the population and the state of the laws generally, in the several countries to which they are sent, in the manner in which the British government now instructs its foreign consuls. The great ameliorations which have lately taken place in the English laws as to imprisonment for debt, were the result of numerous inquiries as to the state of such laws in the United States and other parts of the world by the British government.* What agents so proper for these purposes as ministers, where they have the time? Such an employment would serve to keep them out of that idle, dissipated way of living into which so many of them fall. These reports might be made to embrace any subject which the government thought important. Some have recommended an increase of the salaries of our ministers, and given their reasons for such a

---

* See fourth report in the House of Commons by the commissioners appointed to examine into the practice and proceedings of courts of law. 1832.

measure. Any one acquainted with the preposterous style of living in Europe may give a hundred reasons. I trust that the people of the United States will suffer no such increase to be made. As they have taught Europe many other good lessons, I hope they will add this of economy. A minister has now $9000 a year, and an outfit of $9000, which in four years (and I think that the residences of our ministers even in England, that dearest of all countries, will not exceed a greater average) amounts to $11,250 a year. If an American gentleman cannot live as minister in London for this sum, not as the great there do live, but as the delegate of a republican people ought to live, he had better stay at home. Oxford-street dinners and parading in a coach up and down Hyde Park and Piccadilly will not be looked to as an evidence of the wealth and power of the United States. We shall have other titles to respect in Europe: one of them will be to find our public men conforming in their habits of living to the economical institutions of the country; and the sooner this is insisted on by the people as one of the essential qualifications for office, the better.

67. I also, though I did not participate with Mr. Rush in the glories of the drawing-room, saw some of them. As we were one day going home to our lodgings in a hackney-coach, perceiving at the head of St. James's-street that it was filled with carriages and well-dressed people to an extraordinary degree, we asked the occasion, and were told that it

was the "queen's drawing-room." St. James's-street is immediately in the rear of St. James's Palace, and I believe one of the avenues to it. The street was filled with a striking array of police-men, and there was at the head of it a detachment of horse-guards for the purpose of keeping order, as I supposed. Police-men were stationed also in the neighbouring streets. I went down the street about half its length, and taking my stand against the wall of a house, where I could not be jostled, the scene burst upon me " in a blaze of glory." The street was crammed with the most " splendid" carriages, filled with ladies in full dress. Here were servants in "glowing liveries," from which all the colours of the rainbow were streaming, and horses " in emblazoned harness champing the foaming gold." There were also the coachmen's wigs with their many delicate flaxen curls; the cocked hats, very like those of an American major-general of militia, as I have before remarked; the coachmen's white gloves, white underclothes, and silk stockings; and behind some carriages two, and, I think, three, tall, manly-looking footmen, with their long gold-headed canes. Indeed, it is not possible, by any description I can give, to do justice to what is called the "splendour" of the spectacle. In a country where so many people want bread, it seems to us a very odd use to make of two or three brave-looking fellows, to put them behind a coach with canes in their hands, as though they were placed there like constables, to keep order within.

68. I hope that none of my readers will suppose that I do not know that there must have been among these people some noble-minded, generous, patriotic individuals, who thought it best to spend their money in this way; who believed that it was the highest encouragement they could give to the arts; the most judicious way of imparting comfort to the labouring people, and far better than to scatter their money among beggars, as doubtless it is. No doubt these enormous fortunes thus spent do good. But common sense asks, do they do the most good that can be done with them? Is this the best way of distributing wealth? is it best for the people, after working hard for their money, to put it into the hands of their rulers to make this sort of parade with it? would not the people there, as the farmers, mechanics, and other working people of the United States do, use the money as wisely themselves? Are those exclusive privileges for the happiness of a people, which allow of such a division of property as indulges a very few in this kind of expensive ostentation, which is but a remnant of selfish barbarism, that equally marks these most civilized people and the most savage?

69. In London especially you may see the low estimation in which a human being is held; and this is the moral distinction which is ever present to our minds in Europe between the privileged and unprivileged countries. It is under the benevolent free system alone that man can ever be duly thought of and considered, with all his rights and powers as

a creature of God and as a fellow-man. The occupations of men here and in Europe are so different, that it is impossible to contemplate them as having the same destiny on earth under the two systems. One of the first remarks made by the working people of Europe as they come among us is, that so large a portion of the people here are engaged *in respectable business*, that which becomes a man's duty to perform, and which God has assigned to him as a necessary, indispensable work, be it as master or servant, higher or lower. This makes a serious, reflecting Christian people, who love and respect each other, for they respect each other's occupations; it weans them (though it may be by too slow degrees) from beer-drinking, dram-drinking, cock-fighting, prize-fighting, horse-gaming, from all sorts of gaming and licentiousness, and the lower classes especially from running about at the heels of idle gentlemen, who, in making profligates, fools, and paupers of themselves, by their base example destroy their fellow-men. This is the true glory of a democratic people.

70. The servants of England are a degraded class, and ever have been from the most remote ages; many are still kept for show, as court fools once were. In the reign of Henry VI., the Earl of Warwick, the king-maker, is reported to have had thirty thousand men in his service, who dined daily at his different castles. The men who landed on the rock of Plymouth had no castles. Cavendish, one of Cardinal Wolsey's servants, reckons

his whole number at between four and five hundred, most of whom dined in his hall every day. In the Northumberland household, the earl had three young gentlemen, who attended him as his pages; these pages being called Haunsmen, or Henchmen, from standing at the lord's haunch or side.*

Sumptuousness in these houses and meanness towards the servants was upon an equal footing, as is pretty generally the case down to the present day. In the Northumberland household all joints of meat were entered and accounted for by clerks; if a servant were absent a day his mess was struck off. The under servants ate salted meat throughout the whole year, so that they had a very unwholesome diet; in the same way as some luxurious people among us provide pure butter for the parlour and rancid for the kitchen. In some establishments the rule was, that whoever broke a glass should pay for it (perhaps not a very bad regulation); and if it was not known who broke it, the butler paid for it.

71. The butler of the Anglo-Saxon kings was an eminent noble. The coachman and groom originated early, in the fondness of the English for carriages and horses. Before the invention of stirrups, grooms were kept to assist their master in mounting the horse.†

72. Can there be any wonder, under such a system, that where so many able-bodied men are taken from before the mast, from the cotton-mills and the plough, and fed and clothed at the expense of the

* Domestic Life in England. London, 1835. † Ib.

rest, that many will be without bread, and "that the population (according to Mr. Malthus) must press against the means of subsistence?" Or can there be any wonder that, where men are treated in such a way as to be without any sense of their dignity as Christians, they will, like the poor people of Ireland, and like many in England, breed like animals; and, in such a case, can any one doubt that, if every now worthless acre at Newmarket, Blackheath, Wimbledon Common, or the Hampshire Downs, and all over the rest of the world, was turned into garden ground, there would still be too little bread for the people? The great mistake that Mr. Malthus made (the same that a great many others are making in their political systems) consisted in a false estimate of what human nature is capable; he even mistook the facts as to the progress of the race thus far. This was a fatal mistake, as we are now proving in the United States.

73. *Livery* had its origin in the vanity and pride of the great, which were gratified by the power displayed in a retinue of marked vassals, retainers, and servants. This also is one of the extraordinary sights of London; and though you may see it oll over England, it is elsewhere but seeing little meteors floating about here and there, whereas in London you have the sun, the centre of the system. Blue, it is said, was the most common colour for liveries formerly. The same author tells us that in the year 1623, on the occasion of a wedding, the

Earl of Bristol had thirty rich liveries, with silver lace up to the very capes of the cloaks; the best sorts of which were valued at £80, but that this sumptuousness will not compare with the splendid state liveries of the present times. That the colours of the livery of the kings of England have varied; yellow and red were the colours of the house of Stewart and George I.; scarlet and blue those of George II., III., and IV. That in old times liveries were not only worn by servants, but the *tradesmen* who served a great lord's family wore his livery.

The liveries are so various that I saw every day about London, and particularly on the occasion of " the queen's drawing-room," that it is no more possible to describe them than the milky way or the colours of the kaleidoscope. You may see a white coat turned up with red; a white coat with crimson plush underclothes; a scarlet coat with white underclothes; light blue coat with white underclothes, &c. An observing American lady told me that she never saw pantaloons on a footman, but always " shorts," meaning *breeches*. These expensive personal decorations are considered essential to English greatness; for Sir Walter Scott tells us that the robes worn by the peers at the coronation of George the Fourth cost £400 each—$2000.

The German prince, of whom some of the English critics speak so disparagingly, and for whose accuracy, therefore, I will not vouch, describes the Duke of Devonshire's coach at the Doncaster races.

There were six horses attached to it, the coachman being in flaxen wig and boots; twelve outriders, four grooms on horses of different colours, four footmen in morning jackets, leather breeches, and top-boots; the postillion who rode one of the leaders being in full state livery of yellow, blue, black, and silver, with a powdered wig! I cannot now be sure that the wigs I saw in St. James's-street, upon the occasion of the " queen's drawing-room," were powdered, though I suppose they were; but this I will say, that in the west end of London, at the doors of great houses, I have seen many a powdered servant's head; and why should the servants be marked by these monkey decorations, which taste among the masters has generally discarded?

Mr. Cooper says that in noble houses in London the footmen are selected for their great height and manly port; so that his little man, who just peeped above his master's shoulders as he sat at dinner, could not escape the jeers and laugh of his fellows. It is the business of a footman to stand behind his master's carriage with a gold-headed cane in his hand, to open the carriage-door, and so on; thus we see that, in a country which boasts so much of its advances in political economy, the smallest work is put into the strongest hands. When we were in London we saw a young American, who told us that he did not see the objection to livery, and that he wondered why so many of his countrymen were disgusted with it. No man here can form any adequate conception of the vast sums wasted upon this foppery by a people under a load of eight hundred millions pounds sterling of debt.

74. Let us see, then, if there be any objection to livery, besides its cost. The propriety of livery in a republican country is worth discussing. There are those who do not consider it inconsistent with our republican institutions. They admit that the expensive liveries of Europe are objectionable, but say that livery may consist of a single badge, a yellow button, a gold band, or anything which shall merely denote the condition of the wearer and his relation to his employer; that a master has a right to make such a contract with his servant. What, then, does livery denote? That the wearer is a servant; but why should a servant be distinguished by a servile badge rather than other hardworking people, like the *tradesmen* in ancient times?

The true objection, then, to livery here, is, that it creates one of the European associations of degradation. As an ancient mark of slavery, it is bad enough where it originated; there it has the sanction of custom and antiquity; but in this free country, where a man, however humble his origin, becomes elevated according to the soul that is in him, it is a mean imitation. To make a man dress so as to mark him as an inferior; to compel him to wear his master's coat, his finery, is to exercise a wanton power over him by taking advantage of his poverty. It is a petty tyranny, that is and ought to be disgusting to freemen. Livery, as it

110 PUBLIC AND PRIVATE ECONOMY.

is in Europe, "a coat of many colours," with all its monkey decorations, or livery, plain as it might be, are both creations of pride and folly, that, by engendering hatred and hostility, divide man from man, and are denounced by all pure religion. Our native population despise livery, and will not submit to it. There are a few paltry attempts made just now to renew this servitude, but the inbred disgust of the *native white* American revolts from it. "It is the poverty, and not the will," of the foreigner that consents to it. This poverty need be but a very short-lived excuse with sober and industrious men. It is high time that all the hard-working people of the United States, servants and not servants, should have opinions of their own in all matters that respect their rights and happiness, and exercise them manfully.

75. The secrets of American wealth and happiness will not long remain undiscovered in Europe; and when fully brought to light, they will rouse men as they have never been roused. They lie in practising the principles of Christian benevolence towards all men; in assigning to them respectable and useful occupations; in setting them to work here for a greater proportion of useful objects than have ever been laboured for in other parts of the world, by which, in benefiting not only ourselves, but others, we early obtain just ideas of property. We therefore keep few liveried servants, superfluous grooms, footmen, outriders, and other mere cumberers of the ground, to gratify vanity, pride, and sensual-

ity: the regard in which we hold all men (I speak of the free States), unworthily as this sentiment is yet carried into practice, is our proudest distinction; it is our religion interwoven in our constitutions, theories of government, and institutions generally; it is the universal hope of property, of rising, of gratifying the inextinguishable desires of the mind, that press us on with irresistible energy. The people of the United States are amazed to see the rulers of Europe, many of whom, in other respects, they know to be men of virtue and sense, who have in their hands so great a portion of its property, squandering it upon the mummery of livery, coronations, and other foolish pageants; and they detest the privileged system by which such a power is wielded. They go to the root of the matter, and know that men could not live, and spend, and squander in this way, but through monopolies and abuses; they know perfectly that so many of the rich could not live in the vain, sensual, and wicked way in which they have heretofore, in a free and equal state of society; that, where there is a natural and fair division of property, this will become impossible. They look upon the republican system, therefore, notwithstanding the dangers that seem to surround its infant growth from party selfishness, as at war with the worst vices of men; and expecting from it the most glorious results in purifying and ennobling the human character, they will go on with undoubting faith in our destiny.

CHAPTER VI.

76. The earliest accounts we have of London are from Tacitus about the year sixty-one, when the Romans were driven from it by the Britons, who, in turn, were expelled by the Roman general, Agricola.

I shall in this chapter first state some general facts in regard to London, then speak of the causes of its great population, and make some comparisons between city and country.

London is the rendezvous of what we should call a considerable army. There are generally in London about three regiments of foot-guards, of twelve hundred men each.* Hyde Park, in the west end of London, contains about four hundred acres. The principal entrance to it is through two archways, within a few feet of each other, and in the immediate neighbourhood is Lord Wellington's town-residence, Apsley House. Hyde Park presents one of the most "splendid" exhibitions of the fashion of London. I have taken a stand between the two arches, and gazed at it for a full hour. At high tide, about six o'clock in the afternoon, one might suppose that all the elegant carriages and fashionable people, not in England alone, but in the empire, were collected in Hyde Park. Stages and hackney-coaches are not

---

* England and the English.

allowed to enter.* What a misery it is in these countries not to be rich! It is true enough that the hackney-coach of London is a vile, filthy-looking thing, and the horses are wretched, and the driver is wretched, and the waterman is wretched. Wretched as they are, however, all in London who are not rich are doomed to ride in cabs or hackney-coaches. This hackney-coach is a disgrace to London, and would be to any civilized people; it is so dirty as to be fit only for beggars; when you see it with all its equipments, you would suppose that a company of street beggars had taken it for an airing; and I do not wonder that it is said that fashionable people, who are a little squeamish, are ashamed to see one of them at their doors. Such will be the miserable accommodations, in the end, of all but the affluent, wherever property is mismanaged as it is in England. It is to be hoped that the people of the United States will very early accustom themselves to the enjoyment of *good and respectable things of every kind,* and that they will not shut those who cannot afford to ride in coaches out of their parks and pleasure-grounds. It is equally to be hoped that we shall furnish parks and pleasure-grounds for those poor people who cannot provide them for themselves, which is far from being the case at present. If so, we shall certainly be able to find *profitable and respectable work* for all the working-people, and thus save both rich and poor from spending so

* Guide to London, 1830.

much of their money in the silly, selfish way they do in England. But it is not in England alone that money is so spent. This is one of the remedies by which we propose to rescue the people from so much *overbreeding* and pauperism as there is in England and Ireland, a remedy which we are actually administering here, and which Mr. Malthus could not understand as well as we do who have discovered it, and are using it with success.

77. Mr. Bulwer states the direct cost of royalty thus : Civil list, exclusive of pensions, £411,800; three regiments of horse-guards, £80,000 ; pensions to royal family, £220,000; for servants to different branches of the royal family, £24,000. The whole is usually stated at a million sterling, or about five millions of dollars. How much it is necessary for royalty in England to spend in order to be royalty, it is impossible for us to understand.

78. I have stated, in the second part of this work, some facts to show to what extent gaming has declined in many parts of the United States in a very brief period. This moral and intellectual improvement here is as certain as any other facts in regard to the people.

The great gaming-houses of London are called "hells," and are among its most extraordinary establishments. How a great people, who hope to continue at the head of the world, can support such nuisances, is inexplicable. These hells are not sustained, as one would suppose, by blacklegs, swindlers, and cheats alone, but, in a great measure, by gentlemen, young nobles, and titled men of every degree, such as you see riding in their coaches and on horseback in Hyde Park. I could mention a considerable list of the most eminent men in the empire, of the present and former times, who have been frequenters of these hells; but this is not necessary, and delicacy forbids the use of living names unless it be so. We have our hells too; not exactly in the English style, to be sure; and public men of the greatest distinction who frequent them; but in numbers, in boldness, and publicity, gaming is a very different affair here and in England.

These hells are not in alleys, dark holes, and out-of-the-way places, as would be most becoming, but they stare you in the face in the most beautiful quarters of London. Crockford's, the greatest gaming-house in London, is on the right as you go out of Piccadilly down St. James's-street; and here an honest man is compelled to tread the same pavement with the rogues who live upon what they squeeze from the industrious people; for how else can an idle, gaming, cheating man live? That nine out of ten of all gamblers are cheats, by some direct or indirect device, trick, feigned countenance, or something else that a man of strict honour is ashamed of, every one knows who is at all well acquainted with the matter. One would not believe it possible that the keen, sagacious, hard-working people of the United States, who profess to be a religious people, and among whom religion, true religion, is certainly growing, could ever employ in their honourable service gamblers and spendthrifts, if the disgraceful fact did not stare us in the face. A gambler, in nine instances out of ten, is a cold, selfish, gluttonous, dram-drinking, money-wasting creature, who will, of course, rob the people, directly or indirectly, who employ him. His heart becomes callous, and he cares not for his fellow-man. At one of these hells a man dropped down in a fit. The players thereupon betted upon his coming to life or not. Some person proposed that he should be bled, to which the rest objected, *as it would spoil the bet.* Horace Walpole tells the story.

78. Play, in these houses, is carried on from one o'clock in the afternoon through the night; splendid suppers and choice wines being given to allure customers. The profits of a single hell in one season have been supposed to be £150,000 ($750,000): in a single night a million of money is said to have changed hands.*

Crockford's is said to have been built at an expense of sixty thousand pounds, and furnished for thirty-five thousand. Its interior splendour is not exceeded in London. The saloon is from fifty to sixty feet in length; on each side are two mirrors; the plate alone of the four cost a thousand guineas; the chairs are stuffed with down; the suppers are given by Mr. Crockford; there are 750

---

* Leigh's New Picture of London, 1830.

members of the establishment, who pay twenty guineas entrance money, and ten guineas yearly subscription. Mr. Crockford's cook is the celebrated Ude, whose salary is a thousand guineas a year, five thousand dollars. The cellar out of which the house is supplied contains a stock valued at £70,000, in which there are three hundred thousand bottles on shelves. Young noblemen, just beginning the world in this line, are called " pigeons ;" and are said to be plucked sometimes in a single night to the tune of £5,000, £7,000, or £10,000. The last-mentioned particulars are taken from a book lately published, called " The Great Metropolis," the exact accuracy of which I will not vouch for; but that is not important as to details, when the principal facts as to this enormous establishment, and others of the like kind in London, are well known. And who pay this enormous expense but the working people? if any part of the money has come from a rich father, it is a hundred to one that he never drove the plough to get it; if the members of Parliament voted it, they never earned it; if the king gave it, he never dug for it. Let the working man, then, take heed to his own gaming desires, for he may be sure that these " hells" are all, great and small, lighted up at his expense. I have seen in a single wheat-field in England not less than thirty men and women at work ; some of the women were mothers, and the little children were taken care of under the hedges and shade-trees by the older ones, who should have been at school or at home under their mother's wings; these are some of the harvests that stuff Crockford's chairs with down and fill his cellars with port and Champagne. This is taking bread out of poor people's mouths.

79. The unanswerable reason why the world at large is so poor, and why we in the United States are comparatively so rich and happy, is, that the privileged have been permitted to use the labour of the poor and unprivileged as they chose, and they have chosen, as men will in all such cases, to gratify their pride and vanity.

In part I., section 219, I have given some account of the labour expended in building the pyramids of Egypt, and of the *nutritious food of onions, radishes, and garlic,* with which the labourers were fed while the work was going on. Westminster Abbey and St. Paul's in London, and the palaces and castles spread over the country, are the pyramids of England, and show how an immense portion of the people's labour has been expended. Westminster Abbey was built by Henry III., and finished after fifty years of labour. St. Paul's Church, rebuilt by Sir Christopher Wren, was begun in 1675 and finished in 1761.* A mere niche only in both is devoted to divine service. To build huge temples of stone and mortar in honour of the Deity is

---

* Edinburgh Encyclopedia, tit. London.

not the service he requires of us. If these had been structures for the dissemination of every kind of religious and useful knowledge among the people, all the purposes of infusing a taste for real grandeur and architectural beauty might have been equally answered. But it was not the business of those times to enlighten the people and make them happy in each other.

80. To make people virtuous, you must make them comfortable; misery produces an immense proportion of the desperadoes that infest London. When we were in London we went to see St. Giles's, which is a particular quarter of the city, but which we supposed to consist of a single street. Entering a shop, we asked for St. Giles's; the man said "this is St. Giles's;" upon which we requested him to show us to the most curious parts of it. He directed us to Lawrence-street, as we understood the name; and, indeed, it was such a sight as we had never seen before! No state-prison population that we ever saw could compare with it. The street itself, if it could be called a street, looked more like a long, narrow den than anything else. No man but a resident would dare to enter it even in broad daylight; and we were told that it would not be safe to do so without the protection of the police. As we looked into this den, the people rushed out of their holes, appearing more like wild beasts than human creatures. It was the most painful sight of beings, formed out of the same

dust with ourselves, that we had ever seen. From the looks of the place, not a breath of pure air could ever enter those dark recesses, or a flower ever blossom on a window-sill to delight these miserable people; it seemed as though nature had not made the smallest provision for their happiness. These are the natural evils of an overgrown city; the poor wretches being pent up like sheep which are picked out one after the other for slaughter. Can the lordly palaces, the gorgeous equipages, the liveried and powdered servants compensate for these moral deformities? People who saunter through the west end and rich parts of London may think that it is all gold and glory, but the case is far different from that.

81. To talk of mobs may be thought rather a delicate matter at this period (1838) for a citizen of the United States. If my reader has been in London, he may by chance have been in an omnibus, and seen an Irish country gentleman rush into it breathless, saying that he believed, upon his life, that he had just escaped from the jaws of a *swell mob*. In London a swell mob is composed of a dozen or more desperadoes, as need requires, who, taking occasion of a mob gathered in the streets, or perhaps after stirring up a mob for the express purpose, beset you at midday in the most frequented parts of the town, and then surrounding you, one cries out, "Jack, don't run over the gentleman," another, " Boys, why do

you crowd him ?" and so on, and the deed is done, your watch and pocket-book are gone, and so is the swell mob.

Mr. Jefferson also speaks of mobs. But he does not say " that great cities are great sores," as has been imputed to him ; though he does say " that the *mobs* of great cities add just as much to the support of pure government, as sores do to the strength of the human body. It is the manners and spirit of the people which preserve a republic in full vigour. A degeneracy in these is a canker which soon eats to the heart of its laws and constitution."*

82. After having alluded to the subject of mobs in the United States, it would not be thought doing justice to the subject to leave it here. London has been famous for mobs from the days of Jack Cade down to those of Lord George Gordon, and even later ; and it must be admitted that we have acquired some little notoriety in this way. The design of our Declaration of Independence was to make known to the world a solemn determination to establish and maintain in these then colonies, now United States, the empire of law, reason, and liberty. The question may now, therefore, very properly be asked how far we have persevered in this noble resolution. There has arisen within a very few years, to the astonishment of the rest of the world, and even of ourselves, a spirit of disor-

* Jefferson's Notes on Virginia, p. 245.

ganization, of misrule, of mob-law equally dishonourable to the cause of democracy and fatal to liberty, if persisted in. It has run like a sort of wild fire or pestilential disease through the country, seeking to establish a new sort of law here; not the law of the Declaration of Independence, but the law of the tyrant, who sets aside the law of the people, and says, "I am the Gaul who carries right on the point of his sword;" it is the law of the bludgeon, the dirk, the bowie-knife, the bully, the ignorant, conceited contemners of all that is decent and sacred in society. The shame is the greater, because this mob-law is not natural to the people of the United States; till lately, they have seldom been disgraced by it; there has not been one mob here to twenty in the most civilized parts of Europe for the last fifty years. Many of these mobs (*not all*) have been made up of mere boys and ragamuffins.

At length this mob spirit has burst out in a new form; it is now (1838) overrunning the borders in the greatest state in the Union, in the midst of large towns and an enlightened population; it usurps the reins of government, sets at defiance the laws of honour and neutrality, collects an army on the frontier, and makes war for the nation. There is no name of disgust and abhorrence that these rebels against law and order are not worthy of; and it is this abhorrence which all good people who love the country and reverence its institutions as the gift of God, feel intensely that will put an end to their malpractices. If people will have a government, they must have law; and if they will have a democratic government, they must put in force the law which the majority have made. The very beasts of the field have no worse tyranny than to let each one do as he will according to the length of his claws and teeth.

By the returns of 1831, there were in London 1,646,288 souls; it is supposed that there are now about two millions. Cobbett used to call London the " wen," meaning that it was an enormous pampered excrescence upon the body politic. London has about six or seven times the population of New-York. When any man sees such a city as London, Paris, or New-York, he naturally asks, in amazement, How do these people live? how do they earn their bread in such a narrow space? and, indeed, it seems a mystery which no man can solve. It becomes an important question, then, how far this wonderful population is necessary, healthful, natural. Whence proceed these immense accumulations of property in the hands of a few? how do so many obtain the means of living in idleness and sensuality? whence these lordly palaces? whence these thousands of liveried, powdered slaves, in the name of servants? Whence this unnatural distribution of the comforts that God intended for all his creatures? where is the property that the labourers have worked for and produced? whence this disgusting waste of their earnings in carousing, in midnight banquets, in over-eating and drinking, and other sensual indulgences? How is it that so many wretched, half-fed, half-clothed people are here congregated in holes and dens like wild beasts? how came such an immense number of rogues, thieves, gamblers, swindlers, collected in one little territory not larger than one or two of our country towns? How far is this necessary, desirable, and, if not desirable, how far can it be counteracted in the United States? These are questions well worth the attention of the people. It is generally thought that some cities naturally grow to this enormous size, like London and Paris, just as a tree expands and attains to a great height if circumstances are favourable. Let us see how far this is the case. What are our cities to be?

83. The frogs, being a free nation, says the fable, petitioned Jupiter for a king. He sent them a log, but they found it insensible. They petitioned for a king that should be active; he sent them a stork. The stork gobbled them up. If a people, then, will have a king, a court, a nobility, they must give them privileges by which they can be supported, and, of course, a place in which to spend their money; in England this place is London.

84. What, then, is the cause of this overgrown city? There are many. *First*, One of the obvious causes of a great population in any one place, is the expenditure there of large sums of money. Hume

says that Queen Elizabeth attempted by proclamation to prevent the growth of London, and restrain the people from putting up new buildings; and King James told the nobles to go into the country, for that in " London they looked like ships in the sea, which showed like nothing;" but " that in their country villages they were like ships in a river, which looked like great things."* Hume goes on to say that this was against the policy of all princes theretofore, which had been "to allure the nobility to court; to engage them in expensive pleasures, which dissipate their fortune; to increase their subjection to ministers; to weaken their authority in the provinces by absence; these have been the common arts of arbitrary government." It is the court and nobility, then, who spend such great sums in London that contribute to its enormous size, compared with other parts of the country. Many of the great men in England have houses in London, in which they reside during the fashionable season, which continues from the sitting of Parliament till its close, late in the summer. Then it is that they retire from the cares of the nation to partridge-shooting, commencing about the first of September.

85. *Second*, England attracts to herself, and more especially to London, the wealth of all her colonies. If England had allowed other nations to enjoy freely the same liberty that she loves, their cities and towns would have grown too. Providence has furnished a

* Hume's History, Life of James I.

natural bounty for all mankind. England has a hundred millions of subjects in India; their wealth also has been poured into the lap of London. Few Englishmen go to India meaning to die there, but rather to amass a fortune, and then return and enjoy it in London. The West Indies also, with their seven or eight hundred thousand slaves, have been toiling to the same end; and then the blood of poor Ireland has been made to water this wonderful city. Ireland is a country owned by a comparatively small number of nobles and gentlemen. Many of these have their home in London, in Paris, and all over the world except where it ought to be. The people of the United States have scarcely an adequate idea of the perverted state of existence in Europe. Our working people, for the most part, stay at home, where their estates, farms, and duties are, and so should all men. Give men property enough to live without labour, and nine out of ten of them will lead a vagabond's life, of course. Let the people of the United States, then, beware how they build up cities or anything else by patronage and favour, to be ten times as great as they should be.

86. *Third*, In these various ways an immense number of strangers are constantly collected in London, who are emptying their pockets into it as fast as they can. In London it is said (as I have stated in part second) that a pound a day, that is, five dollars, is a reasonable allowance for a traveller, a single gentleman, living in the hotels. This is given

as a good general rule for people living moderately, prudently, either Americans or English, which is equal to thirty-five dollars a week, and eighteen hundred and twenty-five dollars a year! The main articles paid for are eating, drinking, lodging, washing, servants, seeing sights, hacks, cabs, &c. Clothes, charities, books, and the nameless expenses of a good home, are of course left out. Consider what an immense amount is here for gormandizing and parade; people do not think so now, but they will some day or another. There are no doubt many economical people that live for less; but then, again, to your luxurious, very rich, and fashionable people, this pound a day is a mere bagatelle; they would be ashamed to speak of it, or have it known that they lived in so mean a way. The Clarendon is one of the fashionable hotels of London. I had a friend who stayed at the Clarendon twenty-four hours, and paid twelve dollars, there being nothing extraordinary included in his bill. This is one of the ways in which these great cities are bloated and pampered; in which one man, through ostentation and sensuality, spends ten or a hundred times more than is good either for his body or soul; and another, who, by nature, is as good as he, is not able to scrape together the half of what either his body or soul demands. In the neighbourhood of London I saw some of the poor Essex labourers, who at home worked for ten shillings a week, and who had come to the neighbourhood of London, during the haying season, in the hope of earning a trifle more, leaving their wives and children behind them, and often sleeping in barns and stables at night!

87. We are at an immeasurable distance from the magnificent expenses of London; and then, again, this superb way of living for our country travelling youth, many of whom at home are obliged to groom their own or their father's horses, is not an everyday affair. At the Clarendon, the visiters, or many of them, are the princes, nobles, and gentlemen who own the country; they have the merit, at least, of being dignified and consistent; they live in this style everywhere. This taste for foolish expenses on the part of our country people, who rush into our Clarendons, the fashionable follies of New-York, and other great cities, will not flourish long; we shall become ashamed of it; the natural good sense of our people will break through such extreme folly. Besides, if the labouring people of the United States keep their eyes upon their polar star, *a natural and healthful division of property*, this stupid waste of it will here become impossible; and so will the unnatural and diseased population of London.

88. *Fourth*, It is not difficult to find another reason for the overgrown population of London and the other great privileged cities of Europe. These capitals, being the pets of the kings, queens, and great people, are, as such, cosseted and fed, which, of course, must be done mainly at the expense of the country. We have just had an account of the enormous expense of the queen's coronation. In Europe the people

are legislated for, and plays and amusements provided for them, as we do for children; they, of course, paying for the whistle. Like children, they are ever in the arms of the nurse; that nurse is the government.

Having seen one pageant in London, that is, the commemoration of the battle of Waterloo on the eighteenth of June, we saw another at Paris, the celebration of the *three days of July*. (It was stated, while we were there, how many thousand francs the government paid for this show, but the amount I do not recollect.) The sports took place in the Champs Elysees, Elysian Fields. During the greater part of the three days, an immense concourse of people stretched from the palace of the Tuileries to the Arc l'Etoile, one of the great barriers of Paris, about two miles, over much of which space, booths, tents, and places for theatrical exhibition were built. These sports were adapted to all ages; such as marbles, throwing at joke, flying-horses, stage-plays, mat de cocagne, &c. As I am sure the sight of the last would amuse my country friends, I will describe it as well as I can.

89. The mat de cocagne is a pole about seventy feet high, and twelve or eighteen inches diameter, looking like a small mast, and is placed firmly in the ground. There is a slight enclosure, the ground is covered with tan bark, or some substance of the like kind, and within which are a few police, who regulate the sport. The pole is perfectly round, and *greased*. Some objects were

on the top of it, but I could not distinctly see what. A friend said that on a former occasion there were a gold watch, a silver watch, and a silver knife and fork. The feat to be performed is to climb the pole and bring down the prizes. I was very near, and had a distinct view of the whole scene. The first climber ascended, I think, about four or five feet, and then came down like a log. I cannot recollect all the contrivances to accomplish what seemed to be impossible. Some made the greatest efforts with the arms and knees; some tried their heels; some their toes; some the hollow of the foot. I think it was understood that the raw hands preceded, for I believe that in nearly every case the last man ascended highest. Some got on by violent jerks, and then rested; but the rest was like a man stopping his cart on a steep slippery hill, without anything to block the wheels. Some having ascended a little higher than others, would attempt to rest, when the grease softening under their hands and feet, the descent became inevitable; and the farther that each had got up, the quicker they came down; and one circumstance was universal, there was no stopping in coming down. Some had large pockets, in which they carried ashes to throw upon the pole to assist the ascent. In this case, they were obliged to hold on with knees, feet, and one hand and arm, and scatter the ashes with the other hand. But I could not see that much was accomplished by the expedient. To shorten what might be a longer story,

I stayed till eight or ten had tried in vain, no one of whom ascended higher than ten or twelve feet, at the end of which time I was driven off by the rain. The whole affair seemed to me "like Dame Partington's attempt to sweep out the Atlantic as it was rising into her lower story in a time of high spring tide." But still my friend told me that two years before he had seen every prize carried off. Such is the fun which the great cities in Europe enjoy at the expense of the country people, if it be true that the money is furnished by the nation, and not the city, which I suppose it to be; and if it be not, the moral is much the same, as long as these playthings are provided for by public authority.

90. *Fifth*, Another of the causes of the overgrown population of London is, that cities live upon the follies and vices of the country; I mean *the diseased, the pampered, the "wen" part of them.* Their merchants ransack the world for whatever they can find good or bad, and pour all promiscuously into the country, which they call trade and commerce, and would make us believe that everything that is trade, that employs ships, pays mechanics for building them, and sailors for navigating them, is enriching to a country. This is making "money stir." This is the old story of "the fable of the bees; or private vices, public benefits." Barclay, of whose establishment I gave some account in part second of this work, sends his beer over England, and many other parts of the world. If a man be a strict temperance man, who has given

a pledge of total abstinence, he thinks Barclay's beer poison for people in health; and if he is not, and is a reasonable man, he knows that the people of England drink ten or twenty times more beer than is good for them. Upon all this, be it more or less, Barclay gets the profit; his pockets are filled and the people's are emptied. He is one of the beer gods in London, and the poor creatures in the country are smacking their lips and thinking that so much beer is *good* for them, and making them *strong*, while they are growing poorer and meaner every day.

Here, too, we have impure trade that is constantly impoverishing and demoralizing the country; our own beer, wine, gin, whiskey merchants. I speak here only of excess; and without going into a discussion of the doctrine of the temperance societies, or the teetotallers, the proof is sufficient that we drink of these liquors as the English do of beer, at least as great a proportion, if not greater, than is good for us. Those who vend these liquors in such destructive quantities, if they be successful, build what they call "palaces" in our London, New-York. These practices pollute the morals and corrupt the public taste; and then it follows that the squandering part of the community cover the shoulders of their wives and daughters with thousand-dollar shawls, and give routs at which the guests are so numerous that even the *staircases* are crowded, and so sumptuous that the unhappy, disgraced servants, after draining the half-emptied Champagne bottles, are incapable of setting the breakfast-tables in the morning.

91. These are some of the modes of emptying the wealth of the country into the cities. Then, again, our country youth resort to our Clarendons instead of to economical establishments suited to their fortunes; unfledged boys, the greater part of whom were saved in their father's halls from the seduction of " Brahmin, Lynch, old and superior pale sherry, brown sherry, White Top, Black Top, Eclipse, Joly, Heidsick," &c., by the more bountiful cider and beer barrels. Besides, we have all the electioneering feasts, dinners, sights, pageants, hells, that can possibly be got up in the cities to make the country people who resort to them spend their money like children.

92. And now the great god, Fashion, blows his trumpet on the hills and in the valleys, and away we go to sell our cotton, sugar, wheat, cheese, butter, wool, &c., to buy his wares—the fashions; fans, feathers, flounces, capes, flowers; anything that is blacker, whiter, bluer, greener, rounder, narrower, longer, shorter, larger, smaller than it was the previous season; something that the milliners, tailors, and other fashionable providers in London, Paris, and New-York have got together. Of course, I do not speak of those new, valuable, and beautiful productions which, being introduced by the improvements of successive seasons and ages, are among the great causes of trade and the civilization of

mankind, and which are not to be rejected, except so far as individual prudence and economy require.

People who live by these arts are the leeches that suck the best blood of the country, and never furnish any aliment by which it is restored to the body; in a large city there is, in numbers, an army of those who live by selling fashions; good, bad, or ridiculous, it is all one to them, but not to us. This is grinding the wind for a living; the grinder must be paid, but what does he produce? There are political economists who think it necessary, in the stagnant world in which they have lived, to take things as they are; who do not consider what is best to be done, and only what has been done; who do not even dream of what is going on here, and they tell us that all this "is good for trade; that it keeps people at work, and makes their money stir;" which, in a certain sense, is true, and would be very wise, if there were not more effectual ways in the United States "of making people industrious and their money stir." It must be remembered that it is one thing "to make money stir," and another to make money. All practical political economy must have reference to the intelligence of a people, and the improvements that are going on among them. Those who write here upon economy will write for the *New*, not the *Old* World; their ideas must be graduated upon a scale upon which are marked out vast numbers to be provided for. It is as certain that there will be a revulsion in our moral sentiments upon the subject of our present modes of living, as that there are revulsions in trade; the want of the one creates the other. The extravagant ultras of the present day will become the vulgar by-and-by.

93. The fashions that I have mentioned are a disgrace to a republican people, who divide property equally, or nearly so, among their children; who profess to hate aristocracy and the unnatural accumulation of riches, especially in great cities, and who say that they are determined not to travel the old road, which leads to making the rich richer than they should be, and the poor poorer than they need be. It is with a nation as it is with an individual, the manner in which he spends his money shows what is to become of him; if he spend it for nothing, he will come to nothing.

Let me, then, advise my country friends, who do not see how the great cities grow at their expense, to start from one end of a fashionable shopping-street in a great city, and go up the whole length on one side of it, and come down the other, taking a good look into the shops and stores on both sides, and comparing the ten thousand fine, pretty, dear, fashionable things, the things that are childish, frivolous, or insignificant, and often equally destructive of health and respectability, with what would adorn themselves, their towns and villages; with good, graceful, durable clothing, and enough of it, such as is suited to health and the seasons; with the numberless household comforts that good livers value so much; with good farms, gardens, and their world of fruits and flowers; fine breeds of cattle and horses; roads, trees for shade, pure water for the health, cleanliness, and convenience of villages; with proper provisions for the poor and those bereft of reason; good schools, books, and all the nameless pleasures of hospitality, good society, and Christian civilization. If, however, our farmers, mechanics, and other country people of moderate property will carry their small profits of one, two, or three hundred dollars a year; their kids, goats, and little ewe lambs, to be sacrificed upon the altars of the insatiable fashionable city gods, they must, like all such worshippers, take poverty, leanness, and meanness for their portion.

The useful objects I have above enumerated are in universal demand, or, rather, may be made so; they are things that belong to human nature in every form, which all men want, or should want. I ask, then, if their production will not give vigour to trade, occupation to mechanics and all kinds of labourers, equally with the others, " and make money stir and trade flourish as fast ?"

94. I have thus far feebly illustrated how far London is made up of a diseased, unnatural population, created at the expense of other parts of the country and the world at large. I have shown how much of it is the consequence of monopoly, of patronage, of allowing the government an unreasonable control over the property of the people. I have shown how it is increased at the expense of the country, by the hells, the gin palaces, the su-

perfluous distilleries and breweries: how the money of the people is spent in coronations and other silly pageants; in gormandizing; in wine, gin, rum, brandy, not required for the good of either body or soul; in gewgaws, trinkets, and all sorts of fashionable finery.

Here is a lesson for the people of the United States! Even the people of England, that is, many of them, are getting better thoughts into their minds, and this is true, too, of some of the noble-minded among the great and favoured. Even in that country of strange, unaccountable privileges, no man can observe what is passing in the minds of the more thinking part of the working-people, without seeing that they keep steadily in view as the great cure (that which I have so much insisted upon), *a more righteous and equal division of property*, and that they perceive that this cannot be brought about without knocking off the chains which their own pride, folly, and following after the squandering part of the aristocracy, have put upon them. The enlightened working-people of Europe see that sweating, striving, panting for riches to be thus abused, is a great wickedness and supreme folly. May God speed these patriotic people on their way, and give them a pole star to guide them on an unknown ocean to an undiscovered country. As to ourselves, our freer institutions have given us the chart, the compass, and the courses and distances clearly marked out; may we, then, become a blessing to the poor people of Europe; may our follies be overruled, and may we be set up as a righteous example in this Heaven-favoured land!

95. It would be a very one-sided view of the subject to consider the above as the only causes that have created the vast population of London. As civilization advances, and as a people become numerous, there is a great, natural, and salutary tendency to concentration. Besides, a great and noble cause of the real grandeur of London is the superior freedom of England to that of all the great continental nations. This it is, no doubt, in great part, that has given such celebrity to her merchants, such power to her trade, and made her the mart of the world. This freedom, though still trammelled, is showing what its giant strength will become. The people are proving what they may be under the *new dispensation of a healthful and just division of property*, not brought about by violent revolutions and agrarian disorders, but by their own virtuous, intelligent efforts.

96. Let us now, therefore, look at the other side of the picture; at some of the advantages of a dense, industrious, virtuous population. London is not all "wen." Large cities are not evils or sores, of course, but the vicious and unnecessary parts of large cities are evils. It is an evil to build up by artificial means large cities at the expense of the country. A dense population of happy, industrious beings is an immense advantage, God having created the earth that we should increase, multiply, and replenish it; that is, fill it with excellent things

for the good of all, instead of our own eternal, selfish cravings.

It is in the greatest cities that we see the most perfect specimens of nearly all the work that is performed by man. In London everything nearly, houses, docks, pavements, lights, carts, coaches, &c., &c., are more perfect than in New-York or anywhere in the United States. In large cities, in consequence of the great variety of wants and work, there is a demand for the labour of all poor people, of old and young, and even for those who can do but a little, the lame, the sick, the decrepit; and then there is work, too, for every description of talent.

Then, again, in great cities there is an immense advantage in having a large body of people to do the work that is to be done. In thinly-settled countries more labourers are wanted even to plough the land, erect the houses, and build the bridges. Thinly-settled countries, like Poland and Russia, are poor, compared with those that are thickly peopled, as Holland, Flanders, and England. Wherever there are great numbers there may be, and most often are, the advantages of a *nice division of labour*, which enables us to obtain manufactured things at a vastly less cost than we otherwise should; in other words, *cheap* things, which is desirable to everybody.

97. The advantages of a *nice division of labour*, by which things are made *cheap*, arises from the dexterity which a man acquires by doing one thing

alone, which was pointed out by Xenophon more than two thousand years ago, as plainly as it ever has been since. He says, "Nor are those which have been mentioned the only reasons why the dishes sent from the king's table are grateful to those who receive them; they are in themselves far more delicious to the taste than others. And, indeed, it is not surprising that this should be the case, for, as other arts are practised to much greater advantage in large cities, so the king's viands are dressed in the most exquisite manner. For, in small towns, the same persons are employed to make a bedstead, a door, a plough, a table; frequently, too, the very same man is a house-builder, and thinks himself well off if he finds a sufficient number of employers to enable him to earn a livelihood. It is impossible that a man practising a great variety of trades can be perfect in them all. But in great cities, where there are many who have a demand for each article, an individual gets a sufficient living by exercising a single profession, and not even the whole of that; but one man makes shoes for men, and another for women only. Sometimes, even, one man maintains himself by sewing shoes, and another by cutting them out," &c.*

98. A dense population is most favourable to arts, sciences, discoveries, inventions, and to many of the beautiful and useful refinements of life. Why should the bounty of Heaven be wasted? It is a

* Lord Lauderdale on Public Wealth, ch. v., note.

fancy to suppose that people are the happier for being scattered over an immense surface ; on the contrary, the design of this magnificent system must have been to make many happy, and not a few, one here and there another, each occupying, like a wild animal, more ground than is necessary for his subsistence. Happiness would have been the result if man had been just to his " brother man."

99. However desirable a great population may be, there is no reason to believe that London, compared with inferior cities and the country parts, in a state of free competition, would grow to its present size ; but it has grown not only at their expense, but that of many other portions of the world : nor is there any reason to believe that we shall have so large a population in any one city as London, compared with that of the country, nor is it desirable. The population of London is equal to about one twelfth part that of the United Kingdom ; whereas that of the city of New-York is equal to about the seventh part of that of the State of New-York, and about a fiftieth part of that of the United States. New-York being situated on the sea, and thus having an intercourse with all parts of the world, might be a large city without canals, railroads, and other public improvements ; but Albany, Utica, Rochester, Buffalo, Detroit, and Chicago would be insignificant places. It is, then, plainly the interest of the country to carry *inward* those public improvements which tend to equalize the population, the value of land, and its products. It is also a great public

object to afford the means of a cheap removal of the foreign population from the seaboard to the interior.

100. The rivalry of states and cities is helping on this good work of a *natural equality*, that is equally favourable to the happiness and wealth of the people. The city of New-York is only about a third more populous than Philadelphia and its Liberties; and Philadelphia has about the double of the population of Baltimore or Boston. If all these towns, by some paltry legislation and contrivances of crafty politicians, were crowded into one, we might in a few generations have a "splendid" capital, another London, with its powdered and liveried servants; an enormous mass of wealth, of luxury, of patronage for the luxurious arts, of misery and poverty. But it is far from being as certain that the aggregate wealth and happiness of the country would thereby be advanced. It is certain that it would not. It is a wonder that we have been so long in discovering so plain a truth as that the virtue, happiness, and riches of the people must finally go together. If we see countries where this seems not to be the case, we may be assured that it is a temporary delusion, and that God will not suffer men's eyes for ever to be blinded by it. These truths, so long hidden, are clearly revealed to us, and will be to every people that will make equal laws, practise righteousness, and save the poor from oppression. There must be some plain, natural, common-sense way of accounting for the un-

paralleled prosperity of this free country. It is said in a word ; it is its freedom, *its natural equality ;* the more equal condition of our cities, and the whole people. Let the stream, then, of Heaven's bounty, like the rivers, flow on unobstructed, and benefit whom they will!

101. The great amount of vice and crime in our republican cities is an unnecessary stain upon them. There is not the smallest reason for believing that great cities need contain as miserable and depraved a population as they have. *Physical* evil is one of the great causes of it Moral evil we must have ; much of that portion of it produced by *physical* evil can be removed. Constant bodily discomfort too often produces a selfish mind ; and then there is rankling at the heart the feeling of being poor, forlorn, neglected, and despised by the prosperous. It is the sleeping in garrets and cellars ; the living in holes and dens ; in dirty, unpaved, unlighted streets, without the accommodations of wells, cisterns, baths, and other means of cleanliness and health, by which the poor are subjected to infectious fevers and other diseases; and, what is worse, the infection of their own degradation; these are the causes, in a great measure, of their temptations, their crimes, their over-breeding, and, of course, pauperism. It is cruel of the more prosperous part of the people to say that these evils are unavoidable ; it is criminal to spend their substance sensually, and as they do, while they exist. To remove them is the business of the

richer part of the community, for they have the property ; this is one of the legitimate uses of property ; this they ought to do ; this the poor cannot do for themselves. Then there is education in the cities ! What an immense advantage have they not over the dispersed population of the country in concentrating their efforts, when two or three thousand people can be gathered together at the sound of a bell ! How much happier should we not all be for turning our thoughts from laced coats, fine capes, diamonds, fancy dresses, ten-dollar or five-pound dinners, to these poor people, who have eyes to see the sun, and senses to enjoy the lights of civilization, as well as we !

In England, in the large cities, such miseries as I have above referred to are so common, all classes have been so long accustomed to them, that many revolt from the whole subject in disgust and despair, as from an evil that is helpless, and, therefore, not to be thought of. It is not helpless in our cities, at any rate. There are others who never despair while there is misery before their eyes, and of this number I am sure that England contains a great multitude, and I am as certain that a blessed revolution is following in their steps, which many of them do not even dream of ; that they are angels of mercy, without knowing the exact errand upon which they are sent, which is to enlighten and improve the ignorant, and prepare them for a better government in this world and a happier lot in another. The light which they are carrying in their hands is streaming out into the dark recesses on every side. One would think that this was a charity that could hurt nobody. England has the glory of many such.

102. It was my happiness to see some of these people in England, and to hear of many more. We went to Manchester to see the manufacturing population. The multitude of the people that you see in the streets there oppresses you; you are overborne by numbers nearly as much as in the most frequented parts of London; and then so many of them are dirty, so miserably clad, so sallow, so eye-sunken and forlorn in their whole appearance, that the sight is horrible, and human life seems to be not only wasted, but even worse than thrown away.

103. With one of these, who was a partner in a respectable banking-house in Manchester, we went one night to what they call there " Little Ireland." It is a quarter of Manchester said to contain thirty or forty thousand Irish; a portion of those miserable people who are roaming about the world and picking up crumbs. It is to be hoped that the people of the United States, who must, from the nature of things, have them as fellow-citizens, who, possessing an asylum for them, can save them from hunting for garbage in the gutters, will open their hearts, and duly consider their industry, their tender and interesting family attachments, and their other good qualities; and will regard with compassion their bad ones, made ten times worse by oppression.

The errand of my acquaintance was to collect pennies, sixpences, and shillings for a savings-bank from people who, he said, would never of themselves take the trouble to come to the bank, or might never hear of it. He carried a little deposite-book, going from door to door without knocking. He seemed to enter as an old acquaintance, his first question being, " Anything for me to-night?" Some gave a shilling, some sixpence, and he said that in some cases before he had taken as small a sum as a penny. In every instance but two, the money was given by women and children, and taken out of an old stocking, or some other out-of-the-way place. He collected fifteen or sixteen shillings. He told the people that we were Americans, and had come to see them. They seemed delighted at this; several told us that they had relations in America; one that she had a brother at Lowell. Two said that they wished they were in America " that very night." We did not see a drunken person, or one that did not receive us with civility.

It was a dark, rainy night; most of the streets had not a lam ; in many cases t ere was no sidewalk; the streets being filled with rubbish, we plunged from one mudhole to another, often passing through underground basement passages. The apartments were often wretched, filthy, and comfortless, as one might know from the rent the people paid, some two shillings a week, some one and ninepence. This picture of Manchester has two sides; the fame of its riches has reached every part of the world where a cotton garment is worn.

It is said to be the richest town in England next to London, and they have a saying "that it is rich enough to buy Liverpool (which is about its size) and keep it on hand." A gentleman told me that he thought there were a hundred individuals in Manchester, each of whom had an annual income of £10,000 (fifty thousand dollars); another who was present thought otherwise. These calculations are usually exaggerated.

104. When I was at Manchester they were preparing for a musical festival, which was to be accompanied by a fancy ball. I saw in the newspapers an advertisement by some dealers in that line who had come down from London, of four hundred fancy dresses to be *hired* for the occasion, which dresses were made appropriate to some of the greatest heroes of antiquity; and among the rest I remember that no less a character than *Julius Cæsar* was to display "the light fantastic toe." I have said "hired" dresses. This *hiring of* dresses and other articles, such as glass, lamps, plate, diamonds, &c., is very common in the fashionable world. It is in no way rare for gentlemen to hire dresses for the king's levee. I have heard of an American minister's lady who made no secret of going to the queen's drawing-room in a hired dress. There is no degree of meanness, discomfort, and pinching in useful and honourable expenses in the world of fashion, pride, and folly that is not common; and one would be ashamed to enumerate so many disgusting things of this kind were it not from the hope of instilling into the minds of our working

people an inbred hatred of them. There is in the United States a grasping, devouring passion for riches that causes the hearts of too many to yearn for European pomp and parade, and for those principles by which alone they can be kept up; it is the old enemy of democratic government, and of that natural equality that is our charm, and, as such, whether the people find it in town or country, in friend or foe, in one party or another, for it is everywhere, it ought to be despised, hated, and put down. There is another passion for riches among our industrious, economical, conscientious people, for the good that riches may do, and the useful purposes to which they may be applied, that drives them on with an irresistible energy; and compared with which there is no parallel in Europe, so far as I saw. Besides, I never saw a man who pretended to be a judge of the matter, that did not declare that he found more industry in our free States than in any other part of the world, industrious even as the people of England are. But then you must take the people altogether, for there are many there who work as vigorously and faithfully as people can.

105. Let us now return to the festival and to "Little Ireland." After the festival, I heard it stated that seven thousand pounds ($35,000) were collected upon the occasion, a part or the whole of which was devoted to some charity: charity is a good thing, but, then, as the old saying is, "it is not worth while to burn a barn to roast an egg." And then, again, would it not be a better charity

still to light the lamps, clear out the rubbish, fill the mudholes, and pave the streets in "Little Ireland?" The operators would not need feathers, flounces, and capes for this kind of work. A good stout frock, trousers, and iron-shod shoes, would answer all the purpose. To be serious, this is not *a charity;* it is but the right of the thinking part of the community to apply its property to the improvement of the morals and the enlargement of the physical enjoyment of the people. We have our " Little Irelands" too, and poor people also ; what they can do for themselves, it is best, as a general rule, that they should do ; and the less they are treated like paupers the better for them ; but, then, there are things which they cannot do for themselves : this should be done by taxation, if taxation be necessary, that is, property should do it. There is no economical truth more certain than that these appropriations of property, if prudently made, leave us richer and not poorer ; and then, again, in this way we should be without the pretence of an excuse for wasting our property upon " fancy dresses," and such like paltry devices, in order to give employment to the poor. In the United States, at any rate, we might as well talk about the people not having good air enough to breathe as not having useful work enough to do. Is it not certain, then, that God has set us apart here to the work of perfecting these beautiful democratic institutions ? Is it not certain that they give life to the far-famed industry of our people ?

150   PUBLIC AND PRIVATE ECONOMY.

106. They say that the "*schoolmaster* is abroad." It must be remembered that there are many schoolmasters going about teaching different things. The gentlemen in the "hells" and on the turf have schoolhouses, pupils, schoolmasters of their own. Some have been sent to Manchester to teach the people a different kind of a raffling game from any I have heard of here. It is this. During the week, a number of them deposite with a shopkeeper a shilling each; he keeps the stakes, and receives a trifle for his services. At the end of the week there is a raffle for the purse, and my acquaintance who introduced me into "Little Ireland" told me that when he went to make collections for the savings'-bank, the people often gave as an excuse for not depositing, " that they were making up for the raffle that week." Do our gaming gentlemen know how "infectious" their aristocratic vices are among the poor; how many " Little Irelands" they are peopling, and what a currency they are giving to the infamous, corrupting practice of betting on elections?

107. I have desired to keep in view in this chapter and the last the respective advantages and disadvantages of great cities; how far the great cities of Europe are built up at the expense of the country; how much of their wretchedness and crimes proceed from the want of education, the people being huddled together, neglected by the rich, corrupted by their example, and left without such accommodations as pure water, baths, pavements, lights, pub-

lic squares, and space enough in streets, alleys, lanes, to admit of cleanliness, ventilation, and health.

108. If London had generally the spacious streets of Washington, the noble avenues of New-York, and public squares in proportion, and if the population of it were spread over ten times the present surface, the improved comfort, morals, and happiness of the people arising from such a circumstance, would more than compensate for the supposed advantage in riches of crowding them together for the purpose of contiguity and a nice division of labour. All cities are too crowded. A miserable population is a burden, and not a profit; happiness is the true standard of wealth, not numbers.

109. One of the most important distinctions that exist between Europe and the United States has not yet been taken notice of. It lies in the character of our village and rural population. The travellers of Europe will never understand the people of the United States till they make themselves better acquainted with the strength of the country, the country people. Few have ever formed any adequate conception of them but M. de Tocqueville; and even he better understood the theory of our institutions than the people moulded by them.* The village and country are the natural seed-bed of the equality that reigns here. It has been so from the earliest settlement of the country. Our villages, towns, and counties are natural little republics, where peo-

* This gentleman's admirable work, though liable to objections, ought to be spread far and wide through the United States.

ple with equal privileges, but with very different degrees of knowledge and education, are brought together to take into consideration not only their local affairs, but to discuss nearly every question that is important to them. This equality is the vital spark; it reconciles the poor to the rich, and the rich to the poor; by enabling all to obtain property, it is the best and only perfect protection for it that has ever been conceived of; it brings forth not only all the faculties of men, but of all men; it saves them from crawling, cringing, and flattery, that destroyer of truth; from the imbecility of pride and false ideas of wealth; as it drives out oppression, the heart of man naturally fills up with love and humanity towards his brother man; and thus, by paving the way for the true religion, it is constantly gaining upon the suffrages of mankind.

110. What can be more disgusting in the eye of reason, or odious in the sight of the pure religion of Jesus Christ, than to compel the poor to herd together, to live alone, without the protection and encouragement of the rich? The English village is as unlike ours as well can be. It is generally a collection of poor brick and stone houses, many of them thatched and standing directly on the street, being occupied mostly by tradesmen, mechanics, small shopkeepers, grocers, butchers, bakers, all of whom rank among the low or inferior people in England. Neither the lords nor gentry, lawyers of eminence, fashionable people, those holding respectable offices, or any of distinction, with few exceptions, are to be found in these villages; on the contrary, all such,

as a general rule, live in solitary grandeur in the country, or in London, or some of the large towns. All aspiring people turn their eyes to London as to the sun; like moths, they fly towards that fiery centre; some escape, more perish. What a contrast! Here people of every degree of political power and of private respectability are spread over the well-settled parts of the country; the unfortunate, ignorant, ill-educated do not huddle together; on the contrary, those who have knowledge and education are everywhere spread among them, often living next door to each other, and in habits of neighbourly intercourse. We came to these desolate shores as lovers of republicanism; such we yet are, notwithstanding all that the libellers may say. We have gradually advanced into the country, always carrying our republicanism with us; if we go there, we go to buy, build, and push forward improvements; if we are born there, and move in any direction, it is generally still farther into the country. This proves that a natural equality has an enduring foundation in the United States; that God has here favoured a righteous distribution of property and the good things of this life; that this is to be the scene of a still farther Christian dispensation, and that we may look forward with confidence to a period when the greatness of our cities, constantly invigorated and replenished by our moral country population, shall subsist more upon a virtuous natural trade and superior arts, and less in corrupting the country by foreign vices, impure commerce, paltry shows, and insignificant fashions, than they have heretofore done. As all other unnatural distinctions that elevate wealth at the expense of what is good and virtuous are here melting away, so are those between city and country. The cities will profit by our more virtuous simplicity, and we by their superior refinements. Thus one of the great aims of human society will be answered in making us mutually useful to each other.

111. London is the centre of political power in England; we have no centre; we have no metropolis; we have shaken off all central power of every kind. Here an immense balance of political power is in the country, not by means of numbers alone, but because it has a real, durable foundation in the superior moral strength and intelligence of the country. It cannot be otherwise. There being a superior provision for the human being in the country, men are better, more moral, more religious there. If a man desires political influence in the United States, his chance is far superior in the country than in the cities; a large proportion of those who have had political power or fame in the United States, have been not only country-born, but country-educated people.

It is true that people in the country are not so rich, according to their numbers, as those in our cities; that they are less compact, and therefore have not the same advantages from a nice division of labour; that their mechanical work is generally less perfect; that they are not so intensely active and industrious; that their business is not so promptly and skilfully done as by the industrious part of the citizens. Still the mass of intelligence in the country is greater and the moral tone higher. When speaking of superior intelligence, those few highly-educated people, lawyers, physicians, clergymen, surgeons, artists, men of science, &c., who look to the cities for great reward, are of course excepted. Country people live in the midst of the great and ennobling objects of nature, that give energy to their minds and strength to their arms, which are increased by the very purity of the atmosphere they breathe: a much larger proportion of them are educated; a much smaller oppressed by extreme poverty; they are not so polluted by the vicious part of the alien population; they have more leisure; read more, reflect more; are, of course, more devoted to the interests of religion; their wants being smaller, their contentment is greater; they are less profuse and selfish; they think less of the fashions and the frivolous news of the day; they are less corrupted by that moral leprosy of our cities, foreign vices and fashions; a greater proportion of country people attend to and understand public business; their public assemblies are more quiet and dignified; their amusements more innocent; their youth less subject to temptation; there is less gaming, drinking, feasting, and licentiousness; they are not so liable to mobs and extraordinary excitements; they have a better command of their minds and tempers; are less anxious, careworn, and harassed about their worldly condition; are more independent; their property is more secure; they live less upon patronage and favour, the tricks of trade, underbidding each other, upon rich people and fashionable work, which fails in hard times; they are not so greedy of wealth, nor so often and suddenly transported by insatiable desires to be rich. I readily admit that these strong lines of distinction do not equally apply to all parts of the country.

112. What, then, is the moral of this lesson? It is this. Europe is full of the idolatry of great cities and ill-gotten wealth; let us be freed from it! Let the country exert that moral superiority over the great cities which is a new power here, and greater than ever existed in this form in the world before. Let this be put forth without jealousy or envy of their riches; for it is not riches, but the unnatural inequality, and consequent abuse of them, that destroys the people. The greater the wealth of the cities, the greater will be that of the country, if wisely and morally used. In all healthful trade, the benefit is mutual; and when such a commerce results in building opulent cities and making rich merchants, as it will, so it does in producing a great country, prosperous farmers, mechanics, and labourers of every description. As the country can, then, let it suppress intemperance and all impure trade, by substituting that which has its foundation in a taste for healthful productions, superior arts, and innocent refinements.

THE END.

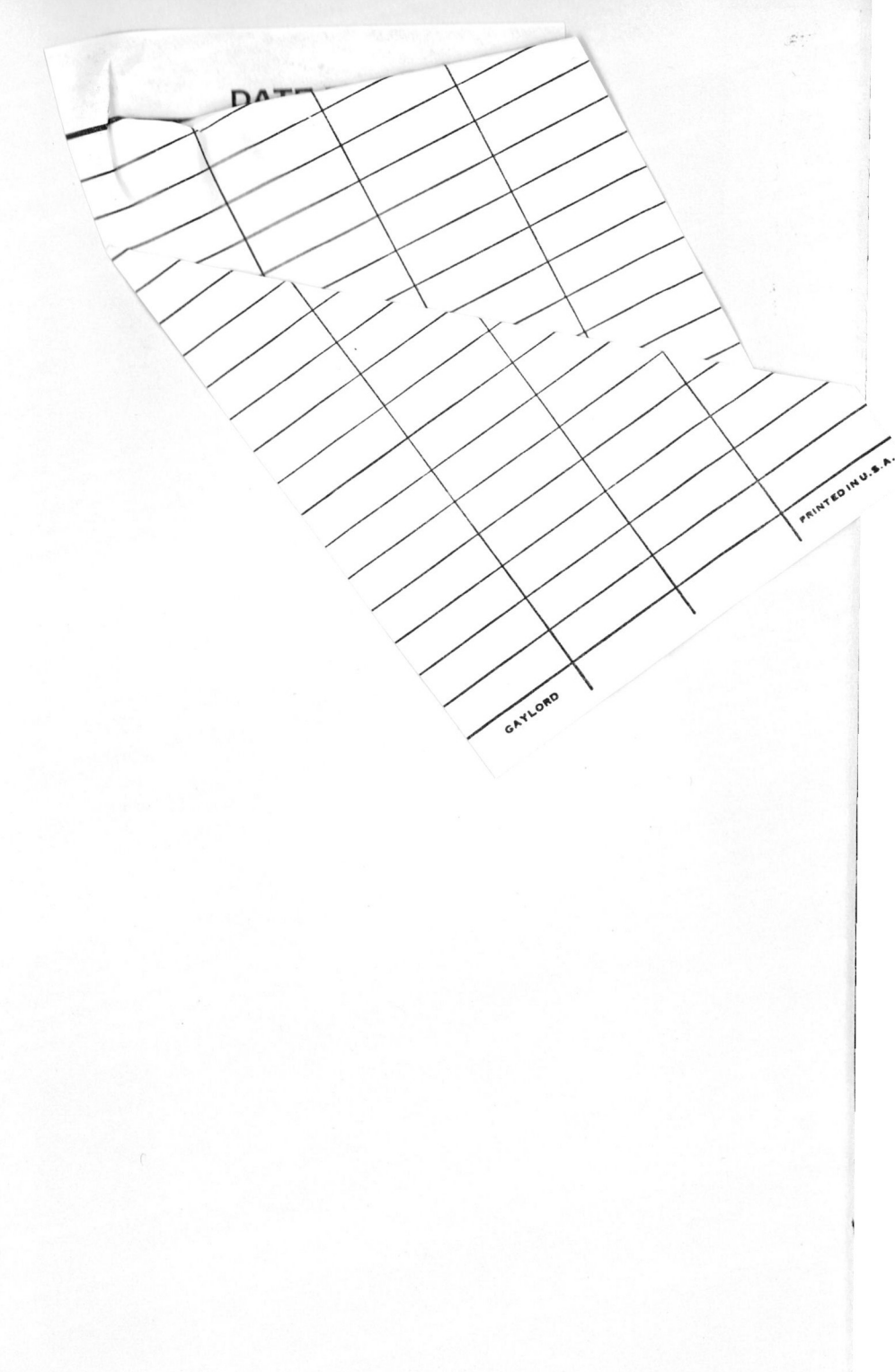